WITHDRAWN

Harvard English Studies 6

The Worlds of Victorian Fiction

The Worlds of Victorian Fiction

Edited by
Jerome H. Buckley

Harvard University Press
Cambridge, Massachusetts
and
London, England
1975

Library of Congress Cataloging in Publication Data
Main entry under title:

The worlds of victorian fiction.

    (Harvard English studies ; 6)
    1. English fiction — 19th century — History and criticism —
Addresses, essays, lectures. I. Buckley, Jerome Hamilton. II. Series.
PR653 W6   823'.8'09   75-5549
ISBN 0-674-96205-2
ISBN 0-674-96207-9 pbk.

Preface

Unlike Marvell's coy mistress and her impetuous lover, the Victorian novelists all seem to have had "world enough and time" to accomplish their objectives. But the concept of "world," as we apply it to their work, is not limited to the ample dimensions of the three-deckers in which they developed character and plot or to the serial publication that permitted a long, leisurely unfolding of theme. The title of the present volume, *The Worlds of Victorian Fiction,* is frankly ambiguous. It was chosen to accommodate a number of essays quite dissimilar in approach and purpose, some tracing a genre or motif throughout the Victorian period, some concentrating on the values of a single author, others on the style and structure of a specific novel. Since each stands as a separate unit, any one passing its critical judgments may differ sharply from one or more of the others. Yet all relate in some fashion to the idea of a fictional "world," and I have grouped them according to my own interpretations of that term.

The Victorian novelist typically strove for the illusion of a complete world; he carefully assigned his protagonist a definite place in an ordered society governed by a general code of manners and morals, which was assumed though not always obeyed. Since realism was the dominant mode of nineteenth-century fiction, the little world of a given novel usually has a close relationship to the real world, the surfaces of which it can often reproduce with a photographic accuracy. The matter of epic or romance may prove incompatible with the realistic bias; as David Staines shows in his essay, the Arthurian theme prominent in Victorian poetry enters scarcely at all into Victorian prose fiction. Yet the degree of realism is at best only approximate; the myth of the romantic Corinne, as Ellen Moers demonstrates, persists in novelists far less flamboyant than Mme de Staël; and even so apparent a realist as Trollope may, as Donald Stone suggests, owe more to a lingering Byronic sensibility than he would ever have cared to admit. If Oscar Wilde was right in believing that nature imitates art, it is possible that the real Victorian world modeled itself to some extent on its fiction. At any rate, Barbara Gelpi argues persuasively that the "true" autobiographies of Mill and Ruskin were influenced by the psychology of the fictive Dickens world.

A "world" of fiction may of course be more specialized and exclusive than its real counterpart. The essays in the fourth section of this volume examine several types or genres, each guided by its own limiting conventions and assumptions. Each kind establishes its own ambiance, the conditions we must accept if we would explore a strange country of the imagination, a new world with its particular expectations. John Maynard explains the intentions of the English historical novel and its ultimate failure to confront the realities of history. Robert Lee Wolff sees "the world of Victorian religious strife" reproduced in miniature for the edification of young Victorians. U. C. Knoepflmacher describes a fictional "counterworld" where illicit anarchic passion overrides middle-class proprieties. Philip Fisher notes the rise of an urban literature with its emphasis on atomism and dehumanization. And Mark Hillegas carries us into a late-Victorian universe of space ruled by scientific law or at least by the formulas of science fiction.

In less generic terms we speak of the "world" of a major novelist — among the Victorians, preeminently Dickens or George Eliot. Here the mark of majority is the power to compel our willing suspension of disbelief, to make us accept the illusion and peculiar emphasis, even the omissions and distortions, as necessary and inevitable, the attributes of a complete and unique world bound in unity by a strong superintending creative vision. In isolating the recurrent figure of the uncle, or the substitute father, Harry Levin offers us a clue to the Dickens world, where all the endlessly varied parts take color from the whole. "What I have been trying to sketch," Professor Levin explains, "is the structure of a consistent mythology, which underlies the totality of his writing." Henry Auster, speaking of George Eliot, points to a modernity of temper as the unifying factor behind all the author's later work, and Hillis Miller and Robert Kiely find George Eliot's use of language, whether in metaphor or dialogue, the essence of her genius. Thanks to a pervasive self-consciousness as narrator, analyzed by Winslow Rogers, Thackeray also achieves a distinctive world. Minor novelists work with less striking individuality, but many hold their mirrors up to nature at characteristic angles and so evoke worlds, or at least small continents, recognizably their own. Charlotte Yonge, for example, as David Brownell presents her, gives us a faithful picture of Victorian domesticity illuminated by her personal sympathies and convictions. A "world" of fiction may be as wide as a novelist's imagination embracing his or her whole canon.

But insofar as every art object deserves appraisal in and for itself, a "world" may also be as narrow — or indeed as comprehensive — as a single book. Several of our essays accordingly focus on a novel rather than a novelist. Professors Kiely and Miller in quite different ways concern themselves with the distinguishing qualities of *Middlemarch*. Melvyn Haberman defines the peculiar bleakness of outlook that identifies the form and mood of *Hard Times*. Richard Stevenson accounts for the curious commingling of tragedy and comedy that sets *Richard Feverel* apart from other Victorian novels. My own brief piece measures the scope of *New Grub Street* and its special relation to George Gissing's literary life, the extent to which an autobiographical novel can attain an autonomous existence.

Whatever their critical method, all the contributors to this volume are convinced of the vitality of their subject matter. As editor I trust that all will chart routes of discovery to some of the many worlds in the galaxy of Victorian fiction.

J. H. B.

Contents

I Views of the Dickens World

The Uncles of Dickens

The Boys of Dickens — that was the title and subject of the first book I remember having read all by myself. At this remove in time I have no impulse to retrace it bibliographically or to identify the Lamb-like adapter who made children's tales out of episodes from the novels. Let it suffice that through his adaptations childhood spoke directly to childhood, so that Dickens' early memories are indelibly mingled with mine, just as they have been with those of innumerable others. Wider and ever widening contexts opened up later on, when I came to read and reread the novels themselves. Yet Oliver, Smike, Paul, David, Jo, and Pip remained at an intersubjective center of consciousness, because it was through such eyes as theirs that Dickens had envisioned his world. Whether there ever was a companion volume entitled *The Girls of Dickens* I do not know, nor whether his readers of either sex could empathize as effectively in the long run with Little Nell, Little Emily, or Little Dorrit. But it is a question not so much of being either a male or a female waif as of having been cut off from a parent or parents; half of Dickens' protagonists are orphans and most of the rest are demi-orphans. We know, of course, from his biography, that the cutting-off was a psychological process in his case. We know too how his imagination returned and took its departure, again and again, from the

1

temporary breakup of his family through his father's imprisonment for debt and his brief personal sentence to child labor at
the age of twelve. "His feeling that his own parents had rejected
and abandoned him," as Harry Stone has stated, "was perhaps
the most shaping emotion in his life."

The resulting impairment of his father-image is personified
with humor in Wilkins Micawber and with bitterness in William
Dorrit. It is attested more deeply and darkly by that condition
of fatherlessness which besets so many of his characters. For
every "Aged P." who gives his blessing, like the elder Wemmick
in *Great Expectations,* there must be at least two fathers who
break with their sons, like both Sir John Chester and John Willet
in *Barnaby Rudge.* And when an ostensible orphan turns out to
have a long-lost father, he may prove as shadowy and unwelcome
as Barnaby's; grim indeed is the irony that reveals Smike as the
dead son of Ralph Nickleby. Dickens' characteristic reversal of
the breadwinner's role extends far beyond *Little Dorrit*: Nell
must keep a sharp eye on her grandfather, Agnes must become a
little mother to Mr. Wickfield, and Sissy Jupe must fend for
herself when she is deserted by her father, the acrobatic clown.
Most explicit is the situation in *Our Mutual Friend,* where the
drunkard "Mr. Dolls" is continually admonished by the dolls'
dressmaker, Jenny Wren: she becomes "his little parent" and
treats him as her "prodigal old son." Harold Skimpole, in *Bleak
House*, indulges himself by pretending to be "a mere child." In
Hard Times Josiah Bounderby, who has a respectable mother,
would rather pose as a foundling; Thomas Gradgrind's educational theories are discredited by the conduct of his son and
daughter. As a devoted paterfamilias, Mr. Dombey is the exception that proves the rule, since his devotion to the sickly Paul is
utterly nullified by his callous treatment of the long-suffering
Florence.

Happy families may be much alike, as Tolstoy has said, while
unhappy families differ in their respective modes of unhappiness.
Tolstoy's own domestic chagrins differed widely from those of
Dickens, although each of them raised a family of patriarchal
proportions. Child of a once-broken home, Dickens went on to
break up his own home, to be separated from his wife under
circumstances of muted scandal. Celebrant of households and

hearthsides and all the familial virtues, he depicted a sequence of marriages which fall surprisingly short of happiness more often than not — from the harsh antagonism of the Dombeys to the bittersweet union of David and Dora, not to mention a lumbering procession of henpecked husbands, ill-used wives, and comic mothers-in-law. Though adulteries are relatively few and far between, the suspicion frequently arises: against the Strongs in *David Copperfield* or the Peerybingles in *The Cricket on the Hearth*. Both of those couples have invited raised eyebrows by the difference in their ages; others must face the consequences of social *mésalliance,* like the Gowans in *Little Dorrit* or the Wrayburns in *Our Mutual Friend*. The jilted specter of Miss Havisham looms as the sworn enemy of marriage; her protégée Estella makes a first match which ignores and justifies that enmity; and *Great Expectations* ends ambiguously without the conventional plighting of troths. *Sketches of Young Couples,* a hack job seldom reprinted, was published anonymously in 1840 — less than four years after Dickens' wedding — to salute the betrothal of Queen Victoria. Couched as a warning to bachelors, it holds up a dozen awful examples, in a light which comes closer to Thackerayan cynicism than to Dickensian sentiment.

Yet we continue to think of Dickens as preeminently the family man among novelists, and he supports this assumption by the number and the variety of *ménages* he has exhibited, for better or for worse. The ideal was not less appealing to him because he felt compelled to show it so imperfectly realized, and the hopes of marital arrangement spring eternal in his happy endings. His relations with his own family, and with his wife's as well, had their close and complicated bearing on his career throughout. John Dickens may have been a feckless provider; but Elizabeth Dickens had a brother, John Henry Barrow, who got young Charles his start in journalism; and it was through her stepnephew, James Lamert, that he had been placed in a blacking warehouse. Not only his father and brother but also his in-laws were, before long, to depend upon the financial successes of "Uncle Charles." Between these human attachments and that artistic detachment toward which he had to struggle, he must have lived in a state of continual oscillation. Joyce, who grew up harboring similar attitudes toward kith and kin, thought of his

Stephen Dedalus as a self-proclaimed stepchild. "He felt that he was hardly of the same blood with them but stood to them in the mystical kinship of fosterage, fosterchild and fosterbrother." Samuel Butler, in his recoil from the Victorian family, became an intellectual father-slayer. Dostoevsky, who had literally seen his father slain, was a spiritual father-seeker. Kafka would enact the dilemma for the twentieth century, in his flight from paternal authority and his search for an accepted identity.

Dickens did not need a surrogate father; Micawber-Dorrit was already too much of a presence in his life. He was temperamentally incapable of committing literary parricide in Butler's sense, yet he took an iconoclastic stance toward the authorities and he sought increasingly to widen his circle of sympathies. He had scant respect for heads of houses, in whatever housing they might appear: country estates or city firms, lawcourts or government offices, mills or mines or anything else that had hardened into an establishment. Schools were a special instance, since they concerned themselves with the young and the schoolmaster stood in loco parentis. But there are as many foes as friends in his long succession of teachers, and his schoolrooms tend to parallel his prisons in their institutional rigidity. To whom then could a child — or we who follow the spectacle through the child's experience — look up? Where are the adults to guide him or, as a sociologist would put it, to be his role-models? Society for Dickens resembles Plato's republic in one respect, if in no other: it is presided over by a class of guardians. When these are blood relatives, they are uncles or occasionally aunts; otherwise, though quasi-avuncular, they may stand in "the mystical kinship of fosterage" to the youthful character involved. Their position coincides with a persistent custom observed by anthropologists in tribes across the world, whereby the maternal uncle plays a part often more responsible than that of his nephew's parents. Sometimes the same part is played by a godparent or *compère,* who retains the power to bless or curse his junior charge.

Hence what Claude Lévi-Strauss has termed *le privilège avunculaire* designates a universal pattern of behavior, which underlies some crucial themes of Dickens. It may be worth our while to browse through his works once more, looking for whatever

might be disclosed through such relationships. A piece of his
discarded machinery suggests a paradigm in its very record of
failure, *Master Humphrey's Clock*. This was to have comprised
the framework for a series of stories, but even a contribution
from Mr. Pickwick failed to strike any spark. Its only reason for
survival is the impetus it gave to one full-length narration, *The
Old Curiosity Shop*. That novel begins with a first-person narrator, Master Humphrey himself, who will bow out after Chapter
Three. Meanwhile the old man, walking the London streets at
night, has encountered Little Nell, who is lost, and has guided
her back home to her grandfather's antiquarian premises. Alas,
that haven is far from secure, and there will be no deliverance
from the longer wanderings that lie ahead for her. Those are
prefigured, along with a frequent plight of the Dickensian protagonist, in Master Humphrey's comment: "It always grieves me
to contemplate the initiation of children into the ways of life,
when they are scarcely more than infants." If they go astray,
Dickens has gone out of his way to imply, they are lucky to
encounter a Samaritan — and not a Herod. Another marginal
comment is suggested in *Sketches by Boz,* between the lines of a
sketch on a favorite *topos,* "A Christmas Dinner." Here in the
usual family gathering, with its aura of good cheer and tension
relaxed, we note that — although Grandmamma and Grandpapa
are alive and present — it is Uncle George who presides.

The displacement is revealing, as is the absence of fathers for
so many of those initiates "into the ways of life." They are bound
to be meeting with other elders, who will either befriend them or
oppose their progress. Uncles ought particularly to be counted
upon when they are not fathers in their own right, when they are
unmarried and well-to-do. Thus the brood of Kenwigses in
Nicholas Nickleby flatters and venerates Mr. Lillyvick, "a public
man" — to wit, a collector of water-rates. They are outraged
when he suddenly marries an actress, Henrietta Petowker, and
not placated until she has run away with a half-pay captain and
they have been reinstated in Lillyvick's will. An additional
sketch by Boz, "A Bloomsbury Christening," features the rich
Mr. Dumps, who is persuaded to stand as godfather to his
nephew's son, despite his lifelong hatred of children. His reluctant

offering, a silver mug, gets stolen along the way, as fate will have it, and his congratulatory speech breaks down into a misanthropic denunciation of progeny. "The Poor Relation's Story," from *Reprinted Pieces,* presents the other and softer side in this conflict of values. "I failed in my expectations to my Uncle Chill," the Poor Relation confesses, "on account of not being as sharp as he could have wished in worldly matters." Having little, he can count on less; accordingly he is rejected by his fiancée; and his lonely existence is mitigated only by his avuncular — if that is still the word — fondness for a cousin's son, Little Frank. All his boasts about his wife and family have been merely "Castles in the Air," pathetic reveries like Lamb's "Dream-Children."

This last example illustrates the two sides of avuncularity, as a moral influence and a source of motivation. Since Uncle is well established in the community, it seems natural that he should be expected to show himself a generous protector, a tutelary spirit looking after the lives of his younger connections. If he disappoints such an expectation, he would seem to be unnatural, hostile and malicious, a proponent of those negative forces which he should be tempering. Nephew, when he seeks through fantasy what has been denied him by reality, points back to the more affirmative view of unclehood and indicates its function as an agency of poetic justice. It is not for nothing that "my uncle" was common slang for a pawnbroker, as it is in the farce so titled, which Dickens wrote in collaboration with his subeditor, W. H. Wills. Moreover, it is the clue to a jocular passage about a certain debt-ridden ancestor of the Chuzzlewits:

> Throughout such fragments of his correspondence as have escaped the ravages of the moths, we find him making constant reference to an uncle, in respect of whom he would seem to have entertained great expectations, as he was in the habit of seeking to propitiate his favor by presents of plate, jewels, books, watches, and other valuable articles. Thus he writes on one occasion to his brother in reference to a gravy-spoon, the brother's property, which he (Diggory) would appear to have borrowed or otherwise possessed himself of: "I have bestowed upon that irresistible uncle of mine everything I ever possessed" . . . This gentleman's patronage and influence must have been very exten-

sive, for his nephew writes, "His interest is too high" — "It is too much" — "It is tremendous" — and the like. (*Martin Chuzzlewit,* chap. I)

Here the heaviness of the double-entendre stresses the duality of the conception: the avaricious loan-shark disguised as a friend-in-need. Edmund Wilson allowed for both possibilities in his seminal essay, "The Two Scrooges." In the *Christmas Carol* Ebenezer Scrooge is expressly presented as an uncle, through his curmudgeonly argument over the holiday with his genial nephew Fred. His relation with his clerk Bob Cratchit places him in a line of hardhearted employers, like Ralph Nickleby and the Chuzzlewits, who are faithfully served by kindhearted employees, like Newman Noggs and old Chuffey. Scrooge's redemption, which converts him into "a second father to Tiny Tim," is morally contrived rather than psychologically motivated. Dickensian characterization, as Wilson recognized, is regularly monolithic: "The curmudgeons of the early Dickens . . . are old-fashioned moneylenders and misers of a type that must have been serving for decades in the melodramas of the English stage . . . They are the bad uncles in the Christmas pantomime who set off the jolly clowns and the good fairy, and who, as everybody knows from the beginning, are doomed to be exposed and extinguished."

This is highly suggestive, if somewhat impressionistic, for it is always illuminating to set the dramatis personae of Dickens against the perspectives of the theater. Beyond the Christmas pantomime or the blood-and-thunder melodrama towered the Shakespearean repertory, and there — beyond even Claudius, King of Denmark — menaced the very archetype of wicked uncles, Richard III. Dickens' scorn for kingship is reflected in *A Child's History of England,* which lingers over such royal waifs as Prince Arthur, "the fatherless boy," murdered at the behest of his uncle, King John. Inevitably, no episode in the chronicle has drawn more sympathy from the chronicler than the set piece that recounts the murder of Richard's principal victims, the two little princes in the Tower. Nor was there any other play of Shakespeare's to which Dickens alluded more repeatedly than *Richard III.* A performance of it at the Theatre Royal in Rochester (the "Dullborough" of *Reprinted Pieces*), when he was six years old, may well have been his earliest theatrical memory. One of the oddest, which must have tested his predilection, was that of a stout lady performing the title role at Brighton in 1848. Boz's sketch on "Private Theatres" mentions Richard first, as the juiciest and therefore most expensive in a list of parts which stagestruck amateurs paid to act. Mr. Wopsle, one such amateur, could not say grace without reminding Pip of the hunchbacked usurper; one of his stage-tricks, "the sliding business," is evoked in Dickens' own play (written and acted with Mark Lemon), *Mr. Nightingale's Diary.* Any villain who enjoys his villainy must walk perforce in those limping tracks — and none more consciously than Quilp in *The Old Curiosity Shop,* characterized by his wife as "a second Richard Crookback."

But what of the other Scrooge, the not impossible but rather improbable alter ego, reformed and turned philanthropist overnight — or, more generally and plausibly, Dickens' good uncles? They have their own prototypes, no less idiosyncratic though hardly so histrionic, deriving mainly from fiction rather than drama. Prominent among them is My Uncle Toby, whose amiable foibles were more congenial to Tristram Shandy than the doctrinaire crotchets of his father. Their descent can easily be traced, via Parsons Adams and Primrose, Hudibras and Doctor Syntax, to that great exemplar who found his own exemplars in knightly romances. Like Don Quixote himself, they were highminded and absentminded as champions, as companions wellmeaning and accident-prone. Mr. Pickwick's central position in that good-natured company has been registered by critics ever since Washington Irving wrote to Dickens: "Old Pickwick is the Quixote of commonplace life, and as with the Don, we begin by laughing at him and end by loving him." Love would so predominate over laughter, in the interpretation of Dostoevsky, that Pickwick and Quixote could be grouped together with Jesus as reincarnations of "the positively good man," the altruist rebuffed whose Dostoevskyan persona would be Prince Myshkin in *The Idiot.* Dostoevsky seems to have been well aware that his reading of Dickens was strained and subjective. *The Pickwick Papers* owed its immediate success and its unique standing among its author's novels to its sustained lightheartedness. Marking his debut as a novelist and making his reputation, its appearance coincided with the cultural watershed of Queen Victoria's accession in 1837.

Consequently *The Posthumous Papers of the Pickwick Club* is Dickens' pivotal work, a starting point for much that follows and a retrospective link with tradition. Though it is less involved with family matters than any of the other novels, though its elderly celibate protagonist is heavily insulated against them, it has farther-reaching implications which ask for our closer scrutiny. Timed to happen a decade before the date of writing, reverting to the last years of George IV, it looks back nostalgically from the cobblestones of London toward the countryside in coaching days. In its loosely episodic construction it revives the precedent of the picaresque genre, as well as of the Sir Roger de Coverly papers. Like those literary forerunners, it achieves a kind of unity through the dominance of an eponymous character. This character, far from having been imagined by the novelist in advance, was gradually and stumblingly adumbrated through the actual course of composition. It is well known that Samuel Pickwick, Esq., was conceived as a cockney sportsman, not unlike the jovial grocer John Jorrocks, whose misadventures in the saddle were bringing current popularity to the humorous sketches of Robert Surtees. Mr. Pickwick is confronted with various sports in the early stages of his jaunts and jollities, but he shies away and shows less and less interest in them. He is trundled to a shooting party, while temporarily lame, in a wheelbarrow; when he takes up the reins of a coach, his horses take occasion to run away. He is not a skater but a slider; he is more sure of himself as a spectator, watching a cricket game pretty much as he watches a military review or a borough election.

Dickens has told us how, as a twenty-three-year-old journalist, he was called upon to supply the text for a series of illustrations by Robert Seymour, an established artist who specialized in hunting scenes. From the outset the fledgling writer insisted on a free hand for himself and a wider venue for his anti-hero: one of the latter's friends and followers, Mr. Winkle, would do his feeble best to maintain the sporting interest; and, after the sudden and tragic death of Seymour between the first and second monthly numbers, Dickens would assert the firmest of upper hands over all his subsequent illustrators — notably Hablôt K. Browne, alias Phiz, to whose wry talent Mr. Pickwick and so many other Dickensian characters owe their graphic identities. It is significant that Pickwick's original image had been tall and thin, and that this was belatedly changed to the physiognomy we recognize: short and corpulent, bald and bespectacled, clad in old-fashioned stock, waistcoat, cutaway, gaiters, and tights. As a city-dweller making excursions to the country, he displays certain characteristics of the bourgeois gentleman. Inasmuch as he has "retired from business and is a gentleman of property," he is truly a *rentier* and man of infinite leisure, free to pursue his fancies, curiosities, and friendships wherever they may lead. Yet speculation can yield no clue as to how he has managed to make so comfortable a fortune. It is hard to think of him functioning daily through a long career in a countinghouse. Temperamentally, he has nothing in common with those wily entrepreneurs and ruthless extortioners who represent the sphere of business for Dickens.

Dickens did have some intention of lampooning pseudoscience, as engaged in by the amateur naturalists and the would-be archaeologists of the recently founded British Association. Mr. Pickwick has attained his eminence in this hazy field through his Theory of Tittlebats, and he crowns his international reputation by discovering — if not deciphering — a runic inscription, successfully resisting the sensible efforts of the hostile haberdasher, Mr. Blotton, to reduce it to a commonplace *graffito*. The learned world conspires to glorify his self-deception; later, on a moonlight escapade of the Pickwickians, a "scientific gentleman" is deliberately deceived into believing that their lanterns are meteors. But the joke of such exposures, whether they hinge on illusion or delusion, is mechanical and limited, set up to be knocked down, as Dickens was to demonstrate in his uninspired *Mudfog Papers*. The territory Swift explored, the island of Laputa, was not to be a destination of the Pickwick Club. The constructive device of a club could pitch the tone at the secretarial level of its minutes, with Boz presenting himself as their editor, and drawing on his background as a reporter to produce a style which combines the scholarly transaction with the parliamentary proceeding. The effect is so extravagantly mock-heroic, when the opening chapter records a meeting, that the mockery gets out of hand. If this be greatness, we are constrained to remember Jonathan Wild. Dickens' ironies would have no anchor, were it not for the heckling interventions of that stolid skeptic, Mr. Blotton. Why he should be present among these gulls, challenging their adulation of Pickwick's arch-gullibility, cannot otherwise be explained.

Their way of meeting his challenge, and somehow containing it, has given us a proverbial formula for the victory of parliamentary usage over common sense. Mr. Blotton is quite right, of course; Mr. Pickwick really is a humbug, insofar as he accepts the credit for his pretentions to serious research and superior intellect. To add that he is a humbug merely "in a Pickwickian sense" seems rather to compound the initial insult than to retract it; for what is Pickwick if not Pickwickian, and who would be Pickwickan if he were not? The alternative would be to suspend the rules and imply that "Pickwick" is synonymous with lack of meaning. Thus our introduction to him inflates his self-esteem in order to puncture it. But that is no more than a beginning, a preliminary explosion which clears the ground for further development. We are not likely to forget that the unregenerate Scrooge described Christmas as "humbug," nor can we negate what Christmas stood for in Dickens' scheme of ultimate values. Mr. Pickwick will develop, then, to the point where Dickens feels obliged to rationalize the "decided change in his character," arguing in the preface that we are struck at first by the "superficial traits" of a whimsical personality, and that we perceive his goodness and other merits as we come to be "better acquainted with him." This, however, is reasoning ex post facto. Pickwick grew into his part as Dickens grew into his craft. Both the character and the novel retain a good deal of what Meredith called "the lumber of imbecility." Scrutinizing the detail of *Pickwick Papers,* we behold such limitations in the process of being outgrown.

"The machinery of the Club, proving cumbrous in the management," Dickens admitted, "was gradually abandoned as the work progressed." Mr. Pickwick becomes less of a gentleman polymath and more of "an observer of human nature." Alfred Jingle, Esq., the strolling player, claims to be one too: "Most people are when

they've little to do, and less to get." The second chapter brings
the members out of their clubroom into the streets, a livelier terrain for observation. There Mr. Pickwick's habit of taking notes
embroils him at once with a cabman. He is extricated from the
encounter by the jaunty and garrulous Mr. Jingle, whose roguish
reappearances will string together some of the numerous loose
ends of the plot. Mr. Pickwick's investigations, like Don Quixote's adventures, usually terminate in anticlimaxes. When he is
caught holding a dark lantern, he is aptly characterized by Sam
Weller as "a amiable Guy Fawkes." Worldly situations tend to
cast him in the role of a guy, a butt, a figure of fun. Yet, even in
his most embarrassing discomfitures, he never relinquishes "his
amiable character." When he awakens from his tipsiness after the
hunters' picnic, he finds himself and his wheelbarrow in the village pound being pelted with vegetables by the villagers. In his
indignation he threatens a lawsuit for false arrest; but his host,
Mr. Wardle, "half-bursting with laughter," warns him that the
respondents might say he "had taken too much cold punch." Indignation rapidly subsides before a more Pickwickian reaction.
"Do what he would, a smile would come into Mr. Pickwick's
face; the smile extended into a laugh; the laugh into a roar; and
the roar became general."

Mr. Pickwick is seldom guyed so unmercifully; but he is continually laughed at; and he has the Falstaffian virtue, as a laugh-
ingstock, of joining in with the laughers and generalizing the
roar. This puts him in a different position from his trio of followers, who seem altogether humorless in the pursuit of their
respective vanities. When Pickwick roundly declares that Tupman is too old and fat to dress up as a brigand, Tupman sees
nothing ridiculous in the masquerade, and touchily attempts to
start a fight. Pickwick is not afraid to put up his fists, as he will
prove again in the prison episode; yet it is he who relents and
relaxes and ends by insisting that the embarrassed Tupman wear
the absurd costume. The Pickwickians are individualized only to
the extent that each of them has his ineffectual aspiration: Tracy
Tupman to be a philanderer, Augustus Snodgrass to be a poet,
and Nathaniel Winkle to be a sportsman. By contrast with their
mentor, they remain in the realm of two-dimensional caricature:
three musketeers marching in quickstep behind an inimitable

Dartagnan. That they have been accorded "a roving license for a year or two, to see something of men and manners" under Mr. Pickwick's supervision, is regretted by the businesslike Mr. Winkle Senior. But the dispensation has freed them from mundane obligations, and something of the Pickwickian disposition has rubbed off on them, together with its "characteristic expression of benevolence." Mr. Pickwick's benevolent countenance, forever beaming with smiles, lights up every scene where he appears: "it was none other than that jolly personage."

The major lesson his disciples learn is that "general benevolence was one of the leading features of the Pickwickian theory." Now benevolence means, literally, well-wishing. Pickwick's true vocation is a mission of good will, junketing up and down the country to wish everybody well, just as Dickens' declared purpose was to help his readers "think better of their fellow men and look upon the brighter and more kindly side of human nature." Yet *Pickwick Papers* conveys intimations of Dickens' darker themes, and its rural rides turn citywards when its hero faces litigation and chooses imprisonment. When we see him sliding on the ice, he cuts an appealingly childish figure; but if his innocence looks both silly and saintly, when it flies in the face of experience, he seems rather a foolish wise man than a wise fool. Clearly this Don Quixote needs a Sancho Panza to cushion his misadventures, if not to ward them off, to keep him in touch with practical realities. After his exploratory sally, Cervantes' knight could never have set forth again without recruiting a squire; similarly, Dickens' novel gets a second start with the entrance of Sam Weller; and the circumstance that presents him blacking boots at the White Hart Inn links him closely with the sharpest recollection of Dickens' childhood. Though he is willing to become a gentleman's servant, when that gentleman happens to be Mr. Pickwick, there is nothing servile about Sam. In a downstairs "swarry" reminiscent of Thackeray, he will put down the supercilious flunkeys of Bath.

Sam has earned, through his metropolitan wisdom, his outstanding place among servants wiser than their masters. Though he has never risen so high as the versatile Figaro, he has undergone the lower vicissitudes, and he knows what it is like to sleep in "unfurnished lodgings" underneath Waterloo Bridge. Many of his comments and anecdotes, delivered with cockney insouciance, have a cutting edge of social criticism. His celebrated Wellerisms — quotations from farfetched contexts twisted into new applications — extend the dialogue, by way of verbal parallels, to a metaphorical plane of trenchant commentary. The very first of these indulges in hangman's humor, apropos of the row of boots he is polishing: "reg'lar rotation, as Jack Ketch said, wen he tied the men up." The special affinity between master and man is underlined by the Christian name they share, and it may be worth incidentally noting that Weller was the surname of a maidservant in Dickens' mother's family (Pickwick was a name on a stagecoach between Bath and London). The classic quotation, whether two can live as cheaply as one, is put by Mr. Pickwick to his landlady with the notion of hiring Sam in mind. She interprets it as a proposal, and it leads to her breach-of-promise suit. But what she discerns in her lodger's eye is not, nor could ever be, "a species of matrimonial twinkle"; for Mr. Pickwick is consecrated to bachelorhood, and to the club as a haven of fellowship, an inner sanctum of masculine camaraderie. Moreover, he is surrounded by object-lessons militating against the hazards of matrimony, such as the conjugal hostilities of Mr. and Mrs. Pott or the Widder's conquest of Sam's philosophical father, "a wictim of connubiality."

Even in those interpolations after the mode of Cervantes which lend a note of lugubrious fantasy to the rough-and-tumble merriment, there are occasions which inform against marriage. In the ghostly tale of the Bagman's Uncle, that dignitary rescues — or dreams he does — a beautiful girl from her captors, though he has had no more preparation for dueling than a private performance as Richard III. But his romance is blighted when she vanishes into the eighteenth century, having exacted from him a vow that he would marry no other. Celibacy sets a seal on avuncularity. When Don Quixote blundered into the wrong bedroom, he could resist the maid of the inn, Maritornes, because he had sworn everlasting fidelity to Dulcinea del Toboso. Mr. Pickwick has no such commitment to protect his chastity, when he makes the same mistake in the Great White Horse at Ipswich, and finds himself sharing the chamber of a middle-aged lady in yellow curl-papers. Nonetheless his response to their confrontation is just as maidenly as hers. "Mr. Pickwick, it is quite unnecessary to say, was one of the most modest and delicate-minded of mortals. The very idea of exhibiting his nightcap to a lady, overpowered him." Ironically, he backs out of the situation into the threat of a duel with her suitor, Mr. Peter Magnus. Mr. Magnus has confided in him and asked his advice on the tactics of courtship. Mr. Pickwick, while emphatically denying that he has "done this sort of thing" in his time, has plotted a successful scenario. His reintroduction to the lady forms a painful recognition scene. Happily the duel is averted by the next set of anti-climactic complications.

Decidedly he is not a marrying man, much less a ladies' man of any sort, and yet he can by no means be considered a misogamist. He takes a vengeful pride in thwarting Jingle's matches and showing up that adventurer's designs. But when he sympathizes with the lovers, he arranges trysts and mollifies parents or rivals, and in the book's four marriages he plays a benign and Cupid-like part. Three of these are quickly subsumed in the closing pages; the other one, the centerpiece of the book, coincides with the celebration of Christmas at Manor Farm, Dingley Dell; and Dickens makes a point of celebrating the nuptial with "other Sports" and attendant customs. While Mr. Trundle, the bride-groom, remains an inconspicuous mute, Mr. Pickwick volubly steps forward to dominate the proceedings. Naturally he is the principal witness, the first to kiss the bride, Isabella Wardle, and the proposer of the toast. In his speech he momentarily — and dashingly — wishes himself young enough to be her husband, and finally rejoices at being old enough to preserve a fatherly attitude. During the evening, having replaced his habitual gaiters with pumps and speckled stockings, he leads the dance; on the following night, Christmas Eve, he is the main attraction under the mistletoe and the leading spirit in blindman's buff. Weddings are licensed subjects for jesting, the author remarks, but he is speaking merely of ceremonies, and indulging in "no hidden sarcasm upon a married life." As it happened, Dickens was married to Catherine Hogarth two days after the first installment of *Pickwick Papers* was published. It was destiny that indulged in hidden sarcasm.

The decisive episode of Bardell versus Pickwick is a trial in

the fullest connotation of the term, a public ordeal testing and
confirming Mr. Pickwick's resistance to marriage. Many of the
satirical touches caught echoes from the contemporaneous
Norton-Melbourne divorce case. When the judicial travesty cul-
minates by upholding Mrs. Bardell's claim, Mr. Pickwick reaffirms his principles by preferring to be imprisoned rather than
to pay damages. As the story proceeds from courtroom to prison,
Dickens' mood shifts from satire to reform, and foreshadows
his deepening humanitarianism: "This is no fiction." The
retrospective preface expresses his satisfaction at the legal and
penal improvements that have come about since his attacks, in
particular the demolition of the Fleet and the revision of —
always a sore point with him — "the laws relating to imprisonment for debt." As contrasted with the verdant pastoralism of
Dingley Dell or even the low comedy of the innyards, Mr. Pickwick's grand tour now takes a realistic direction, a descent into
hell. His relations with his fellow prisoners in the Fleet bring out
that ambivalence for which Thomas Hood coined a punning
phrase, "the goodness of Pickwickedness." Goodness presupposes wickedness, to be sure. The Pickwickian exploration of
men and manners, though it has occasionally suffered from the
impudence and double dealing of Jingle and his ilk, has scarcely
come to grips with radical evil. Later the opposing forces will
cease to be capricious individuals and assume the guise of self-
destructive institutions. Mr. Pickwick's brief sojourn in the
underworld offers him his most genuine opportunity for the
exercise of virtue.

Any taste for revenge would be highly gratified by the incarceration of Jingle at last, together with his scruffy henchman Job
Trotter, to whom Mr. Pickwick's greeting is "Take that, sir."

> Take what? in the ordinary acceptation of such language it
> should have been a blow. As the world runs, it ought to have
> been a sound, hearty cuff; for Mr. Pickwick had been duped,
> deceived, and wronged by the destitute outcast who was now
> wholly in his power. Must we tell the truth? It was something
> from Mr. Pickwick's waistcoat-pocket, which chinked as it was
> given into Job's hand: and the giving of which, somehow or other
> imparted a sparkle to the eye, and a swelling to the heart, of our

excellent old friend, as he hurried away. (*Pickwick Papers,* chap. XLI)

In the holiday circles through which he has previously moved, beaming smiles and paternalistic gestures have been adequate expressions of his innate good will. The Pickwick that emerges from the Fleet is ready to transpose that bland benevolism into serious action. Turning the other cheek to Jingle and Trotter, he passes beyond mere Quixotry toward the Sermon on the Mount, as Dostoevsky hinted. He not only secures their release and arranges their rehabilitation; he is furthermore persuaded to pay the costs for Mrs. Bardell, rather than allow her to be jailed for them, as he has been at her lawyers' instance. As the chapter-heading sums it up: "Mr. Pickwick's benevolence proves stronger than his obstinacy." To moralize in the most general terms, mercy and grace have transcended legalistic and punitive notions of justice — thereby enabling W. H. Auden to interpret the book as another allegory of the Fall of Man. Dickens was suspicious of philanthropy in some of its institutionalized manifestations, but Mr. Pickwick qualifies as a philanthropist by the simple etymological definition of Abou ben Adhem: "one who loves his fellow men." Though he seems bereft of family ties, and avoids domestic entanglements, he is *engagé* in a broader commitment. His unaging "juvenility of spirit," his wholehearted eagerness to be a participant in the fun, without regard for such petty concerns as dignity or prudence, quickens our sense of involvement in other lives than our own. As a patron and problem-solver he is all too fallible; he can be led astray by a clever rogue like Jingle, as he is to the girls' school at Bury St. Edmunds; yet it must be said, as it could be of any leader, that those who depend upon him are more naive and trusting than he.

In the end the club becomes a clan, with Mr. Pickwick as its honorary patriarch. When he settles down into retirement, some of his following are "disposed to think that he contemplated a matrimonial alliance; but this idea the ladies most strenuously repudiated." Their instincts are amply justified when his house-warming party at Dulwich turns out to be the wedding of Snodgrass and Emily Wardle. Her sister, Mrs. Trundle, is permitted to attend in an interesting condition. Among the festive couples are Winkle and the former Arabella Allen, to whose match Mr. Pickwick has reconciled their relatives. Only one of his three clubmen is still unmarried: the ever hopeful Tupman has been disillusioned by the old maid Rachael Wardle, after Mr. Pickwick exposed her scheduled elopement with Jingle. Like his mentor, and like Reginald Bunthorne, "Single will he live and die." But the others have defected and are giving hostages to fortune, the clubbable comradeship of the jolly bachelors has become a thing of the past, and the Pickwick Club is dissolved forever. Mr. Pickwick gathers consolation from the unbroken attendance of the faithful Sam, one of whose duties is to read aloud from the club's memoranda. And after two years more, when the housekeeper opportunely dies, Mr. Pickwick makes his final match; he promotes the pretty Ipswich housemaid Mary to the vacant post, on condition that she espouse her patient fiancé, Sam. The priority of the master's comfort over the man-servant's modus vivendi could not have been more strikingly confirmed. But Sam and Mary will have "two sturdy little boys," and the *ménage à cinq* will live on in happy togetherness.

We could not imagine Mr. Pickwick coping anywhere without Sam Weller, who had even sacrificed his own freedom to continue his service in the Fleet. Obviously the servant is a more competent and better-rounded human being than the man he serves. Yet Pickwick's kindness is authenticated by the loyalties it commands, just as his idealism gains substance from the earthy touch of Sam's realism. The concluding words of the last sentence in the book crystallize their relationship into "a steady and reciprocal attachment which nothing but death will terminate." It is no coincidence that echoes the language of the marriage vow: "till death do us part." After all, the alliance between the two men has been heralded by the ambiguous question that Mrs. Bardell mistook for a marriage proposal. Two can live together more happily than, if not as cheaply as, one; so can five, if necessary; the more the merrier, as long as number one is at the head of his surrogate family. Pickwick's bond with Sam is stronger than Sam's with Mary, stronger than the unions that have mated his ex-colleagues, because it is social and ethical rather than sexual or genetic, because it assumes responsibilities that could have been ignored: Sam's on behalf of Pickwick, and

Pickwick's on behalf of the rest. Both will go on making their pilgrimages to the annual ceremonies at Dingley Dell. Mr. Pickwick will stand as godfather to an expanding new generation of Winkles and Snodgrasses. The posthumous papers of his little society will spread his benediction along with his legend, so that, in the observances of sociability, he will be invoked as a universal uncle.

No other novel of Dickens has a chief protagonist who is nearly as old as Mr. Pickwick; his must therefore be our full-length portrait of benevolent avuncularity. Many of his acquaintance are not much younger, but the novelist was, and he shaded in his elders with a tinge of youthful ridicule: witness Mr. Tupman, dressing up and behaving as if he were still a young man. Children figure mainly as supernumeraries at family parties. If the Fat Boy stands out, it is less for his eating and sleeping than for his precocious Gothic vein: "I wants to make your flesh creep." Subsequently Dickens will train his focus on boys and girls, and — so far as these survive — on young men and women, growing up and learning the ways of the world. Parents, we have noted, take little part in this initiatory process; there are other mentors, both for better and for worse. In the classical epic man's destinies were overseen by the gods, and either guided or persecuted according to the state of affairs in the heavens. So it may be with Dickens' heroes and heroines, scarcely comprehending the intrigues and alignments that lie in wait to descend upon them from on high, alternately hounded by an evil genius or else delivered by a deus ex machina. Those preternatural forces assume the human shape of Good or Bad Uncles, whose archetypal forebears were Don Quixote and Richard III respectively, and whose Dickensian models are Mr. Pickwick and Scrooge in his malevolent pre-Christmas phase. Graham Greene, who is keenly aware of such tensions, aptly points out how the Dickensian melodrama is heightened by "the eternal and alluring taint of the Manichee."

Overwhelming benevolence, which prevails in *Pickwick Papers,* is more evenly matched — and sometimes overwhelmed in its turn — by the powers of malevolence unleashed through Dickens' subsequent novels, where he probes more deeply and

ranges more widely. A rapid survey should allow us to view
them, more or less chronologically, as a series of individual con-
flicts in a continuous psychomachia. There is never any tragic
doubt regarding the basic distinctions between good and evil, yet
the outcome of their spiritual struggle becomes less certain and
more complex as the novelist develops. *Oliver Twist,* with its
subtitle echoing Bunyan, *The Parish Boy's Progress,* comes earliest and closest to explicit allegory. As if the personifications were
not obvious, the author labels them in his prefatory apologia for
the ethical realism of his presentation:

> I have yet to learn that a lesson of the purest good may not
> be drawn from the vilest evil . . . I saw no reason, when I wrote
> this book, why the dregs of life . . . should not serve the purpose
> of a moral, as well as its froth and cream.

> In this spirit, when I wished to show, in little Oliver, the prin-
> ciple of Good surviving through every adverse circumstance, and
> triumphing at last; when I considered among what companions
> I could try him best, having regard to that kind of men into
> whose hands he would most naturally fall; I bethought myself
> of those who figure in these volumes. (*Oliver Twist,* Introduction)

Hence he personified the principle of Evil through characters
from the London underworld, who were then figuring in "mur-
derous melodramas" or "Sensation Novels" of the Newgate
School. The institution he began by attacking was the New Poor
Law and its social consequence, the workhouse system. But
Everychild, in the person of Oliver, moves on into a morality,
which shunts him back and forth between the thieves' kitchen of
Fagin, the wicked Jew, and the comfortable homes provided by
the respectable Mr. Brownlow and his kindly friends, the May-
lies. The title of one chapter, "The Pursuit and Escape," applies
to the larger pattern. Oliver is rescued by his benefactors and
recaptured by the malefactors; no haven seems safe from the
nightmarish apparition at the window of Fagin and the villainous
half-brother Monks. When Bill Sikes murders Nancy, who has
repented of her complicity in the kidnapping, he is hunted down
— a recurrent Dickensian phrase — to a providential retribution.
Fagin, "the merry old gentleman," inducting boys into crime and

thereby perverting the functions of teacher and sponsor, is duly condemned to a ranting execution. Oliver is definitively rescued and restored to his inherent goodness; the foundling is adopted into a family, which is all but his own. It transpires that the old-fashioned Pickwickian bachelor, Mr. Brownlow, is almost his uncle, having once been engaged to Oliver's father's sister long defunct. Even more providentially, the sisterly Rose Maylie turns out to be Oliver's aunt, having been the sister of his dead mother. As the two orphans embrace, "A father, sister, and mother were gained, and lost, in that one moment."

The Old Curiosity Shop, to some extent, retraces the pilgrim's progress of *Oliver Twist.* Its orphan heroine is another babe, wandering through the urban and provincial woods, whose burdens are augmented by the gambling habits of her prodigal grandfather. Daniel Quilp, the dwarfish landlord who evicts them from the shop, persecutes them with a hatred which transcends the profit motive. "A little hunchy villain and a monster," in the words of his mother-in-law, he practices his villainies with a sadistic gusto, croaking and snarling, making faces and taking pleasure in being reprobated as a moneylending fiend. He is complimented when the obsequious lawyer, Sampson Brass, calls him "Quite a Buffoon." His affinity with Richard III, had it not been remarked by his own wife, would be signalized by his headquarters on Tower Hill. Histrionically he indulges in asides and soliloquies, some of them approximating blank verse. He is truly Ricardian when he proposes that Little Nell marry him as soon as his first wife dies. More grotesquely than any of Mrs. Jarley's waxworks, he infests Nell's troubled dreams. To her rescue comes a mysterious stranger, an eccentric but sympathetic traveler, the Single Gentleman, who is revealed to be her great-uncle in the final disentanglement. She and Grandfather Trent are also sheltered by another avuncular type, the Old Bachelor. But such efforts are too little and too late; they are overshadowed by the machinations of Quilp, who keeps popping up in pursuit, "like a head in a phantasmagoria." The Manichaean contest is resolved, for once, by the triumph of darkness over light. Hence the special status of "the Nelliad" among Dickens' works.

Nicholas Nickleby meanwhile had started its hero out from young manhood, and plotted a picaresque course for him after the fashion of Smollett, whose influence extends to the alliterative name. In his quest for a vocation, Nicholas undergoes three successive apprenticeships: with Wackford Squeers at Dotheboys Hall, with Vincent Crummles and his troupe of traveling actors, and finally with the brothers Cheeryble in their countinghouse. The theatrical interlude is a comic divertissement, set between the harsh satire on Yorkshire schools and the philanthropic commercialism of the bourgeois conclusion. The brothers Ned and Charles are identical twins, self-made merchants, and bachelors of course; their twinkling and hand-rubbing, their Pickwickian gaiters, and their reduplicating conversation lend them an air of unreality, though Dickens vouches that they were drawn from life. Their benefactions, which make up all too handily for the deficits of the plot, are balanced against the malefactions of Ralph Nickleby, the wicked uncle incarnate. As a cruel usurer and crafty stock-promoter, he is likewise the embodiment of business in its malign and fraudulent aspects. "In short, the poor Nicklebys were social and happy; while the rich Nickleby was alone and miserable." That would be sufficient reason for waging a remorseless vendetta against his nephew, while exploiting his niece Kate by exposing her to the molestations of the rakish Sir Mulberry Hawk. All Ralph's wiles are foiled, with the revelation of his fatherhood and Smike's death, and he sneers and curses his way to self-destruction. The wheel of flouted obligations comes full circle when Smike's tormentor, Squeers, boasts that "Mrs. Squeers has been his mother, grandmother, aunt, — Ah! and I may say uncle too, all in one!"

Martin Chuzzlewit also follows the rambling Smollett-like form, but the orphaned hero's itinerary stretches across the Atlantic, and the pangs of his American misadventures do more to mature him than the auspices of any preceptor. Mr. Pecksniff moralizes with unction and then plagiarizes from his apprentice; Grandfather Martin deliberately acts out the role of a peevish miser in order to bring their selfishness home to his grasping heirs. The question of their problematic inheritance is raised in a mock-heroic exordium, which claims a noble heritage of "violence and vagabondism" for the pedigree of the Chuzzlewits. One of the nastiest among Dickens' unhappy families, they are introduced in a kind of death-watch, and their intrigues over the "testamentary designs" of their hardy patriarch would confirm the shrewdest suspicions of Ben Jonson or Balzac. Martin's cousin, Jonas Chuzzlewit, is the most guileful of the clan, and one of the most energetic in the sinister crew of Dickens' financial operators. Charity and Mercy have been sardonically twisted into the nicknames of Pecksniff's daughters, Cherry and Merry. Jonas courting the elder and marrying the younger, may remind us again of Richard III: "Was ever woman in such humor wooed?" Is there a slight suggestion here of Dickens' own preference for his wife's younger sister? It is scarcely corroborated when Merry — ha! ha! — gets "blighted and plighted," beaten and broken by her drunken husband. Jonas rushes from bad to worse, from stock-promotion to bankruptcy; having practically committed patricide by putting his father in the way of suicide, he murders his fellow swindler, Montague Tigg; and after such wild flights, he self-destructs, like Quilp and the other ogres.

Business is not a swindling operation but an encroachment upon the family in *Dombey and Son*. Paul, the poor little rich boy, is no less a waif for having a purseproud father, to whom fatherhood means little more than continuance of the firm. "Is Florence an orphan like me?" asks a child she encounters. She is one, in spite of her father's existence, since she has no place at all among his values; nor does her spirited stepmother, Edith, who — like Florence, but with a compromising difference — will be forced into flight. School, as usual, sets exercises in homesickness, while the object-lesson of Paul's death reaffirms those values which money cannot buy. He has been too "old-fashioned" for the times; but so is Mr. Dombey, whose maritime ventures are jeopardized by the new railways and will be wrecked by the loss of the freighter *Son and Heir*. These circumstances are complemented by the fortunes of the adolescent Walter Gay and his doting uncle Sol Gills, "an old-fashioned man in an old-fashioned shop." It may be regarded as a Freudian slip, and likewise as an ironic insight, when Mr. Dombey recognizes Walter in his employ: " 'Oh! you are the son of Mr. Gills the ships' instrument maker.' 'Nephew, sir,' I said. 'I said nephew, boy,' said he." When the uncle leaves to search for his nephew, presumably lost at sea, his salty friend Captain Cuttle takes over the nautical supply store, and becomes a foster-uncle to Florence. All are reunited and reconciled there, where Mr. Dombey will have a grandson to dote on. Character had been ordinarily so fixed and so unmitigated by change, with Dickens, that he felt called upon to defend this softening in his preliminary remarks.

In *David Copperfield* the narrator, engendered from the wounding immediacies of Dickens' own boyhood, is the most internal of his characterizations. Many of the other characters seem larger than life-size because their impact is registered upon his inexperience. All too soon he finds himself an orphan, along with his schoolmate Traddles; both his idol, Steerforth, and his aversion, Uriah Heep, are significantly fatherless; while the little mother, Agnes Wickfield, lacks a mother herself, and must bear increasing responsibility for her weak-willed father. In this thoroughly domestic novel there are few unbroken families. True, the Micawbers will always stick together, as Mrs. M. repeatedly avers — but in a vagrant household, attended solely by an "orfling." The idyllic *ménage* residing in the upturned boat at Yarmouth is fathered by a bachelor uncle, Mr. Peggotty, and mothered by a lone, lorn, sniveling widow, Mrs. Gummidge; the cousins, Ham and Little Emily, orphaned when their seagoing fathers were "drown-dead," are fated not to marry. If David's pathetic first marriage to the child-wife Dora is somewhat autobiographical, he waxes somewhat allegorical when he dubs Agnes and Steerforth his Good and Bad Angels. The greatest moral influence, however, is not exerted by such companions or coevals. Malevolence itself, disguised thinly as righteousness, is wielded by the Murdstones, stepfather and step-aunt. Kindness, hardly masked by crustiness, is dispensed through Betsy Trotwood, great-aunt and fairy godmother. Divorced, and shadily dogged by her former husband, she has given shelter to the homeless simpleton, Mr. Dick. David starts, like Oliver, disowned and cast adrift; his adoption gives him a fresh start and an adult career.

Thus *David Copperfield* graduates from the picaresque morality into the full-fledged *Bildungsroman*. Dickens would return to such first-person narrative and to the development of personality with a darker, more detached, and more tightly constructed work, *Great Expectations*. The second performance is more dramatic in its shift from poverty to affluence, as it is more critical in its attitude toward the slowly maturing protagonist and his two contrasting worlds. The orphan Pip has been brought up "by hand" — the rough hand of his termagant older sister and the warm, large, blacksmith's hand of his brother-in-law, Joe Gargery. The condescension of Miss Havisham and the mockery of Estella combine to make him "feel ashamed of home," so that, when an unaccountable windfall comes his way, he is ready to become a snob and a social climber. Great expectations lapse into *illusions perdues*, and the scales fall from his eyes with the realization that his benefactor has been a malefactor. Unlike David or Oliver, Pip owes his good fortune directly to the traumatic incident of his boyhood, when he was terrified into helping a convict to escape. Now that convict, Abel Magwitch, reveals himself as the rich uncle from the colonies.

> "Yes, Pip, dear boy, I've made a gentleman on you! It's me wot has done it! I swore that time, sure as ever I earned a guinea, that guinea should go to you. I swore arterwards, sure as ever I spec'lated and got rich, you should get rich. I lived rough, that you should live smooth; I worked hard that you should be above work. What odds, dear boy? Do I tell it fur you to feel an obligation? Not a bit. I tell it, fur you to know as that there hunted dunghill dog wot you kep life in, got his head so high that he could make a gentleman — and, Pip, you're him!" (*Great Expectations*, chap. XXXIX)

This recognition scene is especially painful because it entails a moment of self-recognition. Magwitch's triumph means a humiliation for Pip, a reversal of those worldly standards which have measured his rise — and with it, with the ill-fated effort to save the embarrassing "Uncle Provis," a dawning awareness of the ex-convict's human worth. "That's it, dear boy. Call me uncle." His genuine commitment to unclehood is parodied in the figure of the pompous busybody, Uncle Pumblechook, a Dickensian variant of M. Homais. "I was not allowed to call him uncle, under the severest penalties," says Pip. Yet it is he who has launched Pip by conducting him to Miss Havisham's, and who complains widely of Pip's ingratitude to his "earliest benefactor and the founder of [his] fortunes." His formation as a gentleman, under the distant patronage of Magwitch, has its counterpart in Miss Havisham's vengeful upbringing of Estella

— who, it will appear, is only a pseudo-orphan, provided with shady parents by the dénouement. Life has chastened her capriciousness, as well as Pip's snobbery, when they meet and part again. We know that Dickens intended to make the parting final, and that he was persuaded by Bulwer-Lytton to leave open the possibility of a happier ending.

We have anticipated the chronological sequence because of closer links between the two *Bildungsromane*. Three other novels need merely be glanced at together in passing, since their basis in historic events led them to stress the social panorama at the expense of the psychological pattern. The waiflike personage is titular, but marginal to the turbulent action of *Barnaby Rudge*: a half-demented mascot among the mob scenes, with a mascot of his own, the raven Grip. The theme of a revolutionary uprising, which culminates in the storming of a prison, is more effectively handled in *A Tale of Two Cities*. There the parallel between Paris and London is matched by the interchanging identities of the two heroes, Charles Darnay and Sidney Carton. Doubling also brings about the confusions of the underplot, inasmuch as Darnay's condemnation happens to be the people's revenge for the misdeeds of his uncle, his father's twin brother, the profligate and haughty Marquis de Saint-Evrémonde. History is contemporary in *Hard Times,* where the menace of revolution impends in a Lancashire strike. Stephen Blackpool, its public victim, is privately victimized by the marital dilemma that binds him to a drunkard and separates him from his beloved Rachael. The irresponsibility of the authorities is attacked through the industrialism of the not quite self-made Bounderby and the utilitarianism of the laissez-faire apologist, Gradgrind. Manchester capitalism, far from being a system, is — as Stephen puts it — "aw a muddle." Concern for others, conspicuously absent from bank and factory, is manifested only at the circus. Sissy, "the stroller's child," and the ringmaster, Mr. Sleary, help to save the Gradgrind offspring from the consequences of their inhuman education.

In *Bleak House* there are many mansions, as well as several orphans. The substantial middle-class abode so chillingly named is connected through "the network of circumstances" with the country gentry at Chesney Wold, the legal establishment at

Lincoln's Inn, and the slum-dwelling paupers of Tom-All-Alones. The delayed bequest of Jarndyce and Jarndyce will prove a curse for Rick and Ada Carstone, wards in Chancery. As their institutional uncle, the Lord Chancellor seems omnipresent and unavailable, vicariously mocked by the gaseous fate of the junk-dealer, Mr. Krook. As head of the house and acting guardian of the parentless family, John Jarndyce is more humane but no more effectual in protecting them from the entanglements of the law. Esther Summerson, his "little old woman" who tells half the story, is less orphaned than she seems. She is entrusted with housekeeper's keys, and — like Agnes, Nell, and Amy Dorrit — with responsibilities beyond her years. Though Jarndyce steps momentarily out of his uncle's role by proposing to her, he is quickly if gently pushed back into middle-aged bachelorhood. The January-May romances of Dickens' later books may have been inspired by his own affair with Ellen Ternan. Farther-reaching changes in his outlook seem to have affected the structure of his scenarios. His juveniles still meet with help and hindrance on their pilgrimages into life; but life itself is more of a muddle than a progress; and the helping or the hindering may now be attributed to institutions rather than individuals. The philanthropy of do-gooders like Mrs. Jellyby is absurdly misplaced in a dislocated society, whereas so hardened a representative of legalism as Mr. Tulkinghorn is really more of an agent than a villain.

Hence the working title for *Little Dorrit: Nobody's Fault*. The institutions that dominate this book are the Marshalsea and the Circumlocution Office, debtors' prison and government bureaucracy. Dickens gave full scope to his obsession with parental deliquency in the father-figure of William Dorrit. Dubbed "the Father of the Marshalsea" for his long incarceration there, he comports himself as its *doyen,* patronizing his fellow prisoners while expecting tips from them as tributes to his record for insolvency. Dickens' old ideal of elderly patronage is reduced to further absurdity in Christopher Casby, an avaricious landlord whose benign expression and venerable locks equip him to pose as "the Last of the Patriarchs." Pancks, his hired extortioner, turns and exposes him to his tenants, altering his countenance by snipping off his white hair: "What's your moral game? What do you do in for? Benevolence, an't it? YOU benevolent!" Amy Dorrit, "Child of the Marshalsea," is the little mother par excellence, taking care of her father and equally feckless brother while her sister dances in a theater. One of the musicians is their "ruined uncle" Frederick, ruined by William Dorrit, a weak yet "fatherly" personality, who might remind us of Balzac's Cousin Pons. When vicissitude suddenly raises the Dorrits from the "Poverty" of Part I to the "Riches" of Part II, Amy is reproved by them for not adjusting to their new sphere of parvenu pretentiousness, and their gentle uncle is moved to an outburst on her behalf:

> "To the winds with the family credit!" cried the old man, with great scorn and indignation. "Brother, I protest against pride. I protest against ingratitude. I protest against any one of us here who has known what we have known, and have seen what we have seen, setting up any pretension that puts Amy at a moment's disadvantage, or to the cost of a moment's pain . . . It ought to bring a judgment on us. Brother, I protest against it, in the sight of God!" (*Little Dorrit*, part II, chap. v)

Amy's confidant and unlikely suitor, Arthur Clennam, is a tired, sad, and rather ineffectual hero. Coming back to his oppressive home after more than twenty years in China, he breaks with his commercial-minded mother, who actually proves to be his stepmother. Having — like the Dorrits and too many others — invested in the collapsing speculations of the great financier, Mr. Merdle, Arthur too must undergo the purgatory of a sojourn in the Marshalsea. He regains his freedom and gains happiness with Amy through his inventive partner, Daniel Doyce, whose technological pertinacity has overcome the vested inertia of the circumlocution office.

Clennam might be loosely designated, as John Harmon is, *Our Mutual Friend*. Both are aging heroes, "constrained, reserved, diffident, troubled," hovering in the background, playing spectatorial parts, and keeping other characters in touch. Incognito, a self-appointed guardian exercising a clandestine surveillance, Harmon goes beyond the precedent of Magwitch to emulate the Caliph in *The Arabian Nights* or Vautrin in *The*

Human Comedy. His chosen and unknowing ward, the pampered Bella Wilfer, is also schooled and tested by the Boffins, adopting her to share in their sudden affluence. Their legacy, of which Harmon is a secret beneficiary, has its source in dustheaps, accumulations of junk, the decomposing middens of civilization itself. Noddy Boffin, "the Golden Dustman," who is modest, honest, and generous by nature, must impersonate a miser in the charade enacted for Bella's benefit. He carries the impersonation much farther than the elder Chuzzlewit; indeed he reverses Scrooge's conversion from avarice to freehandedness. A comparable paradox is embodied in the characterization of Riah, the good Jew, a character deliberately created to counterbalance and rectify the prejudicial image of Fagin in *Oliver Twist*. Riah nevertheless bears all the stigmata of pinching usury; but he too is acting; for he is compelled to be a mere factor — or *âme damnée* — to the actual usurer, Fascination Fledgby, who may thereby pose as a callow man about town. Riah discloses his innate benignity when he finds a sanctum among his Jewish brethren for the fugitive heroine, Lizzie Hexam. He ends by sharing his own retreat with the crippled Jenny Wren, after she has lost her drunken charge, becoming her "second father" and being quaintly addressed as "fairy godmother."

The mounting complications of Dickens' plots had to be held together by the darkly melodramatic *ficelles* of suspense and disclosure. Characters accordingly became, as Mr. Grewgious describes himself, "particularly Angular." Dickens had already called in a detective, Inspector Bucket, to unravel the mysteries of *Bleak House*. His own death, overtaking him after six monthly installments, left unsolved *The Mystery of Edwin Drood*. Yet John Forster's biography gives away the probable solution, "the murder of a nephew by an uncle," though conjectures diverge as to how it would have been reached. Dickens wrote enough to depict John Jasper, the hypnotic organist, as the most complex of his uncles, professing warm regards and harboring jealous reservations. "Uncle and nephew," he says ambiguously, "are words prohibited here by common consent and express agreement." His schizoid temperament is attuned to the novel's frenetic movement between cathedral choir and opium den, between the precincts of Trollope and those of Wilkie Collins. Jasper is the "guardian and trustee" of the vanishing hero, the naive and brash Edwin, who is temporarily betrothed to another orphan, Rosa Budd. Her guardian is Mr. Grewgious, the lawyer, while the orphans from the Orient, Neville and Helena Landless, are in the charge of a pseudophilanthropist, Mr. Honeythunder. Dickens did not get to work out the interplay between these varying guardians and their various wards; and if the murder was to be a nepoticide, it remains forever shrouded by non-completion. But, writing fifteen novels in thirty-three years, he traversed the distance from the open road and cheery innyard to the nocturnal close and Gothic crypt, and from the Pickwickian model of unclehood to its opposite extreme, the Ricardian.

This summary roll-call can have barely suggested certain lines of thematic continuity which lend a family likeness to all of Dickens' novels. Not that I am proposing a critical reduction to what Joyce would call a "monomyth." The teeming invention and unforgettable detail that give each novel its uniquely intense particularity stand well beyond our question. But creation on any scale — not excluding the cosmic — is bound to involve repetitions, and patterns of recurrence offer keys to the meaning of a writer's work as a whole. Proust discerned key-passages conveying leitmotifs through the writings of such novelists as Stendhal, Balzac, George Eliot, and Thomas Hardy. Henry James's metaphor of "the figure in the carpet" has alerted critics to look closely for some internal source of configuration. David Copperfield learns that "Mr. Dick had been for upwards of ten years endeavouring to keep King Charles the First out of the Memorial; but he had been constantly getting into it, and was there now." Dickens never spoke of his father's term in the Marshalsea or his own apprenticeship in the blacking-factory. Yet the double secret had made an impress on his mind which he could not have kept out of his fiction. The fatherless David is forced to paste labels on bottles, while the prodigal father, William Dorrit, blurts out his humiliating past at a Roman banquet. That compulsion was held in check for the most part, and the original trauma was buried in the depths of Dickens' imagination. There it left its mark on his further impressions, shaping his memorial of events and issues. King Charles's head, as Miss Trotwood understands, is Mr. Dick's "allegorical way of expressing" his own mentality.

Out of this obsessive situation, two archetypal figures emerge —or rather a relationship between them; for we are too readily put off by our habit of regarding the Dickensian cosmos as a troop of separable characters, rather than a network of human relations, a nuclear family with the author/reader at the core. If they seem flat, as they did to E. M. Forster, it is because they must be rounded out by our apprehension of them. These two archetypes are the orphan child, at the center of consciousness, and the surrogate father, who is often quite literally the uncle, and who always mediates between the protagonist and the world, whether as his sponsor or his adversary. Smike, Esther, and Estella are not pure orphans, since parents unexpectedly turn up; but orphanhood is the spiritual state of all the heroes or heroines. Some, like Nell or Paul, are cut off in childhood; with others, as with Oliver and Sissy, the story terminates at adolescence. When the waif is permitted to grow up, he or she may sponsor other waifs in turn, as does Nicholas with poor Smike or Amy Dorrit with the half-witted Maggie. Fatherhood is given a bad name, not only by Mr. Dorrit and the other irresponsibles cared for by their children, but also by those loudly voluble moralists whose children go astray: Gradgrind, Pecksniff, Podsnap. Vicarious parenthood in the earlier novels is exercised by such Pickwickian types as Mr. Brownlow or the Cheerybles. More complex, Betsy Trotwood reincarnates the touchy benefactress of fairy lore who walked out of the christening offended by the sex of her godchild. Magwitch, redeeming his criminality through Pip's career, plays the patron anonymously, a secret sharer.

In the later novels the central male figure tends to be older, and to occupy a halfway position between orphaned youth and middle-aged paternalism. Witness Jarndyce, Clennam, and Harmon, especially the last realizing the voyeuristic role of the unknown guardian. Guardianship is represented more and more by lawyers, such as Grewgious, Jaggers, or — on the side of the enemy — Tulkinghorn. Benefactors tend to be decreasingly powerful, even while the hostile powers are being institutionalized instead of personified. The foes of youth are melodramatic vil-

lains in the Ricardian tradition, who confound themselves like
Fagin, Quilp, and Jonas. That stock impersonation becomes elusive, with the chameleonic Rigaud-Blandois in *Little Dorrit* or
the shadowy Compeyson in *Great Expectations,* and all but fades
away in the vengeful crowds of *Barnaby Rudge, Hard Times,*
and *A Tale of Two Cities.* Yet its ghost returns to make a farewell appearance in the schizophrenic drug-addict John Jasper,
probably a nephew-murderer like Richard Crookback himself,
although the crime is lost in mystery. As Dickens proceeds toward the darker end of the spectrum, his images of authority lose
their avuncular privilege. His establishments are menaced with
portents of disestablishment by the fall of the house of Clennam
or the whiff of spontaneous combustion in the rag-and-bone
shop, Mr. Krook's mock-Chancery. Wrongdoing moves its headquarters from the underworld of Fagin and Bill Sikes to the
upper world of Mr. Merdle, the Barnacles, and the Lord Chancellor. Royalty itself, the highest form of paternity, is mocked in
Mr. Turveydrop's emulation of George IV, through which
Dickens seems to be asking us: what are kings but Models of
Deportment, dandified and parasitical?

   "God and the Devil are always fighting," Dostoevsky attested,
"and the battlefield is the heart of man." This is equally the
animating principle in Dickens, with due allowance for his
graphic skill in externalizing and localizing the endless psychomachia. Despite what Louis Cazamian termed his "philosophy
of Christmas," despite the need to justify Micawber's optimism,
despite a teleological commitment to happy endings, he was less
and less inclined to underestimate the power of the Manichaean
opposition. Cheerlessness is constantly breaking in. Death must
have its way with Little Nell, *Hard Times* concludes in little more
than a stalemate, and darkness seems to be prevailing over *Edwin
Drood.* When the patrons and the persecutors are clearly labeled,
as they are for Oliver Twist, then it is not difficult to distinguish
good from evil. But Nell is understandably confused when the
surly Codlin warns her not to trust his merry partner — "Codlin's the friend, not Short" — and both of them are conspiring
against her, as well as against each other. And though she encounters some true friends on her further peregrinations, they
will be powerless to save her. Would she have been safer if she

had professed the creed of Sampson Brass, "Always suspect everybody"? Mr. Pickwick never suspected anybody, and frequently he found himself in trouble. Truly, the Golden Rule is no easier to live by than the predatory ethic of Jonas Chuzzlewit: "Do other men, for they would do you." Jonas, however, is ultimately done in, by himself and by poetic justice. Benevolism triumphs with Pickwick's "Take that, sir!" when he forgoes revenge to offer charity, and we are invited to rejoice over the reform of two arrant sinners, Alfred Jingle and Job Trotter.

Malevolism will go on rearing its many ugly heads, and the psychic battle will be continually refought through quixotic forays and humanitarian campaigns. But, with the maturation of Dickens' art and thought, moral choice becomes more complicated. There is no development of character in such little pilgrims as Oliver and Nell; they are virtually impermeable to outside influences. But when we turn from the allegorical to the picaresque, semi-heroes like Nicholas and Martin are conditioned somewhat by the adventures through which they pass. Adventure is internalized in the *Bildung* of the autobiographical David or the more objectified Pip; the second novel can be read as a chastened reworking of the first; the providential role of Betsy Trotwood is happier — and luckier — than that of Abel Magwitch. In undermining Pip's expectations, while showing up their shallowness, Dickens comes closest to the paradigm of classic realism from Stendhal to Proust. It might not be inappropriate to think of his personae as members of a repertory company, where the same actor would play both Quilp and Fagin while another doubled as Pickwick and Brownlow. Such parts seem interchangeable precisely because of the attitudes they sustain, for all the histrionic variations. Dickens' personages are not rigidly incapable of growth and alteration, as Mr. Dombey demonstrates, especially when we compare him with Ralph Nickleby. Yet the change is rather a transformation than a modification in the midnight conversion of Scrooge or the split personality of Jasper. An effect of added depth is lent by hypocrisy, only to be theatrically unmasked with Uriah Heep. Riah proves the opposite of Uriah, the hypocrite in reverse, and the discovery of patriarchal benevolence behind his miser's mask helps explain Proust's enthusiasm for Dickens.

Dickens' three historic novels seem grimmer and less successful than most of the others, but they taught him to distance his
material, to decentralize his characterization, and to project a
society on a panoramic scale. From those lessons he profited in
three outstanding successes: *Bleak House, Little Dorrit,* and *Our
Mutual Friend.* His journalistic flair served him well in exploring
new backgrounds, exploiting subjects of current concern, and
varying the individuality of each successive volume. One would
not wish to minimize that seemingly endless variety which has
been a main attraction for the reading public. But it is worth
observing how the vivid particulars fit into a more general outline. The interesting suggestion of Mircea Eliade — that the
major novelists of the nineteenth century, though they incidentally complied with the naturalistic assumptions of their time,
were actually engaged in generating myths — applies to Dickens
with peculiar force. What I have been trying to sketch is the
structure of a consistent mythology which underlies the totality
of his writing. There may be at least a certain sense in which
every writer is *homo unius libri*: all his books may be considered
fragments, in Dostoevskian terms, of a great confession, perforce
his own. This is strikingly exemplified by Proust; *Jean Santeuil*
was merely a rehearsal; and he kept on rewriting and amplifying
The Remembrance of Things Past until it was concluded by his
death. Joyce, again, put everything into *Ulysses,* paving the way
with *Dubliners* and *A Portrait of the Artist as a Young Man,* and
making self-repetition the very essence of *Finnegans Wake.*

Balzac may indeed have covered more ground than any other
novelist, but he regarded *The Human Comedy* as a single comprehensive opus. Moreover, it could almost be epitomized by one
pervasive theme, the young man from the provinces challenging
Paris, even as the fiction of Henry James could be emblematized
by the image of a young American heiress dying abroad. So it
is with Dickens' orphans and uncles. The notion of a personal
myth is a paradox which seems warranted in his case by the
nature of his social involvement, the extent to which he lived his
work. He seldom paused from his strenuous endeavors to meditate upon the creative process. Yet it might be suggestive to
recall a trifling caricature of a minor character, summoned from
the void for a page and then dismissed in *Nicholas Nickleby.*

Miss Knag is telling Kate Nickleby about her brother Mortimer, a "small circulating library keeper" disappointed in love:

> "He is a wonderfully accomplished man — most extraordinarily accomplished — reads — hem — reads every novel that comes out; I mean every novel that — hem — has any fashion in it, of course. The fact is, that he did find so much in the books he read, applicable to his own misfortunes, and did find himself in every respect so much like the heroes — because of course he is conscious of his own superiority, as we all are, and very naturally — that he took to scorning everything, and became a genius; and I am quite sure that he is, at this very present moment, writing another book."

Dickens became a genius a harder way. Yet, like Mortimer, he identified with his heroes; he suffered their anxieties and vice versa; he acted out their rags-to-riches fantasies; he heaped his scorn without reserve on obstruction and oppression; through his novels he extended his fellow-feelings as widely as any man has ever done. In some ideal vision, to which he still adhered strongly, he had conceived the human condition as a happy family. If unhappiness prevailed there, it was because the father had been displaced and the son had been consequently neglected, and would measure each supervening influence by its capacity for filling that empty place — which thus became a matrix for the emergence of avuncular figures. Most men shared that wish-dream of happiness, and many had awakened to something like that nightmare of reality. Dickens could therefore universalize their waking dreams in his. He ended by becoming a kind of uncle to his multitudinous family of readers, as well as to the cast of characters whose fortunes he had looked after through thick and thin. Into those imagining and imaginary lives, his household words brought both the malediction of durance and the benediction of deliverance.

MELVYN HABERMAN

The Courtship of the Void:
The World of *Hard Times*

Hard Times interrogates a society quickly growing industrialized, a society organized, maintained, and sanctioned to a large degree by a philosophy Dickens considers obnoxious. It is true that he has a shallow notion of that philosophy,[1] but the conditions which utilitarianism helps to create and which influence the human relationships depicted in *Hard Times* are worth examining. Let Joseph Conrad sound the keynote: "The material apparatus of perfected civilization which obliterates the individuality of old towns under the stereotyped conveniences of modern life had not intruded as yet; but over the worn-out antiquity of Sulaco . . . that fact — very modern in its spirit — the San Tome mine had already thrown its subtle influence." [2] Rarely did Dickens write such a cumbersome sentence. But in their context in *Nostromo*

1. See, for example, Monroe Engel, *The Maturity of Dickens* (Cambridge: Harvard University Press, 1959), pp. 171–173; John Holloway, "*Hard Times*: A History and a Criticism." *Dickens and the Twentieth Century,* ed. John Gross and Gabriel Pearson (London: Routledge and Kegan Paul, 1962), pp. 159–174; David M. Hirsch, "*Hard Times* and Dr. Leavis," *Criticism,* 6 (Winter 1964), 1–16.
2. *Nostromo* (New York: Holt, Rinehart and Winston, 1961), p. 80.

Conrad's words describe the heavy weight of events under which the men in his novels so often break. A heavy weight matched by the prose: the largely Latinate diction reminds us that the process of industrialization, destroying variety, remains foreign to life, an intrusion. And Dickens, writing some six decades earlier, concurs. This essay will investigate the extent of such an intrusion in *Hard Times* and examine its influence on character and environment.

If Coketown cannot be said to be totalitarian, it is at least totalizing. A mysterious (but by now only too familiar) epidemic afflicts the buildings in the city: "The jail might have been the infirmary, the infirmary might have been the jail, the town-hall might have been either, or both, or anything else, for anything that appeared to the contrary in the graces of their construction." [3] These faceless and uniform buildings inhabit streets which are equally removed from any distinctiveness: Coketown contains "several large streets all very like one another, and many small streets still more like one another" (17). A city, Sartre has written, "derives its reality from the ubiquity of its absence. It is present in each one of its streets *insofar as* it is always elsewhere . . ." [4] Coketown, however, manages to be present everywhere; considered singly, each of its buildings, each of its streets, constructs the town's totality. Its citizens must take account of it — it is there. But exactly what is there is another question.

The constitutive principle in Coketown is fact: "Fact, fact, fact, everywhere in the material aspect of the town; fact, fact, fact, everywhere in the immaterial" (17). And "fact" contrives to realize itself by imposing a strictly regularized order on the town, a regulation apparent as early as the second paragraph of the novel, in the fourfold repetition of the phrase "the emphasis was helped by" (1). If such a system, by means of standardization alone, could transform the ordinarily viscous substance of life into something more precise and available to the human mind, then it might hold a special claim on our attention. But

3. *Hard Times,* ed. George Ford and Sylvere Monod (New York: W. W. Norton, 1966), p. 17. Further page references to this work will be given in the text.

4. Jean-Paul Sartre, *Search for a Method,* trans. Hazel E. Barnes (New York: Alfred A. Knopf, 1963), p. 80.

the demands of the utilitarian program do nothing to help make the world more comprehensible. Those identical buildings, for example, as a direct result of their uniform design, refuse to yield up their secrets: remote from their function, they help to create obscurity in the world of *Hard Times*. Stephen Blackpool, though he may not be aware of it, says as much to Bounderby: "Look how we live, an' wheer we live, an' in what numbers . . . an' wi' what sameness . . . Who can look on 't, Sir, and fairly tell a man 'tis not a muddle?" (114). Sameness, the regularized life, helps to produce the muddle and diminishes our ability to differentiate.

Utilitarianism as a system strains toward bureaucracy. "We hope to have before long, a board of fact, composed of commissioners of fact, who will force the people to be a people of fact, and of nothing but fact" (5), the children in the classroom are told. Its practice reflects a bureaucracy's normal procedure of unifying everything within its purview — and everybody. Those streets "very like one another" are "inhabited by people equally like one another" (17) whose children attend a school the major purpose of which is to manipulate "Heaven knows how many heads . . . into one" (7). The indiscriminate lumping together, then, extends to people, as the bureaucracy of fact attempts to assimilate all to the world view implicit in utilitarianism.

"The material apparatus of perfected civilization," as in Conrad, thus reduces the external world to uniformity, inflicts a technological and abstract pattern on it, and impoverishes the landscape, narrowing the environment in which the characters in *Hard Times* act out their lives. Now Dickens as a novelist was peculiarly attentive to the crucial and delicate negotiations between man and his environment. But the latter, effectively denatured,[5] consists for the most part of Coketown and its environs, which loom so large in the novel that even when the narrator looks on the city from afar, it does not take its place within a coherent vista. It resembles nothing so much as a disjunction in

5. For an excellent study of the relations between the natural and industrial worlds in *Hard Times,* see George Bornstein, "Miscultivated Field and Corrupted Garden: Imagery in *Hard Times," Nineteenth-Century Fiction,* 26 (1971), 158–170.

space; it interrupts the view so that one cannot get beyond it: "Coketown in the distance suggestive of itself" (84). It takes part, that is, in no anticipated spatial sequence; it has no precedent. It is what it is, a "sulky blotch upon the prospect" (84) for which nobody has been prepared. Thus appears Coketown as seen from a distance and through the eyes of one who has a great resistance to it, one who knows other places well. When experienced up close, however, by someone who has lived through little else, its influence grows much stronger.

This is how Stephen Blackpool reacts to it: "Old Stephen was standing in the street, with the odd sensation upon him of its having worked and stopped in his own head" (49). "In his own head" — the town, its constituting and regulating rhythms, incorporates itself into the very texture of his mind. One must have great resources of opposition, as Stephen does, to live in this city with one's humanity intact. Bitzer, on the other hand, does not. He learns his lessons well. His reward is to be digested into the system: "I," he tells Stephen, of all people, "I belong to the Bank" (111). At once without and within many of the characters, the town, as stated earlier, is everywhere. When such a guest confronts the self, little else can inhabit it. The self must be emptied, all its furnishings removed to make room for the mechanical intruder.

Mrs. Gradgrind provides us with a localized variant of this theme. Married to a major proponent of utilitarianism, forced to be hospitable to the system her husband propounds, she utters one of the most amazing statements in the language:

> "Are you in pain, dear mother?"
> "I think there's a pain somewhere in the room," said Mrs. Gradgrind, "but I couldn't positively say that I have got it." (152)

So withdrawn is she from her self, so vacant her being, that she cannot experience her own pain. Lacking any human content, then, the system of fact reaches into the inner lives of the characters and completes its work there. The environment gets the better of the negotiations.

The power of the world of fact objectifies itself in the weakness of the characters: life as lived in the hard world of the novel deforms the human substance: "The chimneys, for want of air to make a draught, were built in an immense variety of stunted and crooked shapes, as though every house put out a sign of the kind of people who might be expected to be born in it . . ." (49). The cultural changes *Hard Times* registers, then, promote corresponding, if not equivalent, developments in the characters; or, to put it in other terms, the impoverishment of the external world leads to psychic impairment. Dickens is perhaps uniquely sensitive to the ways in which the world man has created can penetrate the personality, and his sensitivity, affecting the theme of *Hard Times,* begets a conflict between the social aims and the dramatic needs of the book. We know how the conflict resolves itself, but its origin deserves attention.

"We are," the narrator of *The Old Curiosity Shop* says, "so much in the habit of allowing impressions upon us by external objects . . ." [6] In *Hard Times* that habit is very hard to shake; nor do the characters allow the outside world to impress itself upon their lives. They, like us, have no choice in the matter. Dickens believed fervently that institutions carry men closer to death when they malfunction, that when "incapable or sordid hands" interpose themselves between "Heaven . . . and the things it looks upon to bless," those hands engender "more death than life" (85). The theme of *Hard Times* is tyranny.

Or — to be more prudent — a kind of tyranny. Consider Mrs. Sparsit's words, as she tries to put things in their proper perspective for Bitzer: "I only know that these people must be conquered, and that it's high time it was done, once for all" (87). Her imperialistic hope resides in Bounderby, one supposes ("If Bounderby had been a Conqueror, and Mrs. Sparsit a captive Princess" [87]). And he has, if we believe his story, conquered: after all, he has come a long way, this man who was born in a ditch and then abandoned by his mother and who now is so rich and powerful. His story is a stratagem, of course, one designed to persuade people that his is a self-sustained consciousness and that he is a man liberated from human obligations. Bounderby can be regarded as a parody of a type — the self-made man, the

6. *The Old Curiosity Shop* (Boston, 1882), p. 40.

man who postulates himself in order to produce and reproduce himself, the man who in short incarnates the spirit of capitalism. He is the material enactment of his own hypothesis. (If there were a boy who had been born in a ditch, thrown away, and knocked about, and if that boy had the strength to overcome these disadvantages, then he would be like *me,* Bounderby implies. And his present position merely verifies his initial supposition.) Bounderby is the subject who transforms himself into an object, one he is obviously very proud of. But the man who does so ends by tyrannizing over that self-become-object. Like the people to whom Mrs. Sparsit refers, in a way Bounderby is one of the conquered.

Bounderby represents another version of the self emptied. His autobiography arranges itself around a void. By denying his past, he denies his self, empties it of its history, its density; and his story depends upon an absence, that of his mother. When we are first introduced to him, a number of details emphasize his inner emptiness: "A man made out of coarse material, which seemed to have been stretched to make so much of him. A man with a great puffed head and forehead . . . and . . . a strained skin to his face . . . A man with a pervading appearance on him of being inflated like a balloon" (11). And throughout the novel the imagery connects him to the wind; his mother, for example, seeking any information at all about her son, asks whether he is as healthy "as the fresh wind" (60). Of course he blusters — he has power but no substance.

On all possible occasions Bounderby repeats his autobiographical fiction, loudly, and whenever he does so, he acts in an exemplary manner. The growth of totalitarian tendencies in a given society can be measured by the extent to which it has absorbed private life and transformed it into a political concern, an activity that not only increases the power of the state (for the conversion of private into public life thereby expands the scope of its control) but simultaneously weakens the self. Bounderby's bragging, his public avowal of his "private" life, then, sets an example to which even his opponents adhere. Slackbridge, for instance, invokes the principle in his effort to convince the workers to ostracize Stephen: "Private feeling must yield to the common cause.

Hurrah!" (110). And Stephen's personal reasons for refusing to strike are converted into a public, a political concern. One does not have much to choose from between union and employer in *Hard Times.*

Helpless, lonely, Stephen too encounters an inner emptiness: "He had never known before the strength of the want in his heart for the frequent recognition of a nod, a look, a word . . ." (110). The vacuum must be filled, and something does flow into his self-guilt. "It was even harder than he could have believed possible, to separate in his own conscience his abandonment by all his fellows from a baseless sense of shame and disgrace" (110). Stephen responds suitably to his position, for guilt can be considered a symbolic, though illusory, attempt to regain personal control over a situation the individual can no longer regulate. The guilty party admits, in effect, his responsibility. Guilt then records the deprivations imposed upon the self, registers the individual's impotence in the face of the overwhelming power of the social machinery. A man's inability to pressure the social co-ordinates of his life into conformity with his needs, his social and political helplessness, cultivates guilt. Tom's effort to deflect suspicion onto Stephen for the bank robbery only exploits what already exists, objectifies Stephen's inner complexion. As he awaits someone outside the bank, Stephen "began to have an uncomfortable sensation . . . of being for the time a disreputable character" (125). There is nothing so public, so accessible to manipulation, as our guilt feelings.

Private feeling must indeed yield to the commonest of causes — which amounts to another way of saying that the individual finds himself subjected to the exorbitant demands of an arbitrary social discipline in *Hard Times,* a discipline which if followed forces upon the self an accommodation to "one continuous system of unnatural restraint" (101). The intervention, of course, is in behalf of civilization: we must relinquish in order to build. Early in their lives children are taught the general idea:

"Now I'll try you again. Suppose you were going to carpet a room. Would you use a carpet having a representation of flowers upon it?"

> There being by now a general conviction by this time that
> "No, Sir!" was always the right answer to this gentleman, the
> chorus of No was very strong. (5)

Except for Sissy Jupe and a few others, they understand — they
are learning the principle of negation, that underlying the practice of repression, the "one continuous system of unnatural restraint." According to Freudian theory, however, our systematic
renunciations, the extension of our dependency into adolescence
and the concomitant delay in reaching sexual maturity, culminate
in some real gains — a richer, more intense sexual life than that
experienced by other animals and the formation of life-enhancing
cultural activities. But in *Hard Times* the residents of Coketown
reap no benefits from the denials forced upon them. The workers
endure a prolongation of dependence — "there happened to be
in Coketown a considerable population of babies who had been
walking . . . twenty, thirty, forty, fifty years and more" (38) —
but without a compensatory enrichment of their sexual lives
(consider, for example, Stephen's nonsexual relationship with
Rachael), and they surely enjoy no cultural advantages. Those
from the upper orders receive no immunity: Tom and Louisa
seem never to have lived through childhood, and their sexual
lives are neurotic at best.[7]

Again, something has been taken away and nothing has been
put in its stead, or nothing with any human value; as Tom tells
Harthouse, Gradgrind has had his sister "crammed with all sorts
of dry bones and sawdust. It's his system" (103). It is Gradgrind's system, his harsh regimen, and he too has not been able
to find a privileged position within it. He suffers from the usual
ailment, "his eyes found commodious cellarage in two dark
caves" (1), and he acts as if those newly exposed to the utilitarian method are empty also. As the children sit in the classroom, "ready to have imperial gallons of facts poured into them"
(1), "Thomas Gradgrind now presented Thomas Gradgrind
to the little pitchers before him, who were to be filled full of

7. Daniel P. Deneau goes so far as to suggest an "abnormal" relationship between Tom and Louisa in his article "The Brother-Sister Relationship in *Hard Times*," *Dickensian*, 60 (1964), 173–177.

facts" (2). Gradgrind's system courts the void, celebrates those vacant intrahuman spaces.

Despite the power of Gradgrind's system, when one is subjected to the impediments erected by the constrictive program, one's psyche does not submit without a struggle. The required discipline meets with much resistance. Louisa is perhaps typical in this respect: "In her mind . . . a struggling disposition to believe in a wider and nobler humanity than she had ever heard of, constantly strove with doubts and resentments . . . Upon a nature long accustomed to self-suppression, thus torn and divided, the Harthouse philosophy came as a relief and justification" (127). And Harthouse himself understands Tom's problem: "He rushes into these extremes for himself, from opposite extremes that have long been forced — with the very best intentions we have no doubt — upon him" (132). In Tom's case, self-suppression, by means of an implacable dialectic, necessitates self-indulgence, "recompense," he says, ". . . for the way in which I have been brought up" (40) — for every action an equal and opposite reaction. It is a failed dialectic, of course, one lacking a synthesis. Tom — and Louisa — live in extremity, and in *Hard Times* extremes do not enlarge the possibilities of humanity but maim and tear the human fabric (that is, cause the inner void).

Louisa's inner conflict is informed with resentments engendered "because of the wrong that had been done her" (127). Finding herself unable to direct that resentment outward, toward her father, Louisa tries to contain it, to hold it within herself, but its energy remains and struggles for some expression. The struggle reaches a climax when Louisa, fleeing from Harthouse, returns home, having no resources that will enable her to cope with the emotion he has stirred within her: "A dull anger that she should be seen in her distress, and that the involuntary look she had so resented should come to this fulfilment, smouldered within her like an unwholesome fire. All closely imprisoned forces rend and destroy" (170). The resentment in that passage is aimed inward: the self, enraged to find that the received system provokes an irreconcilable struggle, seeks a way simultaneously to punish itself for its failure to maintain its integrity and to resolve the conflict. Self-hatred yields to the urge for self-destruc-

tion. "When I was irrevocably married, there rose up into rebellion against the tie, the old strife, made fiercer . . . and which
no general laws shall ever rule or state for me, father, until they
shall be able to direct the anatomist where to strike his knife into
the secrets of my soul" (166). In no other character does the
inner devastation reach such an advanced level, but it exists in
some form in almost every person connected with the utilitarians.
Bounderby's fictionalized version of his life suggests his dissatisfaction with himself, and the second paragraph of the novel contains an interesting hint concerning the strain Gradgrind goes
through: "his very neckcloth, trained to take him by the throat
with an unaccommodating grasp" (1). Tom too cannot elude the
inevitable effects of the depredations practiced upon him, and
after telling Louisa "I am sick of my life, Loo. I hate it altogether" (39), he chafes "his face on his coat-sleeve, as if to
mortify his flesh, and have it in unison with his spirit" (39).

Such are the consequences of living in accordance with principles which, when applied, rob man of his stability and force him
to live a life of extremes, on the margins of the possible. Nothing
in the Gradgrindian philosophy fortifies the human emotions, and
the monolithic program, in the service of an all-encompassing
and yet reductive rationalism, rewards materially — it is the only
way it knows or trusts — those who serve its interests, rewards,
and betrays, as we have seen in some detail. It betrays because it
subtracts. In what must be the most rhetorical question in *Hard
Times,* Gradgrind desperately asks Bitzer, "Have you a heart?"
(217). But like Harthouse's chest, Bitzer's contains only a "cav-
ity where his heart should have been" (176). And that vacancy,
Bitzer informs Gradgrind, "is accessible to Reason, Sir . . . And
to nothing else" (218). Anything else — a human psychology
based on emotion, for example — is immediately held suspect,
and this suspicion leads to the general failure of human relationships in the novel.

Husbands and wives, parents and children, discover no intimate and interpersonal glue that will bind them together and
make their socially sanctioned relationships appear necessary; all
traditional and formally constituted human connections seem to
be merely contingent. Mrs. Pegler calls our attention to the issue
when her kinship to Bounderby is revealed publicly: "I have al-

ways lived quiet and secret, Josiah, my dear. I have never broken the condition once. I have never said I was your mother" (198). Her kinship, that is to say, is conditional: she will be treated secretly as a mother, she will receive financial support from her son, provided she neither acts like a mother nor acknowledges the relationship. As consanguinity lapses into affiliation, the ties uniting mother and son dissolve — theirs is a "rationalized" arrangement, organized around money and empty space. "I have admired you at a distance," she says, "and if I have come to town sometimes, with long times between, to take a proud peep at you, I have done it unbeknown, my love, and gone away again" (198). This kind of quantified association also creates empty time — "with long times between" (and thus the ennui that Louisa, her mother, Tom, and Harthouse all testify to). Insofar as this kind of relationship does produce remoteness between people, it mystifies life and accordingly encourages people to spy on one another in order to traverse the distance separating them. Thus "unbeknown" to her son, Mrs. Pegler takes a periodic "proud peep" at him.

The motives of some others are not so innocuous. Bitzer supplements his income nicely by holding "the respectable office of general spy and informer" at Bounderby's bank, and the passage in which we learn this affords some more evidence that spying and the rational ordering of life are somehow interrelated in the world of *Hard Times*: "His mind was so exactly regulated, that he had no affections or passions. All his proceedings were the result of the nicest and coldest calculation" (88). Perhaps the sharpest pair of eyes in the novel are owned by Mrs. Sparsit, who, ever watchful, "sat at her window all day long looking at the customers coming in and out, watching the postmen, keeping an eye on the general traffic of the street . . . but, above all, keeping her attention on her staircase" (159). After the failure of her project, she receives condign punishment: "Regarded as a classical ruin, Mrs. Sparsit was an interesting spectacle on her arrival at her journey's end . . ." (180). Bitzer's and Mrs. Sparsit's watching is a form of aggression, intimating that suspicion is a regulative principle in Coketown (as Rachael says, "'It goes against me . . . to mistrust any one; but when I am so mistrusted — when we all are . . ." [192]).

Less harmful is the "spying" of Tom and Louisa as they try to catch a glimpse of the circus (9). (Dickens repeats the motif at the end of *Hard Times*. When Sissy and Louisa enter the circus, Sleary informs them that Tom is safe and requests that they look at the ring through a "thpy-hole" [214]. They do, and see Tom dressed as a black servant.) Just before Mrs. Gradgrind dies she expresses her belief that her life and the system under which she has lived have been incomplete, that something indefinable has escaped from her: "But there is something — not an Ology at all — that your father has missed, or forgotten, Louisa. I don't know what it is" (153). Both Tom and Louisa recognize this at a much earlier stage in their development, and what they do when trying to peek at the circus represents their awareness of the narrowed confines of their lives, their desire to see something beyond Coketown and the system imposed upon them. Their act illustrates, moreover, not only their hope for transcendence but the limited and relatively impotent forms that that hope can assume in a utilitarian society. Not knowing exactly what, they sense that something has been concealed from them, but they have at their disposal no effective repertoire of gestures and acts that might enable them to uncover an entryway to a world elsewhere. Now something has indeed been kept from their sight, but much more than the circus.

As Sissy Jupe and Rachael walk in the country one autumn Sunday, the day they discover the fractured body of Stephen Blackpool, they manage to avoid "mounds where the grass was rank and high, and where brambles, dock-weed, and such-like vegetation, were confusedly heaped together . . . for dismal stories were told in that country of the old pits hidden beneath such indications" (201). Camouflaging the mouths of the unused mine shafts, the rank and random growth serves to relax the attentiveness of the unwary, but that covering represents an important activity of civilization.

All civilizations, so that they can continue to operate with as much efficiency as possible, do their best to deflect attention from what is terrifying, and most establish institutions and systems designed to prevent their citizens from attending to some of their most serious fears. Clearly, the utilitarian ideology in *Hard Times* is meant to function in exactly that way: utilitarianism is a kind of contract formulated between the men of fact and the rest of society for the vindication of the former and the peace and security of the latter. And no matter if the rest of society has had nothing to do with the drafting of the terms of the contract, it is designed for their benefit. For if the opaque material that makes up reality can be reduced to statistics, to an arithmetical index, then it will appear to be neither mysterious nor fearful but transparent and familiar. The interests of society will have been served, or so a utilitarian might argue. In fact, as we have already seen in some detail, the factual organization of life tends to make it more obscure and to bewilder the senses of the citizens of Coketown.

Let us consider the "old pits": the vegetation merely covers up those dangerous holes, without doing anything to change their reality. The ground appears to be harmless, but the unwary person who steps on the covering will drop, probably to his death, as Stephen Blackpool does, down a deep shaft. If the heavy growth hiding the openings to the unused mine shafts exemplifies the means by which society tries to divert consciousness from the fearful, then what utilitarianism attempts to disguise is the fact that nothingness supports it. For this the text provides some evidence, and when Bounderby occupies his country house we learn that it is "accessible within a mile or two, by a railway striding on many arches over a wild country, *undermined by deserted coal-shafts*" (128, my italics). Some even inhabit the void: before Mrs. Gradgrind dies, her voice seems so feeble "that she might have been lying at the bottom of a well" (151); and, appropriately, her children, speaking in the haircutting chamber one evening, seem to be "overhung by a dark cavern" (40). Mrs. Sparsit, on the other hand, that "lady paramount over certain vaults in the basement," earns her living by "keeping watch over the treasures of the mine" (86). The inner emptiness fostered by the system corresponds to a gulf in the external world; vacant intrahuman space is balanced by interhuman vacancies.

Two details cited above — the "deserted coal-shafts" and "the mine" (in Bounderby's bank, of course) guarded by Mrs. Sparsit — connect Bounderby with Stephen's fatal plunge, and so his early boast that he "was born in a ditch" (12) can in this context take on a new meaning. Bounderby would have us believe that he has mastered the void, that he is the man able to bring life out of nothingness (for, as he says, 'nobody threw me a rope" [13]). Bounderby admits the existence of the void, but only as a challenge, as something else he has overcome in a life punctuated only with marks of success.

Stephen Blackpool too knows of its existence. In his long conversation with Bounderby he associates the gulf with the class structure of Coketown:

> Sir, I canna, wi' my little learning an' my common way, tell the genelman what will better aw this . . . but I can tell him what I know will never do't . . . Agreeing fur to mak one side unnat'rally awlus and for ever right, and toother side unnat'rally awlus and for ever wrong, will never, never do't . . . Let thousands upon thousands alone, aw *leading the like lives* and *aw faw'en into the like muddle,* and they will be as one, and yo will be as anoother, wi' *a black unpassable world betwixt* yo . . ." (115–116, my italics)

A number of important issues congregate in this passage. As we have already seen with respect to the individual, extremes (the absolute segregation of right and wrong) help to shape the abyss, which here seems inseparable from the muddle created by the "rational" ordering of life ("aw leading the like lives and aw faw'en into the like muddle"). That muddle claims the life of Stephen. The regulation he mentions, however, leads not to clarity but to incomprehensibility (the "black unpassable world"), one class remaining unknown to the other. This impenetrable darkness between classes signifies the interruption of human space which, fragmented, bisected by the gulf, is thus inhabited by classes at once isolated and terrifying — isolated for obvious reasons, terrifying because the connecting links between them (that is, the space common to both of them) are merely possible. But at this point we should recall that utilitarianism undertakes to blur our awareness of the terrifying aspects of life.

One way of insuring this faulty vision is to create an educational system which will maintain in the citizens a low level of awareness, a system much like the one we see in *Hard Times,* and which will virtually guarantee an unremitting traffic in error for those whom the schools "educate." The consequences of achieving success on the terms of the system may be observed in Harthouse, who, though we never see him, as we do Bitzer, in the schoolhouse, takes it upon himself to study utilitarianism and coaches "himself up with a blue-book or two" (95): he loses all his ability to make discriminations. "I assure you," he tells Louisa, "I attach not the least importance to any opinions . . . any set of ideas will do just as much good as any other set, and just as much harm as any other set" (99). Utilitarianism, then, organizes and enforces a communal ignorance.

We see it at work when the townsfolk cluster around the placards, listening attentively to someone reading the notices aloud, and all the while staring "at the characters which meant so much with a vague awe and respect that would have been half ludicrous, if any aspect of public ignorance could ever be otherwise than threatening and full of evil" (187). Society, Dickens stresses, should not frustrate cognition, but rather should create structures which stimulate awareness, for like Pope and Milton before him, Dickens believes that evil, recognized as such, evil placed out in the open, can only be defeated, that our perceptions arm us against danger: "When the Devil goeth about like a roaring lion, he goeth about in a shape by which few but savages are attracted. But, when he is trimmed, smoothed, and varnished, according to the model; . . . then . . . he is the very Devil" (137).

The subject of that sentence is Harthouse, but he is not really the Devil, only a moral illiterate. And in a scene distinguished for its dramatic failure, he receives a lesson in elementary morality from the heuristic Sissy Jupe, who, forcing him to make a choice — "I ask you to depart from this place tonight, under an obligation never to return to it" (177–178) — settles upon Harthouse a moral imperative, and applies a corrective to his faulty education: "What will be, will be. *This* will be, I suppose. I must take off myself" (178). The stilted and altogether inappropriate speech of Sissy should not blind us to the crucial moral issue involved in this confrontation between innocence and experience. When in Dickens' novels society is characterized by moral ignorance, innocence, in the absence of any other ethical agency, confers moral obligations upon others, establishes values which society has not realized. Failing, however, to evoke Harthouse's conscience, Sissy succeeds only in raising his self-consciousness; Harthouse, however, is not a good student, and whenever he thinks of this encounter he feels "ashamed of himself" (179).

Yet, like the greatest dramas, Dickens' novels discover a way to overcome the limited awareness of the characters. No matter that a varied and systematized ignorance pervades *Hard Times*; the reader should not overlook what the characters have been unable to perceive. As soon as Sissy Jupe leaves Harthouse's room, the thwarted seducer, contemplating the ruins of his desire, refers to himself as "a Great Pyramid of failure" (179), an apt allusion, carrying with it geometric connotations entirely fitting for one associated with the utilitarians. But the text describes another pyramid, and the passage in which it appears requires some attention.

> The father of one of the families was in the habit of balancing the father of another of the families on the top of a great pole; the father of a third family often made a *pyramid* of both those fathers, with Master Kidderminster for the apex, and himself for the base; all the fathers could dance upon rolling casks, stand upon bottles, catch knives and balls, twirl hand-basins, ride upon anything, jump over everything, and stick at nothing. All the mothers could (and did) dance, upon the slack wire and the tight-rope, and perform rapid acts on bare-backed steeds; none of them were at all particular in respect of showing their legs . . . they were not at all orderly in their domestic arrangements, and the combined literature of the whole company would have produced but a poor letter on any subject. Yet there was a remarkable gentleness and childishness about these people . . . and an untiring readiness to help and pity one another . . . (27, my italics)

The circus people are no more learned than the rest of the characters in *Hard Times,* but the society they form provides them with the opportunity to transcend their ignorance. Theirs is a community founded on cooperation and mutuality, or perhaps it would be better to say that the circus's sense of community grows out of the *risks* it undertakes. The circus creates its own dangers, as we see in the passage above, but at the same time it confronts those dangers openly; nothing intercepts the awareness of the members of the troupe, and each player, recognizing the dangers he faces, recognizes also that he is interdependent. As a result of this shared knowledge, the circus maintains, tenuous though it may be, its communal equilibrium: it is, in a word, socialized. Father helps father, all lend support to the young (Kidderminster is the top of the pyramid), and every person stands ready to aid anyone who needs assistance. The great vitality of the circus's citizens and its countenancing of sexuality, without either feeling threatened or awakening in its members a sense of guilt, disclose the health of the community.

Coketown, on the other hand, promoting ignorance of the dangers inherent in its structure, fails to achieve any balance — as we have seen, it is defined by extremes — and constructs barriers, empty spaces, between class and class, citizen and citizen. At its core is the void, uninhabitable space. As opposed to that kind of space is that which the circus composes. The circus pyramid, for example, gives meaning to space, organizes it so that it coheres to a humanized design (it is made up of people, after all), and so too with the traditional circles within which all the circus acts are performed. The circus, unlike Coketown as seen from a distance, is no mere blotch upon the surface, it energizes and activates space, participates in an ordered sequence, a human arrangement, and its space does not overwhelm the individual. Nor does it achieve its form by exclusion alone: it can utilize the world of fact without being annexed into it. The figures of the circle and the pyramid illustrate the point, as does the advertisement describing the act of Sissy's father, who is said to throw "*seventy-five hundredweight* in rapid succession backhanded over his head, thus forming a fountain of *solid iron* in mid-air" (9). The circus can even on occasion be very useful indeed — as when Sleary's dancing horses and trained dogs help Tom to escape (220). So, far from merely ejecting the factual from its boundaries, the circus establishes the ground on which fantasy and fact can *interact* and produce life.

Utilitarianism in *Hard Times* does not. It seeks to banish everything it cannot fit into the world view implied in its ideology. And yet the nature of its complexity escapes its adherents. "Then," Sissy tells Louisa, "Mr. M'Choakumchild said he would try me once more. And he said, Here are the stutterings —"

(44). Louisa quickly corrects Sissy: the figures are statistics, not stutterings. But Sissy's malapropism is meaningful; the intricate system of numbers the utilitarians want the schoolchildren to master is a form of *language,* though, as her slip implies, it is not a very effective one, and impedes communication. As a language, however, it can cooperate in the creation of fictions: "And he said, This schoolroom is an immense town, and in it there are a million of inhabitants, and only five-and-twenty are starved to death in the streets, in the course of a year." "And he said, Now, this schoolroom is a nation. And in this nation, there are fifty millions of money" (44). The narrator understands the fictional character of the capitalistic ethos informing the world of Coketown:

> "Why can't they do as I have done, ma'am? What one person can do, another can do."
>   This, again, was among the fictions of Coketown. (90)

Bitzer speaks those words to Mrs. Sparsit, who herself, along with Bitzer's employer, knows well what a fiction is. To hear the last two converse, the one insisting on her aristocratic origins, the other on his deprivations, one all pretense, the other all affectation, is to apprehend the mutual and reinforcing fictions that shape Coketown. The advocates of utilitarianism in *Hard Times* would have others believe that their methodology offers the world a shortcut to comprehension, a way of interpreting and understanding itself. As we have seen already, that is not so. Dickens remains convinced that utilitarianism affords no clarification of the human condition but has the status of merely another fiction. As such, it is not exempt from obscurity and ambiguity and, like most fiction, itself demands clarification. And even the reality that industrialization forges seems more fantastic than any reality the characters in *Hard Times* are prepared for. Certainly with its "unnatural red and black" color, its "interminable serpents of smoke" trailing out of its chimneys, its black canal and purple river, and its piston moving "up and down like the head of an elephant in a state of melancholy madness" (17), Coketown is busy creating a new mythology that will take its place among the most lethal fictions the world has known.

Whether cynically, as in the case of Bounderby, or unwittingly, the utilitarians participate in the creation of fictions, but always the participation is at the expense of humanity. The utilitarian dispensation intends to create human beings answerable to the claims of reason, of fact, alone — a lethal fiction if there ever was one. It seeks to improvise a new kind of being, one liberated from imagination and emotion. But the improvisation is faulty, and the organized privations forced upon some of the characters succeed in creating only a different kind of animal. So Gradgrind comments that Thomas and Louisa have been "trained," and even if it is to a "mathematical exactness" (10), his system treats children in essentially the same way that the circus treats its animals (and here we should remember Tom's appropriate nickname, "the Whelp"). Gradgrind cannot avoid the fate his children share, and when Sleary hands Sissy over to him, he does so "as to a horse" (31). Bounderby, that "noble animal" (98), employs a woman, Mrs. Sparsit, who is often compared to a bird (for example, 147), while Gradgrind's employee, Harthouse, feels at one point "as if *he* were the whelp to-night" (178).

As the animal imagery implies, the enlarged social system depicted in *Hard Times* develops manifold ways to diminish humanity. Any prospects for a humane order are seriously attenuated in this novel, especially since the circus, relegated as it is to the margins of society, to a kind of no-man's-land — Gradgrind finds it on "neutral ground . . . neither town nor country" (8) — and forced to move from town to town, cannot consolidate its limited power, and thus can proffer no deliverance, only escape. The circus is, in effect, a kind of communal picaro, but its lot as such suggests that an *individual* can no longer expect to move freely across the country, that if one desires to live through one's experience, one must do so in concert with others. The fictional life projected in *Hard Times* declines to reassure society; the question that Dickens does his best to frame in words is what to make of an augmented thing.

BARBARA CHARLESWORTH GELPI

The Innocent I:
Dickens' Influence on Victorian Autobiography

Through the winter months of 1853–54, just at the time when
Dickens was visiting Preston to get material for *Hard Times,*
John Stuart Mill was writing his *Autobiography.* The fact that
Dickens' fictional version of utilitarian education is remarkably
close to Mill's factual description of his own upbringing has
already been noted,[1] and the resemblances are probably not mere
coincidence. It is surely possible and even likely that when
Dickens described Thomas Gradgrind's catechizing of Bitzer he
had in mind stories which he had heard about James Mill's education of his son, even though he could not, of course, have read
the *Autobiography.* For by the time that John Stuart Mill met
John Sterling in 1828, the story of Mill's childhood training had
already become legend. Mill writes that Sterling "told me how he
and others had looked upon me (from hearsay information) as a
'made' or manufactured man, having had a certain impress of
opinion stamped on me which I could only reproduce." [2] Then,

1. Cf. F. R. Leavis, *The Great Tradition* (London: Chatto & Windus,
1948), p. 228; Edgar Johnson, *Charles Dickens: His Tragedy and Triumph* (New York: Simon and Schuster, 1959), 2:809.
2. John Stuart Mill, *Autobiography and Other Writings,* ed. Jack
Stillinger (Boston: Houghton Mifflin, 1969), p. 93. Further references to
this work will be given in the text.

57

too, by 1854 it seems more than likely that Carlyle, to whom
Hard Times was dedicated and whom Dickens knew well, was
keeping that legend alive — and, since Carlyle and John Stuart
Mill were no longer friends, making the Mills, *père et fils,* both
into mechanical men, satanic Mills to whom the very name of
Gradgrind may punningly allude.[3] So the facts of Mill's life may
have been grist for Dickens' mill; that is a straightforward enough
possibility.[4] Yet is it not also feasible that the fantasies of
Dickens' novels had an effect on Mill's account of his facts?

   In his study of the autobiographical form Roy Pascal has discussed the importance to the Victorian novel of the great autobiographies of Goethe, Rousseau, and Wordsworth. Peter
Coveney in *The Image of Childhood* and Jerome Buckley in his
essay on the *Bildungsroman* have noted the impress particularly
of Wordsworthian autobiographical feeling and beliefs about
childhood upon Dickens and the incalculable but certainly enormous influence that Dickens' vision of childhood had in turn
upon all Victorians.[5] Say then that Dickens, moved by Words-

   3. Carlyle himself may have intended or enjoyed the puns on the
name of Mill that occur in *Sartor Resartus.* For instance, he translates
Novalis's phrase "eine furchtbare Mühle des Todes" exactly and so
describes the universe created by "the Motive-grinders and Mechanical
Profit-and-Loss Philosophies" as "the Mill of Death" (Thomas Carlyle,
Sartor Resartus: The Life and Opinions of Herr Teufelsdröckh, ed.
Charles Frederick Harold [New York: Odyssey Press, 1937], p. 164).
Michael St. John Packe mentions "a series of identifiable puns" in *Sartor
Resartus* on the name Mill and cites one from chap. 10: "Shall your
Science proceed in the small chink-lighted, or even oil-lighted, under-
ground workshop of Logic alone; and man's mind become an Arithmeti-
cal Mill, whereof Memory is the Hopper, and mere tables of Sines and
Tangents, Codification, and Treatises of what you call Political Economy,
are the Meal?" (*The Life of John Stuart Mill* [London: Secker and
Warburg, 1954], p. 168).
   4. J. Fielding completely disagrees with this theory as "unfair to James
Mill and unjustified by what his son wrote in the *Autobiography*" ("Mill
and Gradgrind," *Nineteenth-Century Fiction,* 11 [1956], 148). However,
my point says nothing about the actualities of James Mill's theories and
refers only to Dickens' probable conception of those theories.
   5. Pascal, *Design and Truth in Autobiography* (Cambridge: Harvard
University Press, 1960), p. 52; Coveney, *The Image of Childhood* (Baltimore: Penguin Books, 1967), p. 119; Buckley, "Autobiography in the
English Bildungsroman," *The Interpretation of Narrative: Theory and
Practice,* ed. Morton Bloomfield, Harvard English Studies, vol. 1 (Cambridge: Harvard University Press, 1970), p. 95.

worthian theory and practice and motivated as well by obsessive images drawn from memories of his own childhood, writes *David Copperfield.* The character he portrays draws into himself all his author's ideas and feelings and then becomes a focus, an "archetypal image" if you will, for thoughts and feelings of Dickens' readers. Therefore I think it a mistake to say, as Wayne Shumaker does in *English Autobiography,* that the rise of the novel and of the autobiography are parallel but that one does not stand in "causal relation" to the other.[6] The relationship may not be simply "causal," but neither are the two forms parallel and unrelated. They are interlaced: the rise in the number and quality of autobiographies becomes marked with the beginning of the Romantic period; that rise leads to a new emphasis in early Victorian novels on the mystery of the individual's growth and change through the interaction of all those things that make up his or her character and circumstances; that emphasis in turn brings even greater numbers of mid-Victorians to meditate on the facts of their own particular lives against the backdrop of the novelists' and — since he was the most widely read — especially Dickens' fantasies.

Therefore the nature of those fantasies which a society finds most compelling is very important: like the beautiful statues which pregnant Greek women were to gaze upon in order to produce beautiful children, a compelling story in art works its influence upon life. It forms, and, if it is unbalanced or untrue or misunderstood, it may deform. Both Peter Coveney and Angus Wilson in their studies of the children in Dickens' novels believe that in mediating the Romantic image of the child to the Victorians Dickens marred it and sentimentalized it by his self-pity. Wilson, however, does not entirely agree with Coveney; he, like Jerome Buckley, sees Dickens as growing out of that self-pity by the time he wrote *Great Expectations,* and he has a good argument.[7] But before Pip came Little Nell, Oliver Twist, Paul Dombey, David Copperfield, and Jo the street sweeper. Their

6. Wayne Shumaker, *English Autobiography: Its Emergence, Materials, and Form* (Berkeley: University of California Press, 1954), p. 29.

7. Wilson, "Dickens on Children and Childhood," in *Dickens 1970,* ed. Michael Slater (London: Chapman and Hall, 1970), p. 223; Coveney, *Image of Childhood,* p. 112; Buckley, "Autobiography," p. 98.

stories were read by John Ruskin, John Stuart Mill, and Walter
Pater,[8] and it is my belief that these men in their autobiographical
writings were influenced to "see" themselves as Dickensian waifs,
those small people who cast such long shadows over the Victorian
sensibility. Using Mill's *Autobiography* as a focus, I would like
to consider the similarities between the autobiographers' relation
of facts and Dickens' heart-wringing fantasies.

First: loneliness. When Mill was growing up, his family lived
in a small, cramped house. The large table at which he and his
father worked filled one end of a room occupied also by his
harassed mother and the many younger children.[9] In the *Autobiography* only the table remains and the figure of his father.
Brothers and sisters who must be tutored appear, but only as
potential or actual sources of difficulty, never as companions.
Mill had no friends, or, to put it in his own words, "He [James
Mill] completely succeeded in preserving me from the sort of
influence he so much dreaded" (*Autobiography*, p. 21). Pater
too lived in a small house with his mother, grandmother, aunt,
two sisters, and a brother, but save for a mother and a little
sister, his semiautobiographical figure, Florian Deleal, in "The
Child in the House" is always alone. Ruskin was, in fact, an only
child, born to middle-aged parents; nevertheless he had some
visits with cousins, and from the time he was ten he had his
cousin Mary as a companion. Yet he considers it the "dominant
calamity" of his upbringing that, as he flatly states, "I had nothing
to love" (*Praeterita*, 1:61–62). Like so many of Dickens' children all three writers have little or no sense of emotional bond

8. Mill wrote to his wife, Harriet, in 1854 complaining of the male
chauvinism in *Bleak House* but saying at the same time that the novel
was the only one "that I altogether dislike." The suggestion is, then, that
Mill had read all of Dickens' previous novels (*The Later Letters of
John Stuart Mill, 1849–1873*, ed. Francis E. Mineka and Dwight N.
Lindley [Toronto: University of Toronto Press, 1972], p. 190). Thomas
Wright says that Pater lost his taste for Dickens in middle life but that
in boyhood he had very much liked his work (*The Life of Walter Pater*
[London: Everett and Co., 1907], 2:116). Ruskin in *Praeterita* de-
scribes the excitement with which he and his father, with thousands of
others, waited for each new installment of a Dickens novel and admits
Dickens' influence on "The King of the Golden River" (*Praeterita*
[Sunnyside, Orpington, Kent, 1887], 2:115). Further references to
Praeterita will be given in the text.

9. Packe, *John Stuart Mill*, p. 20.

with loving parental figures, and their interaction with other children, when it occurs at all, if happy, is brief — if unhappy, is only another cause for feelings of alienation.

Like Dickens' waifs too all three autobiographers are extraordinarily observant. The child Ruskin, deprived of almost all toys and turning his quick eyes to "examining the knots in the wood of the floor, or counting the bricks in the opposite houses" (*Praeterita*, 1:17), is a figure to haunt the imagination, and Pater's Florian lives with extraordinary awareness of "the material objects" about him.[10] Can the same be said of Mill, however? There are no descriptions of place in the *Autobiography,* no attempts to describe faces or to give exact conversations. For the effectiveness of his story, however, such particulars are better absent. On what, after all, *should* the eyes of young Mill be fixed? On books. And so they are. The titles of the books lying on that large table, the Greek words written on cards: these come before us with extraordinary clarity. "The green fields and wild flowers" through which he walked with his father, repeating his lessons all the while, are described with only the words I have quoted, but "the account I gave him daily of what I had read the day before," the slips of paper containing notes, the books discussed and what was said about them: all that detail is seen and heard again through the eyes and ears of a quick, docile child (*Autobiography,* p. 6).

Their intelligent sensitivity to impressions and ideas gave all three autobiographers a great need for parental love and understanding to help them deal with the ideas flooding in upon them, but, like Dickens' lonely children, they did not get such love or do not remember getting it. Pater's father died when he was very young, as did the fathers in "The Child in the House" and *Marius the Epicurean.* The mothers in these stories are vaguely beneficent but withdrawn, shadowy figures. Very telling, however, is the note of resentment in "Emerald Uthwart," a story based in part on Pater's experiences at King's School, Canterbury. Since his older brother seems not to have gone to the school, nor, of course, did his sisters, there is significance in the

10. Pater, "The Child in the House," *Miscellaneous Studies* (London, 1895), p. 172.

narrator's comment on Emerald's schooling: "Little by little he [Emerald, youngest of the brothers but "not the youngest of the family"] comes to understand that, while the brothers are indulged with lessons at home, are some of them free even of these and placed already in the world, where, however, there remains no place for him, he is to go to school, chiefly for the convenience of others . . ." [11]

Mill has no sense of having been loved by his father, for none of the considerable attention that James Mill gave him had for the boy any tinge of loving-kindness or concern. Mill writes: "The element which was chiefly deficient in his [James Mill's] moral relation to his children, was that of tenderness" (*Autobiography*, p. 32). He goes on to describe his father as a "typical" Englishman in that, although originally a man of strong feelings, he had habitually repressed them until, to all intents and purposes, they disappeared. Add to this his father's constitutional irritability and the child's continual state of fear, and one gets the result baldly stated in Mill's early draft but then canceled: ". . . my father's children neither loved him, nor, with any warmth of affection, any one else" (*Autobiography*, p. 33).

Surprisingly, it seems to have been Mill's conscious intention in writing the *Autobiography* to pay tribute to his father. At least, after writing it he believed that he had done so. In 1865 he wrote to George Grote, thanking him for a review in which he alluded to James Mill's distinction in history and philosophy. "I am glad," Mill writes, "that you take the opportunity of doing justice to my father. My own contribution to his memory is already written in a MS designed for posthumous publication . . ." [12] So he seems to have remembered what he had written eleven years before, but in fact the scenes described between James Mill and his son can well match those between Mr. Dombey and his daughter Florence, Mr. Bumble and Oliver Twist, or Mr. Murdstone and David Copperfield. Not that Mill's scenes are presented with any of the overt pathos that Dickens uses; they are, indeed, underplayed, but Mill's litotes has its own powerful effect.

11. Pater, "Emerald Uthwart," *Miscellaneous Studies* (London, 1895), pp. 203–204.
12. Mill, *Later Letters*, pp. 1120–21.

In one scene, for instance, we are presented with a three- or four-year-old John and his father sitting at the single table, John working at his Greek, his father writing *The History of India*. No Greek-English lexicon was yet in print, and John, who knew no Latin, could not use the Greek-Latin lexicon. Therefore, "I was forced to have recourse to him for the meaning of every word which I did not know. This incessant interruption he, one of the most impatient of men, submitted to . . ." (*Autobiography*, p. 6). We have all the information we need, and Mill, with filial delicacy, withdraws, leaving it to the imagination of his readers to reconstruct *how* his impatient father submitted to interruption and how he, the child, felt, torn between fear of interrupting and fear of making a mistake in his lesson.

Occasionally Mill allows himself a negative comment. For instance, describing his lessons in Greek elocution he writes: "Of all the things which he required me to do, there was none which I did so constantly ill, or in which he so perpetually lost his temper with me," and adds meekly, "but I even then remarked (though I did not venture to make the remark to him) that though he reproached me when I read a sentence ill, and *told* me how I ought to have read it, he never, by reading it himself, *shewed* me how it ought to be read" (*Autobiography*, p. 16). *Praeterita* is filled with examples of a similar meekness masking still-felt bitterness and at last getting its revenge, not the resounding last word which Betsy Trotwood inflicts on the Murdstones, but powerful nonetheless.

The effect of constant "negative reinforcement" upon Ruskin and Mill as upon Dickens' waifs is a haunting sense of their inadequacy and clumsiness. (In Pater's case there is only the negative evidence that he was too self-conscious about what he took to be his physical ungainliness and ugliness to write about them; his semiautobiographical figures bear no physical resemblance to him.) Just as her father's presence is a constraint upon "the natural grace and freedom" of Florence Dombey's thoughts and actions and as David Copperfield becomes "sullen, dull, and dogged" under the tutelage of Mr. Murdstone, so Mill describes himself as clumsy, inept, and awkward. For these qualities he says that he "merited reproof," but in fact he turns the reproof on his father for harassing him with "severe admonitions" about his "slackness" while providing him with only the stimulus of mental activity (*Autobiography*, p. 23). Ruskin too blames his parents for everything from his shyness in company to his inability to swim or to ride a horse (*Praeterita*, 1:63–64, 157, 329).

Ruskin's situation was the opposite of Mill's in that his mother was the domestic tyrant, his father the passive observer of her rules, and without much reading between the lines one can sense the reproach Ruskin feels toward his father, who might have given him so much more had he not worried about "infringing any of mother's rules" (*Praeterita*, 1:48). The end result was the same for both Mill and Ruskin, however, in that (again like so many children in Dickens' novels) intellectually and emotionally browbeaten yet painfully intelligent and aware, feeling their "backwardness" while at the same time resenting the overbearing figure who made them so conscious of inadequacy, they had no consoling mother to whom they might turn for comfort.

Dickens' children are usually bereft of their mothers through death, that absence being then no fault of the mothers. So Oliver Twist, Little Nell, the Dombey children, David Copperfield, Esther Summerson — all are motherless. As a novelist Dickens was thus able to take much though not all of the sting out of his portrayal of these mothers' inadequacy, but his own autobiographical sketch helps to explain why he took the mothers offstage. After Dickens' father was released from debtors' prison, he quarreled with the relative for whom Dickens worked at the blacking factory, and Dickens lost his job there. His mother went down the next day to try to get it back. "My father said, I should go back no more, and should go to school. I do not write resentfully or angrily: for I know how all these things have worked together to make me what I am: but I never afterwards forgot, I never shall forget, I never can forget, that my mother was warm from my being sent back." [13]

Mill, without the novelist's privilege of killing the mother in symbolic portrayal of the child's utter loneliness, achieves a similar effect, perhaps finally a more telling effect, by never mentioning her at all. The reader is left to suppose that, like the

13. John Forster, *The Life of Charles Dickens* (London, 1872), 1:49.

well-brought-up child, he is saying nothing when he cannot say something nice, and therefore the silence about his mother is a speaking void. It conveys its message even better than the statement made in the early draft of the *Autobiography* and then canceled. There he puts the final "blame" for the coldness and fear of the house in which he was brought up not on his father but on his mother: "That rarity in England, a really warm hearted mother, would in the first place have made my father a different being, and in the second would have made the children grow up loving and being loved. But my mother, with the very best intentions, only knew how to pass her life in drudging for them" (*Autobiography,* p. 33). Mill's bitterness is irrational and his contemptuous dismissal of the drudging unkind. Anything we can infer about James Mill's character suggests that not a single goddess alone but a combination of Aphrodite and Minerva, just for a start, would have been needed to make him a totally different being. Mill's fantasy of an all-powerful, all-healing mother figure is an interesting one, however, and not unrelated to similar fantasies in Dickens' work, but consideration of it lies outside the scope of this essay.

In sum, Mill's descriptions of his childhood self give him the qualities of "typical" Dickensian waif-children, although the method by which he achieves his characterization is the precise opposite of Dickens'. He works more through what he does not say than what he says; an aristocratic and quiet aloofness or a carefully precise concern to give praise or credit where due and assign blame as charitably and quietly as possible: this is his manner. There are in his work no death scenes, no whippings, no descriptions of poverty or loneliness or terror, no denunciations of man's inhumanity — none of the things, in short, that we tend to consider Dickensian. But to take Mill's seeming rationality and his calm interest in pedagogical method at face value is to misread the *Autobiography*. The interior life it describes (albeit unconsciously) is as tempestuous as that of any Dickens novel and indeed closely resembles the Dickensian "plot."

If it be granted that there are parallels between Dickens' fantasies and the autobiographers' remembrance of their facts, what then? How is it significant that the Dickensian waif strays off the written page and into life? A sociologist might find in the similarities between literature and life a proof that Dickens' novels are more factual and less fantastical than they seem, and the parallels open interesting lines of speculation about the "politics" of the Victorian home. That approach, however, deals with these events as facts, and my interest here is not so much with the facts themselves as with what the autobiographers made of the facts — with the incidents and personalities they chose to remember and with the emotions surrounding remembered events in a luminous haze. Since self-pity is dominant among those emotions, the case I have made might be used as further evidence in justification of Coveney's position and Buckley's on the destructive effects of self-pity; it works against "perfection of the life" just as, in Dickens' novels, it was damaging to "perfection of the work."

Thus the self-pity evident in Pater's semiautobiographical pieces might be another explanation besides that of T. S. Eliot for the note of "inexhaustible discontent, languor, and homesickness" in Pater's work.[14] Eliot ascribes it to the loss of genuine religious faith, and his dislike of Pater's ideas makes him overstate his case. The note is not as all-pervasive as he suggests, but it is there, and a curious passage in *Marius the Epicurean* may help to explain it. Marius's mother dies while away from home, and the narrator comments: "For it happened that, through some sudden, incomprehensible petulance of his, there had been an angry childish gesture, and a slighting word, at the very moment of her departure, actually for the last time . . . the thought of that marred parting having peculiar bitterness for one, who set so much store, both by principle and habit, on the sentiment of home." [15] Pater makes Marius's domestic feeling sound like a virtue, but "the sentiment of home," if based on unresolved bitterness, guilt, and self-pity, makes only for awareness of homelessness — makes then for alienation.

Ruskin's self-pity makes him see his life as failed and indeed

---

14. These are the phrases with which Pater describes qualities in the work of Coleridge ("Coleridge," *Appreciations: With an Essay on Style* [London, 1889], p. 105). Eliot thinks them a better description of Pater's own state of mind ("Arnold and Pater," *Selected Essays, 1917–1932* [New York: Harcourt, Brace, 1932], p. 357).

15. Pater, *Marius the Epicurean* (London, 1885), 1:44–45.

does frustrate the full effectiveness of what is nonetheless a towering achievement. Moving restlessly from project to project, he can take little or no pleasure in what he has done but broods instead about unfulfilled and now unrealizable ambitions: "And if only . . . my father and mother had seen the real strengths and weaknesses of their little John . . . they would have made a man of me there and then, and afterwards the comfort of their own hearts, and probably the first geologist of my time in England" (*Praeterita,* 1:157).

The stultifying effect of self-pity may also help to explain the halt in Mill's mental growth after a certain point in his life: "From this time [around 1840] I have no further changes to tell of," he writes in 1854 (*Autobiography,* p. 132). And it is true that once he has described the importance of his relationship with Harriet Taylor, whom he met in 1830, he chronicles external events almost exclusively and describes no further inner changes of attitude. James Olney in his study of autobiography called *Metaphors of Self* attributes this halt to Mill's lack of feeling,[16] but in my opinion his reading of Mill's personality is entirely wrong. Not lack of feeling but violent feelings of pity for his childhood self, of bitterness at the loss of potential selves he could imagine but could not become, may have kept Mill from coming to a final totality of vision.

Just as in *Art and Illusion* E. H. Gombrich has shown Ruskin's aesthetic theory of "the innocence of the eye," the perception of colors as he imagined a child would see them, to be based on a false physiology and a false psychology,[17] so, as Coveney has pointed out, Sigmund Freud earlier proved the theory of an originally "innocent I" to be false psychology creating in turn false pedagogy and false sociology. It is Coveney's hunch that the whole feeling for childhood and innocence in the Victorian period may be an aspect of the Victorians' sexual repression; the child is a symbol of "purity," and when he does not live up to the symbol he embodies, he is treated savagely. Freud, by destroying the idea of childhood's sexual innocence, was actually

16. *Metaphors of Self: The Meaning of Autobiography* (Princeton: Princeton University Press, 1972), pp. 39–41.
17. *Art and Illusion: A Study in the Psychology of Pictorial Representation,* 2d ed. (New York: Pantheon Books, 1961), pp. 296–297.

preserving the "original romantic assertion of childhood's importance, and its vulnerability to social victimization."[18]

That Mill, Ruskin, and Pater all show the effects of Victorian
sexual repression goes without saying. But again, Coveney's use
of Freudian theory turns more on the treatment of actual children
and the children's remembrance of their upbringing than it does
on the idea of the child and the symbolic significance for adults
of their childhood years. There remains the question: what in
the first place (putting aside, perhaps unfairly, for argument's
sake the beauty and power of its language) gave a poem like
"Ode: Intimations of Immortality from Recollections of Early
Childhood" the impact it had on Dickens and through him on
the Victorians? What in turn gave Dickens' fictitious children
such a hold on Victorian imaginations?

The vision of the child for which Wordsworth found expression in the "Ode" and which, of course, our autobiographers experienced through the work directly as well as through its effects
upon Dickens — is one of potential, perhaps infinite potential,
frustrated by finite circumstance. To appreciate the power of the
image Wordsworth called up one must consider not only Freudian theory on the importance of actual childhood but also Carl
Jung's theories about the archetype of the child, an archetype
which, he writes, "symbolizes the pre-conscious and post-conscious essence of man. His pre-conscious essence is the unconscious state of earliest childhood; his post-conscious essence is
an anticipation by analogy of life after death. In this idea the
all-embracing nature of psychic wholeness is expressed." [19] When
he uses the phrase "by analogy" Jung means, as Wordsworth
seems to mean in the "Ode," that the sense of earlier "glory"
leads to a sense of future glory, not necessarily in an afterlife but
in certain states of mind that the notion of "afterlife" symbolizes.
The child is a "mighty Prophet" of the soul's infinity; the sense
of that infinity may time and again be lost, but through the image
of the child it can at moments be recaptured.

Jung's explanation of the symbol, then, would be that it arises

18. Coveney, *Image of Childhood,* p. 302.
19. "The Psychology of the Child Archetype," *Archetypes and the
Collective Unconscious* (Princeton: Princeton University Press, 1969),
p. 178. Further references to this work will be given in the text.

in answer to the human desire for all that is contained by the phrase "fullness of life." His thoughts about the image of the child also help to explain the great importance it takes on in early nineteenth-century literature. It is Jung's belief that the image of the child appears when the unconscious aspects of the psyche have been "repressed to the point of total exclusion" (*Archetypes,* p. 164). Thus it arises — and Blake, Wordsworth, and Coleridge were all consciously so using it — as an answer to the excessive rationality of the eighteenth century's dominant cast of mind. The children in *Songs of Innocence,* the little girl in "We Are Seven," "the limber elf" at the conclusion to part 2 of *Christabel* all effortlessly enjoy a vision, a sense of themselves, that the rational adults around them cannot fathom but can resent and try to frustrate. Dickens in the same way sets up Sissy Jupe's childish wisdom as an answer to Gradgrind's methodology, and in Mill's *Autobiography,* suffering little John becomes a similar reproach against and answer to the systematizing James. Excessive rationality divides mind from feeling and at last destroys feeling, as, according to his son's theory, it destroyed James Mill's feeling. Excessive morality (related to rationality) divides action from instinct as it divided Margaret Ruskin's methods of child rearing from her maternal instinct. The child is an image of wholeness set up against these divisions. "It represents," writes Jung, "the strongest, the most ineluctable urge in every being, namely the urge to realize itself" (*Archetypes,* p. 170) — and to realize itself as a whole: mind and feeling, will and emotion, act and instinct, psyche and soma.

This archetypal significance casts what Jung would call a "noumen" around the image of the child; the portentousness of the child as symbol, then, may offer another explanation besides Angus Wilson's for the mysterious wisdom often found in Dickens' "little people." Wilson calls children like Paul Dombey, Little Nell, and Tiny Tim "gnomic" and sees their characterization as deriving from Dickens' "reminiscence of himself in those castaway months [at the blacking factory]." [20] While interested in these children, Wilson finds fault with the qualities of morbidity and sentimentality in their characterization and blames these

20. Wilson, "Dickens on Children," p. 204.

artistic lapses on Dickens' constant memory of his childhood suffering. Without denying his interpretation, I would add the possibility that in portraying children Dickens is moved not only by self-pity but at a deeper level by the archetypal image of the child. The symbolic "weight" of the archetype is not applicable to any particular child, whether actually or imaginatively "real." In trying to bring the symbol and the fact together Dickens has the same difficulties that Wordsworth suffered when he devoted a stanza of the "Ode" to "a six years' Darling of a pigmy size."

Jung's description of the archetype of the child offers an insight, then, into the meaning of the symbol itself and helps explain as well the significance of its appearance early in the nineteenth century. But perhaps most interesting of all is the rationale his essay gives for those qualities of personality that I found both Dickens' fictional children and the autobiographers' remembered ones to have in common — and here, lest I seem to have set up those qualities with Jung in mind from the beginning, let me say that I had noted the parallels and written my description of them before I came across Jung's essay on the child symbol. An explanation for the relevance of his insights to my theme must lie in what Jung himself might term "synchronicity" and not in scholarly artful dodging.

The child's loneliness and separation from parents are concomitants of the way in which the archetype finds expression in myth, dream, or story because, according to Jung, "the motifs of 'insignificance,' exposure, abandonment, danger, etc., try to show how precarious is the psychic possibility of wholeness, that is, the enormous difficulties to be met with in attaining this 'highest good' " (*Archetypes,* p. 166). He gives another explanation as well: the child symbolizes a move toward greater consciousness, greater understanding than that previously available, and such consciousness is necessarily *"all alone in the world"* (169).

To a world that simply cannot understand it the potentially new consciousness expressed through the child may seem clumsy and stupid, but the awkward-looking child possesses an intelligence and awareness far greater than those around it: "It is a striking paradox in all child myths that the 'child' is on the one hand delivered helpless into the power of terrible enemies and in continual danger of extinction, while on the other he possesses powers far exceeding those of ordinary humanity. This is closely related to the psychological fact that though the child may be 'insignificant,' 'unknown,' 'a mere child,' he is also divine" (170).

The archetype appears, Jung believes, as prognostic of a change in consciousness, and ideally that change should involve a departure from earlier, more restricted ways into a new vision of life and life's meaning. For the process to come to completion, however, the fantasist, poet, visionary, autobiographer, or tale-teller must separate what Jung calls his "personal infantilism" — that is, his memories of himself as an abandoned or misunderstood or unjustly treated child — from his sense of what the memories signify. He must come to see that the oppressed child of his imagination is at least partly the expression of the heart's hunger for totality of being and that the blame laid upon his parents and his upbringing is in fact a cry against all that divides the self. Paradoxically, if he does not make that dissociation, the image of the child instead of serving to integrate consciousness has the effect of creating a deeper alienation because it stirs up the divisive emotions of anger, bitterness, and self-pity, and the vision of an innocent "I" entangles the visionary in an ever deeper loss of innocence.

A way of thinking about Dickens' and the autobiographers' self-pity, then, is to see it as arising from their failure to dissociate the archetypal symbol of the child from memory's image of their childhood selves. Of such a failure the *I Ching* would say "no blame," and besides, of course, all had some cause to pity themselves. Still the genuine pity of it is that the image of the child if properly understood says that no one need feel sorry for himself. It invites us to rejoice.

II George Eliot and the World of Middlemarch

HENRY AUSTER

George Eliot and the Modern Temper

To understand the current of feeling running through the reservations in the reviews of *Romola* and its successors,[1] we should relate it to the antipathy with which the great modernist works were first greeted. In both reactions can be heard the note of fretfulness and anxiety provoked by the writers' impatience with habits of mind and expression that their readers still find comfortable. The difficulty of modern literature (and art in general), once regarded as merely perverse, has long since come to be accepted as natural, reflecting the "variety and complexity" of our civilization.[2] In most cases it has been assimilated by the temper of the age and deprived of its power to shock, intimidate, and exasperate. As T. S. Eliot said:

> A new kind of writing appears, to be greeted at first with disdain and derision; we hear that the tradition has been flouted and that chaos has come. After a time it appears that the new way of writing is not destructive but recreative. It is not that we have repudiated the past, as the obstinate enemies — and also the

1. For a full compilation and account of the contemporary reactions to George Eliot's work, see David Carroll, ed., *George Eliot: The Critical Heritage* (London: Routledge and Kegan Paul, 1971).
2. T. S. Eliot, "The Metaphysical Poets," *Selected Essays* (London: Faber and Faber, 1951), p. 289.

stupidest supporters — of any new movement like to believe;
but that we have enlarged our conception of the past; and that
in the light of what is new we see the past in a new pattern.[3]

George Eliot's late novels do not have the outright formal
challenge of *The Waste Land* or *Ulysses*. *Romola* (1862–63),
Felix Holt, the Radical (1866), *Middlemarch* (1871–72), and
Daniel Deronda (1876) met with respect, sometimes very great,
often mingled with varying degrees of puzzlement or disappointment, but never with the uncomprehension and hostility
that T. S. Eliot and Joyce encountered. But her readers, recalling
their delight in the warmth, ease, and color of her first books, felt
that she was now straining to impede their enjoyment and under
standing with unnecessary abstraction and analytical detail. What
is audible in these reviews are intimations of the wariness with
which the "common" reader has come to view the latest work
of the serious adventuring artist. They were called forth by elements in the novels that were essentially and increasingly modern,
that were recognized as such then, and that can be considered
today to represent the continuity between Romantic, Victorian,
and modern literature that is more and more insisted upon in
our critical and historical discussions. Indeed, the modern preference for her later fiction illustrates the process described by T. S.
Eliot of absorption and assimilation in time of works whose
exploratory novelty is at first received without understanding.

The modern elements in George Eliot's work are diverse and
can be found to some extent in the early fiction (particularly in
The Mill on the Floss and *Silas Marner*), but their growing
prominence and her increasing interest in them begin to be
marked in *Romola* and reach a resonant culmination in *Daniel
Deronda,* her last novel.[4] As a group these four late books can

3. "American Literature and the American Language," *To Criticize
the Critic* (New York: Farrar, Strauss, and Giroux, 1965), p. 57. See
also Lionel Trilling, "On the Teaching of Modern Literature," *Beyond
Culture: Essays on Literature and Learning* (New York: Viking Press,
1965), for a rueful account of some of the consequences of such
assimilation.
4. Some discussion of modern elements in the novels can be found
in David Carroll, *"Silas Marner:* Reversing the Oracles of Religion,"
Literary Monographs, 1 (1967), 167–200: Carole Robinson, "*Romola:* A
Reading of the Novel," *Victorian Studies,* 6 (1962), 29–42; (on *Middle-*

be taken as a particularly interesting case study in any examination of the emergence of the modern outlook in English literature. Of the many strands that are woven into this outlook, certain crucial ones have been recognized in George Eliot's work: her concern with the plight of the individual in a world of changing and decaying values, her acute sense of the erosion in society of long-established traditions, her realism — the insistence on presenting life as it really is in its fullness and complexity, its mystery as well as commonness. Alienation and progress have long been seen in her work as prominent themes with formal consequences, while her feminism has naturally attracted a good deal of attention lately, though its lack of a militant edge sets a limit on the sympathy it can command today. (Her interest in marriage as perhaps the central arena in which the issues of personal identity and fulfillment are decided would have had to be considered modern until about five years ago, when the emerging position of the women's movement, drawing on other currents of thought, called into question the centrality of marriage in our accepted scheme of life.)

Her philosophical bent, her immersion in psychology and the minute analysis of motives, and her recourse to science as a source of allusion and illumination were the most specific grounds for the disgruntlement felt in her own time by the readers of the late books; today they are highly praised. The coherence of the massive, apparently rambling narratives by means of networks of imagery and symbols has particularly appealed to the aesthetic inclinations of modern critics. Another source of affinity has been found in the surprising flexibility and subtlety of her narrative presence in her work. Such qualities stem from and in turn convey to the reader a feeling for character as mysterious and significant. The result is that the late novels in particular, despite

march) Frank Kermode, "D. H. Lawrence and the Apocalyptic Types," *Continuities* (London: Routledge and Kegan Paul, 1968), pp. 122–151; Ann Sedgeley, *"Daniel Deronda," Critical Review,* 13 (1970), 3–19. In "Beyond the Liberal Imagination: Vision and Unreality in *Daniel Deronda," Victorian Studies,* 4 (1960–61), 33–54, Robert Preyer set the tone for many of the later examinations of this novel by calling attention to the way in which it breaks with George Eliot's past practice as a novelist and with her previous attempts as a moralist and student of society and culture to shore up the defenses of Victorian liberalism.

George Eliot's celebrated sense of the actual, carry an impression
of interiority, which has come to be regarded as an essential
quality of modern literature.[5]

But this interiority, unarguably modern though it may be, is
so in a very broad historical sense that is sometimes extended as
far back as the fifteenth century. The other qualities, more or
less familiar to readers of George Eliot, that I have been pointing
to as modern can also be traced far back in literary history, and
some are usually associated with the rise of the novel as a genre.
The argument for Eliot's modernity thus seems to be rendered
paltry by the recollection that modernity itself can in many ways
be considered a venerable phenomenon. The argument is still
further shaken by the awareness that whatever modern elements
we may be able to unearth in her works, the world, the atmosphere, and the ethos that she has created, even in the cosmopolitan, shifting, rootless locale in *Daniel Deronda,* are inevitably
those of the nineteenth century and not our own. Modern in
many respects she may well be, but modern elements do not
overthrow the historically conditioned character of her outlook;
they look ahead only so far as the historical conditions themselves survive in our own time and culture.

What is (and has to be) missing in her presentation of life
is as important in preserving its nineteenth-century essence as its
modern aspects are in foreshadowing the twentieth century. And
what is missing can be summed up in the idea of apocalypse
and its consequences for the imagination. The side of modernism
expressed in such phrases as "connoisseurs of chaos," the "imagination of disaster," "waiting for the end," and by the image
of the abyss is notably absent from the world of George Eliot's
fiction, early and late.[6] She was spared the historical realities of

5. For some important discussions of the term *modern* in connec-
tion with the novel, see José Ortega y Gasset, "Notes on the Novel,"
The Dehumanization of Art and Other Essays on Literature and Culture
(Princeton: Princeton University Press, 1968); Erich Auerbach, *Mimesis*
(1953; reprint ed., Princeton: Princeton University Press, 1968); Ian
Watt, *The Rise of the Novel* (London: Chatto & Windus, 1957); Erich
Kahler, *The Inward Turn of Narrative* (Princeton: Princeton University
Press, 1973).

6. Frank Kermode's interpretation of *Middlemarch* (in *Continuities*)
as a novel of crisis resembling *Women in Love* is in many ways suggestive and valuable, but it remains unconvincing to me in its blurring of

world wars and concentration camps and the full development of a technological society massed on what is increasingly felt to be a shrinking planet. Whatever reservations she may have about social progress, however somber her view of the individual's emotional and moral situation, her outlook is basically hopeful and rests on the assumption of an orderly if complex and not terribly exhilarating world. There is indeed a tragic dimension in her work, but it originates in the tragedy of Sophocles, modern only in Arnold's sense, and has little in common with the tragic sense in Nietzsche, Chekhov, Yeats, or Beckett.

For the notion of the absurd, so expressive of the modern sensibility, there is no room in Eliot, nor for the cynicism or rejections that notion can give rise to, especially in the realm of politics. These we begin to find in Henry James, but in English it is really Conrad and D. H. Lawrence who first fully define this outlook for our time. And because she is still unaware of the full possibilities of fragmentation, the experiments with form in her novels never go far toward the self-conscious disruption of mimetic conventions, the sense of aesthetic order won anew each time from social disarray and psychological confusion to which we have become accustomed in the serious literature of our own time. (The two sustained flashbacks in the first twenty chapters of *Daniel Deronda,* together with the opening remarks about the arbitrariness of beginnings, are an example of her experimentation and show an aesthetic self-consciousness about time that is modern. The importance accorded to memory in all her novels as a help in a character's effort to shape his life is related to that awareness.)

What then remains of George Eliot's modernism? My case for it hinges on two concepts which are neither modern in the sense of having originated in the twentieth century nor so dominant in her late novels as to do more than disturb their Victorian atmosphere. But this disturbance is striking enough to set her somewhat apart from her contemporaries as a writer with sufficient understanding of the spiritual tendencies of her own time to express them in terms that the twentieth century can recognize

---

distinctions between the kinds of crisis, the views taken of it, and the forms of expression and structure in the two books.

as its own. The concepts I have in mind are unity of being and creative imagination. Briefly and plainly, the creative imagination, as it is understood in the Romantic-modernist tradition, can be seen as the activity of the human mind that brings order out of the chaos of sense impressions of which our physical life consists. Whether the sense of order created by the imagination reflects anything objectively real and "out there" is unimportant. The Romantics, on the whole, thought it did, many of the modernists think that it does not, but even if this were so, the reality of the constructed order through which we declare the humanity of our lives remains unaffected. What matters is the sense of harmony — in Romantic literature often called joy — within oneself, with others, and with the physical world achieved by the imagination in its happiest moments of bringing the mind into relationship with external experience. It is this feeling of harmony, this sense of the fullness and vividness of life, of control and mastery that links Wordsworth's spots of time with Joyce's epiphanies, T. S. Eliot's still point, and Yeats's unity of being.

The ultimate purpose of the Romantics in their discovery and exploration of the imagination was celebration; the ultimate result, fully visible only after what may be considered a Victorian adoption amounting to a reaction,[7] was a new faith.

> I am very religious [wrote Yeats], and deprived by Huxley and Tyndall, whom I detested, of the simple-minded religion of my childhood, I had made a new religion, an almost infallible Church of poetic tradition, of a fardel of stories, and of personages, and of emotions, inseparable from their first expression, passed on from generation to generation by poets and painters with some help from philosophers and theologians. I wished for a world where I could discover this tradition perpetually, and not in pic-

7. Arnold's poetry, most of it composed less than fifty years after the seminal writings of Wordsworth and Coleridge, is the fullest, most precise, and most moving expression among the Victorians of "the ache of modernism." The Romantic experience of the creative imagination and unity of being is recalled here only as concept and memory, representing one of the two worlds between which the poet sees himself wandering. His own world is characterized by a profound sense of loss, which provides the subject matter of the poems and determines their tone and shape.

tures and in poems only, but in tiles round the chimney-piece and in the hangings that kept out the draught. I had even created a dogma: "Because those imaginary people are created out of the deepest instinct of man, to be his measure and his norm, whatever I can imagine those mouths speaking may be the nearest I can go to truth." [8]

One has only to recall a poem like Wallace Stevens' "Sunday Morning" to feel that the reclamation by the Symbolists of the Romantic faith answers George Eliot's expressed need for a religion in the future that would "teach us to do without consolation." [9]

But the modern cult of the imagination can be perilous and has exacted a long list of sacrificial victims. Matthew Arnold acutely described in 1858 the price that a life fully committed to creative imagination and unity of being can demand (Yeats's analysis of his contemporaries — "the last romantics" — in "The Tragic Generation" can be said to bear out Arnold's fears):

> People do not understand what a temptation there is, if you cannot bear anything not *very good,* to transfer your operations to a region where form is everything. Perfection of a certain kind may there be attained, or at least approached without knocking yourself to pieces, but to attain or approach perfection in the region of thought and feeling, and to unite this with perfection of form, demands not merely an effort and a labour, but an actual tearing of oneself to pieces, which one does not readily consent to . . . It is only in the best poetical epochs (such as the Elizabethan) that you can descend into yourself and produce the best of your thought and feeling naturally, and without an overwhelming and in some degree morbid effort; for then all the people around you are more or less doing the same thing.[10]

Declining to pay the price required, Arnold instead turned to criticism and social and cultural analysis, essentially in order to

8. W. B. Yeats, "The Trembling of the Veil," *Autobiographies* (London: Macmillan, 1956), p. 116.

9. *The George Eliot Letters,* ed. Gordon S. Haight (New Haven: Yale University Press, 1955), 6:216.

10. *Letters of Matthew Arnold,* ed. George W. E. Russell (London: Macmillan, 1901), 1:84–85.

revive the conditions in which the imagination could flourish. When that revival came it wore a different aspect from what he had had in mind. The way of imagination in a world seemingly committed to matter, the quest for unity when there appeared to be none, were indeed dangerous, but the times did not allow of safe remedies. More and more artists made the commitment from which Arnold had backed off; the strongest (one thinks first of Yeats and Picasso) found strategies for survival. In various guises, creative imagination and unity of being, despite the practical confusions and political aberrations of individuals, have served since the 1890s as the guiding ideals in art's struggle against the dehumanizing forces of the twentieth century.

The modern novel has not been discussed in the light of these concepts as much as modern poetry, perhaps because poetry communicates its vision of life too frequently in terms of itself, of poetry and art in general. The principles of creative imagination and unity of being thus stand forth more sharply than in fiction, where they are usually overlaid by the accumulation of circumstantial detail and concerns of characterization and narrative. But the feeling of what T. S. Eliot called "the dissociation of sensibility" and the search to find a "re-association" are as central in the novels of our time as in the poetry. Examples chosen almost at random from among the significant modern works of fiction in English illustrate the preoccupation with the potential and the dangers of the imagination in seeking to create a sense of unity in a world bereft of meaning and order.

Conrad's Jim pays with his life to turn his shadowy ideal of conduct into substantial reality (confirming in effect Yeats's faith in a religion of imaginative expression), while Marlow, as he evokes and gives words to our fascination by Jim's quest, sets that ideal — a product of the imagination — in the context of all human effort and activity. The touch of sarcasm is characteristic:

> For a moment I had a view of a world that seemed to wear a vast and dismal aspect of disorder, while, in truth, thanks to our unwearied efforts, it is as sunny an arrangement of small conveniences as the mind of man can conceive. But still — it was only a moment: I went back into my shell directly. One *must*

— don't you know? — though I seemed to have lost all my words in the chaos of dark thoughts I had contemplated for a second or two beyond the pale.[11]

In Lawrence the darkness beyond the pale seems more alluring than terrible and invites exploration:

> This world in which she lived was like a circle lighted by a lamp. This lighted area, lit up by man's completest consciousness, she thought was all the world: that here all was disclosed for ever. Yet all the time, within the darkness she had been aware of points of light, like the eyes of wild beasts, gleaming, penetrating, vanishing. And her soul had acknowledged in a great heave of terror only the outer darkness. This inner circle of light in which she lived and moved, wherein the trains rushed and the factories ground out their machine produce and the plants and animals worked by the light of science and knowledge, suddenly it seemed like the area under an arc-lamp, wherein the moths and children played in the security of blinding light, not even knowing there was any darkness, because they stayed in the light.[12]

While this passage, like Lawrence in general, can be read as assuming an order in the natural world, it seems more accurate to me to see in it an urgency to extend the purview of human consciousness: the dark terra incognita of the unconscious is really a construct of the imagination, a paradigm of existence. Thus, the promising symbols of the arch in *The Rainbow* are realized in *Women in Love,* though in considerably subdued and chastened terms, in the equilibrium ("a pure balance of two single beings: — as the stars balance each other") of the relationship of Birkin and Ursula, who must create this image and sense of unity out of a perpetual struggle against the disintegration of their world and their own selves. (As Birkin says to Gerald, "two exceptional people make another world.")[13]

11. Joseph Conrad, *Lord Jim* (Boston: Riverside Press, 1958), p. 225.
12. D. H. Lawrence, *The Rainbow* (New York: Compass Books, 1961), p. 437.
13. *Women in Love* (New York: Compass Books, 1960), p. 197. In this book Lawrence makes an interesting distinction between completeness of being, associated with static or bygone perfection (Breadalby and the way of life there), narrowness (Gerald is said to convey "a sort of

In *Portrait of the Artist as a Young Man* and *Ulysses* the quest for unity through assertion of the synthesizing power of the imagination serves as the theme as well as the structural principle. It plays a similar role in Foster's *Howards End* and in *A Passage to India,* where of the several approaches to life examined Hinduism, particularly in the spiritual exercises of Professor Godbole, is shown to give the greatest scope to the imagination. Not only does it help the consciousness to comprehend more of the teeming multifariousness of life in India, but it also resists most successfully the appalling sense of life's nullity represented by the Marabar Caves.

Unity created by imagination, meaning and mastery won from disorder and indifference, is also the central theme of *To the Lighthouse*. In this poetic fiction, the issues are drawn delicately but clearly and fully. Lily Briscoe has been unable to achieve the synthesizing vision that impels her painting: "Beautiful and bright it should be on the surface, feathery and evanescent, one colour melting into another like the colours on a butterfly's wing; but beneath the fabric must be clamped together with bolts of iron. It was to be a thing you could ruffle with your breath; and a thing you could not dislodge with a team of horses." [14] Lily recalls the magnetic effect Mrs. Ramsay had on her, her ability to create a sense of meaning and harmony out of the circumstances, trivial, accidental, incongruous, of ordinary life. "Like a work of art" of the sort Lily has been dreaming of, Mrs. Ramsay was able to achieve unity of being: "But what a power was in the human soul!" [15] But it is ten years later, Mrs. Ramsay is dead, and only Mr. Ramsay, the philosopher of what George Eliot called "that hard, unaccommodating Actual," survives. Poised between the present and her memory of the past, between

---

fatal halfness, which to himself seemed wholeness"; p. 199), and ultimately death, and change, growth, openness, and life (thus it is said of Birkin: "He is not a man, he is a chameleon, a creature of change"; p. 85).

14. Virginia Woolf, *To the Lighthouse* (Harmondsworth, Middlesex: Penguin Books, 1964), p. 194. Cf. pp. 56–57: "She saw the colour burning on a framework of steel, the light of a butterfly's wing lying upon the arches of a cathedral. Of all that only a few random marks scrawled upon the canvas remained."

15. Ibid., pp. 182–183.

the sight of Mr. Ramsay and her vision of Mrs. Ramsay, between the physical evidences of amorphousness and mutability and her intimations of harmony and an immortality of sorts, Lily comes gradually to understand what was missing from her painting ten years before. As she turns from the canvas she is trying to master to catch a glimpse of the canvas under which Mr. Ramsay with his two sulking, now almost grown children is approaching the lighthouse, she seeks to fuse her vision of Mrs. Ramsay with the sense of actuality embodied by Mr. Ramsay: "Where was that boat now? Mr. Ramsay? She wanted him." [16] Thus she at last finishes her painting because under pressure of common events she has the sense of having grasped the elusive mystery of life and of art: "One wanted, she thought, dipping her brush deliberately, to be on a level with ordinary experience, to feel simply that's a chair, that's a table, and yet at the same time, It's a miracle, it's an ecstasy. The problem might be solved after all." [17]

Tentative and modest as this sounds, it is still infinitely more buoyant and hopeful than the manic, grotesque, guarded, or self-consciously naive forms of expression to which writers of fiction have had to resort more recently in order to affirm the creative power of the imagination. In works like *Under the Volcano, Invisible Man, The Adventures of Augie March, Catch-22,* and *One Flew Over a Cuckoo's Nest,* the imagination in its struggle to generate unity of being finds itself beleaguered not so much anymore by an intractable material world as by a constricting and threatening social world. Society and its institutions, seen so often in terms of disease and madness, are themselves imaginative products, inventions and constructions of the imagination gone wrong. Subjective in origin, they take on an objectivity that comes to obstruct and threatens to stifle the subjectivity of individual life. Civil war, revolution, and divorce thus provide apt imagery for this inner division, which also gives the apocalyptic tone to so much of modern fiction.

In George Eliot's time, however, the dialogue of the mind with itself had not yet reached so violent a stage. Her books are

16. Ibid., p. 230. Cf. S. P. Rosenbaum, "The Philosophical Realism of Virginia Woolf," *English Literature and British Philosophy,* ed. S. P. Rosenbaum (Chicago: University of Chicago Press, 1971), pp. 347–348.
17. Ibid., p. 229.

still based on the capacity of the human imagination to create unity and order. Their somber tone reflects the relative freshness of the perception that neither God nor society can be depended on to create meaning for us and her profound awareness of the perils that attend the exercise of our unasked autonomy. Thus she constantly discriminates between more and less creative, more and less valid interpretations of life. Her protagonists are usually faced with the challenge of infusing with meaning a world that seems to be made up of fragments; with increasing explicitness and emphasis in the later novels, it is the creative imagination that is shown to be most successful in performing this task as it brings the individual psyche, with its tangle of needs, desires, impulses, and confusions, into a vital relationship with the exterior world. The vitality of that relationship stems from its realism: it is based on a respect for the "hard, unaccommodating Actual" — the demands of the selves of others, the necessary web of personal relations, the intricate, involuted operation of social and historical forces — as well as for one's own limitations.

In the tradition of the Romantics, George Eliot sees us all begin in childhood with a spontaneous, effortless exercise of creative imagination and enjoyment of unity of being:

> We could never have loved the earth so well if we had had no childhood in it ... What novelty is worth that sweet monotony where everything is known, and *loved* because it is known? ... These familiar flowers, these well-remembered bird-notes, this sky, with its fitful brightness, these furrowed and grassy fields, each with a sort of personality given it by the capricious hedgerows — such things as these are the mother tongue of our imagination, the language that is laden with all the subtle inextricable associations the fleeting hours of our childhood left behind them.[18]

18. *The Mill on the Floss,* book 1, chap. 5. Cf. book 2, chap. 1: "There is no sense of ease like the ease we felt in those scenes where we were born, where objects became dear to us before we had known the labour of choice, and where the outer world seemed only an extension of our own personality: we accepted and loved it as we accepted our own sense of existence and our own limbs." The Standard Edition of the *Works of George Eliot* (Edinburgh: Blackwood, 1901) is used throughout.

Experience of such harmony and well-being, reminiscent of the totality associated with the heroic naiveté of Homer's epic world,[19] is not to be had anymore in maturity. The most that one can expect in modern life is to win through after confusion, mistakes, and struggles to a view of life and oneself that yields a feeling of integrity and coherence, a sense of being in tune not so much with society and the world but rather with the underlying tendency and significance of events. George Eliot makes us feel, despite the lingering sense of unfulfilled promise running through *Middlemarch,* that Dorothea Brooke does achieve a good measure of such equipoise. But at the end of *Daniel Deronda* Gwendolen Harleth is faced with a psychological and spiritual predicament that is essentially the same as that of a modern protagonist. For her (unlike Deronda, who is "chosen" for a significant, integrated, but exceptional life), the underlying tendency of events, the dynamism of history, are not present as an objective reality with which her imagination can interact to achieve fulfillment. And here one is forced to the conclusion that it is not the heroine who is at fault but her society, which the author sees, at best, as pleasant, unimaginative, not agitated on the whole by the slow but impressive, wide and varied movement for change that pulses through *Middlemarch.* We have the sense, historically false, that for the English large concrete problems no longer exist, and in the absence of such problems, a more basic problem is taking shape, as the society is sliding into a torpor of complacency and even decadence. There seem to be no causes to stir, inspire, and enlarge the individual imagination, since nationalism is something alien that only Jews, Arabs, or Italians are fortunate enough to have to live by and for.

But what can be felt to be a glaring omission in the book's vision gives a peculiarly modern perspective on the predicament of the heroine. Not only is Gwendolen morally and psychologically something of the antiheroic figure characteristic of modern literature, but there is little difference — mainly one of irony, that antiheroic element — between the way that she is contrasted with Deronda and the relationship of the narrator in *Under*

19. See Georg Lukács, *The Theory of the Novel* (Cambridge, Mass.: MIT Press, 1971), especially part 1, chap. 1.

Western Eyes with Razumov, Natalia Haldin, and the revolutionary ethos. Like a modern heroine Gwendolen is left at the end of her story to shape her existence almost despite society and history, relying (after her moral apprenticeship to Deronda) largely on her own psychological resources, above all on her imagination. Similarly Romola, despite being painstakingly placed in fifteenth-century Florence, also resolves her doubts and uncertainties by distilling from the mixed social currents of her world what is presented as a strictly personal gospel. (It is in fact an illustration of the Comtist religion of humanity.) The existential situation is more important here than precise historical rendering (which is given all the same): it is the individual quest for meaning in a world echoing with confused alarms of struggle and flight that interests the author (and the reader) more than the careful topography of the darkling plain and the disentanglement of the clashing armies. Hence the reminder in the proem that "we still resemble the men of the past more than we differ from them" and the focus on the church service as symbolic of the changeless essence in the human situation: "the images of willing anguish for a great end, of beneficent love and ascending glory . . . These things have not changed . . . the little children are still the symbol of the eternal marriage between love and duty; and men still yearn for the reign of peace and righteousness, — still own that life to be the highest which is a conscious voluntary sacrifice."

The marriage of love and duty is the form that the desired synthesis takes in this novel, but it is brought about not through the imagination — at least not directly — but through a degree of self-sacrifice and submission that strikes us as theoretic. Imagination here is regarded with as much suspicion as respect, and the author's wariness in approaching it is reflected in the fact that the heroine is allowed to experience imagination only vicariously through the tainted visionary figure of Savonarola. The impact of his impassioned idealism and zeal is validated, but only after a careful, cumulative dissection of the fleshly corruption which his imagination is heir to. It becomes clear to Romola that "the enthusiasm which had come to her as the only energy strong enough to make life worthy, seemed to be inevitably bound up with vain dreams and willful eye-shutting" (chap. 52).

Savonarola's is "the struggle of a mind possessed by a never-silent hunger after purity and simplicity, yet caught in a tangle of egoistic demands, false ideas, and difficult outward conditions, that made simplicity seem impossible" (chap. 59). Rejecting him and his influence, Romola leaves Florence and eventually finds a role as a secular Madonna in a nameless, plague-stricken village. She then discovers in herself the energy for sympathy and involvement with the lives of others for which she once relied on Savonarola. Only now is she able to affirm the effect he had on her, though she continues to repudiate his mixed nature. Extracting "a sort of faith . . . out of the very depths of despair," she thinks it "impossible that it had not been a living spirit, and no hollow pretense, which had once breathed in the Frate's words, and kindled a new life in her" (chap. 71).

The living spirit is that of human idealism and striving. There are frequent reminders of the secular nature of what is taken by many in the novel's world as miraculous. The crucial influences and interventions are human, and the contradictions that agitate the heroine in her search for "a valid law" — between humanism and Christianity, worldliness and other worldliness, "affections" and "duties," "lawlessness" and "obedience," "inner moral facts" and "external law," self and nature — appear to be resolved with the help of the imagination but without genuine trust in it. The book's conclusion has a dying fall, in contrast with the novels that followed; the desire for happiness and fulfillment seems discredited and its place filled by the melancholy, abstract, unconvincing idealism of self-sacrifice and resignation of the religion of humanity.

Savonarola's imagination, the visionary energy from which Romola draws strength and motive power, flows in a religious channel. But it is emphasized time and again that what inspires her is not his faith or theology but its result: his conviction in translating the spiritual force that drives him into the practical terms of personal and public ethics. In *Felix Holt* the link of imagination (or vision) with religion is made still more tenuous. Christianity is presented with respect but not without a degree of condescension as only one way — and one in danger of being left behind by the pace of events — in which imaginative power finds expression and thus a way of giving shape and direction to life. It is that function that is sacred and not particular forms, which explains the borrowing of religious terminology to describe the imagination at work not only in this novel and its successors but in modern writers like Lawrence and Joyce. When Esther, stirred by Felix Holt's challenges to her complacent gentility, is inspired by Mr. Lyon's story of his love for her mother, she not only takes her stepfather seriously for the first time but is moved to admiration. His pious response and her silence make the difference between them quite clear:

> "But that must be the best life, father," said Esther, suddenly rising, with a flush across her paleness, and standing with her head thrown a little backward, as if some illumination had given her a new decision . . .
>
> "What life, my dear child?"
>
> "Why, that where one hears and does everything because of some great, strong feeling — so that this and that in one's circumstances don't signify."
>
> "Yea, verily; but the feeling that should be thus supreme is devotedness to the Divine Will."
>
> Esther did not speak; her father's words did not fit on to the impressions wrought in her by what he had told her. (Chap. 26)[20]

The action of the book, the interweaving of plots that reach back a generation with the narrative set in the midst of the political activity of the first Reform Bill, is seen as unfolding not according to the Divine Will but, at least in individual lives, the moral law of consequences. The characters are distinguished between those whose imagination is strong and farseeing enough to envision the effects of their actions and who are then guided by their visions, and those who from frustration or self-seeking yield to the pressure of momentary needs and impulses and live with the consequences of their surrender. But all are the authors of their own fates, especially Esther, of whom we even are told that "her life was a book which she seemed to be constructing herself" (chap. 40). The assumption of omniscience that underlies this image — omniscience of both the author and the central

20. Cf. Dorothea in *Middlemarch*, chap. 39: "I have always been finding out my religion since I was a little girl. I used to pray so much — now I hardly ever pray."

characters — stands in contrast to the indeterminacy prevailing in modern fiction. Our faith even in the imagination has diminished since George Eliot's time; we are more impressed than she was by the contingent, unpredictable nature of the world. But whether it is called vision, imagination, or expanded consciousness, the means by which some sense of order is won from life is essentially the same in her novels and those of our time. Mrs. Transome, "seeing nothing that was actually present, but inwardly seeing with painful vividness what had been present a little more than thirty years ago" (chap. 1), Harold Transome, of "narrow imagination which . . . is admiringly called the practical mind" (chap. 8), Mr. Jermyn, startled by the "tall whitewrapped figure which had sometimes set his heart beating quickly more than thirty years before" (chap. 21), all illustrate failure of imagination. Their lives are characterized by images of division, contradiction, incongruity. On the other hand, Felix Holt, who calls himself "a man . . . warned by visions" (chap. 27), and Rufus Lyon, whose "illusions" reflect "a wider vision of past and present realities — a willing movement of a man's soul with the larger sweep of the world's forces" (chap. 16), speak with a moral authority that derives from their imaginative contact with reality.

But it is Esther, the true protagonist of the novel, who most convincingly represents the way of imagination. Unlike Felix, a static and stilted figure for whose heroic qualities we must take the author's word, Esther is seen to grow in complexity, stature, and authority as she moves from a life that is "a heap of fragments" (chap. 15) to one that is like "the best life" that she perceived in her father's story. Her friendship with Felix first rouses a dormant idealism in her; this is given a more precise form by her response to Mr. Lyon's disclosure of her origins. But it is only during her stay at Transome Hall that her imagination, stirred by the stark reality of a way of life the appearance of which she is used to admiring, emerges decisively to guide her to "the choice . . . which gives unity to life, and makes memory a temple where all relics and all votive offerings, all worship and all grateful joy, are unbroken history sanctified by one religion" (chap. 44). Mrs. Transome's bitter unhappiness, Mr. Transome's senility, Harold's bland charm serve to awaken her to the full significance of the qualities in Felix and her stepfather that she has just learned to admire: "Every day she was getting more clearly into her imagination what it would be to abandon her own past, and what she would enter into in exchange for it" (chap. 40).

At a critical point near the end Esther is considering "the parting of the ways" (chap. 44) that will determine the course of her life: "her mind was in that state of highly-wrought activity, that large discourse, in which we seem to stand aloof from our own life . . . 'I think I am getting that power Felix wished me to have: I shall soon see strong visions.' " A short time later, caught up still in this imaginative contemplation, she moves to the window to take up a stance characteristic of George Eliot's heroines at certain key moments in their lives (and recalling Lily Briscoe's situation and perception near the end of *To the Lighthouse*): "She drew up the blinds, liking to see the grey sky, where there were some veiled glimmerings of moonlight, and the lines of the for-ever running river, and the binding movement of the black trees. She wanted the largeness of the world to help her thought" (chap. 49). We thus see her imagination as activity, a movement from self-consciousness to the outside world and back again, very much in the spirit of Coleridge[21] and with a sense of synthesis and unity as its end. Just as at the trial "her woman's passion and her reverence for goodness rushed together in an undivided current" (chap. 46), so at this point, fully aware of the costs, Esther perceives and accepts "the best thing that life could give her" — a sense of unity through "a supreme love, a motive that gives a sublime rhythm to a woman's life, and exalts habit into partnership with the soul's higher needs" (chap. 49).

It is the same need, as the text shows, to face "the largeness of the world," to check the pull of self-centered recrimination and anguish by contact with external reality, that in one of the great moments in *Middlemarch* draws Dorothea Brooke to the window. A similar inward-outward alternation of movement is apparent in the staging of the scene in which she and Will finally

21. See, for example, his use of the motion of the "small water-insect" as "no unapt emblem of the mind's self-experience in the act of thinking" (*Biographia Literaria,* ed. J. Shawcross [London: Oxford University Press, 1954], 1:85–86).

declare their love for each other. It is not fanciful to suggest that what we are watching in such passages is the imagination at its synthesizing, dialectical, creative work of bringing mind and world, subject and object, into relationship with one another. It is a domestic, prosaic, low-keyed version[22] of what Wordsworth in *The Recluse* calls the "Paradise, and Groves Elysian" that result from "the discerning intellect of Man, / When wedded to this goodly universe / In love and holy passion."

In *Middlemarch* the efforts at such wedding provide the central theme. It finds expression, as is well known, in the examination of various marriages, the movement for reform, with its implication that, as Mr. Brooke puts it, "We're all one family, you know — it's all one cupboard" (chap. 51), and the vocational or professional aims of characters like Dorothea, Lydgate, Casaubon, Bulstrode, and Caleb Garth (of whom we are told in chapter 24 that "myriad-headed labour . . . had laid hold of his imagination in boyhood . . . [and] had acted on him as poetry without the aid of the poets"). But most of these characters do not have the degree of fullness and strength of imagination needed to succeed in the quest for unity. In one way or another their sensibilities show the "spots of commonness" that express a less than total commitment to the imaginative visions they espouse. Their incomplete apprehension of reality carries the seeds of their destruction. As the overlapping and intertwined narratives show again and again, whatever in the outside world is ignored, neglected, or left out of account has a tendency sooner or later to assert its claims in such a way as to bring down the flawed construction of reality. While the Dorothea-Casaubon and Lydgate-Rosamond relationships constitute the fullest accounts of such disillusionment, it is Mr. Bulstrode, confronted by Raffles, who most concisely and vividly illustrates the underlying psychological phenomenon: "as if by some hideous magic, this loud red figure had risen before him in unmanageable solidity — an incorporate past which had not entered into his imagination of chastisements" (chap. 53).[23] Rosamond, the supreme

22. Presumably it was her solemn, low-keyed quality that made Yeats dislike George Eliot. See *Autobiographies,* pp. 87–88.

23. The general point and this particular example were suggested by a paper read by David Carroll at the *Middlemarch* conference in Cal-

egoist, the most impervious of all the characters to impressions from the outside, suffers two such shocks of recognition. When Will repudiates her, "all her sensibility was turned into a bewildering novelty of pain; she felt a new terrified recoil under a lash never experienced before. What another nature felt in opposition to her own was being burnt and bitten into her consciousness" (chap. 78). And Dorothea's appeal to her on behalf of Lydgate also makes "her soul totter all the more with a sense that she had been walking in an unknown world which had just broken in upon her" (chap. 81).[24]

It is the inadequacy of Lydgate's imagination, powerful but narrow, that is dissected most precisely as well as poignantly. Not unlike the aesthetes of Yeats's generation, who nonchalantly professed to leave living to their servants, Lydgate does not apply his full powers to life, only to the science and practice of medicine, "bringing a much more testing vision of details and relations into this pathological study than he had ever thought it necessary to apply to the complexities of love and marriage." Only in his work does he manifest the same inward-outward rhythm of the imagination in action to be seen in Dorothea and Esther Lyon: "Fever had obscure conditions, and gave him that delightful labour of the imagination which is not mere arbitrariness, but the exercise of disciplined power — combining and constructing with the clearest eye for probabilities and the fullest obedience to knowledge; and then, in yet more energetic alliance with impartial Nature, standing aloof to invent tests by which to try its own work." He admires "the imagination that reveals subtle actions inaccessible by any sort of lens" but does not see that life, even more than science, challenges him with problems that require the play of such imagination for their solution. Losing sight of the end in his fascination by the means, Lydgate wants to pursue through biochemistry "those minute processes

gary in September 1971. Here a brilliant and witty argument is made for the psychological significance of the Gothic and violent imagery that crops up with startling frequency in the novel.

24. Rosamond presents something of a problem for my argument as the person of least imagination in the novel who nevertheless succeeds through sheer force of egoism to realize her utterly conventional "vision" of life. But the book's scheme of values, in which the reader is made to share, renders her success ignoble and odious.

which prepare human misery and joy, those invisible thorough-fares which are the first lurking-places of anguish, mania, and crime, that delicate poise and transition which determine the growth of happy or unhappy consciousness" (chap. 16). He never clearly recognizes the connection between the passionate articulation of his professional ideals and the melancholy work-ing out of these very same issues in his own life.[25]

Dorothea's imagination is the most adequate to the task of wedding the mind to reality and thus transforming it, however slightly. Not unlike Wordsworth's sister Dorothy in "Tintern Abbey," she is a figure of youthful energy and idealism. Strug-gling to order what seems to her a fragmented and amorphous world, she is gradually educated into the capacity "to conceive with that distinctness which is no longer reflection but feeling — an idea wrought back to the directness of sense, like the solidity of objects" (chap. 21).[26] From the start she yearns "after some lofty conception of the world which might frankly include the parish of Tipton" (chap. 1), but, handicapped by an education "at once narrow and promiscuous" (chap. 2), with its "toy-box history of the world" (chap. 10), she must discover through independent study, as it were, and its attendant mistakes the way to coherence in life. The vast spectacle of human activity, past and present, "seemed nothing but a labyrinth of petty courses, a walled-in maze of small paths that led no whither" (chap. 3). Her impressions of Rome, described in the celebrated passage in chapter 20, reflect her distress and confusion after the assump-tions on which she had set the course of her life have proven false. At this point she is in a state of mind like Coleridge's in the Dejection Ode: "I may not hope from outward forms to win / The passion and the life, whose fountains are within." Her progress through the book is marked by a gradual freeing of those fountains until she becomes, like many a hero and heroine of modern fiction, an artist at living, an example of imagination

25. The analysis of Lydgate's character is consistent with the kind of perspective Arnold took up ten years later in "Literature and Science."
26. The significance of this often noticed passage is well brought out by Norman Feltes, "George Eliot and the Unified Sensibility," *PMLA*, 79 (1964), 132, as he emphasizes the centrality of the concept of the fusion of thought and feeling in the work of George Eliot and of G. H. Lewes.

applied to life, a figure like Mrs. Ramsay in *To the Lighthouse* or Mrs. Gould in *Nostromo*. That is why Will's compliment in their brief exchange about poetic imagination is more than a platitude (even though Eliot mocks his ready conventionality):

> "To be a poet is to have a soul so quick to discern that no shade of quality escapes it, and so quick to feel, that discernment is but a hand playing with finely-ordered variety on the chords of emotion — a soul in which knowledge passes instantaneously into feeling, and feeling flashes back as a new organ of knowledge. One may have that condition by fits only."
>
> "But you leave out the poems," said Dorothea, "I think they are wanted to complete the poet. I understand what you mean about knowledge passing into feeling, for that seems to be just what I experience. But I am sure I could never produce a poem."
>
> "You *are* a poem — and that is to be the best part of a poet — what makes up the poet's consciousness in his best moods," said Will, showing such originality as we all share with the morning and the springtime and other endless renewals. (Chap. 22)

During Dorothea's dismal marriage to Casaubon, her imagination must be repressed and "the sense of connection with a manifold pregnant existence had to be kept up painfully as an inward vision, instead of coming from without, in claims that would have shaped her energies" (chap. 28). Only after his death, when her involvement with the lives of others comes to a crisis culminating in that early-morning vision from her window, does she win for herself the sense that "she was a part of that involuntary, palpitating life, and could neither look out on it from her luxurious shelter as a mere spectator, nor hide her eyes in selfish complaining" (chap. 80). The imaginative contact of self and reality produces in her case a sense of balance and fulfillment, although the book ends on an essentially tragicomic note (especially when the assorted fates of all the characters are taken into account). Dorothea's life is spoken of as a sacrifice; the channels in which "her full nature . . . spent itself . . . had no great name on the earth." But what is important is that her full nature does find expression. She achieves a sense of harmony on the modest scale dictated by "the conditions of an imperfect social state." Although "there is no creature whose inward being is so strong that it is not greatly determined by what lies outside it," Dorothea succeeds, however slightly, in shaping the world more in accordance with the vision of her ardent imagination than it was when she found it: "the effect of her being was incalculably diffusive: for the growing good of the world is partly dependent on unhistoric acts; and that things are not so ill with you and me as they might have been is half owing to the number who lived faithfully a hidden life, and rest in unvisited tombs" ("Epilogue").

In the epilogue there is, then, an attempt at a balanced assessment of the significance of the narrated events. If we consider the heroine's story one of disappointment, it is implied that we have seen nothing yet: "we insignificant people with our daily words and acts are preparing the lives of many Dorotheas, some of which may present a far sadder sacrifice than that of the Dorothea whose story we know." The case of Gwendolen Harleth, who is far from Dorothea's idealism if not from her innocence, may be seen as an illustration of that warning about the prospects for individual fulfillment in the years to come. Yet why sacrifice? Where material hardship is contemplated in terms of having to get by on seven hundred a year and keeping only one servant the word has a peculiar ring. But to think for a moment about its resonance here is to be reminded of the interiority prevailing in these two novels, where crises of character are more important than financial gains or losses. It is true that George Eliot has a rare ability to dramatize both sorts of crisis and make us feel strongly how interconnected they are (as in the case of Lydgate, for example). But in *Middlemarch* and still more in *Daniel Deronda* it is interior space, the mental landscape rather than the physical, that commands attention. We are reminded of the significance and even the primacy of the inner world in many ways. In chapter 51 Deronda's mother says, "thoughts, feelings, apparitions in the darkness are events — are they not?" Deronda himself has already agreed with her in advance when he supports Mirah's Keatsian-Yeatsian faith in the imagination ("If people have thought what is the most beautiful and the best thing, it must be true"): "It is a truth in thought though it may never have been carried out in action. It lives as an idea" (chap. 37). Earlier still, in the spirit of Ruskin and foreshadowing Wilde,

Deronda sees the relationship between art and nature in a way already close to the modern. Commenting on the sculptured cloister at Monk's Topping he wonders "whether one oftener learns to love real objects through their representations, or the representations through the real objects . . . When I was a little fellow these capitals taught me to observe, and delight in, the structure of leaves" (chap. 35).

Such comments, consistently emphasizing the fascination of the "unmapped country within us" (chap. 24), not only prepare the ground for the sustained, eloquent, but meticulously rational defense of the imagination occupying books 5 and 6, but they serve also to justify the interest in Gwendolen's consciousness and its development — a slender and "insignificant thread" in the "mighty drama" of human history (chap. 11). Invoking grand imagery on behalf of both Deronda and Gwendolen — straightforwardly in his case, ironically in hers — the author keeps us constantly aware that "men, like planets, have both a visible and invisible history" (chap. 16). The focus on the latter reflects the book's interior dimension and helps to account for the rarefied social milieu in which most of the action takes place. A chronicle of fine consciousnesses cannot have much to do with the pressure of usual material needs: to carry on their exalted quest for meaning, identity, and "the best of all life" (chap. 32), the characters must be freed (like James's Isabel Archer and many another modern protagonist) from the worry of having to earn a living. Not that such ordinary stress is entirely absent: Gwendolen, after all, must pawn her necklace, and she marries Grandcourt to save her mother from a life of genteel poverty and herself from service as a governess. There are other reminders of the claims of material existence, but all are mere machinery of plot and atmosphere: not one is essential to the modern drama of consciousness, which can best be staged, as is not infrequently pointed out, with the backing of "three or five per cent on capital which somebody else has battled for" (chap. 17).[27]

27. William Myers, in "George Eliot: Politics and Personality," notes that she "habitually psychologizes social fact." With a good deal of justice he criticizes her view "that the real causes of history are 'cultural' — in the spirit behind events, not in the events themselves . . . It is a position which comfortably evades the challenges of slums, crime, dis-

The impressive argument for the imagination at the center of the book occurs in the story of Deronda's discovery of his role as a nineteenth-century Moses and makes use of terms like soul, faith, yearning, vision, ideas, second sight, and divine reason as well as imagination. But despite the strongly religious flavor of the language the direction the argument takes is toward the extension of the average man's notion (chap. 37) of the power of the human mind. Echoing Romantic idealism and looking forward to its modernist version, Eliot refers to inspiration and creativity in science and the arts to celebrate "that passionate belief which determines the consequences it believes" (chap. 41). With his own life as an example, Deronda comes to accept in chapter 55 Mordecai's belief that "visions are the creators and feeders of the world" (chap. 40). And Mordecai urges his view in words that in part recall Stephen's in *Portrait of the Artist as a Young Man*: "The world grows, and its frame is knit together by the growing soul; dim, dim at first, then clearer and more clear, the consciousness discerns remote stirrings. As thoughts move within us darkly, and shake us before they are fully discerned — so events — so beings: they are knit with us in the growth of the world" (chap. 40).[28]

Art and artists, drama and music, as well as references to visionary figures of history, religion, and myth (Washington, Buddha, Moses, Prometheus) are used to provide familiar if not always immediately relevant analogues for Mordecai's passionate claims and Deronda's extraordinary temperament and history. The narrative strains to create a congenial climate for the enjoyment "of those rare moments when our yearnings and our acts can be completely one, and the real we behold is our ideal good"

---

ease and violence which Dickens was prepared to face" (*Literature and Politics in the Nineteenth Century*, ed. John Lucas [London: Methuen, 1971], p. 117).

28. Michael Y. Mason, calling attention to the idealistic philosophy of Whewell and the importance there given to the imagination's role in perceiving reality, cites a strikingly similar passage from G. H. Lewes's *Foundations of a Creed*: "The world grows as we grow; and we grow with the growth of the world. Nothing exists for us, but what is felt. We are the centres to which the intelligible universe converges, *from* which it radiates" ("*Middlemarch* and Science," *Review of English Studies*, 22 [1971], 151–169).

(chap. 63). But while the realization of unity of being through creative imagination is illustrated most fully in the convergence of Deronda's temperament and his Zionist mission, the more problematic, realistic, and moving version of that process is to be found in the story of Gwendolen Harleth. The connections between the two narratives are now generally recognized,[29] and the extremely selective focus here will be excused. Deronda, we are told quite early, has "a fervour which made him easily feel the presence of poetry in everyday events" (chap. 32); the narrative endorses this quality as "the chief poetic energy . . . the force of imagination that pierces or exalts the solid fact" (chap. 33). His interest in Gwendolen must be seen as an expression of this imaginative energy — a recognition of the poetry in her. Her crisis dramatizes more effectively than his fulfillment the real human issues. Terrified as she is of vastness and solitude (chap. 6), blind though she is to "that mighty drama" of history, Gwendolen (like Kurtz's Intended in *Heart of Darkness*) nevertheless embodies an ideal: girls like her "are the Yea or Nay of that good for which men are enduring and fighting. In these delicate vessels is borne onward through the ages the treasure of human affections" (chap. 12). Better than Mirah, Mordecai, or the Cohens, Gwendolen expresses the heroic aspect of the commonplace, the particular human conflict that must become a felt part of Deronda's experience and vision. It is in this sense that she represents an education for him (chap. 35).

She is introduced "at a stage when the blissful beauty of earth and sky entered only by narrow and oblique inlets into the consciousness, which was busy with a small social drama almost as little penetrated by a feeling of wider relations as if it had been a puppet-show" (chap. 14). Contact with Deronda and shock after shock of discovery about herself in the course of her marriage to Grandcourt painfully serve to extend her horizons. She too is imaginative and given to visions, but hers represent neurotic eruptions of fears and perceptions she has tried to suppress.[30]

    29. See especially David Carroll, "The Unity of *Daniel Deronda*," *Essays in Criticism,* 9 (1959), 369–380.
    30. Jean Sudrann, "*Daniel Deronda* and the Landscape of Exile," *ELH,* 37 (1970), 433–445, shows in detail how Gwendolen's "fits of spiritual dread" (chap. 6) rise out of repression. Her analysis of the presentation

Their significance only gradually becomes clear to her. Her movement toward new consciousness, toward an imaginative apprehension of her true position, culminates in the final perturbation by which we see her shaken. After Grandcourt's death her dependence on Deronda, allowed into the open, has grown. When he tells her of his mission and his imminent departure and marriage, "the great movements of the world, the larger destinies of mankind" at last burst in upon her: "she was . . . for the first time being dislodged from her supremacy in her own world, and getting a sense that her horizon was but a dipping onward of an existence with which her own was revolving." The imagery of vastness and solitude, mystery and heroic activity, that had been used previously to indicate Gwendolen's obliviousness is now invoked again, this time to describe her sudden awareness of what Yeats called "the desolation of reality." But the scene ends with a sense of tremulous potential that is itself an achievement for her. Parting kindly with Deronda, first hysterically, later calmly, she accepts the new vision of reality and her responsibility for herself: "I am going to live . . . I shall live. I mean to live . . . I shall live, I shall be better" (chap. 69). The imaginative shaping of life is still in the future, but we are left to feel that the regenerative process inspired by Deronda will maintain its thrust toward the kind of life he has urged upon her: one in which "true affections are clad with knowledge" (chap. 36) and which grows "like a plant" (chap. 65). It is an ideal that has continued to haunt modern writing.

---

of Grandcourt's drowning as a realization of Gwendolen's secret fear and hatred ("I did kill him in my thoughts . . . I saw my wish outside me"; chap. 56) accords well with the tendency in *Middlemarch* of neglected aspects of external reality to assert themselves with a vengeance. Gwendolen's story is acutely interpreted here as one of "modern" alienation as described by Sartre.

her own extraordinary command of words as a critic, translator, and novelist, we have good reason to believe that Feuerbach's attitude toward language was particularly congenial to her. We expect to find — and do find — that the misuse of language on the part of her fictional characters is often regarded as a flaw subject to moral correction. Though she has been accused of writing like a schoolteacher, Eliot's idea of proper usage is not limited to grammatical correctness. One of the striking achievements in her first novel, *Adam Bede,* is the creation of sympathetic characters who express themselves in a rich colloquial idiom. Eliot's idea of good language, like Feuerbach's, is based on its efficacy as a link between human beings. Language as rhetoric, fashion, frivolity, or rule is not of particular interest to her. The object of the word is communication, its life is dialogue.

In the "Prelude" and "Finale" of *Middlemarch,* Eliot refers metaphorically to the historical and social changes which make the heroism of a Teresa of Avila impossible in mid-nineteenth-century England. Before the story begins we are reminded that Teresa had "found her epos in the reform of a religious order." At the end Eliot observes that "the medium in which [Teresa's] ardent deeds took shape is forever gone." "Epos" and "medium" are significant terms since they both call attention to modes of expression without drawing too fine a distinction between language and action. The implication is plain and, to a writer, especially disturbing: in periods of social disorder and incoherence, language is one of the structures that falters. To perceive the problem is not necessarily to be able to name it in such a way as to help others or to begin the healing process referred to by Feuerbach, simply because words are themselves subject to the general malady. Eliot is some distance from Beckett's world of "nameless things" and "thingless names," but the serene reassurances of her "Prelude" and "Finale" cannot conceal the depth of her pessimism about the salvific power of words in a realm between two worlds, "one dead, the other powerless to be born."

Though of no particular importance in the "plot," one of the crucial emblematic scenes of *Middlemarch* is Mrs. Garth's grammar lesson. The episode has all the detail and warmth and mellow sympathetic tones for which Eliot is famous, but these elements should not obscure the fact that the scene introduces in playful form one of the major and most serious preoccupations of the novel: the relationship between language and social structure. The lesson is about "agreement in number," the need to contain complexity within order. In her authorial asides Eliot illustrates Mrs. Garth's lesson with a subtle display of pronouns and an observation about mothers and daughters which moves rapidly from the specific to the general and assumes a social intimacy with the reader:

> Mrs. Garth, with her sleeves turned above her elbows, deftly handling her pastry — applying her rolling-pin and giving ornamental pinches — while she expounded with grammatical fervour what were the right views about the concord of verbs and pronouns with "nouns of multitude or signifying many" was a sight agreeably amusing. She was of the same curly-haired, square-faced type as Mary, but handsomer, with more delicacy of feature, a pale skin, a solid matronly figure, and a remarkable firmness of glance. In her snowy-frilled cap she reminded one of that delightful Frenchwoman whom we have all seen marketing, basket on arm. Looking at the mother, you might hope that the daughter would become like her, which is a prospective advantage equal to a dowry — the mother too often standing behind the daughter like a malignant prophecy — "Such as I am, she will shortly be."
>
> "Now let us go through that once more," said Mrs. Garth, pinching an apple-puff which seemed to distract Ben, an energetic young male with a heavy brow, from due attention to the lesson. " 'Not without regard to the import of the word as conveying unity or plurality of idea' — tell me again what that means, Ben." (Mrs. Garth, like more celebrated educators, had her favourite ancient paths, and in a general wreck of society would have tried to hold her "Lindley Murray" above the waves.)
>
> "Oh — it means — you must think what you mean," said Ben, rather peevishly. "I hate grammar. What's the use of it?"
>
> "To teach you to speak and write correctly so that you can be understood," said Mrs. Garth with severe precision. "Should you like to speak as old Job does?"
>
> "Yes," said Ben stoutly; "it's funnier. He says 'Yo goo' — that's just as good as 'You go.' "
>
> "But he says, 'A ship's in the garden,' instead of 'a sheep,' " said Letty with an air of superiority. "You might think he meant a ship off the sea."

"No, you mightn't, if you weren't silly," said Ben. "How could a ship off the sea come there?"

"These things belong only to pronunciation, which is the least part of grammar," said Mrs. Garth. "That apple-peel is to be eaten by the pigs, Ben; if you eat it, I must give them your piece of pastry. Job has only to speak about very plain things. How do you think you would write or speak about anything more difficult if you knew no more of grammar than he does? You would use wrong words, and put words in the wrong places, and instead of making people understand you, they would turn away from you as a tiresome person. What would you do then?"

"I shouldn't care, I should leave off," said Ben with a sense that this was an agreeable issue where grammar was concerned. (Chap. 24) [2]

The passage "works" as an amusing and instructive scene; there is a fine play on words, but there is no mistaking it for Sheridan or Austen. It is not neat or polished or economical. And it is not quite enough to say that Eliot adds local color, "frilled cap" and "apple puffs," and that makes the whole difference. In this agreeable scene about grammatical agreement, the atmosphere is heavy with potential discord.

The chapter begins with the approach of Fred Vincy, whose affection for the Garths is not shared by his family, who "though old manufacturers could not any more than dukes be connected with none but equals, . . . were conscious of an inherent social superiority which was defined with great nicety in practice, though hardly expressible theoretically." Of course, there is a "connection" between the Vincys and the Garths. Not only does Fred admire Mary and her family, but he has prevailed upon the friendship and kindness of Mr. Garth — who is much poorer than his own father — to underwrite a debt on his behalf. The chapter on good grammar and "right" connections begins with Fred's determination to confess to Mr. Garth the awkward outcome of his irresponsibility and abuse of the friendly tie. The reality, then, is not absence of connection, but a connection which, on one side, is undervalued and mistreated.

Like Feuerbach, G. H. Lewes and Herbert Spencer stressed

2. Quotations from *Middlemarch* are taken from *Works of George Eliot,* 10 vols. (Edinburgh: Blackwood, 1901), vol. 7.

the social dimensions of language. Language, like society, is in a continuous state of change, yet, according to Spencer, certain structures and uses — especially those having to do with religion — retain elementary links to the past and appear almost exempt from the usual flow. In the humanistic religion of George Eliot, Mrs. Garth is a strong matriarch and, like Noah, she is determined to save something in the flood: "In a general wreck of society [she] would have tried to hold her 'Lindley Murray' above the waves." Noah preserves natural creatures in his ark, Mrs. Garth preserves a book, a grammar book, at that, the Word — not as St. John understood it, but as Feuerbach did, an image of an idea, the regulated product of civilization.

The picture of Mrs. Garth holding her grammar above the waves is as comic and informative as that of Becky Sharp tossing Johnson's dictionary out of the coach window at the beginning of *Vanity Fair*. One source of the humor is the apparent serenity and stability of Middlemarch. This is not a Gothic novel; we do not anticipate floods or wrecks, and in any event Mrs. Garth would seem an unlikely savior and a grammar book too trivial to be saved in a time of calamity. But, as one reads on, the story *is* calamitous; society *is* undergoing profound changes, suffering irrevocable losses; and Mrs. Garth's homely conservatism, though it cannot stem the tide, can provide a temporary resting place from which to survey the damage.

For Mrs. Garth, the world is inherently hierarchical; there is a comfortable order implied in her reference to pigs, greedy boys, old Job, Fred Vincy, and the fine gentleman she would like her son to be. At the top of her ladder is a vision of articulate people making themselves pleasant and lucid on the most difficult subjects by putting the "right" words in the "right" places. Agreeable manners, good feelings, clear ideas, and graceful expression are all somehow tied to correct language. The thought of trying to unite these dubious and apparently unrelated ends in any utterance leads young Ben to prefer silence (" 'I should leave off,' said Ben with a sense that this was an agreeable issue where grammar was concerned").

The range of Eliot's perceptions and sympathies is marvelously distilled in this brief scene. She values order and stability, yet sees, and to some extent welcomes, changes which challenge the rigidities of language and society. It is not surprising that she should show indulgence to Mrs. Garth's attentiveness to language, but it is surprising that this loquacious novelist should sympathize with Ben's wish to "leave off." Yet as long and richly wordy as *Middlemarch* may be, it is not a display of unmixed confidence in the power of language and, especially, of dialogue. Despite its double plot and careful pairing of characters, *Middlemarch* is not, like *Pride and Prejudice,* a masterpiece of dialogue; it is a masterpiece of interrupted dialectics, of dialogues broken off, like Ben's with his mother, though on a more serious level, out of frustration and a sense of futility.

The first and most obvious impediment to serious dialogue arises, not surprisingly, when one of the potential pair has no character, that is, no relatively coherent and consistent set of traits, beliefs, ideas that govern a point of view and hence a choice of words. Listening to the conversation of such a person is like rifling through old newspapers, magazines, and torn letters for verbal odds and ends. Dorothea's uncle, Mr. Brooke, is a man of incomplete ideas and unfinished sentences, incapable of participating in an exchange because he is never "there" long enough to be held to a particular position. When he decides to run for Parliament, his enemies call him "retrogressive," his friends call him foolhardy, and those in between call him neither, because they think, rightly, that ideologically he is nothing.

> "Brooke doesn't mean badly by his tenants or anyone else, but he has got that way of paring and clipping at expenses."
>
> "Come, that's a blessing," said Mrs. Cadwallader. "That helps him to find himself in a morning. He may not know his own opinions, but he does know his own pocket." (Chap. 38)

The conversation broadens out into definition. What is the right name for Mr. Brooke? He enters the scene, and Mr. Cadwallader reads from a newspaper:

> "Look here! All this is about a landlord not a hundred miles from Middlemarch who receives his own rents. They say he is the most retrogressive man in the country. I think you must have taught them that word in the *Pioneer*."
>
> "Oh, that is Keck — an illiterate fellow, you know. Retrogres-

sive, now! Come, that's capital. He thinks it means destructive: they want to make me out a destructive, you know," said Mr. Brooke with that cheerfulness which is usually sustained by an adversary's ignorance.

"I think he knows the meaning of the word. Here is a sharp stroke or two. 'If we had to describe a man who is retrogressive in the most evil sense of the word, we should say he is the one who would dub himself a reformer of our constitution, while every interest for which he is immediately responsible is going to decay; a philanthropist who cannot bear one rogue to be hanged, but does not mind five honest tenants being half starved; a man who shrieks at corruption, and keeps his farms at rack-rent; who roars himself red at rotten boroughs, and does not mind if every field on his farms has a rotten gate; . . . But we all know the wag's definition of a philanthropist: a man whose charity increases directly as the square of the distance . . .' " (Chap. 38)

But Mr. Brooke's friends cannot debate with him, because his thoughts are scattered; he repeatedly reaches for an allusion and then trails off into incoherence or silence: "Satire, you know, should be true up to a certain point. I recollect they said that in *The Edinburgh* somewhere — " or: "You should read history — look at ostracism, persecution, martyrdom, and that kind of thing. They always happen to the best men, you know. But what is that in Horace? *Fiat justitia, ruat* . . . something or other" (chap. 38).

The most effective tactic Mr. Brooke's opponents can adopt is not to define him or his positions, since he has none, but to expose his absence of ideas. At a public rally he appears on a balcony to deliver an address, becomes nervous, and "having lost other clues, [falls] back on himself and his qualifications." This leads to aimless meanderings until among the crowd an effigy of him is raised up, "a neutral physiognomy painted on rag." Nothing could be a more accurate or cruel satire of the hollow man as a political candidate. Mr. Brooke sputters on, the effigy echoes and mimics his meaningless words, eggs are thrown until finally the charade of verbal communication is given up. "No voice would have had wing enough to rise above the uproar, and Mr. Brooke, disagreeably anointed, stood his ground no longer."

Mr. Brooke's is an extreme case and, despite moments of pathos, it is treated comically. Eliot has some sympathy for him in his humiliation, but her sympathies are limited and the picture she provides of him is primarily one seen from the outside. But this episode, like that of Mrs. Garth and her grammar book, is not a gratuitous bit of local color. Nothing in *Middlemarch* is, thematically, accidental. Mr. Brooke's fragmented, clichéd, incoherent language is a mark of the man. It illustrates the self-debilitating consequences of unexamined privilege. His position has not only hitherto protected him from tenants, reformers, journalists, and men of ideas, it has, through custom and tradition, provided him with the semblance of an identity and saved him the effort of having to locate a genuine one. In the light of Mr. Brooke and his rally, the phrase a "general wreck of society," though drastic, is not so absurd as it first appears. He cannot put the "right" words in the "right" places, and "Lindley Murray" cannot help him. His relationship to his tenants, his neighbors, and his family is a muddle which plays havoc with his pronouns and predicates. The vigor and meaning of the social structures which produced him have eroded and left him groping for words.

Property and privilege are obviously no guarantees of Mrs. Garth's vision of social order and good talk. Quite to the contrary. Eliot, like Arnold, satirizes an uneducated gentry, but implies more radically that their position more than their lack of schooling is what keeps them ignorant. Far and away more educated than most men and women of her time, Eliot had no illusions about the intrinsic moral or social value of learning. Unassimilated information can be worse than useless because it can create an illusion of substance and meaning where there is none. "Knowledge remains acquisition instead of passing into culture." [3] Like property and rank, scholarship can insulate from the world, though, unlike them, its susceptibility to systematic abstraction can yield a character which, however narrow, is consistent and identifiable. Mr. Casaubon does complete his sentences. He simply does not utter many of them.

---

3. George Eliot, "Silly Novels by Lady Novelists," *The Essays of George Eliot* (New York, 1883), p. 195.

"He talks very little," said Celia.
"There is no one for him to talk to."

Dorothea's rejoinder is prophetic and more literally true than she imagines. Mr. Casaubon is neither confused nor lacking in character. He is not a cipher or a bundle of old rags like poor Mr. Brooke, whose problems can be defined in grammatical terms by his difficulty in locating the pronoun *I*. Mr. Casaubon's trouble is with the second person, singular and plural. He is a solipsist, the only inhabitant of his own universe. Pride, a sense of intellectual superiority, and finally the sheer bulk of data which he is incapable of analyzing form a wall between him and the rest of the world.

A beautifully comic exchange between Brooke and Casaubon illustrates the differences in their characters:

"How do you arrange your documents?"
"In pigeonholes partly," said Mr. Casaubon with rather a startled air of effort.
"Ah, pigeonholes will not do. I have tried pigeonholes, but everything gets mixed in pigeonholes: I never know whether a paper is in A or Z." (Chap. 2)

Mr. Brooke has no system; Mr. Casaubon has one, but it is rigid and self-contained. It does not derive its logic or direction from "outsiders." Indeed, intrusion from without can only destroy such a "system" of thinking and being. The marriage to Dorothea, which is usually viewed in terms of its wounding effects on her, exposes Casaubon's closed system to light, curiosity, and life, thereby turning it to ashes and killing the scholar. Marriage, the most obvious of Victorian emblems of concord and exchange, is the "wreck" of Casaubon's society of one. His death, which is sometimes criticized as an artificially imposed plot device to free Dorothea for Ladislaw, is, in fact, totally in keeping with Eliot's psychological and moral scheme.

Dorothea invades "the anterooms and winding passages" of her husband's mind. While on their wedding trip in Rome, it is she who wishes to repair the "brokenness of their intercourse" and he who tries to keep her at a distance. The immediate references are, of course, intellectual and spiritual, but the physical resonance is perfectly consistent. What she wants is intimacy, and when he answers her questions about Rome "in a measured, official tone, as of a clergyman reading according to the rubric," she presumes to do what no invisible member of a congregation would dare. " 'But do *you* care' was always Dorothea's question." It would be an exaggeration to say that Dorothea's innocent aggressiveness kills Casaubon. More precisely, her vitality and youthful intelligence reveal to him his moral and psychological moribundity and hasten the process by which his body joins his mind.

Readers of *Middlemarch* have always agreed that one of the greatest and most profoundly insightful sections of the novel is that part in which Casaubon learns of his mortal illness and he and Dorothea wait in solitude for his death. The silence of Lowick Manor is unbearable to Dorothea; to break it is impossible for Casaubon. The point is that *his* silence — his inner silence — has once and for all been catastrophically broken by his marriage. The one dialogue between husband and wife which is not jarring or stilted is among the last they have before his death, as Dorothea waits for him at the top of the stairs on his way to bed. It is a touching and truthful summing up of their relationship:

> "Dorothea!" he said with a gentle surprise in his tone. "Were you waiting for me?"
>
> "Yes, I did not like to disturb you."
>
> "Come, my dear, come. You are young and need not to extend your life by watching." (Chap. 42)

Eliot's view of society is that of an organism in a continuous state of flux. Theoretically, she agreed with Comte and Spencer that the process was inevitable and, if accepted and understood, could be turned to the benefit of mankind. She possessed a broad but not simple faith in progress. In this, as in religion, her acute observation of individual cases made her skeptical of abstract doctrine. Whatever one's belief about meliorism and reform, to be a witness to social change as it affects individual lives is like observing biological evolution in an acre of meadowland. Seen at a distance, the change is gradual, minute, and even appealing in its variety. Looked at more closely, devastation and wreckage are the conditions of new life and new forms. Had she been more of a satirist and less of a humanist, Eliot's portrait of Casaubon would have stopped at caricature and left him a corpse incapable of feeling or acting. But her sympathetic imagination persuades us to feel the "disturbance" Dorothea has been to him and to comprehend, if not approve, the jealousy which prompts him to alter his will to her disadvantage should she remarry after his death. It is part of Eliot's perspicuity as an observer of human nature in detail to recognize that there is feeling and power (often destructive) in the death agony, that even gradual, evolutionary change is more than a matter of periodically sweeping dry bones into a closet.

Dorothea, the bride of an elderly scholar, the jeering crowd at Mr. Brooke's political rally, young Ben at his grammar lesson are all disturbers of the peace. Intentionally or not, they challenge the habits and torment the complacent monologues of the old order. The most important and complex of the intruders in Middlemarch is, of course, Tertius Lydgate. Though he is able to carry on conversations of perfect clarity on professional matters and appears to make himself understood by Dorothea, his dialogues with Rosamond are filled with humorous and, finally, painful misunderstandings. The encounter between Lydgate and Rosamond is not an obvious clash of youth and age, radical and reactionary; true, her family has the money and his the older lineage, she has the manners of country gentry and he has medical learning, but neither of them is deeply educated or refined in the way Eliot values. Neither her etiquette nor his knowledge is fully integrated into their moral and spiritual being; their "accomplishments" are not refined by self-knowledge. Thus, they both tend to flaunt them and use them as means by which to condescend to others. "A really cultured woman, like a really cultured man, is all the simpler and less obtrusive for her knowledge . . . She does not give you information, which is the raw material of culture — she gives you sympathy, which is its subtlest essence." [4]

4. Ibid., pp. 195–196.

Rosamond is highly conscious of language, but words are more a symbol of status and fashion to her than a means of communication.

"I shall not marry any Middlemarch young man."

"So it seems, my love, for you have as good as refused the pick of them; and if there's better to be had, I'm sure there's no girl better deserves it."

"Excuse me, Mamma — I wish you would not say, 'the pick of them.' "

"Why, what else are they?"

"I mean, Mamma, it is rather a vulgar expression."

"Very likely, my dear; I never was a good speaker. What should I say?"

"The best of them."

"Why, that seems just as plain and common. If I had had time to think, I should have said, 'the most superior young men.' But with your education you must know."

"What must Rosy know, Mother?" said Mr. Fred, who had slid in unobserved through the half-open door while the ladies were bending over their work, and now going up to the fire stood with his back towards it, warming the soles of his slippers.

"Whether it's right to say 'superior young men,' " said Mrs. Vincy, ringing the bell.

"Oh, there are so many superior teas and sugars now. Superior is getting to be shopkeepers' slang."

"Are you beginning to dislike slang, then?" said Rosamond with mild gravity.

"Only the wrong sort. All choice of words is slang. It marks a class."

"There is correct English; that is not slang."

"I beg your pardon, correct English is the slang of prigs who write history and essays. And the strongest slang of all is the slang of poets." (Chap. 11)

George Eliot agrees that "all choice of words is slang" and that it "marks a class." It is simply another way of saying what she has emphasized throughout the book, that language is a social convention, that it varies from group to group, and that it reflects the changes, innovations, and strains within the multiple intersecting circles of society. What is false and silly about Rosamond is not her use of conventional polite language, but her anxiety as a manufacturer's daughter to conceal her origins and very often her meaning with language which she imagines to be upper class.

When Fred first mentions Lydgate to his sister, she shows an interest, but as usual there is a fuss about how to name people and things — not so as to know and understand them — but in order to determine whether they are "above" or "below," to be envied or despised.

"There was a Lydgate at John's who spent no end of money. I find this man is a second cousin of his. But rich men may have very poor devils for second cousins."

"It always makes a difference, though, to be of good family," said Rosamond with a tone of decision which showed that she had thought on this subject. Rosamond felt that she might have been happier if she had not been the daughter of a Middlemarch manufacturer. She disliked anything which reminded her that her mother's father had been an innkeeper. Certainly anyone remembering the fact might think that Mrs. Vincy had the air of a very handsome, good-humoured landlady, accustomed to the most capricious orders of gentlemen.

"I thought it was odd his name was Tertius," said the bright-faced matron, "but of course it's a name in the family. But now, tell us exactly what sort of man he is."

"Oh, tallish, dark, clever — talks well — rather a prig, I think."

"I never can make out what you mean by a prig," said Rosamond.

"A fellow who wants to show that he has opinions."

"Why, my dear, doctors must have opinions," said Mrs. Vincy. "What are they there for else?"

"Yes, Mother, the opinions they are paid for. But a prig is a fellow who is always making you a present of his opinions."

"I suppose Mary Garth admires Mr. Lydgate," said Rosamond, not without a touch of innuendo.

"Really, I can't say," said Fred rather glumly as he left the table, and taking up a novel which he had brought down with him, threw himself into an arm-chair. "If you are jealous of her, go oftener to Stone Court yourself and eclipse her."

"I wish you would not be so vulgar, Fred. If you have finished, pray ring the bell." (Chap. 11)

The exchange sparkles with irony. Rosamond casually equates "rich" with "good"; Fred describes himself even more accurately than Lydgate in his definition of "prig"; he reveals his own jealousy in accusing Rosamond of it; and finally Rosamond identifies plain speaking with vulgarity. In short, the feelings being revealed in this exchange are commonplace and coarse while the right choice of words is endlessly disputed. Language becomes a mask, inadvertently and ironically revelatory. Since it is not a genuine mingling of mind and heart with social convention, it is an inadequate instrument through which two creatures can come together. Fred and Rosamond understand one another because they are alike, but the meeting of Rosamond and Lydgate is the beginning of another social calamity.

The humor and satirical bite of conversations within the Vincy family have an eighteenth-century flavor partly because there is so much conscious artifice and posing which a good dose of common sense could eliminate if properly applied. Instead of the eighteenth-century device of the sensible servant, Eliot makes a direct appeal to the "common reader" who will conclude in his own way that these characters should knock it off and talk straight. The point is that it looks as if they could if only they wanted to. But the difficulties in communication are far graver for Rosamond and Lydgate. The roots of the problem are deeper; the resonances may be comic at first, but they soon become grim and painful; and rational solutions — obvious or obscure — are not to be found.

The first conversation between Rosamond and Lydgate looks like a conventional flirtation. The ostensible subject is trivial, the tone flattering and coy on both sides.

> "Tell me what you saw in London."
>
> "Very little." (A more naive girl would have said, "Oh, everything!" But Rosamond knew better.) "A few of the ordinary sights, such as raw country girls are always taken to."
>
> "Do you call yourself a raw country girl?" said Lydgate, looking at her with an involuntary emphasis of admiration, which made Rosamond blush with pleasure. But she remained simply serious, turned her long neck a little, and put up her hand to

touch her wondrous hair-plaits — an habitual gesture with her as
pretty as any movements of a kitten's paw. Not that Rosamond
was in the least like a kitten: she was a sylph caught young and
educated at Mrs. Lemon's.

"I assure you my mind is raw," she said immediately; "I pass
at Middlemarch. I am not afraid of talking to our old neighbors.
But I am really afraid of you."

"An accomplished woman almost always knows more than we
men, though her knowledge is of a different sort. I am sure you
could teach me a thousand things — as an exquisite bird could
teach a bear if there were any common language between them.
Happily, there is a common language between women and men,
and so the bears can get taught." (Chap. 26)

Through the polite teasing, both speakers utter truths about
themselves. Rosamond is, as becomes more and more apparent
after their marriage, "afraid of talking" to Lydgate. She is not
well educated, but her false modesty with regard to her intellectual resources conceals a moral rawness of a more serious kind.
Through social position and wealth, she wants attention and
power over others. As Eliot says, she is a sylph — a creature
without a soul — and it is that undeveloped spiritual and moral
center which she contrives to hide with modest protestations
which she knows will flatter Lydgate and draw his attention to
her "accomplishments" and social station.

Lydgate is not a flawless victim in this exchange. He too uses
"innocent" comparisons which reveal to the reader, if not to
Rosamond, a fatal insensitivity on his part. Her condescension
toward him is based on her wealth and status in Middlemarch
society; his condescension to her is based on his sex. His
"pretty" analogy of the bird and bear can only have been the
kind of masculine flattery that would send shivers down Eliot's
spine. It concedes delicacy and vulnerable beauty to women and
retains power for men. The bird can teach the bear "a thousand
things," but there is no mention of the bear teaching the bird.
The polite meaning is, of course, that the bear is crude and has
nothing to teach. The real meaning, given Lydgate's intelligence
and learning, is that the bear's power of mind, like his power
of body, is simply not communicable to the bird. Despite his

"happy" conclusion, it is doubtful that Lydgate does believe in a common language between the sexes. With respect to Rosamond and himself, the doubts are well founded.

The scene in which Lydgate and Rosamond become engaged is without directly quoted dialogue. Eliot refers to it as "a moment of naturalness," that is, a moment in which physical attraction and emotional intensity make polite conversation impossible. On seeing Rosamond's distress, Lydgate asks, "What is the matter?" Her response is wordless, and the "power" of the moment obscures to him the true character of the relationship. Lydgate acts out the role of conqueror and protector in such abstract confidence of his masculine strength as to be totally unaware of the force of Rosamond's will and of her psychological hold over him.

> Rosamond had never been spoken to in such tones before. I am not sure that she knew what the words were; but she looked at Lydgate and the tears fell over her cheeks. There could have been no more complete answer than that silence, and Lydgate, forgetting everything else, completely mastered by the outrush of tenderness at the sudden belief that this sweet young creature depended on him for her joy, actually put his arms round her, folding her gently and protectingly — he was used to being gentle with the weak and suffering — and kissed each of the two large tears. This was a strange way of arriving at an understanding, but it was a short way . . . In half an hour he left the house an engaged man, whose soul was not his own, but the woman's to whom he had bound himself. (Chap. 31)

It is no accident that the chapter concludes with a discussion of death as well as marriage and another of the many references to right words in right places. When Lydgate calls on Rosamond's father to ask for her hand, he finds Mr. Vincy anticipating the death of old Mr. Featherstone:

> The felicitous word "demise," which had seasonably occurred to him, had raised his spirits even above their usual evening pitch. The right word is always a power and communicates its definiteness to our action. Considered as a demise, old Featherstone's death assumed a merely legal aspect so that Mr. Vincy could tap

his snuff-box over it and be jovial, without even an intermittent affectation of solemnity; and Mr. Vincy hated both solemnity and affectation. Who was ever awe-struck about a testator or sang a hymn on the title to real property? Mr. Vincy was inclined to take a jovial view of all things that evening . . . and when his approbation of Rosamond's engagement was asked for, he gave it with astonishing facility, passing at once to general remarks on the desirableness of matrimony for young men and maidens and apparently deducing from the whole the appropriateness of a little more punch. (Chap. 31)

"Demise" and "matrimony for young men and maidens" are not merely polite locutions, they are terms so general and neutral as to be detached from all emotional specificity. That is precisely what Mr. Vincy wants — no disruption of the orderly routine, no embarrassing expressions of strong feeling. Mr. Vincy is not using language to conquer intense emotion in himself. We have good reason to believe that the bland and detached words he uses are accurate reflections of his state of mind. But he also uses certain kinds of language to ward off unwanted efforts at serious articulation of feelings by others. If one part of sincerity is the approximate matching of words and thoughts, Mr. Vincy is sincere enough. He is not particularly concerned about the death of Featherstone or the love life of his daughter, and that, without being positively insulting, is what his words convey. The trouble is that that kind of sincerity discourages, almost to the point of making impossible, the kind of sincerity Lydgate might have attempted with a different prospective father-in-law and, more important, with a different fiancée. To wish that Mr. Vincy would use "better" words is to wish him a better man. Like Brooke and Casaubon, Rosamond and Lydgate, Mr. Vincy is less given to affectation and verbal deception than we may at first think. He is pretty much what his words show him to be. His language is a fair label of his spirit, but it is not an agent of exchange, of growth, of expansive communication. To speak, for him as for many of the characters in *Middlemarch,* is to participate in the prevention of dialogue.

Mr. Vincy's tendency to generalize is, in a minor key, analogous to Lydgate's difficulties in perception and expression. Though an able scientist with a capacity to study details and

generalize fruitfully from them, Lydgate's mental processes, in
regard to human beings — especially women — are often shown
to work in reverse. He has general preconceptions into which he
assumes individual cases will fit. After his marriage to Rosamond,
he finds himself deeply in debt because of her extravagance and
is unable to talk with her about it. Thinking of an earlier love
affair, he wonders if she would kill him if she wearied of him.
"And then, 'It is the way with all women.' But this power of
generalizing which gives men so much the superiority in mistake
over the dumb animals was immediately thwarted by Lydgate's
memory of wondering impressions from the behaviour of another
woman . . ." (chap. 58).

Thoughts of Dorothea trouble Lydgate's masculine generalization, but they come too late to alter it or help his marriage. From
the beginning, he and Rosamond have regarded each other as
types, capable of being dominated but not understood. But what
is treated as a source of attraction in their courtship becomes a
disaster in marriage. When Lydgate finally attempts to speak with
her about their financial trouble, Rosamond leaves the room. "It
seemed [to Lydgate] that she had no more identified herself with
him than if they had been creatures of a different species and
opposing interests." That is, of course, true of Rosamond. Lydgate still does not realize that it has been equally true of him.

Their "reconciliation" is even more depressing than their
quarrel. Neither makes any further effort at speech. Words have
not served them well, and they fall back into their roles as "bird"
and "bear," each as isolated and deluded as they had been from
the start.

> He only caressed her; he did not say anything, for what was there
> to say? He could not promise to shield her from the dreaded
> wretchedness, for he could see no sure means of doing so. When
> he left her to go out again, he told himself that it was ten times
> harder for her than for him: he had a life away from home and
> constant appeals to his activity on behalf of others. He wished to
> excuse everything in her if he could — but it was inevitable that in
> that excusing mood he should think of her as if she were an
> animal of another feebler species. Nevertheless she had mastered
> him. (Chap. 65)

Imperfect communication is a literary subject which antedates *Middlemarch* and the novel as a genre. What is striking in *Middlemarch* is the frequency, extent, and finality of the failures of dialogue. Male, female, old, young, rich, poor, learned, ignorant, idealists, materialists — all seem to have the problem. And what is particularly interesting is that Eliot, though seeing the profound moral consequences of it, exposes the origins of the difficulty more often in psychological and sociological terms than in moral ones. Her characters may have choices to make and wills to govern, but their choices and wills are hemmed in by inherited attributes and circumstances for which they are not responsible and which they have little or no power to change.

On one hand, the range and flexibility of language are limited by the psychological and experiential differences among individuals. Most writers recognize this, but few have accentuated the oppressive and destructive effect of it more seriously than Eliot. Part of her pessimism may be derived from her friend Herbert Spencer, who faced this issue, like so many others, with melancholy resignation: "The necessity is that in dealing with other beings and interpreting their actions, we must represent their thoughts and feelings in terms of our own. The difficulty is that in so representing them we can never be more than partially right, and are frequently very wrong." [5]

On the other hand, Spencer, Conte, Feuerbach, and Lewes — all important and congenial to Eliot's thought — stressed the collective nature of language. Everything that we know and say is shaped not only by individual traits and tendencies, but by conceptions and patterns of thought accumulated through generations of group experience. In emphasizing the value of language and thought in their communal aspect, Lewes acknowledges the limitations of individual choice and initiative. "Individual experiences being limited and individual spontaneity feeble, we are strengthened and enriched by assimilating the experience of others. A nation, a tribe, a sect is the medium of the individual mind . . . We may say with Comte that the past more and more dominates the present, precisely as in the individual case it is the

5. *The Study of Sociology* (Ann Arbor: University of Michigan Press, 1961), pp. 103–104.

registered experiences which more and more determine the feelings and opinions. Human knowledge is pre-eminently distinguished from animal knowledge by this collective experience . . .
The consolations of convergent thought in social forms, scientific theories, works of art, and above all, language, are in-
cessantly acting on me." [6]

Though denying total passivity, Lewes depicts individual man
as "acted upon" by his family, nationality, and religious tradition.
In examining Middlemarch as a community, Eliot adds class,
education, and sex to the list. Caught between idiosyncrasy and
inherited modes of group thought and expression, each character
speaks a language which, even when grammatically correct, is a
disturbingly imperfect or useless instrument of communication.

The dissatisfaction many readers have felt with the ending of
the novel stems from many things — an unconvincing portrait
of Ladislaw, a too sudden change in Dorothea, and so on — but
one of the major problems is the enormous burden placed on
these two characters to love intelligently, that is, to feel intensely
and think well, and to share their emotions and thoughts amid
the wreckage of the failed efforts of most of the other characters
in the novel. Eliot has provided overwhelming evidence against
the chances of success.

The dialogue between Will and Dorothea in their crucial love
scene near the end of the book has none of the imagery, wit, or
irony of most of the other talk in the novel. It is simple to the
point of being childlike. And that, in fact, is what George Eliot
calls it. Will says that they can speak "to each other without
disguise," and then they stand "with their hands clasped, like
two children" watching a noisy storm through the window. The
chapter concludes with Dorothea's renunciation of her wealth
uttered in "a sobbing, childlike way." As in Eliot's picture of
Mrs. Garth and her grammar book, they stand apart from the
flood and appear to be exempt from the general wreck of society.

It is perhaps Eliot's Feuerbachian version of Christ's injunc-
tion to "make yourselves like little children" in order to enter
the kingdom of heaven. But deprived of its spiritual and mystical

6. George Henry Lewes, *The Study of Psychology* (London, 1879),
pp. 165–166.

overtones, the advice is mere romantic sentimentality. Feuerbach also said that "to speak is an act of freedom." Dorothea and Ladislaw are able to speak to one another, albeit in simpler terms than will sustain them for very long. Given what we have seen and heard throughout the novel, Eliot is asking us to make an exceptionally generous act of faith in their future and that of the society in which they will live. Like Thackeray's puppets, Dorothea and Will, seen as children watching a storm, appear to be a familiar Victorian evasion of a familiar but darkening Victorian vision of a reality which is becoming more and more difficult to name and, in naming, to control.

J. HILLIS MILLER

Optic and Semiotic in *Middlemarch*

> . . . this power of generalising which gives men so much the superiority in mistake over the dumb animals.
>
> George Eliot, *Middlemarch*

George Eliot's apparent aim in *Middlemarch* (1871–72) is to present a total picture of provincial society in England at the period just before the first Reform Bill of 1832. She also wants to interpret this picture totally. She wants both to show what is there and to show how it works. This enterprise of totalization, as one might call it, is shared with an important group of other masterworks of Victorian fiction, including Thackeray's *Vanity Fair* (1847–48), Dickens' *Bleak House* (1852–53), *Little Dorrit* (1855–57), and *Our Mutual Friend* (1864–65), and Trollope's *The Way We Live Now* (1874–75). All these novels have many characters and employ multiple analogous plots. They cast a wide net and aim at inclusiveness, in part by a method of accumulation. Nevertheless, since the actual societies in question were unmanageably complex and multitudinous, some strategy of compression, of economy, had to be devised in each case. As George Meredith puts it in the "Prelude" to *The Egoist,* "the inward mirror, the embracing and condensing spirit, is required to give us those interminable mile-post piles of matter . . . in essence, in chosen samples, digestibly." [1] The means of condensation used vary considerably, however, from novelist to novelist.

Dickens, for example, achieves inclusiveness by making the part explicitly stand for the whole. He emphasizes the synecdochic, representative, emblematic quality of his characters. Mr. Krook, the rag and bottle shopkeeper in *Bleak House,* stands for the lord chancellor, his shop for the Court of Chancery. Chancery, in turn, is a synecdoche for the state of "wiglomeration" of English society as a whole. In the same novel, Sir Leicester Dedlock is presented as an example of the whole class of aristocrats; Gridley, the Man from Shropshire, is an emblem for all the suitors who are destroyed by the delays of Chancery, and so on. Moreover, the range of examples includes by this method of synecdoche all of England. Characters from the country and from the city, from the lowest level of society to the highest, are presented.

George Eliot is more straightforwardly "realistic" in her procedure. *Middlemarch* presents a large group of the sort of people one would in fact have been likely to find in a provincial town in the Midlands. Their representative or symbolic quality is not insisted upon. This would be the wrong track to follow, I believe, in a search for her methods of totalization. Moreover, Eliot does not present examples from the whole range of English society. The relation of Middlemarch to English society is rather that of part to whole, or that of a sample to the whole cloth, according to a metaphor I shall be examining later. The relationship is once more synecdochic, but the kind of synecdoche in question is different from the one used by Dickens. In *Bleak House* the member of a class is presented as a "symbol" of the whole class. In *Middlemarch* a fragment is examined as a "sample" of the larger whole of which it is a part, though the whole impinges on the part as the "medium" within which it lives, as national politics affect Middlemarch when there is a general election, or as the coming of the railroad upsets rural traditions. Eliot's strategy of totalization is to present individual character or event in the context of that wider medium and to affirm universal laws of human

1. *The Works of George Meredith,* Memorial Edition (London: Constable, 1910), 13:2.

behavior in terms of characters whose specificity and even uniqueness is indicated by the completeness of the psychological portraits of each — Dorothea, Lydgate, Casaubon, Bulstrode, Fred Vincy, Mary Garth, and the rest. This fullness of characterization and the accompanying circumstantiality of social detail in *Middlemarch* have been deservedly admired. They make this novel perhaps the masterwork of Victorian realism.

The subtitle of *Middlemarch* is *A Study of Provincial Life*. This may put the novel under the aegis of a kind of painting, a "study from life." The more powerful association of the word, however, is with a scientific "study." In *Middlemarch* Eliot is attempting to fulfill for the life of a provincial town that enterprise she had mapped out in her important early essay on the German sociologist of peasant life, Wilhelm Heinrich von Riehl. In that essay, "The Natural History of German Life" (*Westminster Review*, 1856), she had implicitly proposed the writing of works of fiction which would do for English life what Riehl had done for the German peasant: "Art is the nearest thing to life: it is a mode of amplifying experience and extending our contact with our fellow-men beyond the bounds of our personal lot. All the more sacred is the task of the artist when he undertakes to paint the life of the People. Falsification here is far more pernicious than in the more artificial aspects of life." [2] Much of *Middlemarch* is modeled on the sociologist's respect for individual fact George Eliot so praises in this essay. The experience of each character in *Middlemarch* is described in such detail that the reader is encouraged not to forget its differences from the experiences of the other characters.

Nevertheless, the narrator of *Middlemarch* assumes throughout that the behavior of these unique people manifests certain general and universal laws. These laws may be formulated and are in fact constantly formulated, as when the narrator says: "We are all of us born in moral stupidity, taking the world as an udder to feed our supreme selves." [3] The special mode of

2. *Essays of George Eliot,* ed. Thomas Pinney (New York: Columbia University Press, 1963), p. 271.

3. *Middlemarch,* Cabinet Edition (Edinburgh and London: William Blackwood and Sons, n.d.), chap. 21. Further references to this work will be given in the text.

totalization in *Middlemarch* is this combination of specificity, on
the one hand, and, on the other hand, generalizing interpretation
on the basis of specificity. Such generalizing is proposed as valid
not just for all people in the particular middle-class society of
Middlemarch, and not just for the English society at a specific
moment of its history of which Middlemarch is a part, but for
all people in all cultures in all times.

I intend here to explore one mode of this generalizing interpretation, the presentation by the narrator of certain all-
encompassing metaphors which are proposed as models for
Middlemarch society. Such metaphors are put forward as a
means of thinking of all the people in Middlemarch in their
interrelations through time. Each metaphor is an interpretative
net which the reader is invited to cast over the whole society,
to use as a paradigm by means of which to think of the whole. I
shall argue that there are three such totalizing metaphors, or
rather families of metaphors. Each group of metaphors is related
to the others, fulfilling them, but at the same time contradicting
them, canceling them out, or undermining their validity.

The recurrence of such metaphors throughout *Middlemarch*
and their assumed validity affirms one of the most important
presuppositions of the novel. The unique life of each of the characters is presented as part of a single system of complex interaction in time and space. No man, for Eliot, lives alone. Each
exists in "the same embroiled medium, the same troublous fit-
fully-illuminated life" (chap. 30). The nature of this "medium"
and of the interaction of character with character within it is
analyzed throughout by the narrator. The voice of the narrator,
sympathetic certainly, but also clairvoyant in his insight into
human folly, is in *Middlemarch,* as in Victorian novels generally,
the most immediate presence for the reader and the chief generating force behind the stylistic texture of the novel.

text . . . from Medieval Latin *textus,* (Scriptural) text, from
Latin, literary composition, "woven thing," from the past par-
ticiple of *texere,* to weave.[4]

4. *American Heritage Dictionary of the English Language,* s.v. "text."

Perhaps the most salient totalizing metaphor presented as a model for the community of Middlemarch is in fact a family of related metaphors. Each member of this family compares Middlemarch society or some part of it to a spatially or temporally deployed material complex — a labyrinth, or flowing water, or woven cloth. There are two important implications of these metaphors as they are used in the novel. The first is the assumption that a society is in some way like a material field and therefore is open to the same kind of objective scientific investigation as may be applied to such a field, for example, to flowing water. The other is the assumption, reinforced by many passages in the novel, that the structure or texture of small-scale pieces of the whole is the same as the structure or texture of the whole and so may be validly described with the same figures. This is the assumption of the validity of one kind of synecdoche. The part is "really like" the whole, and an investigation of a sample will lead to valid conclusions about the whole. If Middlemarch society as a whole is like flowing water or like woven cloth, the mental life of each of its inhabitants may also be validly described in the same metaphors. In a similar way, when the reader or the narrator focuses on the relation between two of the characters out of the whole lot, the metaphors will be found to be valid on that scale too. In the other direction, as I have suggested, it is implied that what is true in Middlemarch is also true for English society as a whole, or even for any human life anywhere and at any time. *Middlemarch* is full of such shifts in perspective from close up to far away and back to close up again, according to that law of scientific method which Lydgate admirably formulates: "there must be a systole and diastole in all inquiry," and "a man's mind must be continually expanding and shrinking between the whole human horizon and the horizon of an object-glass" (chap. 63). Eliot's assumption is that in the social world, at least, such changes in scale reveal a strict homogeneity between the large-scale and small-scale grain or texture of things. As Will Ladislaw phrases it, "the little waves make the large ones and are of the same pattern" (chap. 46).

The most persistent of these structural metaphors, as has often been noticed, is the metaphor of the web. One explicit application

of the image of a web to the whole range of social relationships
in the novel comes in the passage where the narrator distinguishes
his[5] enterprise from that of Fielding. Whereas Fielding lived in
more spacious times and could allow himself the luxury of the
famous "copious remarks and digressions," "I at least," says
the narrator, "have so much to do in unravelling certain human
lots, and seeing how they were woven and interwoven, that all
the light I can command must be concentrated on this particular
web, and not dispersed over that tempting range of relevancies
called the universe" (chap. 15). The narrator's effort is not
merely that of observation. He must, like a good scientist, take
apart the specimen being analyzed, unravel all its fibers to see
how it is put together, how it has been woven and interwoven.
That the texture of Middlemarch society as a whole may be accurately represented in a metaphor of woven cloth is taken for
granted throughout the novel. It appears in many apparently
casual texts as a reinforcement of more elaborate passages in-
viting the reader to keep the paradigm of the web before his
mind. Lydgate, to give one example from early in the novel, finds
himself for the first time "feeling the hampering threadlike pressure of small social conditions, and their frustrating complexity"
(chap. 18).

The metaphor of a web, however, is also used repeatedly in
Middlemarch to describe the texture of smaller-scale entities
within the larger social fabric. The lovemaking of Rosamond and
Lydgate, for example, is described as the collective weaving of
an intersubjective tissue:

> Young love-making — that gossamer web! Even the points it
> clings to — the things whence its subtle interlacings are swung —
> are scarcely perceptible; momentary touches of finger-tips, meet-
> ings of rays from blue and dark orbs, unfinished phrases, lightest
> changes of cheek and lip, faintest tremors. The web itself is made
> of spontaneous beliefs and indefinable joys, yearnings of one life
> towards another, visions of completeness, indefinite trust. And
> Lydgate fell to spinning that web from his inward self with won-

5. Her? After all, the fiction of the male narrator is still maintained
in *Middlemarch*. To speak of the narrator as a "he" allows the reader
to keep firmly in mind the distinction between the author of the novel,
Marian Evans, and the created role of the storyteller, George Eliot.

derful rapidity . . . As for Rosamond, she was in the water-lily's expanding wonderment at its own fuller life, and she too was spinning industriously at the mutual web. (Chap. 36)

Another important use of the metaphor of a web is made in the description of Lydgate's scientific researchers. Lydgate's attempt to find the "primitive tissue" is based on the assumption that the metaphor of woven cloth applies in the organic as well as in the social realm. His use of the figure brings into the open the parallelism between Eliot's aim as a sociologist of provincial life and the aims of contemporary biologists.[6] Lydgate's research is based on the hypothesis that all the organs of the body are differentiations of "certain primary webs or tissues": "have not these structures some common basis from which they have all started, as your sarsnet, gauze, net, satin and velvet from the raw cocoon?" (chap. 15). If Lydgate assumes that biological entities may be described as tissues, the narrator of Middlemarch makes the same assumptions about the subjective lives of the characters. Of Lydgate, for example, the narrator says that "momentary speculations as to all the possible grounds for Mrs. Bulstrode's hints had managed to get woven like slight clinging hairs into the more substantial web of his thoughts" (chap. 31). Much later in the novel, basing the generalization again on Lydgate's psychology, the narrator asks: "Is it not rather what we expect in men, that they should have numerous strands of experience lying side by side and never compare them with each other?" (chap. 58). This image of mental or intersubjective life as a reticulated pattern like a grid is implicit when a few pages earlier the narrator says of Rosamond and Lydgate that "between him and her indeed there was that total missing of each other's mental track, which is too evidently possible even between persons who are continually thinking of each other." The image of mental or social life as traveling along tracks which may or may not intersect with others is also latent in an earlier remark about Ladislaw: "There are characters which are continually creating collisions

6. For the relation of Lydgate's researches to the science of Eliot's day, see W. J. Harvey, "The Intellectual Background of the Novel," *Middlemarch: Critical Approaches to the Novel,* ed. Barbara Hardy (London: University of London, Athlone Press, 1967), pp. 25–37.

and nodes for themselves in dramas which nobody is prepared to act with them" (chap. 19).

To the metaphor of the web, however, must be added the metaphor of the stream. Collective or individual life in Middlemarch is not a fixed pattern like a carpet. The web is aways in movement. The pervasive figure for this is that of flowing water. This figure is homogeneous with the figure of the web in that flowing water, for Eliot, is seen as made up of currents, filaments flowing side by side, intermingling and dividing. Flowing water is, so to speak, a temporalized web. Casaubon, for example, is said, in a fine series of phrases, to have possessed "that proud narrow sensitiveness which has not mass enough to spare for transformation into sympathy, and quivers thread-like in small currents of self-preoccupation or at best of an egoistic scrupulosity" (chap. 29). Lydgate, after he has met Rosamond, "had no sense that any new current had set into his life" (chap 16). Of his life as a whole when it is in the midst of being lived (in the middle of its march, as one might say), the narrator asserts that it has "the complicated probabilities of an arduous purpose, with all the possible thwartings and furtherings of circumstance, all the niceties of inward balance, by which a man swims and makes his point or else is carried headlong," for "character too is a process and an unfolding" (chap. 15). In another place, the narrator speaks of "the chief current" of Dorothea's anxiety (chap. 22), and, as opposed to the egotistic scrupulosity of Casaubon's small soul, "in Dorothea's mind there was a current into which all thought and feeling were apt sooner or later to flow — the reaching forward of the whole consciousness towards the fullest truth, the least partial good" (chap. 20). In the climactic scene of Dorothea's renunciation of her fortune to marry Will, "the flood of her young passion bear[s] down all the obstructions which had kept her silent" (chap. 83).

One final element must be added to complete the description of Eliot's admirable development of a quasi-scientific model to describe the subjective life of the individual, the relations of two persons within the social "medium," and the nature of that medium as a whole. This element has already been anticipated in what has been said about the correspondence, in Eliot's view of things, between small- and large-scale structures. This idea, however, is but one aspect of a larger assumption, that is, the notion that any process in any of the three "scales" is made up of endlessly subdividable "minutiae." Anything that we call a "unit" or a single fact, in social or in mental life, is not single but multiple. A finer lens would always make smaller parts visible. The smaller parts, in turn, are made up of even smaller entities.

One corollary of this vision of things is the rejection of that straightforward idea of single causes which had characterized, for example, *Adam Bede*. In *Middlemarch* Eliot still believes in causality, but in the psychological and social realms the causes are now seen as unimaginably multiple. No fact is in itself single, and no fact is explicable by a single relationship to a single cause. Each fact is a kind of multitudinous node which exists only arbitrarily as a single thing because we happen to have the microscope focused as we do. If the focus were finer, the apparently single fact would subdivide and reveal itself to be made of multiple minutiae. If the focus were coarser the fact would disappear within the larger entity of which it is a part. A single momentary state of mind, for example, exists in relation to all its latent motives, the minutiae of mental life which underlie it, in relation also to its own past and future, and in multiple relation to what is outside it, all the other people to whom the person is socially related. The metaphor of the variable lens of a microscope is in fact used by Eliot to make this point:

> Even with a microscope directed on a water-drop we find ourselves making interpretations which turn out to be rather coarse; for whereas under a weak lens you may seem to see a creature exhibiting an active voracity into which other smaller creatures actively play as if they were so many animated tax-pennies, a stronger lens reveals to you certain tiniest hairlets which make vortices for these victims while the swallower waits passively at his receipt of custom. (Chap. 6)

One might ask, parenthetically, how and why the metaphor of the microscope has been contaminated here by another apparently unrelated metaphor, that of money, taxes, and "custom." This interpretation of one metaphor by another metaphor is characteristic of Eliot's use of figure. An attempt to explain fully this linguistic habit must be postponed, but one can say that the displacement of one figure by another is asymmetrically parallel to the displacement of the weak lens by the strong lens of the microscope. In each case, one vision of things is replaced by another. The optical visions are apparently reconcilable, whereas the two metaphors interfere with one another even if they are not wholly contradictory. The text of *Middlemarch,* in any case, goes on to apply the metaphor of the double-lensed microscope to a particular case in the novel: "In this way, metaphorically speaking, a strong lens applied to Mrs. Cadwallader's match-making will show a play of minute causes producing what may be called thought and speech vortices to bring her the sort of food she needed."

The phrase "play of minute causes" is echoed throughout the novel by similar phrases keeping before the reader the idea that the mental and social events being described are extremely complex. This complexity is essential to their mode of existence. The narrator speaks, for example, of "a slow preparation of effects from one life on another" (chap. 11), or of an ardor which cooled "imperceptibly," like other youthful loves ("Nothing in the world more subtle than the process of their gradual change!" chap. 15), or of "the minutiae of mental make in which one of us differs from another" (chap. 15), or of Lydgate's "testing vision of details and relations" (chap. 16), or of "the suppressed transitions which unite all contrasts" (chap. 20), or of the "nice distinctions of rank in Middlemarch" (chap. 23), or of "the living myriad of hidden suckers whereby the belief and the conduct are wrought into mutual sustainment" (chap. 53), or of a "fact" which "was broken into little sequences" (chap. 61), or of the way Bulstrode's "misdeeds were like the subtle muscular movements which are not taken account of in the consciousness" (chap. 68).

All this family of intertwined metaphors and motifs[7] — the

7. What, exactly, is the nature of the resemblance which binds together the members of this family and makes it seem of one genetic stock? Why, if Eliot's goal is to describe what is "really there," objectively, must there be more than one model in order to create a total picture?

web, the current, the minutely subdivided entity — make up a single comprehensive model or picture of Middlemarch society as being a complex moving medium, tightly interwoven into a single fabric, always in process, endlessly subdividable. This medium can be seen and studied objectively, as if there could be an ideal observer who does not change what he observes and who sees the moving web as it were from all perspectives at once, from close up and far away, with both gross and fine lenses, in a continual systole and diastole of inquiry. The storyteller in *Middlemarch* is in short the ideal observer of Victorian fiction, the "omniscient" narrator. His aim is to do full representative justice to the complexity of the condition of man in his social medium. There are many admirable passages in *Middlemarch* giving examples of what the narrator sees, each a new application of the model I have been describing. None is perhaps so comprehensive an exploitation of the totalizing implications of this family of metaphors as an admirable passage in chapter 11 describing "old provincial society":

Old provincial society had its share of this subtle movement: had not only its striking downfalls, its brilliant young professional dandies who ended by living up an entry with a drab and six children for their establishment, but also those less marked vicissitudes which are constantly shifting the boundaries of social intercourse, and begetting new consciousness of interdependence. Some slipped a little downward, some got higher footing: people denied aspirates, gained wealth, and fastidious gentlemen stood for boroughs; some were caught in political currents, some in ecclesiastical, and perhaps found themselves surprisingly grouped in consequence; while a few personages or families that stood with rocky firmness amid all this fluctuation, were slowly presenting new aspects in spite of solidity, and altering with the double change of self and beholder.

Therefore speak I to them in parables: because they seeing see not; and hearing they hear not, neither do they understand. (Matthew 13:13)

. . . er hat das Auge nicht dafür, das Einmalige zu sehen; die

Ähnlichseherei und Gleichmacherei ist das Merkmal schwacher Augen.[8]

"Double change of self and beholder"! I have said that my first family of metaphors in *Middlemarch* does not raise problems of perspective, or that in any case it presupposes the possibility of an ideal observer such as that assumed in much nineteenth-century science, in the days before operationalism, relativity, and the principle of indeterminacy. This is true, but in fact an optical or epistemological metaphor has already introduced itself surreptitiously into many of my examples. The narrator must concentrate "all the light [he] can command" (chap. 15) on his particular web in order to see clearly how it is woven. Study of the web requires constant changes of the lens in the systole and diastole of inquiry. Any conceivable observer in Middlemarch will be changing himself along with all the other changes and so will change what he sees.

A pervasive figure for the human situation in *Middlemarch* is that of the seer who must try to identify clearly what is present before him. This metaphor contaminates the apparently clear-cut objectivist implications of the metaphor of the flowing web. As more and more examples of it accumulate, it struggles with a kind of imperialistic will to power over the whole to replace that objectivism with a fully developed subjectivism or perspectivism. The "omniscience" of the narrator, according to this alternative model for the human condition, can be obtained only because he is able to share the points of view of all the characters, thereby transcending the limited vision of any single person. "In watching effects," as the narrator says, "if only of an electric battery, it is often necessary to change our place and examine a particular mixture or group at some distance from the point where the movement we are interested in was set up" (chap. 40). The narrator can move in imagination from one vantage point to another, or from close up to far away. He can be, like the

8. Friedrich Nietzsche, *Die Fröhliche Wissenschaft,* para. 228, in *Werke,* ed. Karl Schlecta (Munich: Carl Hanser Verlag, 1966), 2:152–153; ". . . they lack eyes for seeing what is unique. Seeing things as similar and making things the same is the sign of weak eyes" (*The Gay Science,* trans. Walter Kaufmann [New York: Vintage Books, 1974], p. 212).

angel Uriel, "watching the progress of planetary history from the Sun" (chap. 41), and at the same time share in that microscopic vision of invisible process, perceptible only to inward imaginative vision, so splendidly described in a passage about Lydgate's method as a scientist. It is a passage which also describes covertly the claims of Eliot's own fictional imagination. Lydgate, the narrator says, is endowed

> with the imagination that reveals subtle actions inaccessible by any sort of lens, but tracked in that outer darkness through long pathways of necessary sequence by the inward light which is the last refinement of Energy, capable of bathing even the ethereal atoms in its ideally illuminated space . . . he was enamoured of that arduous invention which is the very eye of research, provisionally framing its object and correcting it to more and more exactness of relation; he wanted to pierce the obscurity of those minute processes which prepare human misery and joy . . . (Chap. 16)

The metaphor of the complex moving web, the "embroiled medium," is, one can see, further complicated, or even contradicted, by the metaphor of vision. Each of those nodes in the social web which is a separate human being is endowed with a power to see the whole. This power is defined throughout the novel as essentially distorting. Each man or woman has a "centre of self, whence the lights and shadows must always fall with a certain difference" (chap. 31). The "radiance" of Dorothea's "transfigured girlhood," as the narrator says, "fell on the first object that came within its level" (chap. 5). Her mistakes, as her sister Celia tells her, are errors in seeing, of which her literal myopia is a metonymy. "I thought it right to tell you," says Celia apropos of the fact that Sir James intends to propose to Dorothea, "because you went on as you always do, never looking just where you are, and treading in the wrong place. You always see what nobody else sees; it is impossible to satisfy you; yet you never see what is quite plain" (chap. 4). Mr. Casaubon, however, is also "the centre of his own world." From that point of view he is "liable to think that others were providentially made for him, and especially to consider them in the light of their fitness for the author of a 'Key to all Mythologies' " (chap. 10).

Of the inhabitants of Middlemarch generally it can in fact be said that each makes of what he sees something determined by his own idiosyncratic perspective, for "Probabilities are as various as the faces to be seen at will on fretwork or paperhangings: every form is there, from Jupiter to Judy, if you only look with creative inclination" (chap. 32).

Seeing, then, is for Eliot not a neutral, objective, dispassionate, or passive act. It is the creative projection of light from an egotistic center motivated by desire and need. This projected radiance orders the field of vision according to the presuppositions of the seer. The act of seeing is the spontaneous affirmation of a will to power over what is seen. This affirmation of order is based on the instinctive desire to believe that the world is providentially structured in a neat pattern of which one is oneself the center, for "we are all of us born in moral stupidity, taking the world as an udder to feed our supreme selves." This interpretation of the act of seeing is most fully presented in the admirable and often discussed "parable" of the "pier-glass" at the beginning of chapter 27:

> An eminent philosopher among my friends, who can dignify even your ugly furniture by lifting it into the serene light of science, has shown me this pregnant little fact. Your pier-glass or extensive surface of polished steel made to be rubbed by a housemaid, will be minutely and multitudinously scratched in all directions; but place now against it a lighted candle as a centre of illumination, and lo! the scratches will seem to arrange themselves in a fine series of concentric circles round that little sun. It is demonstrable that the scratches are going everywhere impartially, and it is only your candle which produces the flattering illusion of a concentric arrangement, its light falling with an exclusive optical selection. These things are a parable. The scratches are events, and the candle is the egoism of any person now absent — of Miss Vincy, for example. Rosamond had a Providence of her own who had kindly made her more charming than other girls, and who seemed to have arranged Fred's illness and Mr. Wrench's mistake in order to bring her and Lydgate within effective proximity.[9]

9. Although several hypothetical originals, including G. H. Lewes, have been suggested for the "eminent philosopher," N. N. Feltes argues

This passage is perhaps more complicated than it at first appears. It begins with an example of what it describes, an example which implicitly takes note of the fact that Eliot's own "parabolic" method, in this text, as in many other passages in *Middlemarch,* is a seeing of one thing in the "light" of another. The word "parable," like the word "allegory," the word "metaphor," or indeed all terms for figures of speech, is of course itself based on a figure. It means "to set beside," from the Greek *para,* beside, and *ballein,* to throw. A parable is set or thrown at some distance from the meaning which controls it and to which it obliquely or parabolically refers, as a parabolic curve is controlled, across a space, by its parallelism to a line on the cone of which it is a section. The line and the cone may have only a virtual or imaginary existence, as in the case of a comet with a parabolic course. The parabola creates that line in the empty air, just as the parables of Jesus remedy a defect of vision, give sight to the blind, and make the invisible visible. In Eliot's parable of the pier glass the "eminent philosopher" transfigures "ugly furniture," a pier glass, by "lifting it into the serene light of science," but also makes an obscure scientific principle visible. In the same way, the candle makes the random scratches on the pier glass appear to be concentric circles, and so Rosamond interprets what happens around her as being governed by her private providence, just as Eliot sees provincial society as like a woven web, or the ego of an individual person in the light of a comparison to a candle. The same projective, subjective, even egotistic act, seeing one thing as set or thrown, parabolically, beside another, is involved in all four cases.

At this point the reader may remember that the narrator, in a passage I earlier took as a "key" expression[10] of Eliot's use of

---

persuasively that the philosopher was Herbert Spencer and that the image may be traced back from Spencer to a passage in Ruskin. See "George Eliot's 'Pier-Glass'; The Development of a Metaphor," *Modern Philology,* 67, no. 1 (August 1969), 69–71.

10. The metaphor of the key, which I have borrowed for the language of the novel to use as language about the novel, contains exactly the ambiguity I am exploring here. A "key," as in the "Key to all Mythologies," is both an intrinsic pattern organizing from within a large body of apparently heterogeneous material and at the same time something introduced from the outside which "unlocks" an otherwise hidden pat-

a model of objective scientific observation, says "all the light I can command must be concentrated on this particular web." With a slight change of formulation this could be seen as implying that the subjective source of light not only illuminates what is seen but also, as in the case of the candle held to the pier glass, determines the structure of what is seen. Middlemarch society perhaps appears to be a web only because a certain kind of subjective light is concentrated on it. The passage taken in isolation does not say this, but its near congruence with the passage about the pier glass, a slightly asymmetrical analogy based on the fact that the same metaphorical elements are present in each allows the contradictory meaning to seep into the passage about the web when the two texts are set side by side. Each is seen as a modulation of the other. The same key would not open both, though a "master key" might.

In spite of the disquieting possibilities generated by resonances between two similar but not quite congruent passages, the narrator in various ways throughout *Middlemarch* is clearly claiming to be able to transcend the limitations of the self-centered ego by seeing things impersonally, objectively, scientifically: "It is demonstrable that the scratches are going everywhere impartially." This objective vision, such is the logic of Eliot's parable, shows that what is "really there" has no order whatsoever, but is merely random scratches without pattern or meaning. The pier glass is "minutely and multitudinously scratched in all directions." The idea that reality is chaotic, without intrinsic order or form, and the corollary that any order it may appear to have is projected illicitly by some patterning ego, would seem to be contradicted by the series of totalizing metaphors I have explored — web, flowing water, and so on — as well as by the generalizing, rationalizing, order-finding activity of the narrator throughout the book. It would seem hardly plausible, at this point at least, to

tern. A key is a formula which cracks a code, as when George Eliot in *Daniel Deronda* says, "all meanings, we know, depend on the key of interpretation" (chap. 6). The meaning of a text is both intrinsic to that text and yet present in it only when it is projected by a certain extrinsic set of assumptions about the code or "key." This shifting from intrinsic to extrinsic definitions of "key" is present in the various meanings of the word, which include mechanical, architectural, musical, and botanical senses.

say that reality for Eliot is a chaotic disorder. It might seem more likely that this is an irrelevant implication of the parable, an implication which has by accident, as it were, slipped in along with implications which are "intended." A decision about this must be postponed.

Among the "intended" implications, however, may be one arising from the fact that a pier glass is a kind of mirror, while the examples of the "flattering illusion" Eliot would have encountered in Herbert Spencer or in Ruskin lacked this feature. Ruskin, for example, speaks of the path of reflected moonlight seen across the surface of a lake by a spectator on the shore.[11] The pier glass would, after all, reflect what was brought near it, as well as produce its own interfering illusion of concentric circles, and the candle is a displacement or parable for the ego, of Rosamond or whomever. Rosamond would of course see her own image in the mirror, Narcissus-like. This implication of the parable links it with all those other passages, not only in *Middlemarch* but also in *Adam Bede,* for example, or in *Daniel Deronda,* where egotism is symbolized by the admiration of one's image in a mirror, or where the work of representation is expressed in the traditional image of holding a mirror up to reality. A passage in chapter 10, for example, apropos of the low opinion of Mr. Casaubon held by his neighbors, says that even "the greatest man of his age" could not escape "unfavourable reflections of himself in various small mirrors." This apparently uses the figure of the mirror in a way contradicting the parable of the pier glass. The mirror is now the ego rather than the external world. In fact, however, what is always in question when the mirror appears is narcissistic self-reflection. This may be thought of as seeing our own reflection in the mirroring world outside because we have projected it there. Or it may be thought of as our distortion of the world outside in our reflecting ego, so that it takes the configurations of our private vision of things. Any two subjectivities, according to this model, will face one another like confronting mirrors. If Casaubon was "the centre of his own

11. See Feltes, "George Eliot's 'Pier-Glass,' " p. 69, for a discussion of the passage from Ruskin's letter of February 1844 to the *Artist and Amateur's Magazine,* reprinted in *The Works of John Ruskin,* ed. E. T. Cook and Alexander Wedderburn, Library Edition (London, 1903), 3:656–657.

world," had "an equivalent centre of self, whence the lights and
shadows must always fall with a certain difference," the people
in whom he seeks the reflection of his own sense of himself are
not innocent mirrors, but are themselves instruments of distortion: "even Milton, looking for his portrait in a spoon, must
submit to have the facial angle of a bumpkin" (chap. 10). The
projection of one's selfish needs or desires on reality orders that
random set of events into a pattern, the image of the mirror
would imply. This pattern is in fact a portrait of the ego itself,
an objective embodiment of its subjective configurations. The
terrible isolation of each person, for Eliot, lies in the way each
goes through the world encountering only himself, his own image
reflected back to him by the world because he (or she) has put
it there in the first place, in the illusory interpretation of the
world the person spontaneously makes.

The narrator of *Middlemarch,* it would seem, can escape from
this fate only by using perspective to transcend perspective, by
moving from the microscopic close-up to the panoramic distant
view, and by shifting constantly from the point of view of one
character to the point of view of another. Such shifts will give
a full multidimensional picture of what is "really there," as when
the narrator, after a prolonged immersion within the subjective
experience of Dorothea, asks: " — but why always Dorothea?
Was her point of view the only possible one with regard to this
marriage? I protest against all our interest, all our efforts at
understanding being given to the young skins that look blooming
in spite of trouble . . . In spite of the blinking eyes and white
moles objectionable to Celia, and the want of muscular curve
which was morally painful to Sir James, Mr. Casaubon had an
intense consciousness within him, and was spiritually a-hungered
like the rest of us" (chap. 29).

The word "interpretation," however, which I used just above,
will serve as a clue indicating the presence within the optical
metaphors of an element so far not identified as such. This element contaminates and ultimately subverts the optical model in
the same way that the optical model contaminates and makes
more problematic the images of the web or of the current. All
the optical passages in fact contain elements which show that

for Eliot seeing is never "merely" optical. Seeing is never simply a matter of identifying correctly what is seen, seeing that windmills are windmills and not giants, a washpan a washpan and not the helmet of Mambrino, to use the example from *Don Quixote* cited as an epigraph for chapter 2. Seeing is always interpretation, that is, what is seen is always taken as a sign standing for something else, as an emblem, a hieroglyph, a parable.

Superimposed on the models for the human situation of the objective scientist and the subjective perspectivist, interlaced with them, overlapping them in each of their expressions, is a model for the situation of the characters and of the narrator which says all human beings in all situations are like readers of a text. Moreover, if for Eliot all seeing is falsified by the limitations of point of view, it is an even more inevitable law, for her, that we make things what they are by naming them in one way or another, that is, by the incorporation of empirical data into a conventional system of signs. A corollary of this law is the fact that all interpretation of signs is false interpretation. The original naming was an act of interpretation which falsified. The reading of things made into signs is necessarily a further falsification, an interpretation of an interpretation. An important sequence of passages running like Ariadne's thread through the labyrinthine verbal complexity of *Middlemarch* develops a subtle theory of signs and of interpretation. Along with this goes a recognition of the irreducibly figurative or metaphorical nature of all language.

I have elsewhere discussed George Eliot's theory of signs, of interpretation, and of figurative language in *Middlemarch*.[12] Limitations of space would in any case forbid discussion of this third model for the human situation here. It is possible, however, to conclude on the basis of what I have said about two families of metaphors in *Middlemarch* that the models are multiple and incompatible. They are incompatible not in the sense that one is more primitive or naive and gives way to a more sophisticated

12. In "Narrative and History," *ELH* 41 (Fall 1974), 455–473. I have also tried to indicate in this essay the alternative positive theories of history, of individual human life, and of the work of art with which Eliot, in *Middlemarch,* replaces the "metaphysical" theories, governed by concepts of totality, of origin, of end, and of substantial analogy, which she so persuasively dismantles in the novel.

paradigm, but in the sense that any passage will reveal itself when examined closely to be the battleground of conflicting metaphors. This incoherent, heterogeneous, "unreadable," or nonsynthesizable quality of the text of *Middlemarch* jeopardizes the narrator's effort of totalization. It suggests that one gets a different kind of totality depending on what metaphorical model is used. The presence of several incompatible models brings into the open the arbitrary and partial character of each and so ruins the claim of the narrator to have a total, unified, and impartial vision. What is true for the characters of *Middlemarch,* that "we all of us, grave or light, get our thoughts entangled in metaphors, and act fatally on the strength of them" (chap. 10), must also be true for the narrator. The web of interpretative figures cast by the narrator over the characters of the story becomes a net in which the narrator himself is entangled and trapped, his sovereign vision blinded.

George Eliot's insight into the dismaying dangers of metaphor is expressed already in an admirably witty and perceptive passage in *The Mill on the Floss,* published over a decade before *Middlemarch,* in 1860. Here already she formulates her recognition of the deconstructive powers of figurative language, its undoing of any attempt to make a complete, and completely coherent, picture of human life. This undoing follows from the fact that if we can seldom say what a thing is without saying it is something else, without speaking parabolically, then there is no way to avoid the ever present possibility of altering the meaning by altering the metaphor:

> It is astonishing what a different result one gets by changing the metaphor! Once call the brain an intellectual stomach, and one's ingenious conception of the classics and geometry as ploughs and harrows seems to settle nothing. But then it is open to some one else to follow great authorities, and call the mind a sheet of white paper or a mirror, in which case one's knowledge of the digestive process becomes quite irrelevant. It was doubtless an ingenious idea to call the camel the ship of the desert, but it would hardly lead one far in training that useful beast. O Aristotle! if you had had the advantage of being "the freshest modern" instead of the greatest ancient, would you not have mingled your praise of metaphorical speech, as a sign of high intelligence, with

a lamentation that intelligence so rarely shows itself in speech without metaphor — that we can so seldom declare what a thing is, except by saying it is something else? (Book 2, chap. 1)[13]

13. It is worth noting that George Eliot's rueful complaint about the proliferating contradictions of metaphor, which has arisen apropos of Tom Tulliver's difficulties in school, is followed almost immediately by an ostentatious and forceful metaphor, as if Eliot were compelled, in spite of herself, to demonstrate that we cannot say what a thing is except by saying it is something else: "At present, in relation to this demand that he should learn Latin declensions and conjugations, Tom was in a state of as blank unimaginativeness concerning the cause and tendency of his sufferings, as if he had been an innocent shrewmouse imprisoned in the split trunk of an ash-tree in order to cure lameness in cattle."

III Private Worlds

Thackeray's Self-Consciousness

A perilous trade, indeed, is that of a man who has to bring his tears and laughter, his recollections, his personal griefs and joys, his private thoughts and feelings to market, to write them on paper, and sell them for money. Does he exaggerate his grief, so as to get his reader's pity for a false sensibility? feign indignation, so as to establish a character for virtue? . . . affect benevolence or misanthropy? . . .

How much of the paint and emphasis is necessary for the fair business of the stage, and how much of the rant and rouge is put on for the vanity of the actor? His audience trusts him: can he trust himself? How much was deliberate calculation and imposture — how much was false sensibility — and how much true feeling? Where did the lie begin, and did he know where? and where did the truth end in the art and scheme of this man of genius, this actor, this quack? [1]

This passage, from Thackeray's famous attack on Sterne for emotional hypocrisy, has more relevance to Thackeray's own work than he would have admitted. Thackeray was obsessed

1. From the lecture on Sterne and Goldsmith in *The English Humourists of the Eighteenth Century* (1853), in *The Oxford Thackeray* (hereafter cited as *Works*), ed. George Saintsbury, 17 vols. (London: Oxford University Press, n.d. [1908]), 13:665–666.

with the question of how to know and trust his own feelings. His trade was "perilous" to him in the same way he describes Sterne's as being. In conceiving of his novels as "a sort of confidential talk between writer and reader," [2] he denies himself a comfortable distance between his life and his writings. The danger is that of being overwhelmed by his private thoughts and feelings and of not being able to give them artistic shape. Under cover of attacking Sterne, he is asking penetrating questions about his own art.

As in all of Thackeray's best writing, the questions he asks here turn out to be less rhetorical than they at first seem. The playfulness of tone is what makes possible the disturbing confrontation with difficult truths, although it also means that they will be only confronted, not resolved. Though he does not see his way to getting rid of rouge and paint altogether, he still asks "how much" of it is necessary. The passage does not suggest the possibility of finding a way of measuring emotional honesty, but still asks us to try. As with Sterne, we shall never be able to say just how much Thackeray was a "man of genius," how much an "actor," how much a "quack"; yet these questions are constantly and uncomfortably before us.

Thackeray's self-consciousness and its effect on his work has not been fully assessed, since critics tend to praise it when they like the result and deplore it when they do not. Self-consciousness in Thackeray means more than his notorious habit of breaking the fictional illusion. He nervously turns against all of the fictional devices and conventions that are his stock in trade. Sometimes he explicitly draws attention to the artificiality of his writing: "I know that the tune I am piping is a very mild one. . ." [3] Sometimes he undermines his own effects, by not allowing them to have the impact he presumably intended. He denies even modest expectations of suspense: "I do not . . . condescend to keep candid readers in suspense about many matters which might possibly interest them . . . Phil's first love affair, to which we are now coming, was a false start. I own it at once." [4]

2. "Preface," *The History of Pendennis,* in *Works,* 12:xxxi.

3. *Vanity Fair,* ed. Geoffrey Tillotson and Kathleen Tillotson (Boston: Houghton Mifflin, 1963), chap. 6.

4. *The Adventures of Philip* (1861–62), chap. 8, in *Works,* 16:103.

He is nervous about the inner lives of his created characters and falls back on the insinuations of gossip or on cynical or senti-mental caricatures, as in his description of Laura Bell's affection for Helen Pendennis: "It was devotion — it was passion — it was all sorts of fondness and folly; it was a profusion of caresses, tender epithets and endearments, such as it does not become sober historians with beards to narrate. Do not let us men de-spise these instincts because we cannot feel them. These women were made for our comfort and delectation, gentlemen — with all the rest of the minor animals." [5] He openly chides himself for his cynical and digressive habits: "Be quiet. Don't pursue your snarling, cynical remarks, but go on with your story." [6] He wavers between contradictory attitudes toward the world his characters inhabit, sometimes castigating it fiercely, sometimes acquiescing in its materialism: "It is all vanity to be sure: but who will not own to liking a little of it? I should like to know what well-constituted mind, merely because it is transitory, dis-likes roast-beef? That is a vanity; but may every man who reads this, have a wholesome portion of it through life, I beg . . ." [7] The effect of these shifts and juxtapositions is often not a bal-ancing of opposed perspectives, not a creative irony, but rather a nervous retreat, closing off a discussion that has got out of hand: ". . . I am trying to turn off the sentence with a joke, you see — I feel it is growing too dreadful, too serious." [8]

As a result Thackeray cannot develop larger structural ironies. No event in a Thackeray novel can have a stable meaning; no character can be finally known. For all its energy, *Vanity Fair* (1847–48) tends to become an endless spiral of reflections and reverberations, mirrors and echoes. Though the narrative perspective is more fully controlled in *The History of Henry Esmond* (1852), this novel is a sort of optical illusion, facing now one way, now the other. Critics have traced out numerous thematic and psychological patterns in the other two major novels, *The History of Pendennis* (1848–50) and *The New-comes* (1853–55), but they still bring to mind James's phrase,

5. *Pendennis,* chap. 21, in *Works,* 12:252.
6. *Philip,* chap. 5, in *Works,* 16:56.
7. *Vanity Fair,* chap. 51.
8. *The Newcomes,* chap. 11, in *Works,* 14:151.

"large loose baggy monsters," for they are large and loose and baggy in their "patterns" as well as in their massiveness.[9]

Wendell Stacy Johnson effectively describes the tradition of Victorian self-consciousness exemplified by Thackeray. He summarizes the possible artistic consequences of a writer's uncertainty about himself:

> Sometimes, depending on the clarity and the artfulness of a dramatic method, the result is an impressive representation of human life with its moral ambiguities and mixed feelings. The painfully self-conscious performer, emotionally committed to his role, who turns stage fright into energy through his art can be more moving than the too calm master technician. Sometimes, too, the result of this nervous combination is vagueness or stuttering, is incoherence.[10]

Evaluating self-conscious art, however, is more difficult than Johnson suggests. Successful self-conscious art, says Johnson, depends on "the clarity and the artfulness of a dramatic method," but the performer's "stage fright" would seem to rule out clarity and artfulness. Yet if his stage fright has been transcended, how do we tell the result from that achieved by the "too calm master technician"?

The fact is that Thackeray's art achieves effects we cannot evaluate with critical terms derived from a conception of novels as autonomous organic wholes. Johnson's account depends on those terms. Recent critical studies of Thackeray by Juliet McMaster and Barbara Hardy show this problem more fully.[11] Both studies maintain a tone of generous enthusiasm for Thackeray, but only because the authors fail to recognize the intensity

9. "Preface," *The Tragic Muse* (New York: Scribner's, 1908). For the tracing of thematic and psychological patterns in the novels, see James H. Wheatley, *Patterns in Thackeray's Fiction* (Cambridge: MIT Press, 1969), and Bernard J. Paris, *A Psychological Approach to Fiction* (Bloomington: Indiana University Press, 1974).

10. "Victorian Self-Consciousness," *Victorian Newsletter,* no. 21 (Spring 1962), p. 5. For a broader perspective see Masao Miyoshi, *The Divided Self* (New York: New York University Press, 1969).

11. McMaster, *Thackeray: The Major Novels* (Toronto: University of Toronto Press, 1971); Hardy, *The Exposure of Luxury: Radical Themes in Thackeray* (Pittsburgh: University of Pittsburgh Press, 1972).

of Thackeray's self-consciousness. They praise the complexity brought about by his shifting perspectives, without seeming aware that the same shifting perspectives produce results we can only call incoherent or even cowardly. Hardy avoids these questions by limiting her study to the "content" or "subject-matter" of the novels, avoiding their form (13). McMaster is more ambitious; she continually asserts that the shifting perspectives are successfully controlled to bring about satisfying artistic wholes. Here is how she comments on the passage about Sterne I began with: "For Thackeray and Pendennis, actor and quack are necessarily facets of the artist, and honesty consists partly in the admission of them, and in the ability to define the limits of their influence" (81). The notion of "defining limits" is foreign to the passage on Sterne, and in fact its "honesty" consists in its recognition that we can *never* completely separate lie and truth.

Because of his self-consciousness Thackeray has been particularly intriguing to two literary theorists who have attacked the critical language of organic wholes and controlled meanings, Morse Peckham and Wolfgang Iser.[12] Both use Thackeray to illustrate concepts of "discontinuity" and "indeterminacy" that they feel are at the heart of the artistic experience. Far from trying to reconcile the apparent inconsistencies of *Vanity Fair* by showing hidden thematic or psychological patterns, they commend those inconsistencies as explicit examples of what other artists do more indirectly. Such a radical redefinition of the novel, with the chaotic narrative of *Vanity Fair* at its center, is at best quixotic; it makes Thackeray into a more fashionably modern writer than he is. Surely the interaction of continuity and discontinuity, determinacy and indeterminacy, is the heart of the artistic experience.

Thackeray remains the most problematical of the Victorian novelists; a coherent assessment of his work will be achieved only by steering between the alternatives discussed here. We must get back to the self-consciousness and its workings and not merely praise some of its results as controlled ambiguities

12. Peckham, *The Triumph of Romanticism* (Columbia: University of South Carolina Press, 1970); Iser, "Indeterminacy and the Reader's Response in Prose Fiction," in *Aspects of Narrative,* ed. J. Hillis Miller (New York: Columbia University Press, 1971), pp. 1–45.

while dismissing others as mindless sentimentalities. It is just as bad to oversimplify the novels by pulling out neat patterns as to lose oneself in the elegant convolutions of the Thackerayan mind.

Of Thackeray's four major novels, *Pendennis* and *The Newcomes* are most useful in exploring some of the consequences of Thackeray's self-consciousness. Much critical attention has been paid to the structural means by which he focused his self-consciousness in the other two novels — the metaphorical framework suggested by the title of *Vanity Fair* and the eighteenth-century memoir form of *Henry Esmond*. *Pendennis* and *The Newcomes* are looser works, and in them we can see Thackeray's narrative personality given its fullest embodiment. The personality revealed is that of the "implied author" of these novels.

What is the meaning of the implied author's presence in and behind the fictional world of *Pendennis*? [13] One of the first problems we are aware of is Thackeray's uneasy relationship to his characters. He is overwhelmed by surfaces, appearances, gestures, and roles and has a deep uncertainty about human identity. At times he feels that the inner life of any other person is sacred and unknowable, but he is just as ready to assume that what cannot be known does not exist and that his characters are merely painted puppets.

Two related problems of characterization arise from these uncertainties. Limited to a static conception of human character, he nevertheless writes a long novel which seems to show the protagonist developing and growing. In addition, many characters — especially Pen's mother Helen Pendennis — bear the apparent marks of Thackeray's emotional obsessions, insufficiently mastered and controlled.

Thackeray's particular conception of human character is most fully expressed in chapter 59 of *Pendennis,* where he says that "we alter very little," much less than we like to think, and that

13. For a further account of the critical problems raised by *Pendennis,* see Sylvère Monod, " 'Brother Wearers of Motley,' " *Essays and Studies,* 26 (1973), 66–82. J. A. Sutherland in *Thackeray at Work* (London: Athlone Press, 1974), pp. 45–55, shows how the novel confronts the problem of a writer's selling his private feelings for money.

"circumstance only brings out the latent defect or quality, and does not create it." [14] This is a limited conception of human character, an odd basis for a novel portraying in detail the growth of an artist. *Pendennis* reads like a *Bildungsroman* without a *Bildung*. It takes all of Thackeray's ingenuity to maintain our interest over this long novel in a protagonist who merely goes on revealing his essential nature over and over in different situations.

Some of the ways in which Thackeray overcomes this structural problem have been discussed by others, but too much effort has been spent finding coherent patterns in the novel.[15] What has not been sufficiently observed, I think, is a deviousness in Thackeray's relationship to Pen and to his readers. More than anything else, his deceptiveness is what raises and then holds our interest in *Pendennis*.

Thackeray does not make clear how much he is indulging Pen's adolescent fancies, how much criticizing them. And he is, as we saw, skeptical about personality change. Throughout the novel he hints that Pen is growing and learning from his mistakes, but these are isolated gestures. He is less interested in moral growth than in the human weaknesses and self-deceptions that make a character (or a reader) think it has taken place. By pretending to show growth, and then revealing that Pen is subject to the same self-deceptions hundreds of pages later, Thackeray makes us share as well as criticize Pen's limitations. The narrator's undependability and the alertness it demands of us partially make up for the lack in *Pendennis* of the teeming social world of *Vanity Fair,* in which a different kind of richness is achieved by the juxtaposition of so many different forms of selfish striving. In *Pendennis* Thackeray is trying to encompass in his own narration the richness of response that can give life to the portrayal of a static character.

A similar deviousness rescues the portrait of Helen Pendennis from sentimentality. In chapter 2, for example, we are intro-

14. *Works,* 12:766, 767.
15. In addition to the books by Wheatley, McMaster, and Hardy cited above, see Martin Fido, *"The History of Pendennis:* A Reconsideration," *Essays in Criticism,* 14 (1964), 363–379; Jean Sudrann, " 'The Philosopher's Property': Thackeray and the Use of Time," *Victorian Studies,* 10 (1967), 359–388.

duced to her in a couple of pages of formal but characteristically equivocal summary. Contradictory opinions of her by Pen, Major Pendennis, the neighbors, and the narrator are adroitly kept in suspension with Helen's own conception of herself. Instead of the resolution of these perspectives there is a pretended conclusion that raises more questions than it answers: "That even a woman should be faultless, however, is an arrangement not permitted by nature, which assigns to us mental defects, as it awards to us headaches, illnesses, or death . . . [A]s for her son Arthur, she worshipped that youth with . . . ardour . . . This unfortunate superstition and idol-worship of this good woman was the cause of a great deal of the misfortune which befell the young gentleman who is the hero of this history . . ." We are rightly put on our guard by the ease of these generalities. They pretend to dispose of an issue that has not been settled. The incompatibility between Helen as a saintly figure and Helen as the earthly jealous mother remains. Throughout the novel Thackeray continues to give partial and unreconciled glimpses of Helen Pendennis; this is an unusual but effective method of characterization.

Of course there are problems in the presentation of Pen and his mother. Helen's deathbed scene (chap. 57) is clearly a moment at which something is radically wrong. Here the two contradictory images are present, but Thackeray seems to insist on reconciling them. Thackeray has Helen die in relief at Pen's assurance that he did not seduce Fanny Bolton and that he is still her virginal son. The complexities of Pen's feelings for Fanny and of Helen's for Pen, fostered throughout the novel by Thackeray's indirect presentation, are abruptly and unsatisfactorily denied. Instead of giving us teasing glimpses that suggest a complexity beyond what the narrative explicitly formulates, Thackeray forces conclusions that draw a curtain over the more interesting reality hinted at earlier.

The ending of the novel is also weak because Thackeray cannot maintain his deviousness. He wants to show Pen essentially unchanged, but at the end he cannot help implying that Pen is worthy of marrying Laura Bell. He tries to keep up a duality of response, suggesting that Pen is still playing a part (though a more attractive one) and that he is lucky to come off so well. But the impression persists that by choosing Laura over Blanche Amory he has achieved a self-mastery beyond the limitations of a static character. In *Pendennis* (unlike *The Newcomes*) Thackeray is still too dependent on the conventional Victorian happy ending. The problem is not self-consciousness, but a lack of complete confidence in his self-conscious narrative method.

The Newcomes is a far more successful novel than *Pendennis* and is beginning to get the critical appreciation that it deserves. In it Thackeray's self-consciousness shows itself best in his creative use of temporal perspectives. Readers have long realized that Thackeray's special appeal is related to his fascination with the passage of time and the nature of reminiscence and memory. But most critics who have written perceptively on this issue have overstated the successes of his temporal manipulations and have ignored the uncertainty that often appears in his handling of time.[16]

Just as Thackeray will often hold contradictory opinions about a character without reconciling them, he often expresses inconsistent attitudes about the past and the passage of time. We expect the greatest historical fiction to achieve a temporary resolution, enabling us to assent to both the remoteness of the past and its essential closeness. In Thackeray's novels the two feelings appear side by side but usually remain distinct. Either the past is all quaint trappings and queer ceremonies or it is indistinguishable from the present. The fictional world being created is either a remote fable-land or an everyday world just around the corner from our own.

The reader first senses the passage of time in *The Newcomes* through the agonizing slow pace of the novel. As Saintsbury says, "*The Newcomes* is scarcely even a microcosm; it is almost the world itself . . ."[17] The reader senses various patterns, such as the ongoing counterpoint between the language of financial

16. See works cited by McMaster and Sudrann, as well as John A. Lester, Jr., "Thackeray's Narrative Technique," *PMLA,* 69 (1954), 392–409. An exception is Sutherland, *Thackeray at Work,* especially pp. 35–44.

17. "Introduction," in *The Newcomes,* in *Works,* 14:xxiv.

materialism and the language of romance, but it is difficult to see why the counterpoint should be so unemphatic and repetitive. The vague and inconsistent chronology is another source of perplexity. Thackeray too often contradicts himself about the passage of years or the age of a character.

More significant and more bewildering is the variety of temporal perspectives through which the story is filtered. It is an oversimplification to praise Thackeray as "a master at switching between [the] two time scales" of immediate experience and the long perspective of the past.[18] The narrator, Arthur Pendennis, is presented as the editor, some quarter-century later, of the doings of his friends and acquaintances. He retells the story with constantly changing aesthetic distance, sometimes striving for dramatic immediacy, sometimes for a long perspective of reminiscence. And some temporal manipulations go beyond those Arthur Pendennis could have supplied. The events of *The Newcomes* are laid over those of *Pendennis,* and Thackeray brings in or has characters mention other figures from his earlier novels. Pendennis's evocation of the events of twenty-five years ago competes with the novelist's reminders of his other books, as he gathers them together into a continuous fabric. The controlling hand of the novelist is even more obvious in the secondary characters' allegorical names and in passages in which he discusses his own manipulations: ". . . [Ethel Newcome], I say, is in a very awkward position as a heroine; and I declare if I had another ready to my hand (and unless there were extenuating circumstances), Ethel should be deposed at this very sentence" (chap. 45).

A further temporal realm that seems beyond Arthur Pendennis's vision is the allusive world of fable-land that permeates the novel. The opening chapter presents "a farrago of old fables" that linger in the background throughout the novel to broaden the frame of reference. No one has described this method of "allusive irrelevancy" so brilliantly as G. K. Chesterton:

> When Thackeray wished to hint a truth which was just not true enough to bear his whole weight, his way was to wander off into

18. McMaster, *Thackeray,* p. 152.

similes and allegories which repeated and yet mocked the main story like derisive and dying echoes . . .

He falls away into philosophizing not because his satire is merciless but because it is merciful; he wishes to soften the fall of his characters with a sense and suggestion of the weakness of all flesh . . . He says that all men are liars, rather than say directly that Pendennis was lying. He says easily that all is vanity, so as not to say that Ethel Newcome was vain.[19]

Chesterton recognizes liabilities in this method and admits that Thackeray came to "use this rambling style without its old subtle purpose of suggestion." [20] But he does not tell us how we can determine whether any given irrelevancy has its "subtle purpose." And he makes the method sound more generous than it is. The merciful quality Chesterton describes applies to Thackeray when he takes the long perspective; yet, when emphasizing the presence of the past, Thackeray will mount scornful attacks on forms of exploitation and snobbishness that are still with us and ask us to condemn them.

There are other allusive effects that are not as graceful as Chesterton's account suggests. For example, more than once in *The Newcomes* he falls into the exact metaphorical scheme of *Vanity Fair* ("as keen as the smartest merchant in Vanity Fair"; chap. 45). These references invoke a more particular and limited frame of reference than he has been working with and make us feel he is nodding.

Yet the discrepancies we are discussing, even the most unsuccessful ones, are essential to his achievement in conveying the feel of human memory. Just as he thinks that "we alter very little," he thinks that we rarely in our own lives transcend our confused everyday attitudes about the past. Most of the time we hold contradictory notions in our minds without being aware of the conflict — responding now to the unchanging and permanent aspects of human affairs, now to the ever-changing flux of experience. His art is an attempt to find a way to go on expressing this inconsistency in our memories, not to transcend it as so many other artists have tried to do. He is trying neither to

19. *Thackeray* (London: George Bell and Sons, 1909), pp. xxiii, xxiv.
20. Ibid., p. xxv.

recapture the past nor to find one satisfying image of it, but rather to render the texture of our feelings about that past.

How do we decide whether Thackeray succeeds in expressing confusion or is merely confused? His works are unsatisfying to readers in search of a fictional experience in which a clear and constant distance is maintained between the novelist and his created world. Attempts to neaten up *The Newcomes* by correcting factual details or expunging moments at which the aesthetic distance suddenly changes will always fail. Nor can we successfully separate the events and the commentary on those events and measure them against each other.

Thackeray's presentation makes us try to articulate a response beyond any that is explicitly put forth amid the contradictory textures of *The Newcomes*. The last page of the novel is the place to see how we can put together the partial and limited perspectives:

> Anything you like happens in fable-land ... [A]nnoying folks are got out of the way; the poor are rewarded — the upstarts are set down in fable-land, — the frog bursts with wicked rage, the fox is caught in his trap, the lamb is rescued from the wolf, and so forth, just in the nick of time. And the poet of fable-land rewards and punishes absolutely. He splendidly deals out bags of sovereigns, which won't buy anything; belabours wicked backs with awful blows, which do not hurt; endows heroines with preternatural beauty, and creates heroes, who, if ugly sometimes, yet possess a thousand good qualities, and usually end by being immensely rich; makes the hero and heroine happy at last, and happy ever after. Ah, happy, harmless fable-land, where these things are! Friendly reader! may you and the author meet there on some future day! He hopes so; as he yet keeps a lingering hold of your hand, and bids you farewell with a kind heart. (Chap. 80)

As McMaster suggests, our response to this passage is not the simple sentimental one that the sentences pretend to be evoking; we know enough to add ironic qualification to the assertions that seem so harmless here.[21] Although the narrator says that "anything you like happens in fable-land," we know that the

21. McMaster, *Thackeray*, pp. 170–173.

description does not really fit the world he has given us. By having Clive and Ethel marry, but only in this fable-land, Thackeray does justice both to the hunger for conventional happiness and to the intractability of human affairs. Our recognition of the irrelevancy of this passage gives weight to the pretended lightheartedness and enables us to sense a unity in *The Newcomes* through the deviousness of the self-conscious novelist.

Sylvère Monod in his study of *Pendennis* carefully considers some of the inconsistencies I have been discussing and the arguments of Thackeray's apologists. But he finally despairs of settling the critical controversy about Thackeray. The only way he can account for the strong differences of opinion about Thackeray's achievement is to point to temperamental differences among Thackeray's readers. Taking a term from *Vanity Fair,* he calls those who most enjoy Thackeray "brother wearers of motley":

> A brother wearer of motley is a man who does not mind being shown that he is a fool or a buffoon and thus enjoys the close relationship and identification with a writer without illusions, part mountebank, part highly intelligent analyst of the weaknesses of mankind, moving at a subdued moral level, using variegated lights, shapes and colours. Such a reader may well feel that, even where there is perplexity as well as complexity, he is eventually helped in his difficult effort to come to terms with his own foibles and with the human predicament.[22]

This is an excellent description of what Thackeray has to offer; I willingly cast my lot with the brother wearers of motley. But to avoid being dismissed as cranks, brother wearers of motley ought to be able to say what is inadequate about the critical standards by which Thackeray is found wanting. Thackeray had no interest in autonomous literary structures, and he knew he was not at his best when trying to carry his readers away from themselves into an independent fictional world. He was

22. Monod, " 'Brother Wearers of Motley,' " p. 82.

aware of himself as a man and as a storyteller, and he self-consciously made that awareness part of the story he was telling. The best of his novels justify themselves by the energy with which he gives voice to so many different impulses and intentions in continuous conflict, those of author and reader as well as those of characters. The illusion is created that every possible human perspective will be taken up, that even the meanest character or reader will have things seen his way for a moment. Though his personal strivings will be ultimately seen as vanity, they will be noticed and be given momentary dignity and plausibility.

This is not to say that Thackeray belongs with Sterne, Joyce, and Nabokov, novelists whose interest in characters and events is an excuse to explore the secondary fictional world of the novelist's relationship to his writing and to his readers. The most plausible attempt to place Thackeray in this tradition underestimates his interest in his characters and their actions and overestimates his conscious control of fictional techniques.[23] Thackeray belongs in no one else's camp. The successes he achieves come from an unusual conception of himself as a writer. He refuses to take himself seriously as an artist, refuses to create impersonal, independently existing fictions. That refusal was caused by an inability to make disciplined demands on himself. The result is fortunate, as his mind is most interesting when most free and unforced, when his reflections can follow one another according to his momentary inclinations. But this method makes its own demands: constant nervous energy to keep up a flexibility of response and a continuing readiness to turn on one's own formulations and assert the contrary.

Behind Thackeray's decline is an impatience with this kind of storytelling, combined with an inability to avoid it and work out for himself some other conception of his art. The late novels are spoiled not by self-consciousness but by his refusal to be as thoroughly self-conscious as he had been earlier. In his late years he lost patience with human diversity and complexity and grew unable to continue doing justice to its endless ramifica-

23. David L. James, "Thackeray's Secondary Fictional World." Ph.D. dissertation, University of British Columbia, 1970.

tions. He more and more tended to fall back on one particular sentimental voice as the last word. At his best he created fictional works of great power because of the self-conscious awareness that no person, not even the omniscient author, deserves that final word.

DAVID BROWNELL

The Two Worlds of Charlotte Yonge

Charlotte Yonge, like every novelist, had two worlds — the one that made her, and the one that she made. Since she was a domestic realist, her created world resembles closely the world in which she grew up. She portrays an aspect of Victorian life not shown by better-known Victorian novelists — growing up in large middle-class High Church families. Yonge's novels offer many insights into Victorian family life. The relationship between her real and created worlds shows still more about Victorian families, as well as something about the nature of the creative process: the virtues of her best novels, which succeed as works of art, and the flaws of her uneven or inferior novels all result from her background.

Both of Yonge's worlds have narrow boundaries. She lived for seventy-seven years (1823–1901) in the village of Otterbourne, Hampshire, four miles south of Winchester. There she lived with her parents until her father died in 1854 and her mother in 1868, and there she took care of her only brother's invalid sister-in-law for twenty-four years. She taught in the village Sunday school for seventy years, and provided religious instruction in the village schools as well. There she edited her magazine for Anglican girls, *The Monthly Packet,* from 1850 to

1893, and there she wrote the two hundred fifty works she published — novels, historical novels, stories of village life, history for children and adolescents, natural history, biographies, and religious instruction books.

Her devout parents, both children of ministers, fearing to spoil Charlotte, never told her that she was clever and attractive. In teaching her, her strict father set high standards and scolded her fiercely when she failed to meet them. Much was demanded of her as the oldest — and, for six and a half years, the only — child. Her handwriting had to be neat in the conventional way — so she was broken of being left-handed. The Fifth Commandment, she was taught, was the most important: any wish of one's parents not prohibited by religion should be regarded as a command. The child should always yield his will to his parents'. Women, as a result of Eve's sin, were inferior in talents to men, and any action taken by a woman without male advice and supervision might lead her to disaster.

During the first thirteen years of Charlotte's life the most exciting events were the Yonges' annual visit to Mr. Yonge's native Devon, where Charlotte could play with her ten cousins and escape the responsibilities of being a strictly regulated oldest child. In Otterbourne she had few playmates, and her brother was too much younger to be a companion. In her loneliness she began imagining playmates — a family of children about whom she told herself stories. Her imagining continued in adolescence, since the family trips to Devon stopped when she was thirteen: Mr. Yonge was devoting his income to building a new church at Otterbourne, under the direction of the new vicar, the Reverend John Keble; also, feeling that the Yonge family had had too many marriages between cousins, he told Charlotte she was now too old to correspond with her male cousins.

Keble, the man whose sermon on "National Apostasy" had begun the Oxford Movement and whose *Christian Year* was the most popular work of religious verse of the age, had a major influence on Charlotte, whom he prepared for confirmation. He reinforced her devoutness and her view of life as religious duty; he strengthened her feeling that she must yield her will to that of others and accept whatever happened to her as the will of God; and he taught her that reserve, which he regarded as a prime poetic virtue, was necessary on important subjects, and that one avoided discussing one's deepest feelings. She thoroughly repressed any adolescent rebelliousness she may have felt, and learned to reject the assumptions of Romanticism: she did not believe that the individual was entitled to achieve his desires against the rules of society and the constraints imposed by duties to others.

In compensation, religion provided an absorbing interest. A friend denied that the lives of members of the Keble circle were "quiet to dullness":

> To those who at that time were their nearest neighbours, their lives were wonderful examples of the self-controlled vivacity of high spiritual existence ... Theology was to them a thrilling interest, and they moved and spoke and thought with unseen presences round them, not physical or fancy-spiritual, but as realizing the angels round about the Throne and the solemn awe of the Throne. In order to be able to think reverently, soberly, and highly about it, all their powers of culture, of insight, of commonsense, of religious observance, and of social interest were to be fully trained and used for the purpose.[1]

Within this framework Charlotte looked for a way to be useful. Her grandmother ran the house, her mother the village charities: apart from her teaching, Charlotte had no job of her own. The two writers she knew — Keble and Marianne Dyson[2] — encouraged her to believe she could do useful work by writing. Without realizing it she had already prepared herself for a career as a writer by her imagined families, by her Boswellian habit of recording conversations during visits away from Otterbourne, by her Christian self-examination, which led her to know herself,

1. Charlotte Anne Elizabeth Moberly, *Dulce Domum: George Moberly: His Family and Friends* (1911; reprint ed., London: J. Murray, 1916), pp. 8–9. Miss Moberly, first head of St. Hugh's at Oxford, will be remembered for her experience when she and a friend, while walking in the gardens of Versailles, found themselves spending their afternoon in the gardens as they had been more than a century earlier. See her *An Adventure.*

2. Miss Dyson, an older woman whom Charlotte met through Keble, was the author of *Ivo and Verena,* a children's book about a heroic youth who converts family and tribe to Christianity in an unconvincing Scandinavian setting. As the title indicates, the book was influenced by de la Motte Fouqué's *Sintram and His Companions,* which was also a favorite of Yonge's. Dyson ran a small boarding school, and she and Yonge corresponded intensively about their pupils and how best to teach them.

and by her observing, writing about, and writing for her school-children as part of her efforts to become a better teacher.

Having been told that her writing was useful, Yonge could regard it as a duty to be done instead of a pleasure better sacrificed. To satisfy her conscience, throughout her life she wrote nonfiction along with her stories; usually she had three works in progress at the same time, of which only one was fiction: she would write a page of each work in turn. Her stories may have offered an escape from her family into an independent life, but she did not acknowledge or recognize this motive: she could not have allowed herself her escape if she had recognized it as an escape. To avoid excluding her family from her created world, she talked out her plots with them during the long period she gave to forming each story. Her father and Keble read through her manuscripts, altering words, phrases, or plot developments they disliked; Yonge, deferring to superior masculine judgment, accepted their emendations with gratitude, though the examples of Keble's help she cites in her tribute to him seem finickin.

The boundaries of her created world are closely related to those of the world Yonge lived in. She usually limits it to the small villages or towns of southwestern England and to the members of the middle and upper classes (servants play no important part). Though characters who are not High Church Anglicans appear — even dissenters — and though they are not presented as evil or infidel, the central figures share Yonge's own religious sentiments.

One boundary of Yonge's created world is established by the subjects that she will not treat. Like Austen, whom she greatly admired, Yonge prefers to let other pens dwell on guilt and misery. She will not study attractive sins or sinners, ministers delinquent in their duty, or subjects such as hereditary insanity which readers with such family problems may find too painful. She will not treat skepticism or problems of faith. She is not interested in industrialization, invention, or social change, though her characters may cope with the consequences of urbanization by raising a new church or burying a new sewer.

Her religious beliefs also limit the ways she views her subject matter. Her Christianity keeps her from seeing any tragedy other than a failure to use one's talents — and those who fail in this way do not achieve the stature of a tragic hero. Even their deaths are not tragic, as signs of repentance allow their survivors at least some hope.

Yonge's world is a moral ecosystem of considerable complexity: every action has a result, and no by-product can be eliminated from the closed system. Every deed sends ripples to the farthest shores of the pond. It is not a simple world; there are no instantaneous conversions or miraculous events. Indeed, Yonge would doubt the possibility of an instantaneous conversion: she is too conscious of the infinite number of small daily efforts a convert would have to make to change ingrained habits before he could lead a Christian life which would meet her exacting standards. If the possibility of individual reform always exists as a means of preventing a character's line of development from leading him to disaster, nevertheless such a conversion is never as sudden or dramatic — as sentimental — as it might be in, say, Dickens. If Yonge had included Eugene Wrayburn in a novel, the reader would understand that even after his marriage to Lizzie he would remain a person whose habits of idleness would make effort difficult and whose snobbish attitudes might occasionally lead him to be embarrassed by his wife. The Christian life is never simple or easy in Yonge's world because her firm grasp on the real world always underlies her religious emotions, and she refuses to idealize the details of life, even at the most solemn moments: when several characters kneel to pray around a deathbed in *The Young Stepmother* (1861), for example, she knows, and records, that after some time had passed, "Fred had grown exhausted with kneeling and had been forced to sit on the floor, and Maurice's voice waxed low and hoarse." [3] Reverence is not diminished by bodily weakness, but cannot be expected to overcome it either.

In Yonge's world details count, and add up. Harriett Mozley, whose novels for children served as a model for Yonge, expressed a basic assumption which Yonge shared: "If we do not accustom our minds to seek truth in detail, and in the small occurrences of

3. *The Young Stepmother* (London, 1861), p. 394.

life, it is in vain to expect we shall be so favoured as to attain it
on a grand scale, or in deep religious views." [4] Yonge builds up
her world through the slow accretion of small daily happenings,
each of which influences the formation of character. As a four-
year-old she taught herself to read from *Robinson Crusoe,* and
perhaps that work shaped her idea of what a story should be:
her works are as full of detail, of day-to-day routine, as Defoe's,
though considerably subtler morally. She imagines her characters
and their setting completely, and her novels offer the reader a
total effect which, like that of a Victorian painting, depends
upon the careful placing in relation to one another of an enormous number of details.

Yonge allows her characters to reveal themselves dramatically,
through action, or, more frequently, through conversation. They
need no explanation on her part, but occasionally she pauses to
analyze or comment on their behavior if she feels the need to un-
derline a contrast or point out an irony resulting from a character's imperfect understanding of himself or another. Her humor
is quiet and usually emerges from observation of her characters
behaving in character: like Austen, she enjoys showing the various ways in which people disguise from others and themselves
their indulgence of their own selfishness. Each incident in her
best works is carefully prepared, and clearly the result of the
characters of those involved; each also leads to further understanding of their personalities and forms the groundwork for
further episodes. Her dialogue is always convincing — never dull
in daily chitchat and never melodramatic in big scenes. Indeed,
when her characters are gripped by strong emotion their reserve
makes them less articulate than usual.

Yonge's characters are her great triumph. Her starting point
in planning most of her novels seems to have been an image of
contrasting characters confronting one another. Like Anthony
Trollope, she considered herself to be less skilled at plot construction than most of her contemporaries; but, again like Trol-

4. *The Lost Brooch: or, The History of Another Month: A Tale for
Young People,* 2 vols. (1841; reprint ed., London, 1848), 1:264. Mozley
was Newman's sister: see Kathleen Tillotson's "Harriett Mozley" in her
Mid-Victorian Studies.

lope, by avoiding elaborate plots she never violates the integrity of her characters to further the plot, as so many other Victorian novelists did. Yonge's people almost never act out of character.

The typical Yonge novel is about a large family of devout High Church principles. Yonge focuses on relationships within the world of the family. Even neighbors hardly figure in these novels, in contrast to such village novels as Martineau's *Deerbrook*. Indeed, the children are expected to find their friends within their family, and those who find a closer friend outside it are regarded as showing an unhealthy taste. Within the family Yonge is more apt to be interested in the children than in their parents, in the daughters than in the sons, in a younger daughter than in the eldest (perhaps because she herself would have preferred not to be the eldest child), and in a daughter who constantly has to struggle to meet the standards imposed on her than in one who is naturally ladylike. *Countess Kate* (1862), a children's story, has as its heroine the little girl most closely resembling its author of all her characters. Kate is clever, shy, lonely, untidy, and noisy, and she usually feels guilty because she is not satisfying adults' expectations. The book offers in purest form a chance to examine a source of tension that animates all of Yonge's best books: while the author remembers vividly the feelings and desires of a child, and identifies emotionally with the child characters who engage her imagination, she has sufficiently accepted her parents' system of values to judge her characters by these standards, and to condemn the characters with whom she sympathizes.

Yonge never questions the lessons she was taught as a child; accordingly her characters have a limited range of possible actions. But often she gives them more chance to develop than she herself had: in many of her stories the child in whom she is most interested is afforded some sort of insulation from parental authority which enables him to mature by carrying responsibility and accepting the consequences of error. The parents may die, go abroad, or be too sick to be consulted. Yonge can then allow her child to resent the restraints imposed on him — a resentment which would be an unthinkable crime if directed against a parent's authority. Even in the absence of parents, however,

a child ought to obey those adults who are in loco parentis —
any Yonge child who disobeys the adult taking care of him
will come to grief.

In those rare cases where a Yonge child resists the parental
will, severe punishment overtakes him: daughters who reject the
family's values by marrying irreligious men or sons who do so
by giving themselves to a worldly way of life are unable to
found families themselves and die fruitlessly. Most severely
punished are daughters who attempt to obtain their own way
by pressuring their parents — and most ill-fated of all are those
who attempt a career unsuitable for a woman. In the early,
rather crude *Henrietta's Wish; or, Domineering* (1850), Henrietta Langford is made to feel guilty of her mother's death because she has urged that vacillating lady to move to a place
where Henrietta and her brother Fred will be with their cousins
— an obvious parallel to a wish of Charlotte's. In *The Clever
Woman of the Family* (1865), Rachel Curtis, Yonge's Emma,
attempts to cure social ills by acting on her own judgment without
the guidance of a man and in opposition to the wishes of her
feeble mother, who would prefer that Rachel do no more than
other young ladies. She becomes the victim of a swindler in a
situation that leads to a child's death; only the love of a good
man redeems her. And worst of all is Janet Brownlow in
Magnum Bonum (1879), who wants to become a doctor: her
reliance on her own judgment leads to her marriage to a quack,
the death of several people, including her own child, and eventually her own death. Yonge dislikes Janet so strongly that she
is unable to be fair to her — which is unusual for Yonge, who,
like Trollope, always at least seems to be fair to her characters
and to allow even the worst of them some virtues.

As these brief summaries suggest, acts of rebellion by daughters against parents are so unthinkable to Yonge that the rare
books in which they occur are deformed by the energy of their
suppression. Yonge, who repressed any such desires she may
have had, had to convince herself that there was no possibility
of escape from the family structure and that the desire to escape
was a crime: the most effective means of convincing anyone that
he has committed a crime is to punish him; the most effective

means of convincing him that his crime is heinous is to punish him severely.

But in the best Yonge novels, where punishment of children who rebel against the family and its standards is only a minor theme, Yonge shows the workings of a large Victorian family with considerable subtlety. In *The Daisy Chain* (1856) the reader becomes thoroughly familiar with the eleven May children and their doctor father; in *The Pillars of the House* (1873), with the thirteen orphaned Underwood children. The details of their daily life are absorbing.

Much of the family's life style in these novels is determined by economic considerations. New strains are put on family finances in a world where, for the first time, 90 percent of the children born will survive infancy.[5] If the boys of the family want to go to university they must win scholarships, and sometimes they suffer from the pressures of fierce competition. Any advantage given one boy may be at a sibling's expense: sending one Underwood son to a better school, away from bad companions, will cost an additional thirty pounds a year, which can be afforded only when one of his older brothers decides to apprentice himself to a trade instead of aiming at university. The Underwood children are able to remain together after the death of their parents only because Felix, the oldest son, gives up his hopes of a university career leading to ordination and lowers himself in the social scale by accepting a job in trade.

In these families financial resources are used without question for the education of the boys, who can use their learning profitably; girls have no potential life outside the household of brother, parent, or husband unless their relatives let them undergo the hard fate of becoming a governess. The older daughters serve as unpaid nursemaids and governesses at home anyhow, because the parents do not have time to take care of everyone. (Even in a small family, Charlotte was her brother's first Latin tutor.)

Economic pressure may lead to sons being urged toward a career in any field where the family can use connections to give him a start. Yonge feels parents should not push children into

5. Duncan Crow, *The Victorian Woman* (London: Allen & Unwin, 1971), p. 278.

careers for which they are not suited — especially the ministry; but if their parents favor the career, the child should regard accepting the decision as his duty.

Another effect of a stretched income is often an enforced lack of privacy. If the entire family gathers in the drawing room in the evening, the cause is less likely to be some Victorian ideal of togetherness than that only one room in the house not already occupied by servants has a fire and light enough to work by. If the entire family must use the same room in the evening, and all their various tasks must be carried out there, mutual forbearance and self-repression are not merely virtues, but necessities.

Another result of the crowding caused by a large family is fierce competition among the children for attention. Each child has to find an acceptable role in the family, a role that brings him recognition, approval, and satisfaction. An almost Darwinian struggle results for enough sunlight and space to grow in. The oldest children in looking for roles define themselves as "the helpful one," "the friendly one," "the dutiful one," or "the beautiful one" (who is usually headed for trouble). Occasionally, despite themselves, they accept the role of "the slow one" or "the clumsy one"; their siblings may endeavor to keep them in such undesirable positions in order to make their own talents more valued. Yonge displays skillfully this jockeying for position. But often the children who are undervalued develop into Yonge's heroes — she feels that whatever promotes humility may be good for the child.

The middle children have to struggle harder for recognition. They tend to be thicker-skinned than their elders, and perhaps more aggressive. The successful ones become "the cleverest one," "the most manly one," or "the most feminine one." Dropouts may become "the difficult one" or "the sickly one." (Yonge is aware that the Victorian invalid can provide roles for two sisters — invalid and nurse.)

The youngest children echo the achievements of the eldest, though the youngest girl may go in for being "angelic" — a pose that wins much praise. Yonge is usually suspicious of children who are unduly pious and suggests that parents should not encourage such behavior by notice and praise.

Modern readers are apt to feel that the children — particularly the daughters — are forced to surrender their very personalities in order to win family approval. Ethel May in *The Daisy Chain,* one of Yonge's most appealing heroines, likes learning Latin and Greek and takes pride in keeping up in these studies with her brilliant older brother; but after a carriage accident causes the death of her mother and the crippling of her oldest sister, she no longer has time enough to keep up her share of tutoring the younger Mays and maintaining the house, and still pursue her studies. Learning is not valued in a lady, and Ethel has been made to feel somewhat ashamed of her Greek: she keeps her learning a secret from outsiders. As a good Yonge heroine she gives up her private pleasure — although she is told she can work on it in her occasional spare moments. But ceasing to keep up with her brother causes her genuine grief.

Ethel's family unite to break her of her clumsiness and untidiness, which are in part the result of being nearsighted but not being allowed to wear eyeglasses (which were believed likely to cause the eyesight to worsen, as well as being unattractive on a lady). With as much effort as "winding up a steam engine to thread a needle," [6] Ethel directs all her mind to altering her habits and becomes the mainstay of the family and her father's confidante — a role she inherited after her sister became engaged since "Ethel was now more entirely the Doctor's own than Margaret could be after her engagement." [7] Victorian fathers occasionally resemble the bull of the herd. Ethel flees the one young man who is intelligent enough to recognize her charms, feeling it her duty to stay with her widower father. She remains his friend and housekeeper in *The Trial* (1864), a sequel dealing with the May family, and in the series of linked novels in which the various families Yonge created make cameo reappearances up through *Modern Broods* (1900), the year before Yonge's death.

Ethel's relationship with her father is an arrangement not uncommon in Yonge's works: when one parent dies, a child is

6. *The Daisy Chain; or, Aspirations: A Family Chronicle* (1856; reprint ed., London, 1882), p. 101.
7. Ibid., p. 317.

promoted to become a replacement, and a consort to the surviving parent. The promoted child, however, never feels fully
secure in his authority and remains a child as well as a parent.
Sons in this position become rather sexless; daughters feel it
almost a duty to flee marriage.

Yonge's characters seem to fear sexual involvement and frequently end up in cross-generational marriages or mock-mar-
riages. Her heroines often marry men a generation older who
have been surrogate fathers to them (as if Esther Summerson
did marry John Jarndyce); her young men cannot marry older
women, but sometimes end up living with them in mock-mar-
riages. Frequently two women or two men end as companions
for life in a relationship Yonge explicitly compares to a marriage.
Usually they seem to be avoiding the responsibilities imposed
by becoming a fully sexed adult.

The modern reader may decide from my summary of *The
Daisy Chain* that Ethel May is fearfully exploited by a society
run by and for males. But she and the other Yonge heroines
find satisfaction in the roles they assume and would not be
comfortable at turning their backs on what they see as their
duty. Ethel has the pleasure of being the most important woman
in the life of a superior man — her father; the interest of being,
in fact if not in theory, the executive of the May family, a position offering the interest of running a household larger than
some small businesses, what with children and servants; and the
challenge of finding a way to build a school and church for
Cocksmoor, a new industrial settlement in the area too far from
existing churches to receive clerical attention. All these roles
and responsibilities contribute to her knowledge that she is
useful and valued in the world, and to the ease that comes from
doing what she believes is virtuous. There is no way in Victorian
England for her to feel it right to pursue her intellectual interests
by escaping and abandoning her family.

Yonge's presentation of family life clarifies aspects of other
Victorian novels, and of the lives of other Victorian novelists
— for example, why Florence Dombey feels she *must* be reconciled with her father, or why Maggie Tulliver, unable either
to be reconciled with her family or to leave and forget them,

can only find a way out of her dilemma through a natural catastrophe and an opera heroine's death. Yonge's picture of the family world makes clearer how the Victorian family could be at once sustaining and imprisoning for a child, supporting him while crippling him for life outside. In some ways her picture of the family life she accepts as right is as frightening as Samuel Butler's attack on it — and her picture seems more accurate and fairer. From Yonge's world one can understand more clearly how much a Victorian could be traumatized either by remaining within the family, as Ruskin did, or by escaping it, as George Eliot and Dickens did.

Yonge herself remained within the family world all her life: she had two periods in which her best works were produced. The first began with *The Heir of Redclyffe* (1853), her first mature novel, published shortly before her father's death, and continues through 1865, with ten important works. A period of ill health followed by nursing her mother during a long last illness led to several unproductive years. Then, with as few family burdens as she was ever to have, Yonge began her second period of major accomplishment with her best novel, *The Pillars of the House,* and her best biography, that of her cousin, the martyred missionary bishop John Coleridge Patteson; both books were written concurrently and published in 1873. A house guest reports that the books ran so parallel that Yonge at lunch one day said, "I have had a dreadful day; I have killed the bishop and Felix [her novel's hero]." [8] In this second period Yonge made her most interesting experiments with the form of the novel and wrote the one novel in which she deals with adult life and marriage, *The Three Brides* (1876), which shows real insight into marital interactions. Thereafter her work gradually weakens: none of her books after 1879 are of even her second-best quality. The liveliest of the later books are those in which she deals with memories of her own childhood or picks up the stories of families she had already created, who were still living in her brain. She retreats into her own past. But some source

8. Ethel Romanes, *Charlotte Mary Yonge: An Appreciation* (London: A. R. Mowbray, 1908), p. 128.

DONALD D. STONE

Trollope, Byron, and the Conventionalities

Despite the seeming oddity of the conjunction, there are interesting reasons for linking the most solidly realistic of the major Victorian novelists, Anthony Trollope, with the most flamboyantly Romantic of nineteenth-century poets, Lord Byron. The specter of Byron haunts Trollope's characters with such frequency as to remind us of the great Romantic's enormous appeal to the youth of Trollope's generation, some of whom, in becoming spokesmen for the Victorian values of their adult generation, had to turn upon their childhood idol with savage force. The standard of reality and the redefinition of the hero and heroic conduct, which many Victorian novelists developed in their writings, are often veiled critiques of their own youthful predilections. For example, when Johnny Eames, who strongly resembles the young Anthony Trollope, is described as knowing "much, — by far too much, — of Byron's poetry by heart," [1] the author is pointing up that flaw in Johnny's character which will cause him grief in The Small House at Allington and The

1. The Small House at Allington, chap. 14. Further references to this work will be given in the text. The dates of the novels, which are noted only when important, refer to the year the book was completed, not published. The Byron text is that of the one-volume Poetical Works (London: Oxford University Press, 1945).

179

Last Chronicle of Barset. When Phineas Finn charges Byron with falsity (*Phineas Finn,* chap. 14), he is speaking for Carlyle, who condemned Byron for lacking sincerity and for being "a dandy of sorrows" and "a sham strong man." [2] For disoriented young men like Johnny Eames or Charley Tudor (in *The Three Clerks*), however, Byron offered a theatrical role, "the character of a Don Juan" (*Small House,* chap. 4), scoffing at social conventions and playing at being in love. Johnny defends his posturing with pseudo-Byronic self-justification: " 'Love is one thing and amusement is another,' he said to himself as he puffed the cigar-smoke out of his mouth; and in his heart he was proud of his own capacity for enjoyment" (*Last Chronicle,* chap. 46).

The lure and danger of Byron, both in his personal life and in the imaginative appeal of his poetry, were such as to be connected in the minds of novelists like Charlotte Brontë with the lure and danger of the creative imagination itself. That the power of the imaginative faculty which called a new world into being could also be linked with heterodox standards of personal behavior frightened the author of *Jane Eyre* into continual acts of penance for the possession of such gifts. It becomes necessary for her heroines, therefore, to suppress their imaginative natures in favor of the restraints of reality, even though it was their author's own intense imagination that called them into being in the first place. Trollope was born in 1815, one year before Charlotte Brontë. They were in their teens, therefore, when the first volume of Thomas Moore's biography of Byron appeared in 1830. This work, more than anything else written about Byron, created the image of the poet-genius which Victorian writers grew up on — and, in many cases, reacted against. "There is something divine in the thought that genius preserves from degradation, were it but true," Charlotte Brontë once wrote; "but Savage tells us it was not true for him; Sheridan confirms the avowal, and Byron seals it with terrible proof." [3]

As was the case with Brontë, Trollope ascribed to his "dan-

2. Quoted in Samuel Chew, *Byron in England* (reprint ed., New York: Russell & Russell, 1965), pp. 250–251.
3. *The Brontës: Their Lives, Friendships, and Correspondence,* 4 vols., ed. T. J. Wise and J. A. Symington (Oxford: Shakespeare Head Press, 1932), 2:210.

gerous mental practice," while a lonely and insecure youth, of imaginary "castle-building" the source of his ability in later years to write novels. Even so, he insisted, his boyhood fantasies were bound "down to certain laws, to certain proportions, and proprieties, and unities. Nothing impossible was ever introduced, — nor even anything which, from outward circumstances, would seem to be violently improbable." Unlike Charlotte Brontë, whose fantasies at times controlled her rather than the reverse, Trollope was always able, he claimed, to impose order on his imagination. "I learned in this way," he asserts, "to maintain an interest in a fictitious story, to dwell on a work created by *my* own imagination, and to live in a world altogether outside the world of my own material life." Trollope described his novels as "shorn . . . of all romance" and noted how in *Rachel Ray,* for example, *he* had "attempted to confine [himself] absolutely to the commonest details of commonplace life among the most ordinary people, allowing myself no incident that would be even remarkable in every day life." [4] But the artistry that conceals imaginative intensity may be as powerful as the artistic impulse which exposes what Arnold called in Byron's case "the pageant of [one's] bleeding heart." Despite the modesty expressed toward his artistic gifts in the *Autobiography,* the insistence that he was no "genius," his "amazing ability" (as his recent biographer notes with regard to Trollope's writing *Doctor Thorne* while on a postal mission to Egypt) "to abstract himself from his surroundings and be lifted by his imagination back into Barsetshire" [5] is proof of the author's imaginative power. The world of *Doctor Thorne,* moreover, was enhanced with romantic values that Trollope refused to see in those Mideastern lands which afforded such possibilities for Byronic description.

Trollope's definition of the artist is far more Romantic than

4. Trollope, *Autobiography,* ed. Frederick Page (London: Oxford University Press, 1950), pp. 42–43; Trollope, *Letters,* ed. Bradford Booth (London: Oxford University Press, 1951), p. 138.

5. James Pope Hennessy, *Anthony Trollope* (Boston: Little, Brown, 1971), p. 167. Other proofs of Trollope's intensely active imagination are his ability to work on two novels simultaneously, to live intimately with his characters, and, as he claimed, to be able to pick up the thread of a work left dangling for years and return to it with his memory still fresh.

the *Autobiography* would suggest, although some of the evidence can be found in it. While he ranked the novelist lower than the poet, Trollope acknowledged that "the lessons inculcated by the novelists at present go deeper than most others." The novelist would not "dream that the poet's honour is within his reach; — but his teaching is of the same nature, and his lessons all tend to the same end. By either, false sentiment may be fostered; false notions of humanity may be engendered; false honour, false love, false worship may be created; by either, vice instead of virtue may be taught. But by each, equally, may true honour, true love, true worship, and true humanity be inculcated; and that will be the greatest teacher who will spread such truth the widest." Trollope's belief in the instructive capabilities of the novelist represents a sublimated expression of the Romantic will to power. In *The New Zealander* (1855) he describes the writer as one to whom it "is given in a certain degree to guide mankind," either for good or for ill. The writer who preaches truthful conduct, "be he poet, historian, romancer, or what not, is the true leader of the people," and the one person capable of delaying, for a time, the decay which Trollope felt must befall England.[6]

This expression of faith in the power of literature is an admission of Trollope's own susceptibilities as a reader. In his lecture in defense of fiction "as a Rational Amusement," Trollope recalls the impact of Mrs. Radcliffe's novels on him and doubts "whether in these practical and unpoetic days there is left, even among the young, enough of the true spirit of romance to comprehend even what was once the effect of these wonderful compositions." "To be too romantic is not the fault of our time," he acknowledges, almost regretfully, and credits the Victorian novelists for having replaced the romantic attitude of his youth with a "manner of looking at life . . . [that] is realistic, practical, and, though upon the whole serviceable, upon the whole also unpoetical rather than romantic." But the novel itself, he observes, evolved out of the desire for "unreal ro-

6. "Novel-Reading," *Nineteenth Century* (January 1879), p. 25; *Autobiography,* pp. 217–218; *The New Zealander,* ed. N. John Hall (London: Oxford University Press, 1972), p. 186. (The echo of Shelley seems curious coming from Trollope.)

mance";[7] and while Trollope's fiction evolved out of a childhood hunger for the ordinary pleasures denied him, a deprivation that enabled him to poeticize domestic bliss as the highest of human pleasures, his literary career was also determined by the ambition to attain the sort of artistic power, without the artistic license, which Byron more than anyone else had displayed earlier in the century. In a famous passage of the *Autobiography* he admits to a lifelong desire to " 'hew out some lump of the earth,' and to make men and women walk upon it just as they do walk here among us, — with not more of excellence, nor with exaggerated baseness, — so that my readers might recognize human beings like to themselves, and not feel themselves to be carried away among gods or demons." [8]

The story of Trollope's childhood suffering, his awareness of being cut off from his parents and despised by boys his age, is well known, and his biographers have seen in the contrast "between the outward assurance [of his manner] and the inward uncertainty; between the seeming asperity and the actual tender-heartedness; between the rough insensibility of gesture and the delicate transparency of mind," the effects of his "tormented childhood." His friend T. H. Escott laid special stress on Trollope's "recurrent moods of indefinable dejection and gloom," the underlying melancholy which Trollope attributed to his pessimistic nature.[9] One thinks of the traumatic effects of Byron's unhappy childhood, his sense of being scorned because of his physical infirmity, and how he too had a dual capacity for high spirits and melancholy, which found dual expression in his writings in sparkling satire and morbid self-analysis. Trollope's recommendations to aspiring writers that they avoid intruding their personality into their work and that they resist the temptation to satire are reminders of his Victorian determination to escape the demands of the ego. Byron's satire was morally blunted, he claimed, because he could not help giving the im-

7. "On English Prose Fiction as a Rational Amusement," *Four Lectures,* ed. Morris Parrish (London: Constable, 1938), pp. 104, 112, 117.
8. *Autobiography* p. 145. The words in single quotes are Hawthorne's.
9. Michael Sadleir, *Trollope: A Commentary* (reprint ed., London: Oxford University Press, 1961), pp. 339–340; Escott, *Anthony Trollope: His Work, Associates, and Literary Originals* (London: John Lane, 1913), p. 170.

pression that he was avenging "himself upon a world that had injured him" rather than aiming to correct the abuses of his age. Trollope also warned himself against indulging in the excesses of satire and romance, which had led his mother to "the pitfalls of exaggeration." Mrs. Frances Trollope possessed humor and compassion in abundance, gifts which her son inherited and learned to express in a more restrained manner than she had in her writings. In contrast to his morbidly self-indulgent and intellectually wasted father, Trollope's mother overflowed with romantic emotions and energies. "She raved . . . of him of whom all such ladies were raving then," her son recalled, "and rejoiced in the popularity and wept over the persecution of Lord Byron." [10] Trollope's portraits of romantically inclined women, such as Lady Glencora Palliser, and of self-suffering men, such as Louis Trevelyan, contain more than a hint of his parents.

Byron's family background was far more disorganized than Trollope's, but the novelist may well have compared himself to the poet who had also been a student at Harrow, where some of Trollope's unhappiest childhood experiences occurred, and had shared his own tutor, Henry Drury. Trollope's sporadic periods of study at Harrow and Winchester took place at the time when, as Henry Taylor noted, "enthusiasm for Lord Byron's impassioned but often rather empty moroseness and despair . . . had passed away from some of the more cultivated classes, and found, perhaps, its surest retreat in the schoolboy's study and in the back shop." [11] As a mildly dissolute young postal clerk in London, Trollope was proud of his acquaintanceship with Shakespeare, Scott, and Byron; and no doubt, like Johnny Eames, he considered himself then "a deep critic, often writing down his criticisms in a lengthy journal which he kept" (*Small House,* chap. 14). He wrote a critique of Byron's disciple, Bulwer-Lytton, about this time[12] and may also have written quires of romantic verse, poor in expression but rich in poetic feeling, like his seemingly prosaic heroine, Miss Mackenzie.

The immediate cause of Trollope's change from an unhappy

10. *Letters,* p. 266; *Autobiography,* pp. 33, 22.
11. Quoted in Chew, *Byron in England,* p. 253.
12. Bradford Booth, *Anthony Trollope: Aspects of His Life and Art* (Bloomington: Indiana University Press), pp. 141–142.

clerk, uncertain of his future, to a respected and self-regarding official and novelist was his reassignment to Ireland. Here Trollope received the fellowship he had craved and a pleasant taste of power as a postal official. Here, too, Trollope's imagination was stirred by the sight of so much decay and wasted energy — reminders of his own past life. The result was a novel, *The Macdermots of Ballycloran,* which powerfully describes the collapse of an Irish family, partly as a result of their uncontrollable passions. ("The Irish character is peculiarly well fitted for romance," he writes in the *Autobiography;*[13] and Ireland offered Trollope the chance in several novels to warn against the excesses of romantic feeling.) His mother's *Domestic Manners of the Americans* had been a monumental demonstration of how a frustrated adventure could be salvaged by being written up, and *Childe Harold's Pilgrimage* had provided the evidence that one's personal sufferings and wanderings could be transmuted to art. The Byronic danger, which Browning as a young poet faced as surely as Trollope did as an aspiring novelist, was that one might not be able to put a sufficient distance between oneself and one's subject matter. To achieve an illusion of authorial neutrality became Trollope's and Browning's goal; and while the Victorian poet's magnificent use of the point of view of his characters has always inspired praise, it is only recently that Trollope's own adroit use of the differing angles of vision of his characters to achieve comic or tragic effects has been appreciated. The various characters who adopt Byronic attitudes or perform Byronic actions, for example, are generally the victims of their own highly colored self-projections, not projections of Trollope's own views as he wrote. But there were sufficient similarities between Byron and Trollope in outlook and writing habits to force the novelist to chastise the Byronic streak in himself, at times with vindictive energy.

The points of similarity beween the two men are noteworthy. They were both compulsive travelers who preferred a cosmopolitan sense of values to the insular prejudices of their native land. Trollope's remark that "one is patriotic only because one is too small & too weak to be cosmopolitan," his attack on en-

13. *Autobiography,* p. 156.

forced conscription ("a man should die rather than be made a soldier against his will"),[14] and his dislike of martial glory are expressions of an independent spirit which, like Byron's, refused on occasion to bend to the dictates of convention. At least three of his works were refused or criticized on the grounds of impropriety. (One of them, "A Ride across Palestine," involves a woman who disguises herself as a man, like the page Kaled in *Lara.*) Both writers spoke against cant wherever they saw it, and both indulged in self-deprecation as if to chastise their own weaknesses. The mood of ironical self-deflation in Trollope's *Autobiography* is reminiscent of the self-criticism indulged in by Byron in his journals. Byron's notorious speed as a writer was more than matched by Trollope's; and both men defended their haste on the grounds of being more truthful as well as more inspired as a result. In *The Bertrams* Trollope extols Byron's letters as the finest models of the genre. One might mention here that Byron's work was criticized by Keats for being a description of what he observed rather than what he imagined, the very charge that reviewers habitually used against Trollope.[15] Byron's declared aim in *Don Juan*, "to show things really as they are," might also serve to characterize Trollope's goal in early works like *The Three Clerks* (1857) and *The Bertrams* (1858) or in later novels like *The Eustace Diamonds* (1870) and *The Way We Live Now* (1873):

> for I avow,
> That till we see what's what in fact, we're far
> From much improvement with that virtuous plough
> Which skims the surface, leaving scarce a scar
> Upon the black loam long manured by Vice,
> Only to keep its corn at the old price.

(12.40)

14. *Letters,* pp. 118, 117.
15. R. H. Hutton (Trollope's favorite reviewer of his works) contrasted Trollope's reliance on observation with Charlotte Brontë's capacity to draw from her imagination to Trollope's disadvantage. See David Skilton, *Anthony Trollope and His Contemporaries* (London: Longman Group, 1972), and the *Critical Heritage* volume devoted to Trollope (ed. Donald Smalley [London: Routledge and Kegan Paul, 1969]).

Byron's attacks on the materialistic values and hypocritical attitudes in his society were sufficient to enable Victorian writers to see him as their ally in behalf of noble and truthful conduct: Ruskin, for example, admired his devotion to justice, Arnold his assault on the fortress of philistinism, Meredith his refusal to "pander to the depraved sentimentalism of our drawing-rooms." [16] Trollope, while respectful of the aim, was mistrustful of the results. Like Byron, Trollope saw in man's essential frailty, his inability to "hear the devil plead, and resist the charm of his eloquence" (*The Three Clerks*, chap. 9), the cause of the sorry state of his society. But where Byron and his heroes stood aloof from the world, refusing to "yield dominion of his mind / To spirits against whom his own rebell'd" (*Childe Harold*, 3.12), Trollope and his protagonists often reconcile themselves to the faulty ways of the world. "His novels," Michael Sadleir observes, "are almost without exception novels of a conflict between individual decencies and social disingenuities," and often enough the protagonist "yields to the pressure or to the temptations of convention." [17] This makes for tragic effect, on occasion, but the concession to social values is also sometimes necessary. In *The Last Chronicle of Barset,* for example, Trollope, instead of using the almost Byronically proud and antiworldly figure of Josiah Crawley as a moral standard to measure the world of Barset-shire by, uses the world as a means of putting this noble but flawed figure into perspective. Trollope allows his comfortable, worldly pastor Mark Robarts the right to "question whether the man was not served rightly by the extremities to which he was reduced. There was something radically wrong within him, which had put him into antagonism with all the world, and which produced these never-dying grievances" (chap. 21). In a Trollope novel a figure like Manfred or Childe Harold becomes a lesson in self-destructive pride and can be saved only by the enjoyment of worldly goods, as in Crawley's case, or by marriage

16. Meredith, *Letters,* 3 vols., ed. C. L. Cline (London: Oxford University Press, 1970), 1:297. Arnold's essay on Byron appeared in the second series of *Essays in Criticism.* For Rushkin's views of Byron see Chew, *Byron in England,* pp. 235–236, 267–268.

17. *Trollope,* pp. 153–154.

to someone like Violet Effingham, as in Lord Chiltern's case (in *Can You Forgive Her?*).

The area of human concern where Trollope unequivocally calls for truthful conduct is that of human love relations; and here one must disagree with the critic of Trollope who, noting correctly enough that "no one has ever confused Trollope with Byron," maintains that he was "not a romantic figure, and . . . idyllic love did not affect him profoundly." [18] The love stories in his novels are not, in the main, concessions to popular taste. They are exhibitions, most of the time, of lovers' capacity for integrity which establish a necessary contrast to the demonstrations of frailty and culpability in the other figures in his novels. (The integrity of the lovers in *Lady Anna* was such as to outrage public taste.) Here Trollope shows the influence of Byron sublimated into the Victorian myth of domestic happiness. One must credit Charlotte Brontë, not Trollope, with converting the proud and dedicated slave-maidens of Byron's romantic tales into loyal Victorian housewives. Henry James paid special tribute to the "clinging tenderness" and "passive sweetness" [19] of Trollope heroines like Lucy Robarts and Mary Thorne, whose one function in life is to cling to the men they love. They cling very prettily, for the most part, and show a becoming Jane Eyre-like pride of spirit on occasion, although their devotion, Trollope indicates in the cases of Emily Hotspur and Lily Dale, can harden into obstinacy or self-destructiveness. Love on such women's part is displayed in terms of adoration. The heroine frequently rejects a more qualified suitor because she cannot bow to him as to a god, and she often admits (as does Mary Masters in *The American Senator*) that she "would sooner marry a man I loved, though I knew he would ill-use me" (chap. 59). There are instances when a woman like Lady Glencora abandons the "romance of her life" — her devotion to a man she knows "to

18. Booth, *Anthony Trollope,* p. 166. For Booth, Trollope's love stories were mostly written in "deference to the taste of the lending library" and are thus a sign of "superficiality" on his part. Cf. Ernest Baker on this matter (*The History of the Novel* [reprint ed., New York: Barnes & Noble, 1963], 8:144).

19. "Anthony Trollope," reprinted in *The Future of the Novel,* ed. Leon Edel (New York: Vintage Books, 1956), p. 256.

be a scapegrace, and . . . liked . . . the better on that account"
(*Can You Forgive Her?* chap. 69) — in favor of the "rich
reality" of a life with Plantagenet Palliser.[20] But the tenacity
with which women like Gertrude Woodward or Hetta Carbury
or Emily Hotspur cling to inferior men proves the cynical admission Trollope made to Escott "that in love affairs women
are generally without discrimination." (Gertrude's devotion to
her criminal husband, Alaric Tudor, may have suggested the
similar case involving Mrs. Bulstrode's loyalty to her husband
in *Middlemarch.*) One remembers the words of one of Byron's
slave heroines, who muses that women can "love whom we
esteem not." [21]

Examples of such devotion among Trollope's male characters
are less frequent, although there is the wonderful exception of
Ontario Moggs in *Ralph the Heir.* The bootmaker's romantic
son is devoted to Polly Neefit with a fervor that his sister, who
reads him "the story of Juan and Haidee" and implores him to
"be true to her; — if it's for twenty years" (chap. 48), obviously
approves. (The most theatrical examples, and the truest, of romantic passion sometimes occur among such lower-class or vulgar characters in Trollope as Aunt Greenow in *Can You Forgive
Her?* or Tom and Gertrude Tringle in *Ayala's Angel.*) The
chivalric devotion among Trollope's older male figures toward
the women they love frequently goes unrewarded, although
Plantagenet Palliser is a conspicuous example where gentlemanly virtues prove more potent in the end than Byronic im-
petuosity and good looks. Another sublimated version of Byronic
devotion involves the intense dedication of sisters to brothers
in Trollope. Kate Vavasor's devotion to her vicious brother
George, Charlotte Stanhope's machinations in behalf of idle
Bertie Stanhope, or Mrs. Harold Smith's efforts to save her
brother, Sowerby, from ruin are examples of such relationships
which show the woman's loyalty to a worthless man. On occasion, however, Trollope satirizes the aspirations to Byronic devotion on the part of Mrs. Dobbs Broughton, who imagines

20. *Autobiography,* p. 183.
21. Escott, *Anthony Trollope,* p. 207; *Sardanapalus,* 1.2.645.

herself "with suicidal hands, destroy[ing] the romance of her own life," yet fears lest "some poet did not immortalize her friendship in Byronic verse" (*Last Chronicle,* chap. 51).

Trollope's younger male figures have a tendency to be weak under pressure, especially in matters of love; and Trollope admits the impossibility of heroic action among men in novels like *Ralph the Heir* and *The Eustace Diamonds.* Since men must act in the world, their capacity for integrity becomes dulled, while women, whose duty it is in life to *be* rather than do anything, can maintain high standards of moral purity. As Lady Fawn reasons in *The Eustace Diamonds,* "a man out in the world had so many things to think of, and was so very important, that he could hardly be expected to act at all times with truth and sincerity" (chap. 46). Men may play at being Don Juans and then repent, as in the case of Harry Clavering or Paul Montague or John Caldigate; but their tyranny over women is such that even the exaggerated double standard which the bigoted Madame Staubach upholds in *Linda Tressel,* and which Trollope here deplores, is not so very far from the Byronic (and Thackerayan) male-female distinctions that one often finds in the novels:

> Such women seem to think that Heaven will pardon that hardness of heart which it has created in man, and which the affairs of the world seem almost to require; but that it will extend no such forgiveness to the feminine creation. It may be necessary that a man should be stiff-necked, self-willed, eager on the world, perhaps even covetous and given to worldly lusts. But for a woman, it behoves her to crush herself, so that she may be at all points submissive, self-denying, and much-suffering. (Chap. 1)[22]

Remove the religious sanction from this account of men and women and we are back in the realm of Byron's Don Juans and corsairs, whose names are "link'd with one virtue, and a thousand crimes." In Trollope, however, that "one virtue" — fidelity in love — is sometimes missing too.

22. Among the several homilies in *The Small House at Allington* which strain toward a Byronic cynicism of tone is the following: "But men are cowards before women until they become tyrants; and are easy dupes, till of a sudden they recognize the fact that it is pleasanter to be the victimiser than the victim, — and as easy" (chap. 14).

Trollope frequently inserts a male protagonist with Byronic tendencies and features who compels attention from others in the manner of one of Byron's "Fatal Men" [23] into his realistic narratives. Sometimes the man must be expelled, as in the case of George Vavasor or Ferdinand Lopez, while on other occasions the man is allowed to prosper, as in the case of Daniel Thwaite. The imperious Luke Rowan in *Rachel Ray* (1863), for example (the novel Trollope claimed to have "shorn of all romance"), is described as "conceited, prone to sarcasm, sometimes cynical, and perhaps sometimes affected. It may be that he was not altogether devoid of that Byronic weakness which was so much more prevalent among young men twenty years since than it is now" (chap. 4). Walter Marrable, the dark, swarthy young man (in *The Vicar of Bulhampton,* 1868) who has "received much injury" in his life and whom Mary Lowther prefers to the gentlemanly Harry Gilmore, is distinguished by "a certain ferocity" of expression (chap. 13). The most ferocious and tyrannical of these Byronic figures is George Vavasor (of *Can You Forgive Her?* 1864), who sports in addition to the requisite dark hair and glowering eyes a Byronic wound — in his case an ugly facial scar. Trollope's ability to put a Byronic convention to new and interesting use is exhibited in the tailor hero of *Lady Anna* (1871): "Daniel Thwaite was swarthy, hard-handed, black-bearded, — with a noble fire in his eyes, but with an innate coarseness about his mouth which betokened roughness as well as strength" (chap. 10). Thwaite has the dilated nostrils, slightly parted lips, and commanding expression which typify the physiognomy of a Lara; but by transposing the Byronic model to the lower classes, Trollope anticipates D. H. Lawrence's attempt to make romantic supermen out of working-class men.

The Byronic males whose energy is seen as a necessary component of the society they marry into appear less frequently in Trollope, however, than the Byronic figures whose individualist values, or lack of them, pose threats to their well-being and, in extreme cases, to the society they prey upon. There are at least

23. See Mario Praz's colorful account of the Byronic "Fatal Man" in *The Romantic Agony,* trans. Angus Davidson (reprint ed., London: Oxford University Press, 1970), chap. 2.

four categories into which such males fit, although the men often share characteristics of more than one Byronic type. (In Byron the protagonist often exhibits all four traits.) These are the Don Juan figure, the romantic adventurer, the man of destiny, and the defier of convention; and Trollope's feelings toward each of the types is as ambivalent as his attitude to Byron himself. The Don Juan posture is an affectation adopted by displaced clerks like Charley Tudor and Johnny Eames to give a semblance of poetic meaning and entertainment to their lives, or by bored young men with time on their hands like Bertie Stanhope in *Barchester Towers* or Jack De Baron in *Is He Popenjoy?* Trollope treats such posing with comic indulgence. A more complicated case is that of Eames's successful rival for Lily Dale's hand, Adolphus Crosbie, who tries to disguise his shabby, and ultimately self-punishing, conduct by telling himself that the "world" has ever treated its Don Juans like "curled darlings" (*Small House,* chap. 25). Trollope underscores the passive nature of his would-be Don Juans by showing how they are manipulated by the women they think they are winning over and how, moreover, they crave punishment for their offense. (Crosbie wishes that Lily had "a dozen brothers" who would avenge her.)

In his important attack on Byron in 1834, Henry Taylor described Byronic heroes as "creatures abandoned to their passions, and therefore weak of mind. Strip them of the veil of mystery and the trappings of poetry, resolve them into their plain realities, and they are such beings as, in the eyes of a man of masculine judgment, would certainly excite no sentiment of admiration, even if they do not provoke contempt." [24] Taylor might have been describing Trollope's aim in *An Eye for an Eye* (1870), the anti-Byronic tragic novel he wrote immediately after his great anti-Byronic comic novel, *The Eustace Diamonds.* Fred Neville is no "villain," Trollope protests, "simply a self-indulgent spoiled young man who had realized to himself no idea of duty in life" (chap. 12). Neville repeatedly disguises his wasteful actions as romantic "adventures"; and he deludes him-

24. "Preface," *Philip Van Artevelde* (London, 1834), p. xviii. Trollope thought highly of this "long, sustained and precious song" (*New Zealander,* p. 175).

self into thinking that, after he has seduced the Irish girl who is passionately devoted to him, the Irish priest Father Marty "might be persuaded to do for him something romantic, something marvelous, perhaps something almost lawless" (chap. 14).

Other versions of the adventurer in Trollope appear as commercial pirates. The Corsair is transformed into Ferdinand Lopez (in *The Prime Minister*, 1874), "a self-seeking, intriguing adventurer, who did not know honesty from dishonesty" (chap. 24), but who, like Byron's pirate, is capable of love. Melmotte, in *The Way We Live Now* (1873), is the apotheosis of the adventurer, a swindler whom everyone respects because he is so successful at his game. "There's nothing like being a robber," one of his admirers declares, "if you can only rob enough" (chap. 32). Trollope had already shown how commercial fraud is disguised by romantic rhetoric in an early novel, *The Struggles of Brown, Jones, and Robinson* (1861), showing "the way in which we all live" (chap. 1). "The groundwork of advertising is romance," observes the central figure in that book. "It is poetry in its very essence. Is *Hamlet* true? . . . Advertisements are profitable, not because they are believed, but because they are attractive" (chap. 10). Melmotte wins the admiration of the reader, at times, for his mixture of romantic persiflage and self-awareness. Knowing that his days as a swindler are numbered, he looks "up at the bright stars," Trollope notes in a passage of comic brilliance laced with Byronic wistfulness:

> If he could be there, in one of those unknown distant worlds, with all his present intellect and none of his present burdens, he would, he thought, do better than he had done here on earth. If he could even now put himself down nameless, fameless, and without possessions in some distant corner of the world, he could, he thought, do better. But he was Augustus Melmotte, and he must bear his burdens, whatever they were, to the end. He could reach no place so distant but that he would be known and traced. (Chap. 62)

Trollope's variation on the Byronic figure ostensibly manipulated by fate is best seen in Louis Trevelyan in *He Knew He Was Right,* which I will discuss separately. Byron's most vivid case of the individual who feels "a power upon me which withholds,

/ And makes it my fatality to live" is Manfred (1.2.23–24), whose manifestation of self-will leads to a desire for self-oblivion. The most extreme case in Trollope of a man driven by a "Fury" and "conscious of being so driven" is that of George Vavasor (*Can You Forgive Her?* chap. 56). Trollope is more sympathetic to such figures lacking in self-control as Owen Fitzgerald in *Castle Richmond,* Burgo Fitzgerald in *Can You Forgive Her?* and Mountjoy Scarborough in *Mr. Scarborough's Family.* Such characters genuinely cannot control their self-destructive impulses. In most instances, however, Trollope shows that a figure like Trevelyan, who blames fate for his misfortunes, has only himself to blame. "Fate is a good excuse for our own will," as Byron pungently observed in *Don Juan* (13.12), deflating the very notion of the "Fatal Man."

It is as the defier of convention that the Byronic character exerts perhaps its most suggestive and dangerous influence on Trollope and his characters. The description of Johnny Eames's boyish desire for license gives way to accounts of individuals living in such violation of convention that they cut themselves off from the human community, where true happiness flows in Trollope. The path of exile taken by Childe Harold is followed by such diverse figures as the Stanhope family in *Barchester Towers,* Lord Lovel in *Lady Anna,* and the Marquis of Brotherton in *Is He Popenjoy?* all of whom prefer the relaxed moral climate in Italy.[25] The lure of bohemianism is best expressed by Madame Goesler in *Phineas Finn* (1867): "it is so pleasant to feel oneself to be naughty!" she tells Phineas, "there is a Bohemian flavour of picnic about it which, though it does not come up to the rich gusto of real wickedness, makes one fancy that one is on the border of that delightful region in which there is none of the constraint of custom, — where men and women say what they like, and do what they like." "It is pleasant enough to be on the borders," Phineas replies (chap. 72) — and Trol-

25. For an interesting description of the Stanhopes see Robert Polhemus, *The Changing World of Anthony Trollope* (Berkeley: University of California Press, 1968), pp. 39–45. Trollope's accounts of the marriages between Lord and Lady Lovel (*Lady Anna*) and the Sir Hugh Claverings, incidentally, bear a resemblance to the popular versions of Byron's marriage.

lope's sympathies are of a borderline nature. He could show the need to defy conventions in a late novel like *Dr. Wortle's School* (1879). ("It is not often that one comes across events like these, so altogether out of the ordinary course that the common rules of life seem to be insufficient for guidance," says Dr. Wortle. "To most of us it never happens; and it is better for us that it should not happen. But when it does, one is forced to go beyond common rules"; chap. 7.) But he worries about the effects of flouting convention in the persons of Crawley or Trevelyan or Julius Mackenzie (in "The Spotted Dog," 1870). Mackenzie's desire to assert himself in contempt of the "conventional thraldom of so-called 'gentlemen' " results in a life of perpetual self-degradation. The Editor who narrates this moving tale observes at the end, after Mackenzie has been driven to suicide: "This was the upshot of his loud claims for liberty from his youth upwards; — liberty as against his father and family; liberty as against his college tutor; liberty as against all pastors, masters, and instructors; liberty as against the conventional thraldom of the world!" [26] Trollope's individualistic streak was no doubt the reason that he told Kate Field that "nature intended me for an American rather than an Englishman." Yet he preferred "to be a bad Englishman . . . than a good American," [27] perhaps because of the security from the threats of unconventionality and excessive self-reliance which his more orderly society provided.

The destructive potential of the human will, self-alienated from human ties and social conventions, is the main subject of *He Knew He Was Right* (1868).[28] This brilliant novel and *The Eustace Diamonds* (1870) are the key masterworks in Trollope showing the dangerous effects of Byronic defiance when translated out of the world of corsairs and Laras and into the real world. But where Trollope treats Byronic attitudes with devastating satire in *The Eustace Diamonds,* he shows the tragic effects

26. "The Spotted Dog," *Editor's Tales* (London, 1870), pp. 236–237, 319.
27. *Letters,* p. 118.
28. See Polhemus, *Changing World,* p. 163; J. Hillis Miller, *The Form of Victorian Fiction* (South Bend, Ind.: University of Notre Dame Press, 1968), pp. 123–139.

of stiff-necked pride in the account of Louis Trevelyan's pursuit of humiliation and self-destruction. The initial cause of Trevelyan's decline into madness is the attention paid to his wife by an elderly acquaintance who enjoys being mistaken for a Don Juan by her husband. Both husband and wife feel that the other should apologize — he for being suspicious, she for refusing to obey his orders — and the unwillingness of either to give way reinforces each one's opinion that he alone is right in this matter. The desire to be proved right drives Trevelyan to wish that the adultery he has feared might happen in fact. "They who do not understand that a man may be brought to hope that which of all things is most grievous to him," Trollope remarks, "have not observed with sufficient closeness the perversity of the human mind" (chap. 38). From refusing to believe in his wife, Trevelyan grows to disbelieve in everyone and everything. Self-exiled to Italy, he gloats to his former best friend that it has been his "study to untie all the ties; and, by Jove, I have succeeded. Look at me here. I have got rid of the trammels pretty well, — haven't I? — have unshackled myself, and thrown off the paddings, and the wrappings, and the swaddling clothes. I have got rid of the conventionalities, and can look Nature straight in the face" (chap. 92).[29]

But what can Trevelyan see other than that he has caused his own ruin? Mad as he is, believing himself "to have been the victim of so cruel a conspiracy among those who ought to have been his friends" as well as the victim of "the terrible hand of irresistible Fate," Trevelyan still has glimmers of the truth. He half suspects "that he had brought his misery upon himself by being unlike to other men" (chap. 84). Even so, he relishes the sense of his tragic role: "He almost revelled in the idea of the tragedy he would make" (chap. 45). Once again Trollope's use of a character's point of view is displayed to great effect. It is Trevelyan, not Trollope, who conceals the real ignominy of his position by investing himself with the trappings of Othello and Lear. Trollope had seen in his father an example of self-inflicted

29. See A. O. Cockshut, *Anthony Trollope: A Critical Study* (reprint ed., New York: New York University Press, 1968), for a suggestive account of the "destructive" effects of freedom on Trevelyan and others (p. 172).

suffering, and he had presented a related kind of suffering in Josiah Crawley, who is deluded into considering himself a latter-day St. Paul. Perhaps the best precedent in Byron for this kind of destructive pride is Lara, "a stranger in this breathing world" and a "thing of dark imaginings," who has been the instrument of his own moral degradation:

> But haughty still, and loth himself to blame,
> He call'd on Nature's self to share the shame,
> And charged all faults upon the fleshly form
> She gave to clog the soul, and feast the worm;
> Till he at last confounded good and ill,
> And half mistook for fate the acts of will.

Trollope expunges the criminal element from Byron's self-doomed figures but retains the

> . . . strange perversity of thought,
> That sway'd him onward with a secret pride
> To do what few or none would do beside.
>
> *Lara,* 1.18

The pursuit of a tragic role in life is a self-defeating enterprise in Trollope, an expense of spirit in a waste of shame. To offset the gloomy aspect of the Trevelyan sections of *He Knew He Was Right,* Trollope employs three romantic counterplots, plus a comic subplot, to show the advantages of "self-abnegation" in a love relationship. The bohemian journalist Hugh Stanbury, for example, learns to find in domestic life the romantic dreams of his youth. Charles Glascock's gentlemanly conduct in behalf of others prompts his American fiancée, who abandons her countrymen's ethic of self-reliance, to note that "the heroes of life are so much better than the heroes of romance" (chap. 85). Dorothy Stanbury's love for Brooke Burgess, on the other hand, enables her to mature from an overly passive maiden to a young lady with a newly won sense of self-importance. Even the comical-pathetic clergyman Gibson provides a parody of Byronic attitudes. Wavering between the desire to play Don Juan to both of the French sisters and to escape their matrimonial nets, Gibson

ascribes his weakness to "some mysterious agency [that] inter-
feres with the affairs of a man and drives him on, — and on, —
and on, — almost, — till he doesn't know where it drives him"
(chap. 65).

It is this comic-pathetic side of the imitation of Byron which
Trollope stresses so successfully in *The Eustace Diamonds*.
Lizzie Eustace is the comic counterpart of Louis Trevelyan:
obstinate, self-willed, defiant of conventions. She, too, by her
perverse refusal to understand and act on the truth, cuts herself
off from the respectable world. But Lizzie is so shallow a creature, so lacking in identity, that hers may be called the comedy
of a lack of will, just as Trevelyan's is the tragedy of an abundance of will. Trollope frequently shows how a character's over-
responsiveness to Byronic or Shakespearean description of
behavior colors his own personality. "Half at least of the noble
deeds done in the world are due to emulation, rather than to the
native nobility of the actors," he declares in *The Last Chronicle
of Barset* (chap. 31). Lizzie's defect is that she is all performance: half of her life consists of the absorbing of lies and the
other half of the mangled transmission of them. "She liked lies,"
Trollope says of her, "thinking them to be more beautiful than
truth. To lie readily and cleverly, recklessly and yet successfully,
was, according to the lessons which she had learned, a necessity
in woman and an added grace in man" (chap. 79).

From a novelist who can provide sympathy for even his worst
villains, the vitriol lavished on so comparatively harmless a being
seems odd at first glance. Lady Eustace is compared at various
points in the novel to "a witch whistling for a wind, and ready to
take the first blast that would carry her and her broomstick somewhere into the sky" (chap. 35); to Tennyson's Vivien, the se-
ductress of Merlin; and to Spenser's Duessa, who finally appears
"soiled, haggard, dishevelled, and unclean" (chap. 76) to the
young man she has hoped to entrap. Part of the reason for his
hostile attitude undoubtedly lies in the fact that in this, the third
volume of the series of political novels he was working on,
Trollope wished to show that just as romantic feeling is debased
by Lizzie into Byronic posturing, so too has politics been turned
into a rhetorical game by mountebank politicians like Daubeny-
Disraeli. *The Eustace Diamonds* enabled Trollope to mount an

indirect attack on Disraeli, whose novel *Lothair* had recently appeared (and received perhaps the highest price paid for a work by a major Victorian novelist). Trollope's description of Disraeli's fiction in the *Autobiography* sounds very much like an account of Lizzie's romantic fantasies: it contains the "flavour of paint and unreality," "the glory of pasteboard," "a wealth of tinsel," "the wit of hairdressers," "the enterprise of mountebanks," "a feeling of stage properties, a smell of hair-oil, an aspect of buhl, a remembrance of tailors, and that pricking of the conscience which must be the general accompaniment of paste diamonds." [30] When Trollope observes of Lizzie that "there was no reality about her" (chap. 61), he is comparing her to one of Disraeli's characters — a point that is underscored when he doubts "whether paste diamonds [instead of her famous necklace] might not better suit her character" (chap. 17). It is "poetic" justice that she ultimately is captivated by the rhetorical audacity of the Jewish adventurer, Emilius: the incarnation of Disraeli himself. "Presuming, as she naturally did, that something of what he said was false," Trollope remarks, "she liked the lies. There was a dash of poetry about him; and poetry, as she thought, was not compatible with humdrum truth" (chap. 73).

The connection between lies and poetry is at the center of Trollope's satire — a satire directed against himself and his reader, as well as against Lizzie Eustace. The plot involving a stolen necklace allowed Trollope to poke fun at the popularity in the mid-Victorian period of mystery novels, containing romantic villains and elaborately contrived plots.[31] Trollope's determination to keep no secrets from his reader is a violation of the code of the genre, as is his reminder to the reader that he is presenting reality instead of fiction. Trollope's insistence that the novel be "truthful" if its readers are to learn lessons in realistic conduct is perhaps his central article of artistic faith. But even the most realistic of fictions remains a fiction. It was Trollope's goal, as he noted in the *Autobiography,* to pass the creations of his imagination off as human beings like his reader. It was the sense of power as a writer, and the forcibleness of his suscepti-

---

30. *Autobiography,* pp. 259–260.
31. See Henry Milley, *"The Eustace Diamonds* and *The Moonstone,"* *Studies in Philology* 36 (1939), pp. 651–663.

bilities as a reader, that prodded Trollope into becoming a writer; and the satire in *The Eustace Diamonds* is directed at the creative and the absorptive processes alike. This is the novel, after all, where Trollope stages a performance of his own unproduced play, *The Noble Jilt,* so that it can be attacked on the grounds of improbability.

Lizzie Eustace's belief in the existence of corsairs because she has read Byron is a naive and eloquent testimony to the powers of art. For Lizzie, every man she meets is a potential Conrad, possessing "that utter indifference to all conventions and laws which is the great prerogative of Corsairs" (chap. 44). When her necklace is stolen, she admires the most eligible candidate for the role of corsair and thief, Lord George; and she considers that his disposal of his accomplice, Patience Crabstick, by dropping "the girl overboard, tied up in a bag, . . . would [be] a proper Corsair arrangement" (chap. 62). (Lord George, to her disappointment, turns out to be innocent and brutally honest.) She feels that there would "be a certain charm in being . . . mastered" by such a man (chap. 51); and she imagines that being "hurried about the world" with him, "treated sometimes with crushing severity, and at others with the tenderest love, not to be spoken to for one fortnight, and then to be embraced perpetually for another, to be cast every now and then into some abyss of despair by his rashness, and then raised to a pinnacle of human joy by his courage — that . . . would be the kind of life which would suit her poetical temperament" (chap. 44). Even Lizzie's romantically derived masochism is a sham masochism. She lacks real emotional feeling. Poetry for her, whether from Byron or the Bible, is a matter of intoxicating words only; and when Emilius makes his floridly worded proposal to her, she finds in it "a taste of the Bible" mixed with the flavor of the "Juan and Haidee" episode (chap. 79). Lady Eustace reappears, somewhat subdued in character, in *Phineas Redux* and *The Prime Minister*. In the latter book her corsair finally appears in the shape of the adventurer Ferdinand Lopez, who dares her "to escape with [him and her fortune] from the cold conventionalities, from the miserable thraldom of this country bound in swaddling clothes." "Mr. Lopez," she replies, "I think you must be a fool" (chap. 54).

One should keep in mind that it is the response to Byron, rather than Byron himself, which is satirized in *The Eustace Diamonds*. And one should not forget that Trollope's master in the deprecation of Byronism was Byron himself, who was able in *Don Juan* to mock the sort of "Poeshie" (as he once called it) which had inspired such popularity. Trollope's descriptions of fashionable life in his novels contain echoes from the English cantos of *Don Juan*. (Lady Dumbello, née Griselda Grantly, might have stepped out of Byron's satire; and there is even a suggestive description of a fox hunt in *Don Juan*.) Trollope's personal respect for Byron at this period is evident in a letter written two months before he began *The Eustace Diamonds* in which he dismissed Harriet Beecher Stowe's famous attack on the poet as the most "outrageous piece of calumny — in the real sense of the word — . . . ever published." [32]

In three late novels, *Is He Popenjoy?* (1875), *Ayala's Angel* (1878), and *Mr. Scarborough's Family* (1881), Trollope once more employs Byronic figures and attitudes for part of his subject matter, but his treatment of them is mellower than in the past. The would-be Don Juan, Jack De Baron, and the dissolute Marquis of Brotherton are both allowed an element of poignancy. Like Trollope's other Byronic defiers of convention, the marquis exiles himself to Italy; but he must eventually face the meaninglessness of his existence: "It had been the resolution of his life to live without control, and now, at four-and-forty, he found that the life he had chosen was utterly without attraction" (*Popenjoy,* chap. 53). In *Ayala's Angel* Trollope describes an elderly artist living in defiance of all conventions in Rome ("Conventions are apt to go very quickly, one after another, when the first has been thrown aside"; chap. 17) who threatens to cast off his son for wanting to live in conventional domestic bliss in England. The central figure of this charming book is a bohemian artist's daughter, who dreams of an "Angel of light" whom she can adore in the manner of one of Byron's slave-maidens. Her angel materializes in the figure of a satirically minded, red-haired "Angel of the earth." Reality is invested with romance; and Colonel Stubbs, Ayala's high-spirited angel, speaks in favor of both values: "I

32. *Letters,* p. 247.

don't mind a little Byron now and again," he concedes, "so there is no nonsense" (chap. 18).[33]

It is in one of Trollope's last novels, *Mr. Scarborough's Family,* however, that he paid the fullest tribute to the power of Byronic romance and acknowledged publicly at last his own relish of authorial power. Old Scarborough's defiance of justice and truth would be a self-punishing moral offense in *Orley Farm* or *The Eustace Diamonds*; yet Scarborough gets his way again and again without feelings of remorse. Like a romantic plot maker, he creates alternate versions of the truth in order to mystify and fool the world. He has two legally valid sets of marriage certificates, one made before and one after his elder son's birth, so that he can apply the laws of primogeniture to whichever son is worthier of inheriting his large estate. Each son seems an expression of the Byronic polarities of romance and satire: Mountjoy, who has the features of a corsair, is extravagantly self-destructive, while Augustus is cynical and vindictive. In a sense they are his literary creations as well as his sons. Scarborough's doctor sees a decidedly "romantic" quality in him: "he has within him a capacity for love, and an unselfishness, which almost atones for his dishonesty," he declares. "And there is about him a strange dislike to conventionality and to law which is so interesting as to make up the balance" (chap. 53). Scarborough makes a Byronic defense of his actions to his principled lawyer:

> "You don't understand the inner man which rules me, — how it has struggled to free itself from conventionalities. Nor do I quite understand how your inner man has succumbed to them and encouraged them."
>
> "I have encouraged an obedience to the laws of my country [Grey replies]. Men generally find it safer to do so."
>
> "Exactly; and men like to be safe. Perhaps a condition of danger has had its attractions for me." (Chap. 19)

"One cannot make an apology for him," the doctor admits after Scarborough's death, "without being ready to throw all truth

33. See Ruth apRoberts, *Trollope: Artist and Moralist* (London: Chatto & Windus, 1971), pp. 191–197.

and morality to the dogs. But if you can imagine for yourself a state of things in which neither truth nor morality shall be thought essential, then old Mr. Scarborough would be your hero" (chap. 58). The key word here is "imagine": put into the real world, Scarborough and his excessively individualistic standards would subvert social harmony, but set within the realm of romance, where all things are permissible, he becomes a romantic hero. A romantic demon existed in most of the major Victorian novelists; that in the thirty-five years of his writing career so obviously "realistic" a writer as Trollope devoted so much attention to the exposure of romantic illusions proves that the demon was never fully exorcised. In old Scarborough Trollope allows his romantic sensibilities full rein at last. At the end, it is true, Scarborough chooses to revert to the truth with regard to the inheritance of his estate before, like Prospero, breaking his wand forever. But in the meantime, he enables Anthony Trollope to exhibit his fascination with Byronic romance and, in so doing, to assert his own artistic power; and the novel allowed him, within sight of his own death, to dare the conventionalities.

RICHARD C. STEVENSON

Comedy, Tragedy, and the Spirit of Critical Intelligence in *Richard Feverel*

George Meredith's pronouncements on the nature of comedy can be both a help and a hindrance to understanding the world of his fiction. The famous *Essay on Comedy,* along with the cryptic "Prelude" to *The Egoist* and passages in a number of the poems, has provided readers with a variety of critical touchstones useful in assessing the novels. A point often overlooked, however, is that only one of Meredith's works — *The Egoist* — is ever referred to in these extrafictional commentaries, and then only indirectly in the "Prelude." The "Prelude" confirms what is already evident from the subtitle and the novel itself: *The Egoist* is a "Comedy in Narrative" close in spirit to the comedy of manners that Meredith brilliantly analyzes in the *Essay.*

But when one moves beyond novels like *The Egoist* or *Evan Harrington* which fall more or less neatly within the generic limits of the *Essay* and other commentaries, the generally accepted critical predisposition to view the world of a Meredith novel as essentially comic may, in some cases, *create* problems of interpretation rather than solve them. This is most true in the novels that take a somber or "tragic" direction. The hero of *The Tragic Comedians,* for example, is described by one recent critic as

205

being "handed over to the Comic Muse" because he falls short
of the "nobleness" required of the tragic hero in Meredith's 1887
poem, "The Two Masks." [1] It is certainly true that Alvan, the
hero, remains a flawed character and that there are comic aspects
to his history — that would seem to be part of Meredith's point.
But to imply that such a history can be dealt with adequately
under the aegis of the "Comic Muse" is, I think, to narrow the
range of the novel unnecessarily. What Meredith actually suggests about Alvan's career, which is based upon the life of
the brilliant German Social Democrat, Ferdinand Lassalle, is
summed up at the work's end, after the hero has died in a dual:
"The characters of the hosts of men are of the simple order of
the comic; not many are of a stature and a complexity calling for
the junction of the two Muses to name them" (15:200).[2] Meredith's meaning here seems clear: a simple generic distinction does
not suit the "complexity" of the world of Alvan and his betrothed, Clotilde, and hence the novel's title.

  Much the same may be said about the story of Richard and
Lucy in *The Ordeal of Richard Feverel*. Joseph Warren Beach,
who established the contention that the comic spirit makes the
"chief distinction" of Meredith's fiction,[3] solved the difficulty of
the somber elements in the novel by dividing it into two parts:
the tragedy of Richard and Lucy and the comedy of Sir Austin
and his System. Beach then proceeded, logically enough, to de-
vote his discussion of comedy to the latter. More recent critics
have seen the fallacy in this selective approach and have recognized and dealt with the anticomic elements in the novel. But
repeatedly these same critics have returned to Beach's basic
premise — *Richard Feverel* is or ought to be essentially comic
— and have treated the novel as comedy manqué. J. B. Priestley,
for example, says that "*Richard Feverel* is presented as a comedy, and has a tragic ending thrust upon it, quite arbitrarily." [4]

  1. I. M. Williams, "The Organic Structure of *The Ordeal of Richard
Feverel,*" *Review of English Studies,* 18 (1967), 18.
  2. This and all subsequent quotations from Meredith's fiction are
taken from *The Works of George Meredith,* Memorial Edition, 29 vols.
(New York: Scribners, 1909–12).
  3. *The Comic Spirit in George Meredith* (New York: Longmans,
Green, 1911), p. 1.
  4. *George Meredith* (New York: Macmillan, 1926), p. 145.

Among more recent critics, Joseph C. Landis has argued that the failure of many of Meredith's novels is due to their "violation of Meredith's comic formula and the resulting forced mating of incompatible elements destructive of the aesthetic unity of the work[s]." *Richard Feverel,* we are told, "is marred by a similar distortion of the formula": "the suffering of the major figures in the novel . . . [is] a violation of aesthetic propriety." [5] John W. Morris, in "Inherent Principles of Order in *Richard Feverel,*" makes essentially the same point: "Richard's suffering destroys the previously established comic decorum of the work." [6] Morris's main authority for what constitutes this decorum, however, is not the "formula" of Meredith's *Essay* but the "generic archetype" of New Comedy. I. M. Williams, as a final example, begins his essay on *Richard Feverel* by defining Richard as a comic hero but ends with the observation that he is "more than comic": "the reader is forced to feel a sympathy which takes him too close to the character to leave him free at the end of the novel to make the objective estimate which is necessary to the author's comic purpose." [7]

It seems to me that those who take this view of *Richard Feverel* have transferred notions of decorum derived from stage comedy intact to the novel, without adequate recognition of the fact that the novel is a radically different — and more flexible — form of literary art. Meredith's *Essay,* it is worth recalling, is primarily a discourse on the theater, not a generic theory of fiction. "The narrow field, or enclosed square" (23:44–45) that Meredith describes as the province of the comic dramatist in the *Essay* is not necessarily the province of Meredith the novelist. And further, as Robert Scholes and Robert Kellogg have pointed out in *The Nature of Narrative,* "the decorum of separate tragic and comic formulations had given way by the nineteenth century to a powerful new impulse [in novelists] to find a common vehicle which would unite the neoclassical realism of social type and the romantic realism of unique individuality. The novel's great virtue lay in finding a way to combine the tragic concern

5. "George Meredith's Comedy," *Boston University Studies in English,* 2 (1956), 27, 29.

6. *PMLA,* 78 (1963), 335.

7. Williams, "Organic Structure," p. 29.

for the individual with the comic concern for society." [8] Scholes
and Kellogg remind us that this point sums up the main lesson
of Erich Auerbach's *Mimesis*; it also sums up one of the main
virtues to be found in *Richard Feverel*. To treat Meredith's experiments with mutigeneric techniques in this novel as a breach
of comic decorum is, as Gillian Beer has acutely observed in
commenting upon the Morris essay, "to flatten and resolve precisely what is energetic and equivocal in Meredith's handling of
plot. Like Thackeray in *Vanity Fair,* Meredith is not just repeating well-known literary forms, nor even composing variations on them; he invokes them as emblems, as possible but
limited ways of looking at his world. He discards them as his
characters move into experiences not within the compass of, say,
Menander's comedy. He counterpoints literary patterns against
life." [9]

It is not my purpose, however, to claim that such a "counterpoint" makes the *Essay* and other commentaries irrelevant to the
anticomic portions of novels like *Richard Feverel, Rhoda Fleming,* or *The Tragic Comedians*. Rather, what I find to be of first
importance in the *Essay* is a prevailing attitude that lies behind
genre or "literary pattern," a quality central to the comic spirit
and at the same time antecedent to it in all of Meredith's art. It
is this attitude that, for purposes of convenience, I shall call the
spirit of critical intelligence.[10] This is the same primary critical
spirit which Ramon Fernandez had in mind when, in his 1926
essay, "Le message de Meredith," he noted that "Meredith . . .
nous convainc bientôt que l'exercice de l'intelligence est indis-
pensable, non seulement pour la pleine compréhension, mais
encore pour la parfaite *realisation* de la vie, que l'on vit plus
intensément et mieux à proportion qu'on est plus lucide." [11]

8. *The Nature of Narrative* (New York: Oxford University Press,
1966), pp. 230–231.
9. *Meredith: A Change of Masks* (London: Athlone Press, 1970), p.
16.
10. I am indebted here to Norman Kelvin, who in *A Troubled
Eden: Nature and Society in the Works of George Meredith* (Stanford:
Stanford University Press, 1961) notes that "what Meredith really meant
by 'common sense' was critical intelligence" (p. 103).
11. *Messages,* 1st ser. (Paris: Librairie Gallimard, 1926), p. 128.

The premium that Meredith places on lucidity, on seeing life clearly, steadily, and whole, is a characteristic that is of the essence to tragic as well as to comic art. For all their differences, *Oedipus Rex* and *Tartuffe* are alike in that they are informed with a profound commitment to the "exercise of intelligence" in the struggle against the forces of self-ignorance. And because Meredith feels free in his fiction to move from the comic to the tragic implications of this struggle, it seems to me that the role played in his art by the spirit of critical intelligence — or "common sense" — is a more reliable basis for assessment of such matters as character, point of view, and structural unity, particularly in the "problem" novels, than the generic distinctions that have traditionally so preoccupied his critics. What I propose to do first in this paper, then, is to define Meredith's notions of humane sanity and rational balance, particularly as they are developed in the *Essay* in relation to the work of Molière, Meredith's master in the art of common sense. Then I shall return to *Richard Feverel,* the most important of the problem novels, to illustrate how an understanding of the characteristic Meredithian tension between the true spirit of critical intelligence and various sophistic and perverted uses of intelligence can aid in assessing the world of his fiction, including the transitions from comedy to tragedy which have disturbed so many readers.

In the *Essay,* when Meredith wishes to illustrate clarity and steadiness of vision he turns repeatedly to Molière: "The source of his wit is clear reason: it is a fountain of that soil; and it springs to vindicate reason, common sense, rightness and justice" (23:17). Indeed, at times one has the feeling that but for the grace of Molière and the fragments of Menander Meredith would have given up the entire enterprise for lack of examples of the pure comic. And it is precisely in this guise — as the quintessence of the "school of stately comedy" (23:9) — that Molière presents an illuminating standard by which to examine Meredith's notions of "clear reason," first as they coincide with Molière's tactics within the boundaries of comedy, and then as they contrast when Meredith moves beyond these limits.

The anonymous *Lettre sur la comédie de l'Imposteur* provides

some interesting correspondences between the theoretical position of Molière and that of Meredith in the *Essay*. The *Lettre* appeared in 1667 in defense of *Tartuffe,* which had been banned
as a result of pressure exerted on Louis XIV by religious con-
servatives. The authorship of the pamphlet has been the subject
of some critical dispute, but it may quite possibly have been
written by Molière himself.[12] In any case, the second part of the
Lettre contains a useful analysis of his theory of comedy, one
which, along with the rest of the pamphlet, became a standard
appendix in editions of Molière and would have been readily
available to Meredith. According to this analysis, the source of
the ridiculous is to be found in any departure from sound sense:
"Le ridicule est donc la forme extérieure et sensible que la providence de la nature a attachée à tout ce qui est déraisonnable,
pour nous en faire apercevoir, et nous obliger à le fuir. Pour
connoître ce ridicule, il faut connoître la raison dont il signifie
le défaut, et voir en quoi elle consiste. Son caractère n'est autre,
dans le fond, que la convenance." [13] For Molière, then, *raison* is
a loaded term — "understanding, perceptiveness, sensitivity, balance," as one critic has defined it[14] — a term very close to
Meredith's use of "common sense."

The argument of the *Lettre* continues: if *raison* is manifested
in a sense of harmony and fitness — "la convenance" — then
"le ridicule consiste dans quelque disconvenance [et] il s'ensuit
que tout mensonge, déguisement, fourberie, dissimulation. toute
apparence différente du fond, enfin toute contrariété entre actions qui procèdent d'un même principe, est essentiellement
ridicule" (4:564). And in the familiar peroration of Meredith's
Essay it is this same *disconvenance,* an essential incongruity or
disharmony resulting from men's dishonesty to others and to
themselves, that is seen as the true subject of the "unsolicitous
observation" of the comic spirit:

12. For arguments in favor of Molière's authorship, see René Robert,
"Les commentaires de première main sur les chefs-d'oeuvre de Molière,"
Revue des sciences humaines, 81 (1956), 19–49. For arguments against
Molière's authorship, see J. D. Hubert, *Molière and the Comedy of
Intellect* (Berkeley: University of California Press, 1962), pp. 106–108.
    13. *Oeuvres de Molière* (Paris, 1878), 4:560.
    14. Paul Lauter, *Theories of Comedy* (Garden City, N.Y.: Doubleday,
1964), pp. 143–144.

Whenever they wax out of proportion, overblown, affected, pretentious, bombastical, hypocritical, pedantic, fantastically delicate; whenever [the Comic Spirit] sees them self-deceived or hoodwinked, given to run riot in idolatries, drifting into vanities, congregating in absurdities, planning short-sightedly, plotting dementedly; whenever they are at variance with their professions, and violate the unwritten but perceptible laws binding them in consideration one to another; whenever they offend sound reason, fair justice; are false in humility or mined with conceit, individually, or in the bulk — the Spirit overhead will look humanely malign and cast an oblique light on them, followed by volleys of silvery laughter. (23:47)

In short, both Molière and Meredith place the highest premium on common sense and the knowledge of self and society that the term implies; both, in turn, see a departure from this norm as a self-betrayal into absurd conduct, conduct which is signaled by the incongruity of men "at variance with their professions." The similarity of these views is not surprising; Molière and Meredith are alike in their sympathy with the classical tradition that stresses reason and moderation. It could be argued, in fact, that the offhand remark put in the mouth of Socrates by Plato in the *Philebus* — that the comic or ridiculous originates in self-ignorance[15] — provides us with the rationalist basis for the views of both writers. But what is finally of most importance here is what becomes of the theory in practice: what may be revealed by looking at Meredith and Molière as practitioners, respectively, of narrative and dramatic art.

There is one aspect of Molière's technique that is of special interest to an examination of the rationalist bias in Meredith's fiction; this is Molière's use of the *raisonneur,* or spokesman for common sense. Cléante in *Tartuffe,* Chrysalde in *L'école des femmes,* Philinte in *Le misanthrope,* Ariste in *L'école des maris*[16] — all of these characters play roughly similar roles in that they dramatize a moderate and sane point of view in con-

15. *Philebus,* no. 48.
16. For discussion of the *raisonneur* in Molière, see G. Michaut, *Les luttes de Molière* (Paris: Librairie Hachette, 1925), pp. 227–229; W. G. Moore, *Molière: A New Criticism* (London: Oxford University Press, 1964), pp. 143–144.

trast to the antics of men of deformed reason like Orgon and
Arnolphe. The *raisonneur* is also a familiar figure in Meredith's
fiction — Austin Wentworth in *Richard Feverel,* Merthyr Powys
in *Sandra Belloni,* Gower Woodseer in *The Amazing Marriage,*
Vernon Whitford in *The Egoist,* to name a few. Besides their
reasonableness, however, these figures share another trait: they
are all more or less uniformly predictable and dull. The reason
for this is that in both Meredith and Molière the real artistic and
moral interest is found less in the rational men than in the figure
who is *déraisonnable,* who illustrates a violation of the "unwritten
but perceptible laws binding [us] in consideration one to another," and who shows where that violation leads. It is these
figures, as J. B. Priestley has put it, who "are so much more vital
and arresting than the characters who are right." [17] Yet the man
who is "right" is also present for a clear purpose: he helps to
keep our eyes set clearly on the norm that is being violated. As
W. G. Moore has pointed out, Molière's *raisonneurs* "ensure
symmetry and roundness of comic presentation. Excess is the
more distinguishable if its opposite is exhibited at the same time.
Sense shows up nonsense, sobriety offsets bad temper. To insist
that one should be 'sage avec sobriété' is a piece of rather flat
moralizing unless and until it is put in contrast to a man doing
the precise opposite." [18]

To limit ourselves to the rational men, however, as Priestley
and Moore do when referring to this figure, is to ignore what is
for me the most interesting aspect of the question, the strategic
role played by the *raisonneuse.*[19] It is an aspect of which Meredith himself was fully aware: "Comedy lifts women to a station
offering them free play for their wit, as they usually show it,
when they have it, on the side of sound sense. The higher the
Comedy, the more prominent the part they enjoy in it" (23:14).
For Meredith, Célimène of *Le misanthrope* is the epitome of the
comic heroines whose wit is "on the side of sound sense": "Célimène is a woman's mind in movement, armed with an ungo-
vernable wit; with perspicacious clear eyes for the world, and a

17. *George Meredith,* p. 123.
18. *Molière,* p. 74.
19. Priestley does note later, in another context, that "woman is the
ally of the Comic Spirit" (*George Meredith,* p. 129).

very distinct knowledge that she belongs to the world, and is most at home in it. She is attracted to Alceste by her esteem for his honesty; she cannot avoid seeing where the good sense of the man is diseased . . . He is only passively comic. Célimène is the active spirit" (23:21–22). When we turn from Philinte to Célimène, then, or from Cléante to Dorine in *Tartuffe*,[20] we find common sense characterized in a manner that clearly is "vital and arresting." The role of the heroine in Meredith's fiction is linked even more consistently than in Molière to the spirit of critical intelligence, and no critic has ever been moved to object to Lucy Desborough, Clara Middleton, or Carinthia Jane Kirby as being "dry sticks." [21] But to mention these figures is also to begin to raise some important distinctions between the role of critical intelligence in the art of Molière and in that of Meredith — between dramatic art that remains strictly within the bounds of comedy and narrative art that ranges both within and beyond the "narrow field, or enclosed square" of the comic dramatist.

A major point of difference may be seen at once in the fact that Molière's commonsensical women tend to arrive on stage with their intellect fully formed: Célimène's "perspicacious clear eyes for the world" are at work from the moment of her first appearance. Such is generally not the case with Meredith's women. Typically, the heroine of a Meredith novel must undergo a painful re-education in order to overcome her inherited views of self-effacement; it is only through innate intelligence and a developing ability to see things as they are and as they should be that she may eventually assume a role in relation to her male counterpart approaching that of Célimène to Alceste. This process of education — education leading away from the sentimental and uncritical notions of the world and men that most of Meredith's heroines initially hold — is experienced by such level-headed young women as the Princess Ottilia in *The Adventures of Harry Richmond,* Aminta Farrell in *Lord Ormont and His Aminta,* and Carinthia Jane in *The Amazing Marriage.* In each of these novels the heroine comes to act as a rational foil to the irrational excesses of, respectively, Harry Richmond, Ormont,

20. Meredith describes Dorine as "common-sense incarnate" (23:14).
21. Priestley's term for Meredith's "philosophical heroes" (*George Meredith,* p. 124).

and Fleetwood. In *The Egoist* this pattern is repeated no less than three times, and in each case Sir Willoughby Patterne's arrogance and utter lack of rational perspective are highlighted by a woman's discovery of her own intelligence. By the time the Egoist has joined his hand with Laetitia Dale's at the novel's end, he has met his match in a wife who is to become not only resident *raisonneuse* at Patterne Hall but also Willoughby's sole chance of salvation from his love of self.[22]

Although the process by which Constantia Durham, Clara Middleton, and Laetitia Dale gain their wisdom is a painful one, *The Egoist* remains a "Comedy in Narrative" as Meredith intended. More typical of the range of Meredith's fiction is *Richard Feverel* — more typical because in it he tries to go in so many directions at once: farce, comedy, romance, and tragedy[23] are all important components of this extraordinarily ambitious first novel. Here one can see the artistic impulses that led to more somber works like *Rhoda Fleming, The Tragic Comedians,* and *One of Our Conquerors,* as well as to comic narratives like *Evan Harrington* and *The Egoist.* As for the heroine of *Richard Feverel,* Lucy Desborough is a spiritual sister to Molière's *raisonneuses* in that her intuitive common sense illuminates the perverted reason of the Feverels, father and son; she is unlike Molière's heroines in that she must suffer anguish and finally death in her futile efforts to transform the promptings of her intelligence into action. It seems to me that in a case like this a critical approach limited to notions of comedy is, finally, an inadequate instrument with which to assess Meredith's art. The part played by Lucy in *Richard Feverel* helps to demonstrate not only the comic implications of the role of critical intelligence in Meredith's fiction but also the potentially tragic result when reason is flouted for too long.

22. For an extended treatment of Laetitia Dale's role, see my "Laetitia Dale and the Comic Spirit in *The Egoist," Nineteenth-Century Fiction,* 26 (1972), 406–418.

23. I use the terms "tragic" and "tragedy" in a loose sense, meaning approximately what Northrop Frye has suggested by the terms "low mimetic or domestic tragedy" (*Anatomy of Criticism* [1957; reprint ed., New York: Atheneum, 1965], p. 38).

When she is described on the banks of the river just before the opening of the "Ferdinand and Miranda" chapter, Lucy is a "daughter of Earth," one of Meredith's natural women. Like many of the heroines who were to follow (Ottilia, Renée, Clara, Aminta, and Carinthia are all most at home in natural settings), Lucy is in perfect harmony with her surroundings in this scene and at peace with herself. She is set against an opulent background of "green-flashing" water, "lilies, golden and white," and meadowsweet hanging "from the banks thick with weed and trailing bramble" (2:116).[24] Identified with Earth, she is the possessor of a unified personality, a balanced embodiment of Meredith's triad of blood, brain, and spirit. True common sense for Meredith involved this same synthesis of human powers, the control and interdependence of mind and emotion that he depicted in "The Woods of Westermain":

> Blood and brain and spirit, three
> (Say the deepest gnomes of Earth),
> Join for true felicity.
> Are they parted, then expect
> Some one sailing will be wrecked.
> Separate hunting are they sped,
> Scan the morsel coveted.
> Earth that Triad is: she hides
> Joy from him who that divides;
> Showers it when the three are one
> Glassing her in union.[25]

These lines act as a gloss not only on Lucy but on the fragmented personalities that inhabit Raynham Abbey and Belthorpe Farm as well. It is, of course, Sir Austin and Richard who progressively harden their corrupted intelligence and consequently part the triad, who out of egoism and self-ignorance allow blood,

24. In chap. 42 (chap. 46 in the original version), "Nature Speaks," Richard thinks that he smells meadowsweet in the Rhineland forest and thus Meredith links the early scenes in which Lucy predominates with Richard's later—and temporary—return to natural common sense.

25. *The Poetical Works of George Meredith,* ed. G. M. Trevelyan (London: Constable, 1912), pp. 201–202.

brain, and spirit to come into conflict and thus finally condemn
Lucy to shipwreck and death.

A significant feature of Lucy's personality, one which recalls
Noorna bin Noorka in *The Shaving of Shagpat* and has obvious
affinities with the comic spirit, is her sense of humor. The laughter
in the novel before Lucy's appearance is of a distorted, unhealthy
quality — Adrian's cynical asides and Richard's and Ripton's
raucous guffaws at the expense of Farmer Blaize. Lucy's laughter
is healthiness personified. Practically her first reaction to Richard
in the "Ferdinand and Miranda" chapter is to laugh at his excessive, sentimental behavior. After he has leaped into the water
to retrieve her lost book, he emerges to claim, "in all sincerity,"
that he does not feel wet:

> Her blue eyes lightened laughter out of the half-closed lids.
> "I cannot help it," she said, her mouth opening and sounding
> harmonious bells of laughter in his ears. "Pardon me, won't you?"
> His face took the same soft smiling curves in admiration of her.
> "Not to feel that you have been in the water, the very moment
> after!" she musically interjected, seeing she was excused.
> "It's true," he said; and his own gravity then touched him to
> join a duet with her, which made them no longer feel strangers,
> and did the work of a month of intimacy. (2:122)

Lucy's good-natured humor is contagious and allows Richard to
see himself as she does. The scene shows not only that Lucy has
common sense but also that Richard, were it not for the System
lurking at Raynham, would be quite capable of benefiting from
her insight.

The freedom and enchantment of the early scenes when Lucy's
instinctive intelligence is ascendant, give way as the novel progresses to an increasing sense of constriction as Richard's single-
minded egotism gains control. By the time Richard hustles her
into Mrs. Berry's house, Lucy is no longer Miranda, but "a captive borne to the sacrifice" (2:239). Richard, in removing Lucy
from the arbitrary authority of Farmer Blaize and Sir Austin,
places her, "like a dutiful slave" (2:253), under his own equally
inplacable brand of authoritarianism. Her good sense directs her
to the more reasonable course: "Your father may be brought to
consent by and by, and then — Oh! if you take me home

now — " (2:255). But Richard's rebellion against the creator of the System in no way frees him from the wrongheaded presumptions fostered by the System itself. His sentimental and self-pitying arguments ("Would you have me lost? . . . I have staked all I have on you" [2:254]) act as a thin veil to his position of power: any resistance on Lucy's part is made to appear as a repudiation of her fidelity. In the end, her only option is "to shut out wisdom; accept total blindness, and be led by him" (2:255).

The transition from comedy to tragedy taking place in this section of *Richard Feverel* is consistent and well prepared for. As various commentators have shown,[26] there are a number of structural, symbolical, and rhetorical devices used by Meredith from the beginning to undercut the novel's comic tone and to foreshadow its outcome — the recurring image of the cypress, the elaborate role played by the infallible System, the narrator's foreboding comments, and the motif of knight errantry are all examples. This last is especially important in tracing the development of Richard's potential for his tragic role as instigator of the disastrous duel with Mountfalcon. Early and late in the novel, Richard's chivalric posturing acts as an index of his egotism and self-ignorance, for Meredith the primary sins against the spirit of critical intelligence. As U. C. Knoepflmacher has said in his discussion of the novel's ending, "by falling back on his notions of heroism and honor, [Richard] escapes the harder task of reconciling himself to his own faults . . . He shows himself to be his father's son, for, like Sir Austin's system, his chivalric notions stem from a fear of confronting man's potential for

26. See especially Gladys W. Ekeberg, " 'The Ordeal of Richard Feverel' as Tragedy," *College English,* 7 (1946), 387–393; William E. Buckler, "The Artistic Unity of 'Richard Feverel': Chapter XXXIII," *Nineteenth-Century Fiction,* 7 (1952), 119–123; Phyllis Bartlett, "Richard Feverel, Knight-Errant," *Bulletin of the New York Public Library,* 63 (1959), 329–340; Charles J. Hill, "Introduction," in *The Ordeal of Richard Feverel* (New York: Holt, Rinehart and Winston, 1964); David E. Foster, "Rhetorical Strategy in *Richard Feverel,*" *Nineteenth-Century Fiction,* 26 (1971), 185–195; U. C. Knoepflmacher, *Laughter and Despair* (Berkeley: University of California Press, 1971), pp. 118–128; Jerome Hamilton Buckley, *Season of Youth* (Cambridge: Harvard University Press, 1974), pp. 63–82. Buckley, while noting "the darker implications of theme or plot" in *Richard Feverel,* makes the important additional point that "the ironic stance of the novelist scarcely prepares us for a final tragedy" (pp. 80–81).

evil." [27] Richard's arrogant and self-deluding playacting, amusing and even at times attractive in the earlier part of the novel, takes on an increasingly serious aspect as he reaches manhood and must assume the responsibilities of husband and father.

What has especially disturbed so many readers, however, is that Meredith appears to provide Richard with a conversion from this theatrical behavior in the late "Nature Speaks" chapter, and then, in J. B. Priestley's phrase, "quite arbitrarily" allows him to take up his heroics where he had left off as the novel moves to its tragic denouement. But to view the failure of Richard's conversion as arbitrary, it seems to me, is to wish to impose a convention on the novel that is at least as arbitrary as the form Meredith chose. The reconciliations and happy endings of romantic comedy, as is so evident in Shakespeare, are typically highly stylized, true to the comic mode that is by nature "arbitrary" in that it rules out the darker side of human experience. If Meredith were to have brought his main characters together in reconciliation at the end of *Richard Feverel,* he would have in large part canceled the increasingly serious implications of the Systematic development of Richard's character and invalidated what David Foster has rightly called "the formative principle of the novel's structure" — its "shift from the comic mode to the tragic." [28] As it is, Meredith uses the "Nature Speaks" chapter to recapitulate the novel's central thematic opposition between nature and artifice, an opposition that he effectively embodies in the style of the chapter itself.

Jacob Korg has recently observed that in *Richard Feverel* the "first function" of the narrative voice "is that of embodying the various states of mind represented in the novel in parodistic styles laced with irony," [29] and this is precisely the technique at work at the beginning of "Nature Speaks." In an extravagant mock-heroic style Richard is compared with Briareus of the hundred hands, "reddening angrily over the sea," and Orestes, "the Furies howling in his ears" (2:498–499). It is a style that neatly sums up Richard's sentimental and rather excessively flat-

27. *Laughter and Despair,* p. 124.
28. "Rhetorical Strategy," p. 195.
29. "Expressive Styles in *The Ordeal of Richard Feverel,*" *Nineteenth-Century Fiction,* 27 (1972), 260.

tering view of himself ("Had he not been nursed to believe he was born for great things?" [2:501]), a style that epitomizes the problem of artifice, as departure from common sense, which the novel is about:

> Far in the West fair Lucy beckons him to come. Ah, heaven! if he might! How strong and fierce the temptation is! how subtle the sleepless desire! it drugs his reason, his honour. For he loves her; she is still the first and only woman to him. Otherwise would this black spot be hell to him? otherwise would his limbs be chained while her arms are spread open to him . . . Ah, happy English home! sweet wife! what mad miserable Wisp of the Fancy led him away from you, high in his conceit? Poor wretch! that thought to be he of the hundred hands, and war against the absolute Gods. (2:498–499)

The ironic narrative tone is maintained for several pages as Richard is depicted with Lady Judith, "adrift . . . on floods of sentiment . . . , over-riding wrecks of Empires!" or affecting a Carlylean melancholy as "he watches the young men of his own age trooping to their work. Not cloud-work theirs! Work solid, unambitious, fruitful!" (2:500–501). Once nature asserts herself in the Rhineland forest, however, Richard's Titanic visions appear to vanish as the narrative makes its transition from a style that is, to borrow a phrase from the *Essay,* "overblown, affected, pretentious, bombastical . . . , pedantic, [and] fantastically delicate" (23:47) to one of direct simplicity: "He was in other hands. Vivid as lightning the Spirit of Life illumined him. He felt in his heart the cry of his child, his darling's touch. With shut eyes he saw them both. They drew him from the depths; they led him a blind and tottering man. And as they led him he had a sense of purification so sweet he shuddered again and again" (2:508).

Thus in this chapter Meredith states the opposition between the values fostered by Sir Austin and those represented by Lucy. What is often overlooked, however, is that there is no guarantee offered here that Richard's "conversion" from the style of the first part of the chapter to the simplicity and humbleness of the last part is in any way permanent. The picture of him as "a blind and tottering man," in fact, suggests something quite different.

Besides specifically preparing for the last lines of the novel,[30] the image stresses Richard's passivity in the scene; the effect is that his "purification" is not self-achieved but comes from without. His return to familiar melodramatic form on receiving news of Mountfalcon's apparent indiscretions in the next chapter, then, seems consistent not with the requirements of romantic comedy but with all that we know about Richard's upbringing and character as they have been portrayed from the outset.

The final scene between Lucy and Richard produces the novel's most affecting contrast between naturalness and artifice, between her humane common sense and his sophistic notions of male honor as he prepares for his duel with Mountfalcon. Lucy's instincts are shown to be consistently sound: with Richard safely returned from the Rhineland, her entire purpose is to keep him with her and the child. When she says, "Come: lie on my heart" (2:537), her impulse is to follow nature, to heal the breach between herself and Richard through sexual union. Although he is strongly moved by Lucy's directness, Richard's response throughout the scene is characteristically centered in his ego: "He must stab her to the heart, shatter the image she held of him" (2:532). His effort to replace this "shattered image" with one even more exalted — that of avenging lover — completes his transition from the romantic and comic hero of the first part of the novel to the tragically misguided husband of the last part, hell-bent on pursuing his Systematized ideal of conduct at any cost: "It was over in an instant. She cried out his name, clinging to him wildly, and was adjured to be brave, for he would be dishonoured if he did not go. Then she was shaken off" (2:537).

It is not difficult to trace Richard's self-ignorance and perverted intelligence to Sir Austin, his System, and the Great Shaddock Dogma. Sir Austin's relation to the spirit of critical intelligence in the novel is made clear by Meredith throughout. While posturing under the banner of scientific humanism, he is intent not on being objective or humane but rather on an elaborate scheme of retribution which he himself cannot fully recognize. In a letter written just after the publication of the novel, Mere-

30. "Have you noticed the expression in the eyes of blind men? That is just how Richard looks, as he lies there silent in his bed — striving to image her on his brain."

dith noted succinctly that "the 'System' . . . had its origin not so much in [Sir Austin's] love for his son, as in wrath at his wife, and so carries its own Nemesis." [31] The System acts as a constant reminder of Sir Austin's betrayal of his own intelligence, his attempt to deify mind through denial of emotion and thus his parting of the Meredithian triad of blood, brain, and spirit. As William Buckler has summed up the case, "The System, having grown out of a mad self-deceit and unrelenting wrath, is implacable: it will not permit the natural affection and paternal love of Sir Austin to grant forgiveness to his son after he has deceived him; and it has so imbued the systematized youth with abstract principles and sentimentality that he cannot fight his father's egoism until all is lost." [32]

Still another illuminating case of corrupted intelligence in the novel is that of Adrian Harley, a character whose sins of omission coincide with the more active intellectual blundering of Sir Austin and Richard to propel events from their comic beginnings to the novel's tragic denouement. Adrian's perverse "objectivity" is developed as a negative complement to his patron's "Science"; where Sir Austin is blind and acts decisively, Adrian sees relatively clearly and is content to look on in amusement. He is used as a means to provide incisive and often accurate judgments, particularly of Sir Austin, but the judgments are always made at a safe distance, in order not to threaten the security of his position. Adrian is both parasite and consummate hypocrite: the chief supporter of the System in public, he is its chief critic in private. For him, humanity is "a supreme ironic procession, with laughter of Gods in the background. Why not laughter of mortals also? Adrian had his laugh in his comfortable corner. He possessed peculiar attributes of a heathen God. He was a disposer of men; he was polished, luxurious, and happy—at their cost" (2:10). The last phrase is important, for in it lies Adrian's condemnation. His view is that of Meredithian critical intelligence gone bad, without the moral sense or humane optimism that assumes man capable of—or worth—redemption. The irre-

31. Meredith to Samuel Lucas, July 7, 1859, *The Letters of George Meredith,* ed. C. L. Cline (London: Oxford University Press, 1970), p. 40.
32. "Artistic Unity," p. 123.

sponsibility of his intellectual negativism, then, acts as a foil to
the spirit of critical intelligence represented by Lucy and embodied in the narrative voice of the novel, a voice that repeatedly
alerts us to the dangers inherent in this perversion of common
sense. Through his broad satiric treatment of the porcine "Wise
Youth," the narrator illuminates Adrian's style of life for what
it is, a constant violation of the "unwritten but perceptible laws
binding [us] in consideration one to another." [33]

The "unwritten but perceptible laws" referred to in the *Essay*
are premised upon acknowledgment of the supreme importance
of the powers of the intellect when tempered by compassion. And
the persistent lack of "consideration" in Adrian's comfortable
cynicism, Sir Austin's demented theorizing, and Richard's self-
indulgent heroic posturing establishes patterns of conduct that
are at once comic and sobering; in this first novel social comedy
is joined with a "tragic concern for the individual" in a manner
that was to become distinctively Meredithian. Meredith works —
and of course not always successfully — to evoke responses that
dramatic tradition has schooled us to keep separate. Like
Molière, he repeatedly dramatizes the tensions that develop in
human relationships between commonsensical behavior (in the
full sense of that term) and its opposites; unlike Molière, in a
number of his novels Meredith pursues this subject to its full
implications, a pursuit in which traditional boundaries between
the worlds of comedy and tragedy simply become irrelevant.

33. See Frank Curtin's essay, "Adrian Harley: The Limits of Meredith's Comedy," *Nineteenth-Century Fiction,* 7 (1953), 272–282, for
an interesting examination of Adrian's role in *Richard Feverel* as the
novel's prime representative of the comic spirit. My quarrel with
Curtin's position is that it fails to recognize adequately how the fact
that Adrian "had no heart" makes his lucidity deeply perverse in
Meredith's view and hence a parody, not a representation, of the comic
spirit. As I have already argued, Lucy Desborough seems to me to be
the most important and interesting touchstone of common sense in the
novel. In addition, as Gillian Beer has observed, Lucy is distinguished in
an essential way from figures like Adrian or the rather pedestrian
raisonneur, Austin Wentworth: "In a book where the characters are
persistently subjected to irony, [Lucy] is the one character who has
remained unsatirized: an ideal being, gentle and strong" (*Meredith: A
Change of Masks,* p. 14).

JEROME H. BUCKLEY

A World of Literature:
Gissing's *New Grub Street*

One of the many luckless authors who drift into George Gissing's *New Grub Street* is a wispy alcoholic named Sykes, who is writing his autobiography, "Through the Wilds of Literary London," for a provincial newspaper. Few readers, Sykes complains, will credit the grim veracity of his narrative: "Most people will take it for fiction. I wish I had the inventive power to write fiction anything like it." Gissing himself could have said the same for much of *New Grub Street,* where he depends far less on inventiveness than on his personal acquaintance with the London literary jungle.

On its appearance in 1891 the novel was both attacked and defended as a grimly "realistic" exploration of the lower depths of an urban society. Yet the "realism" is strictly limited by the author's well-defined interest in his narrow theme: the struggle for survival of the late Victorian man of letters. Gissing does indeed present sharp impressions of mean streets and dreary lodgings, but only as they contain the lives of his defeated protagonists. He shows no interest in the tribulations of the unaesthetic London poor, their resilience, courage, and laughter; he has no concern with social reform or political protest. He is repelled by indigence and its paralyzing hold on the illiterate unaspiring masses, and firmly convinced, like his Henry Rye-croft, that the average man born to penury cannot suffer so intensely as the impoverished artist, for the "intellectual needs" of most Englishmen are merely "those of a stable-boy or a scullery wench." [1] His sympathy in *New Grub Street* lies with the sensitive, gentle Harold Biffen, a novelist celebrating the "ignobly decent," rather than with the drunken wretch whom Biffen abandons in order to rescue a manuscript from a burning hovel. H. G. Wells found Gissing himself lacking in "social nerve" and bumbling in all practical affairs, with "some sort of blindness towards his fellow-men, so that he never entirely grasped the spirit of everyday life." [2] Gissing's "realism," if it is to be called such at all, does not reach far beyond his private and acutely self-conscious experience.

Within the limits of its vision, however, *New Grub Street* achieves a considerable range. Though not precisely a roman à clef, it offers us a veritable Dunciad of the early 1880s, and we may be sure that the aggressive Jasper Milvain, the gossipy Mr. Quarmby, the redoubtable, querulous Clement Fadge, and a score of others had their living counterparts in the new journalism. Whelpdale's *Chit-Chat* with its blatant appeal to the vulgarity of "the quarter-educated" clearly parodies *Tit-Bits,* the penny paper on which George (later Sir George) Newnes built his fortune. *The Study* and *The Wayside* evidently corresponded to familiar monthlies of the time, and *The West End* and *All Sorts,* representing popular weeklies, actually furnished the titles for new periodicals in the later nineties.[3] Milvain talks knowingly

1. *The Private Papers of Henry Ryecroft* (New York: Boni Liveright, 1918), p. 11. See also Gissing's own comments on the lower classes, some of which are less harsh than Ryecroft's, in *George Gissing's Commonplace Book,* ed. Jacob Korg (New York: New York Public Library, 1962), pp. 52–54. Gissing's attitude toward urban realism in fiction is especially relevant: "The outcry of ordinary people that they cannot find interest in novels of common life is intelligible enough. The true interest of such books is in their *workmanship,* of which these readers understand nothing whatever" (p. 53).

2. Quoted by Thomas Seccombe, "The Works of George Gissing," in Gissing, *The House of Cobwebs and Other Stories* (New York: Dutton, 1906), p. xxvi.

3. Gissing himself claimed that these titles had been drawn from *New Grub Street.* See his letter of March 26, 1899, in *The Letters of*

of the demands of the new "market," and Whelpdale projects a quite modern literary agency with a variety of syndicated services. Alfred Yule, on the other hand, insists doggedly on the standards of an old-fashioned pedantic scholarship, and Marian Yule, his daughter and amanuensis, learns to regard herself as a literary machine and to deplore "the hateful profession that so poisons men's minds." From beginning to end we hear much of the jealousies of authors and the scheming rivalries of publishers, of sharp editorial practices, commissioned articles, hostile reviews, rejected manuscripts, ephemeral successes, advertising puffs, libels, and always the drudgery of endless plodding hackwork. And over nearly all of the characters, at some stage of their careers, if not continuously, broods the huge dome of the British Museum, beneath which hosts of readers sit "at radiating lines of desks" like "hapless flies caught in a huge web, its nucleus the great circle of the Catalogue."

Though the detail with which this literary world is evoked is altogether vivid and convincing, the author's attitude toward it is a good deal less than completely objective. Gissing makes no pretense at maintaining the severe disinterest of the thoroughgoing "realist." Many of his opinions and reactions slip naturally enough into the copious shoptalk of his characters, their circumstantial accounts of their projects, aesthetic principles, and journalistic misadventures. But his presence is felt also behind the narrative, and his personal judgment, either as direct commentary or as grim irony, not infrequently obtrudes upon the action. He is not above haranguing the reader with irritable sarcasm:

> The chances are that you have neither understanding nor sympathy for men such as Edwin Reardon and Harold Biffen. They merely provoke you. They seem to you inert, flabby, weakly envious, foolishly obstinate, impiously mutinous, and many other things. You are made angrily contemptuous by their failure to get on; why don't they bestir themselves, push and bustle, welcome kicks so long as halfpence follow, make a place in the world's eye — in short, take a leaf from the book of Mr. Jasper Milvain? . . .

George Gissing to Gabrielle Fleury, ed. Pierre Coustillas (New York: New York Public Library, 1964), p. 122.

It was very weak of Harold Biffen to come so near perishing of
hunger as he did in the days when he was completing his novel . . .
He did not starve for the pleasure of the thing, I assure you.
(Chap. 31)

Gissing seems to be indicting the reader as much as Amy
Reardon when he describes her belated expression of sympathy
for Biffen as "so often the regretful remark of one's friends, when
one has been permitted to perish." We may guess the depth of his
pessimism — outside the fiction — from his complaint, as cheer-
less as a remark by Hardy's little Father Time, that any pleasure
he might have found in observing the antics of a baby was destroyed by "the thought of the anxiety it [was] costing in the
present, and of the miseries that inevitably [lay] before it." [4] And
we may see a like morbidity in the novel itself in the author's
identification of a literary hack and his threadbare wife ("They
had had three children; all were happily buried") or even in the
naming of an indigent surgeon ("I was christened Victor —
possibly because I was doomed to defeat in life"). We are left in
little doubt about Gissing's outlook, his loyalties, or the direction
of his antipathies.

Written with such prepossessions, *New Grub Street* hovers
between embittered satire and a waveringly defensive sentiment.
At first glance the satiric element may seem the more conspicuous. The novel was possibly conceived as Jasper Milvain's
story, for it begins and ends with Jasper — his is the first voice
we hear and his the last word. As the title of the opening chapter
suggests, Jasper is "a man of his day": he is emphatically on the
side of the "new," and his alignment determines his success, just
as Reardon's commitment to the past underlies his abject failure.
Jasper's presence, his characteristic gesture, provides a frame:
near the beginning he reclines on a sofa, his hands behind his
head, as his sister plays the piano; at the end he lies back "in
dreamy ease," while his wife, Amy, widow of the defeated
Reardon, plays and sings for him. He is preeminently the
practical man, selfish, ambitious, adroit, shrewd in his estimate of
competition, charming when amiability seems politic, caddish
when betrayal appears profitable. He has no delusions of genius

4. *Commonplace Book,* p. 22.

or even of great talent as a writer; his objectives are simple and cynical: "Never in my life," he tells Reardon at the outset, "shall I do anything of solid literary value; I shall always despise the people I write for. But my path will be that of success. I have always said it, and now I'm sure of it." Later he warns Marian Yule with the same bluntness, "I shall do many a base thing in life, just to get money and reputation . . . I can't afford to live as I should like to." Marian of course is unwilling to credit his admission, until her inheritance proves too meager to be useful to him and she finds herself accordingly sacrificed to his advancement. Though he is convinced that he can be pleasant if only he has money, his corruption actually increases with his affluence. The very day that the jilted Marian and her father, now blind and broken, leave London, Jasper publishes his calculated eulogy of Yule's old enemy Fadge, to whose post as editor of *The Current* he is shortly to succeed. In the end, when his time-serving strategies have been richly rewarded, he assures Amy, who is likewise practical, that he cannot regret his decision to abandon Marian: "My dearest, you are a perfect woman, and poor Marian was only a clever school-girl. Do you know, I never could help imagining that she had ink-stains on her fingers . . . It was touching to me at the time, for I knew how fearfully hard she worked." We could scarcely ask a more caustic portrait of the cad as man of letters.

As the novel proceeds, however, the satiric intention yields to a stronger autobiographical impulse. Jasper, relegated before long to the background, where he pursues his vision of success, comes forward only at intervals as a foil to less opportunistic and more vulnerable characters. Some of these Gissing attempts to view with a measure of detachment and obliquity, for he diffuses and to some extent disguises his subjective concern. To Whelpdale, who is an essentially comic figure, he assigns his adventures in America, in retrospect more ludicrous than painful: his contributions to the Chicago *Tribune,* his brief career as photographer's assistant, and his resort to a diet of peanuts when penniless in Troy, New York. Alfred Yule, a sharply drawn study of a cantankerous pedant, reflects his respect for scholarship and his trying experience of marriage to a woman beneath him socially and intellectually — though good, long-suffering Mrs. Yule is a steadier more devoted wife than the unfortunate Mrs. Gissing. With Harold Biffen he has a far less constrained sympathy. Often subsisting simply on bread and dripping, Biffen never escapes the dire poverty that Gissing himself knew at least for short periods. As Gissing once did, Biffen plods miles of London streets in the early morning to earn a pittance by tutoring so that he may spend the rest of the day working at his unprofitable novel. If the finished *Mr. Bailey, Grocer* is apparently not much like Gissing's fictions, it suffers similar censure from reviewers who see no excuse for his "grovelling realism" or his failure "to understand that a work of art must before everything else afford amusement." [5] Biffen speaks for Gissing when he describes the dangers of refusing to compromise one's conviction in a world where sensibility can survive only by masking itself in "genial coarseness." And by his last desperate gesture, his death by his own hand, Biffen brings to quiet fulfillment Gissing's recurrent suicidal moods.

When Edwin Reardon, who is the real protagonist of *New Grub Street,* complains that he should have married "some simple, kind-hearted work-girl" instead of the genteel, ambitious, middle-class Amy, Biffen rebukes his fantasy:

> "What a shameless idealist you are! . . . Let me sketch the true issue of such a marriage. To begin with, the girl would have married you in firm persuasion that you were a "gentleman" in temporary difficulties, and that before long you would have plenty of money to dispose of. Disappointed in this hope, she would have grown sharp-tempered, querulous, selfish. All your endeavours to make her understand you would only have resulted in widening the impassable gulf. She would have misconstrued your every sentence, found food for suspicion in every harmless joke, tormented you with the vulgarest forms of jealousy." (Chap. 27)

Gissing here writes from sad experience, for Biffen, imagining what Reardon has escaped, pictures just such a union as Gissing endured — and indeed, at the time of writing, was about to

5. *New Grub Street* itself suffered a similar fate. In his *Commonplace Book* (p. 55) Gissing dismisses as "twaddle" the judgment of *The World:* "By selection of grim subjects he is endangering his otherwise indubitable claim to rank among the first of rising novelists."

repeat. But apart from his marriage to Amy, Reardon's career and character run remarkably close in most details to Gissing's.[6] When we first meet him, Reardon has already reached thirty, the age at which Gissing began the novel. Like Gissing, he has had a sound classical education in a provincial town, has come to London to write, taken miserable lodgings in a back street off Tottenham Court Road, worked for a while as secretary in a hospital, and written several novels, one of which has been successful enough, in terms of sales, to permit him a memorable trip to the Mediterranean. Like Gissing, he eagerly buys old books when he has a spare shilling and reluctantly sells them off when hard pressed for funds. And like Gissing, he is oversensitive to reviews, impatient with people, and badly affected by inclement weather. His conduct surely commands a measure of Gissing's respect. Yet his portrait is no mere exercise in self-justification; it rests upon a deep and far from complacent self-knowledge.

Biffen describes Reardon the novelist as "a psychological realist in the sphere of culture" rather than a devotee of graphic fact and vulgar circumstance; and Gissing himself, in presenting Reardon's character, is very much the psychologist, intensely interested in the analysis yet often clinically detached from it. Despite his manifest virtues, his insight, intelligence, and candor, Reardon is an insecure, unhappy man, subject to sudden revulsions of feeling, a creature of self-pity and irritable pride as well as meekness and compassion. His wrangling with Amy reveals him at his worst, both defiant and abject, now scorning the wife's practicality, now cringing before her common sense. He craves affection and is willing to grovel for it, but when his tears accomplish nothing, then "the feeling of unmanliness in his own position torture[s] him into a mood of perversity," and he becomes cruel in his angry retorts. Ultimately he nourishes his despair; in defeat he regards his seedy clothes "with pleasurable contempt" as "tokens of his degradation," and in the evenings once or twice a week, the masochist of his emotions, he haunts the street where Amy is comfortably housed, so that he may go home hungry to his garret "with a fortified sense of the injustice to which he [is]

6. See Jacob Korg, *George Gissing* (Seattle: University of Washington Press, 1963), pp. 158–159. On Gissing's second marriage, see pp. 150–153.

submitted." [7] His deterioration, paranoid or schizophrenic, is chronicled with an almost Balzacian power and dispassion: "An extraordinary arrogance now and then possessed him; he stood amid his poor surroundings with the sensations of an outraged exile, and laughed aloud in furious contempt of all who censured or pitied him." When we consider the extent of Gissing's identification with this lonely man, we cannot but be shaken by the terror of the self-appraisal.

Reardon's alienation, carrying him at times close to derangement, arises simply from his maladjustment to the new world of literature and his inability to admit the reality of any alternative existence. Gissing himself, though often disappointed at the reception of his books, was never so great a failure, and his extrapolated fears rather than his direct experience inspired his account of Reardon's collapse. Nonetheless, he shared his hero's commitment to the literary life and especially his literary enthusiasms. Like Reardon, he delighted in the Greek classics and responded warmly to the Greek setting as a reminder of the vanished ancient glory. From Athens in 1889 he wrote lyrical letters of the ruins glowing in the evening light:

> The sunsets are of unspeakable splendour. When you stand with your back to the west and look towards the Acropolis, it glows a rich amber; temples, bulwarks and rock are all of precisely the same hue, as if the whole were but one construction . . . Impossible for you to imagine what I mean. Impossible for any painter to render such scenes . . .
>
> One of the sunsets was rendered extraordinary by the fact that, at the same time, there was a perfect rainbow circling over the whole of Athens, from the foot of one mountain to that of another; the colours of the hills were unimaginable.[8]

A year later, writing *New Grub Street,* he granted Reardon the same aesthetic satisfaction, in almost identical terms. Enraptured

7. Cf. the behavior of Widdowson (in Gissing's 1893 novel, *The Odd Women*), who similarly spies on his estranged wife.

8. Letters of November 29 and December 16, 1889, to his brother and mothers, in *Letters of George Gissing to Members of his Family,* ed. Algernon Gissing and Ellen Gissing (London: Constable, 1927), pp. 295–296, 300.

by the memory, Reardon tells Biffen of "that marvellous sunset at Athens":

> "I turned eastward, and there to my astonishment was a magnificent rainbow, a perfect semicircle, stretching from the foot of Parnes to that of Hymettus, framing Athens and its hills, which grew brighter and brighter — the brightness for which there is no name among colours ... The Acropolis simply glowed and blazed. As the sun descended all these colours grew richer and warmer; for a moment the landscape was nearly crimson." (Chap. 27)

Biffen thinks it self-torture to remember such pleasures, but Reardon insists that he is sustained by his lost dream: "Poverty can't rob me of those memories. I have lived in an ideal world that was not deceitful, a world which seems to me, when I recall it, beyond the human sphere, bathed in diviner light." Antiquity thus tempts him to escape the human sphere altogether and so to transcend the concerns of a psychological realism and all the demands of his own fiction, which by comparison with the great classics seems "so wretchedly, shallowly modern." And the past awoke a similar vain nostalgia in Gissing himself; *By the Ionian Sea*, the most serene of his books, concludes with the sigh of the classicist manqué: "I wished it were mine to wander endlessly amid the silence of the ancient world, to-day and all its sounds forgotten."

In both his commonplace book and the autobiographical *Henry Ryecroft,* Gissing defines art as "a satisfying and abiding expression of the zest of life." [9] Yet, as Frank Swinnerton observed,[10] there is very little true zest in Gissing's own art and little or no exuberance or striking vitality in his characters. Reardon, convincing in his quiet despair, becomes intensely animated only on the subject of Greece, but it is hard to imagine Reardon's novels, sensitive though they may be, as really zestful on any

9. *Commonplace Book,* p. 69. Cf. *Henry Ryecroft,* p. 50: art is "an expression, satisfying and abiding, of the zest of life ... The artist is moved and inspired by supreme enjoyment of some aspect of the world about him; an enjoyment in itself keener than that experienced by another man ..."

10. *George Gissing* (Port Washington, N.Y.: Kennikat Press, 1966), pp. 170–171.

subject. Like Gissing, Reardon is apparently a careful craftsman with limited range. Gissing is indeed describing much of his own earlier work when he tells us that Reardon's stories, lacking "local colour" and exciting action, are "almost purely psychological" in interest, devoted as they are to the intellectual dilemmas of people of intellect. And even as he is chronicling Reardon's difficulties in padding out the second volume of a three-decker, he himself is facing the problem of inventing appropriate incidents to complete the three-volume structure in which Reardon has his being.

Though it self-consciously contains its own criticism, *New Grub Street* attempts a larger, more general literary statement. Like many later works of fiction and poetry, it concerns itself with the artist, the medium, and the aesthetic act; it is essentially a novel about novelists and the writing of novels. Throughout it is informed by a writer's understanding of the cruel demands of composition, the challenge of the blank page to be filled, the frequent recalcitrance of words, the refusal of the torpid paragraph to come to life and move with grace and logic. When spared the grosser distresses of hunger and poverty, Reardon still knows the anxieties and frustrations of his craft: "Sometimes the three hours' labour of a morning resulted in half a dozen lines, corrected into illegibility. His brain would not work; he could not recall the simplest synonyms; intolerable faults of composition drove him mad. He would write a sentence beginning thus: 'She took a book with a look of ——'; or thus: 'A revision of this decision would have made him an object of derision.' Or, if the period were otherwise inoffensive, it ran in a rhythmic gallop which was a torment to the ear." Gissing himself experienced similar woes, but also, we gather from his notebook, moments of a satisfaction usually denied to Reardon: "The pains of lit. composition. How easy any other task in comparison. Forcing of mind into a certain current, the temptation of indolence with a book. Yet the reward, when effort once made." [11] His em-

11. *Commonplace Book,* p. 67. Ellen Gissing (*Gissing to Members of His Family,* app. C, p. 405) reports that Gissing was an extremely moody writer, sometimes exuberant, but "if the work had not gone well that day, the dejected look and the deeply lined forehead gave him almost a haggard appearance."

phasis, however, falls less on the art of the novel than on the temperament of the novelist as a man apart, the sensibility that seeks creative expression and so sentences itself forever to the discipline of an isolating and harassing creativity.

Harold Biffen, we are told, "belonged to no class." Reardon, too, is an unclassed literary hero, aloof from the grades of society, fallen from a bourgeois economic status and dissociated in any case from philistine tastes and prejudices, living among the poor yet not of them, respecting the rare independent imaginative thinker, impatient with all vulgarity of thought or gesture. Both Biffen and Reardon could declare with Henry Ryecroft (and so with Gissing): "The truth is that I have never learnt to regard myself as a 'member of society.' For me, there have always been two entities — myself and the world — and the normal relation between these two has been hostile." [12] Nonetheless, both draw the materials and settings of their art from the hostile society rather than from an imagination able to transcend or transmute the commonplace. Especially in studying Reardon, Gissing appraises his own attitude and practice with some dispassion and not wholly favorable judgment. *New Grub Street* at its best is a stocktaking rather than a naive apologia.

The Private Papers of Henry Ryecroft, on the other hand, which followed twelve years later, wears a thinner fictional disguise and suffers the burden of a more directly engaged self-defense. Spared Reardon's fate by a timely legacy, Ryecroft has retired to the seclusion of a Devon cottage, where he may cultivate his roses and cherish his solitude. "I do not enjoy anything nowadays," he insists, "which I cannot enjoy *alone*." [13] Though he has rejected journalism as a "squalid profession," he has always valued the career of letters for "its freedom, its dignity." Self-absorbed and self-opinionated in his voluntary exile, he is now free to extol his difference from other men. He has escaped the London literary struggle for survival; but in withdrawing he has lost his subject matter. The most vivid of his papers record his sufferings as a young writer in the city, hungry days remembered with a proud self-pity and even a degree of nostalgia. In his

12. *Henry Ryecroft,* p. 17.
13. Ibid., p. 125.

aloneness he can now believe that all reality is subjective — that no one, for example, can share his memory of a Suffolk landscape, since, as he tells us, "the place no longer exists; it never existed save for me. For it is the mind which creates the world about us, and, even though we stand side by side in the same meadow, my eyes will never see what is beheld by yours, my heart will never stir to the emotions with which yours is touched." [14]

Though likewise personal and private in many of his reactions, Reardon has no such illusions about the real substance, the grim otherness, of the milieu in which Milvain and Fadge succeed and he and Biffen fail. If there is as much of Gissing in Reardon as in Ryecroft, Reardon nonetheless gains a solidity and dramatic independence as a character, far beyond Ryecroft's, from the cogent depiction of the intellectual setting in which and about which he must write. The physical conditions of authorship have surely changed in many ways since 1891, but the problems of the commercialization of literature and the challenge to aesthetic integrity, which Gissing recognized as never before, remain real and inescapable. *New Grub Street,* the most obsessively literary of Victorian novels, leaves us no doubt about the objective reality of its world.

14. Ibid., p. 89.

IV Other Worlds

JOHN MAYNARD

Broad Canvas, Narrow Perspective:
The Problem of the English
Historical Novel in the Nineteenth Century

With a few very good, but hardly ever splendid, exceptions, the
nineteenth-century English historical novel, in the great age of
the historical novel, is a poor subject. The only general study of
it, Avrom Fleishman's recent *The English Historical Novel*,[1] follows the wise example of Georg Lukács's general discussion of
the European historical novel in not attempting a catalogue
history of the type.[2] To do so would be to write not criticism of

1. *The English Historical Novel* (Baltimore: Johns Hopkins Press,
1971). Hugh Walpole's graceful "Scott and the Historical Novel," in
Sir Walter Scott To-Day, ed. H. J. C. Grierson (London: Constable,
1932), pp. 161–188, provides the broadest brief survey of the limitations of the English historical novel. Though Walpole really brings
no critical approach to the problem that he observes and though he introduces the artificial notion of a certain number of years of pastness
as a test for the genre, Walpole's wide-ranging survey of the English
historical novel is sensible and properly critical. Dora Binkert, *Historische
Romane vor Walter Scott* (Berlin: Mayer & Müller, 1915), surveyed
briefly the forerunners of Scott. Sir John Marriott, *English History in
English Fiction* (London: Blackie & Son, 1940), is a guide to fiction
on English history organized by historical period.
2. Lukács, *The Historical Novel,* trans. Hannah Mitchell and Stanley
Mitchell (1937; trans. ed., London: Humanities Press, 1962). Lukács

237

literature so much as a study of a popular minor subgenre which quickly degenerated from Scott's romantic realism into mere pot-boiling romance. The endless fictionalizations of Mary Queen of Scots or the sex life of Elizabeth I, like our contemporaries' interest in hearing Adolf Hitler speak as he was wont to do, provide, of course, ample grazing for the omnivorous student of culture who can plot in changing fashions about the past the changing moods of escapism in different decades. But if we look above this level in the English context we find very little of substance for the student of greatness in the novel. Above all, we find no *War and Peace,* no *Le rouge et le noir,* a Thackeray but not a Balzac, a Reade but not a Manzoni or a Pushkin, hardly even a Victor Hugo. That is, if there are competent and interesting English novels written in a historical context, there are few, if any, works which can fit Herbert Butterfield's description of the historical novel as historical epic, "a mighty production, a great conception minutely worked out, a piece of architecture . . . the novel carried to a higher power . . . It grapples with Destiny and dares to look the universe in the face." [3] There are few works which present through the medium of the novel a profound awareness of man's largest historical situation and destiny. This said, one may wish to put forth a brief for the importance of the grand vision (if one has the grand leisure to master it) of Scott's cycle of novels on the English and Scottish past, or, as Fleishman remarkably does not, for the breadth of social and historical perspective that George Eliot brings into her study of Middle-march.

Without trying to ignore or pass over these successes, I wish to focus on the problem of the nineteenth-century English historical novel, the relative weakness of fictional works on the subject of history in an otherwise strong tradition of the novel. Of course, the problem thus defined is problematic, though at least not uninteresting, because there can never be more than a probability in an attempt to explain why a given phenomenon fails, or

---

(1885–1971), a native of Hungary, left Berlin in 1933 for the Institute of Philosophy of the Soviet Academy; after the war he became professor of philosophy at Budapest University.

3. *The Historical Novel: An Essay* (Cambridge: Cambridge University Press, 1924), p. 85.

partially fails, to appear. History here is certainly the sum of innumerable biographies, and we should have to go through writer after writer citing particular reasons for his or her failure to find major expression in the area of historical fiction. Rather than this exhausting task, I propose merely to suggest, from the admittedly partial evidence of a few examples of historical fiction by major writers, the kinds of problems that seem to beset this work for English writers from Scott on. Such an approach cannot tell us when and why the English *War and Peace* was not written, but it should at least help to explicate the English historical novel as we do have it and to provide a basis for comparative evaluation.

The historical novel in English is, it should be confessed, one of those fair fields needing folk which graduate students on the lookout for dissertation topics whisper about among themselves and which others may wish could be made permanently virgin land free as Scott's wild highlands from the inroads of the modern critical temperament. The scouting work by Lukács and Fleishman, the first a splendidly engaged, wide-ranging, and rather personal work of criticism grounded on a dialectical materialist's faith in history, the second a competent series of analyses of individual writers' attitudes toward history, have at least set the right standards for wise use of this rather limited (at least in the English context) resource. Not only have they both focused on quality in their explorations, leaving the ordinary historical romance lands in their natural tangled abundance; more important, they have avoided the narrow concern for formal definition and genre which, most of all, can turn an exciting new territory into a deadly dull set of plots waiting for critical homesteaders to nest. Both think of the historical novel not as a tight fictional kind with specific requirements but rather as a novel with a peculiarly strong kind of commitment to man's life in history and to the problems of historical thinking themselves. Lukács's insights into the construction of the historical novel are extraordinary in a formalist school of criticism for being empirical observations drawn from the model of Scott and the early classics. Lukács is above all careful to speak of the historical novel not as a special genre with rules of its own but as a natural growth of the English realist novel of the eighteenth century into greater historical awareness to match its early development of social analysis. At its fullest development, it is not so much a new kind of novel as a new third dimension added to the realist novel. Though he partially cripples himself by insisting on an arbitrary number of years of pastness to the action of the historical novel, Fleishman otherwise follows Lukács in defining "historical" in terms of interest and philosophy, not plot construction or picturesque detail.

Such an approach to the English historical novel spreads a wide net. That there should be so few big fish to fill it seems even more extraordinary when one considers the context of the English novel in the nineteenth century, the time when the historical novel, after its first significant development by Scott, goes on to reach its greatest heights in continental literature. England is, first of all, the seedbed of the historical novel in the strong realistic tradition of the eighteenth century; and then Great Britain is the scene and subject of its first great triumph in the Waverley novels. Even more notably, England, from the time of Burke, Scott, and Coleridge, is the fondest home of the organic historical thinking which John Stuart Mill characterized as the Coleridgean tradition. Not only did historical and organic conceptions and metaphors dominate both scientific and political thinking throughout most of the English nineteenth century; history became in England, with the generation of Carlyle and Macaulay, a hugely popular subject and a major form of literary art in itself; and biography, closest cousin to the historical novel, became, from the time of Johnson and Boswell on, another major popular mode in which English interest in history found expression. Both in the early development of a diffused political base for power and in the early growth of a commercial foundation for the industrial revolution of the nineteenth century, Britain was, as other Europeans normally recognized, in the forefront of European history; and Britons became increasingly conscious of history itself as they became aware that they were not so much entrenched on an island as moving in the river of change.

For the Marxist critic who wishes perhaps only somewhat more than other historical critics to fine hew the connection between history and literary development, Scott presents a rare opportunity, one which it remained for a Hungarian critic writing in exile in Russia to realize fully. Lukács rightly sees the greatness of Scott's achievement: standing at the forefront of English, and therefore of European, history and at the forefront of interest in the past for its own sake, Scott, in Lukács's appreciation, creates the history of civilization right up to the progressive middle-class culture coming into predominance in his day. With or without benefit of a vision of a proletarian future, Marxist and non-Marxist can agree that Scott admirably masters the major evolution of English history up to his time.[4] Whatever mistakes or inaccuracies, even theoretical misperceptions, he may bring into his novels from the limitations of the history of his day, Scott makes the overall movement of history splendidly conscious in the mind of the present. Reinterpreting Scott in the light of his successors in the European historical novel, Lukács pays full honor to the significance of this first major infusion of historical awareness into the novel; and he celebrates Scott's virtual discovery of a new realm for the novel. As Lukács becomes better known in the English-speaking world, he thus opens to us new awareness of the value of a writer who was getting to be something of a dusty heirloom.

What remains, unfortunately, is the job of balancing the ledger in a less Whiggish (or opto-Marxist) context and noting the limitations of Scott as a historical novelist. For, to the historian of the English historical novel, unlike the historian of its continental counterpart, it is not Scott's strengths but his weaknesses which must seem most indicative. Nor is the exercise perverse, for in a writer of Scott's power and originality strengths and weaknesses are more than casually related. To underscore the problems that Scott's special genius allowed him largely to bridge over is to see not only the pitfalls into which his successors more often and grievously fell but also to realize, by contrast, his achievement. Indeed, the major difficulties take us really to the essential difficulty of all work in the hybrid genre of historical

4. Fleishman, *English Historical Novel,* p. 49, unhelpfully stresses the differences between Lukács's progressivism and Scott's; they are obvious, but the similarities in their attitudes about the significance of the emergence of the middle-class nineteenth century are significant. They show not that Scott was a proto-Marxist hiding in a tartan but that he had a sophisticated awareness of social development.

fiction. This is, as Butterfield's modest but thoughtful essay long ago suggested, above all the problem of relating two visions of human life. On the one hand there is the normal material of the novelist, the lives of specific individual humans as they work to fulfillment or frustration, to moral fortitude or failure, to understanding or confusion. On the other hand, the historical novelist must come to terms with another view of human life which the ordinary novelist can normally choose to ignore in his focus on the individual and the immediately human. This is history itself; this may be one of any number of ways of conceiving of history, from a passion play of divine significance to a completely meaningless series of unrelated events. But however the novelist conceives of history, he will find it, as we all do when we turn from our private and immediate concerns to view our lives in the great stream of time in which we are a mere bobbing less-than-mote, a large idea, full of time and people, which easily sweeps away his vision of individual men and women in its course and is only with difficulty related to the private aspirations and developments of those individuals. Such is the inevitable mismatching of infinitesimal cog with infinite cog which we feel most obviously coming into play each time the historical novelist moves us, with whatever grace he can summon, from his great vision of history in, say, the thirteenth century to the poor figure of our hero driving toward night across a wide and desolate plain bound for what great adventure with his fate we shall know, full well, only too soon. Such, likewise, is the melodramatic confrontation of great things with what are small which we have come to expect when we read about some poor ant in history, whom we have come to know and care for (or hate), being thrown suddenly into the company of some great figure, a Richelieu, Bismarck, or Kissinger. Poor ant (more poor for being not unlike ourselves), he must thenceforth carry, along with all his private problems and concerns, the greater burden of knowing his own minute place in the great movements of historical events.

Scott's great legacy to the historical novel, above and beyond all mere authenticity of dialect, manners, or scenery, is, as Lukács perceived, a competent solution to the problem of uniting these two poles, private and public, personal and historical, in the hybrid art. First, he deliberately avoids entering history, in the manner of historical drama, through the main gate: he eschews focusing on a hero from the great world of history who must then be somehow sufficiently humanized to maintain ordinary human sympathies and interests. Instead, he enters by a wicket, choosing for his hero what has been called the Waverley character, a man who, without great premeditation, finds himself a small participant in major historical events. With such a hero, amiable but often somewhat slow to catch on to the significance of the events he witnesses, we have an ideal mediating agent between the personal and impersonal: a man primarily concerned with his private affairs, with whom we may feel the usual novel reader's sympathy through identification; yet a man whose somewhat accidental role in the larger events of his time allows him to be a moving lens through which we may view history itself. The original, young Edward Waverley, in *Waverley,* for instance, pays a private visit to an old friend of his uncle's only to find himself drawn ineluctably into a minor role in The Forty-five, thus serving for us as a firsthand reporter of the contrasts between Hanoverian and Jacobite and finally as an eyewitness to the Young Pretender himself. Or, young, somewhat foolish Frank Osbaldistone in the later novel *Rob Roy,* a fugitive from a career in his father's business in the name of his own mediocre poetic talents, finds himself an intimate observer of another plot on behalf of the House of Stuart and a splendid guide to Scott's social vision of nascent capitalism growing up alongside an expiring feudal order. Both heroes have this one explicit "romance" with history in a life that is then resolved back into a private sphere. Finally, Scott, as Lukács again perceives, makes of his "mediocre" hero as broad a mediating agent as possible, using an outsider, a traveler, a man drawn to both sides at once, as a way of focusing the different forces at work in the history of his age. Waverley and Osbaldistone both have cause to sympathize with both Jacobite and Hanoverian. In the socially deeper exploration of *Rob Roy,* Osbaldistone, son of a great merchant who leans back toward the aristocracy, is an ideal vehicle for letting us experience at first hand the social and economic cleavage of the age. Through such a figure, Scott finds a way to bring home his vision of the dual nature of historical progress, the loss of what is good in the old and the emergence of new good in the

coming order, and to bring it home not as historical abstraction
but as experience felt in individual terms through his hero's
experience.

Such, rather baldly stated, is Scott's great solution to the problem of all historical fiction. What Lukács does not dwell upon is
the price he pays, for here too there is a logic of loss and gain,
for the solution. In fact, the debits are little more than reminders
of weaknesses long acknowledged even by Scott's admirers
among English-speaking readers. First, there is the tendency to
maintain, within the general atmosphere of historical realism,
many of the motives and gratifications of sophisticated romance
plots. Most obviously, for instance, in both *Waverley* and *Rob
Roy,* there is the age-old marriage plot, working toward its
peculiar but undeniable kick of pleasure in the unreal happily-
ever-after ending. The novels thus focus not only on the romance
of an ordinary life in its one touch with the movement of history
but also on the more ordinary romance of love triumphant over
baffling circumstances. Then there is in addition the romance, always ascribed to Scott, of escape into a past seen in its most
exotic characteristics, the romance in *Waverley* and *Rob Roy* of
Highland primitivism and, elsewhere, the romance of medieval
chivalry or implacable Covenanters. Perhaps most indicative,
there is a villain, a Vich Ian Vohr or Rashleigh Osbaldistone,
whose nearly Gothic machinations give to the stories the interest
of great fables of Romantic damnation. All such tidy plot constructions place side by side historical realism and romance,
mitigating the unpleasantness of seeing individual lives in a long
and devaluating historical perspective by offering the reader the
immediate emotional gratification of romance. Scott's slight
predecessor Clara Reeve had remarked that she wrote historical
romance because she found human nature as seen in history
"alas, too often a melancholy retrospect!" [5] Scott more cannily
preserves the pleasures of romance while working around them
an honest vision of history. Yet the effect is to throw back on
history an aura of romance, to keep us from experiencing the
destiny of individuals and mankind in history at the level of highest seriousness. At his best Scott keeps the romance from

5. Quoted in Fleishman, *English Historical Novel,* pp. 21–22.

falsifying history; many of his successors simply turn to pure romance or fable, subordinating all vision of historical reality to a plot fashioned to heart's desire.

In one other way Scott weights the scales against historical perspective and provides additional consolations to himself and his readers as individuals subject to awareness of their own insignificance and impotence against history. While he uses the Waverley hero as a mediating wedge to enter into the complexities of history, he at the same time uses him for just the opposite purpose: as a *fil d'Ariane* to extricate himself at last from the intensity of his own vision. For the special quality of the Waverley hero is that he is at once involved and uninvolved; a participant spectator, he can return, at his author's convenience, to the role of simple spectator. Both Waverley and Osbaldistone, having completed the "romantic adventure" of life, are effectively freed from the historical complexities, in which they have played as boys at grown-up games, in order to take on their timeless lifetime roles as eighteenth-century gentlemen. Meanwhile, great characters, whose different fates we have glimpsed for a while, drift back into the big folio volumes in the estate library and the angry gods of history are placated by the convenient sacrifice of a Rashleigh or a Vich Ian Vohr. Though Scott tells us, whenever hundreds die in battle, that history notoriously slays the just and the unjust, his plots tell us that gentlemen heroes are always spared, villains get theirs in the end, and picturesque characters, like Waverley's father-in-law, the Baron of Bradwardine, are always restored to their lost estates and hereditary honors.

Inasmuch as we all aspire to be mediocre heroes, the arrangement, by which we live happily ever after in a timeless world of the better gentry, suits us as readers. One need not go far into Scott's own biography, with its history of Scott's tragic failure to find the security on an estate granted to so many booby squires without a trace of his genius or a fifth of his passion for the gentlemanly life, to realize the consolation to him of such a perspective on history. More than just a tool of the author, as Lukács takes him, for getting into history, the Waverley hero, properly speaking, establishes the way in which the author chooses to look at history. And this, for all the brilliance of Scott's creation and the breadth of his vision, is decidedly that of the armchair historian, looking out on the pageant of history as a distant and curious tale with which his own happily private life has little connection. The mediocre hero is his man on the spot in Edinburgh or Loch Lomond but able, when the going gets too hot, to turn back into Edward Waverley of Waverley-Honour, Gent., at ease in his spacious Gothic high-arched library or into Richard Osbaldistone, Lord of Osbaldistone Manor, musing over his youth in leisured tranquillity.

Scott thus tempered his historical perspective on human life by romance elements and a deliberate distance from involvement in history which made him decidedly a genial historian to the readers of his day and which will continue to make him a lovable historian to generations to come. While some of his continental followers saw through this geniality into the seriousness of his historical intentions and chose to imitate what was newest and best in Scott, his English followers were drawn rather to imitate his most popular characteristics. In a writer of high popular character like Bulwer-Lytton, for instance, history is exploited almost entirely for its romance interest and for its romantic possibilities. His best-known work, remembered for its title if not for its excellence, *The Last Days of Pompeii* (1834), shows this tendency at its most blatant. If it were merely exotic escapism projected into the past, as in Flaubert's much greater classical re-creation, *Salammbô,* it could be looked upon as a flight of pure fancy. Certainly it is this. But what makes it such a striking example of the flight from history in the English historical novel following Scott is the awesome and terrible historical reality of its subject. Although Bulwer-Lytton could at least show some sophistication in political analysis in his other historical novels on less fatal themes,[6] when he settled near Pompeii to meditate this most

6. Curtis Dahl, "History on the Hustings: Bulwer Lytton's Historical Novels of Politics," in *From Jane Austen to Joseph Conrad,* ed. Robert Rathburn and Martin Steinmann, Jr. (St. Paul: University of Minnesota Press, 1958), pp. 60–71, discusses the strengths and weaknesses of Lytton's more explicitly political novels, especially *Rienzi* and *The Last of the Barons.* Though less fantastic than *The Last Days of Pompeii,* these works suffer from modernization and moralization of history, a tendency to melodrama in the plots, and, working uneasily against these, an excessive concern for antiquarian accuracy.

obvious example of the vanity of human wishes in the uncertain chances of existence, he abandoned all serious historical perspective. The historical interest is reduced, as Fleishman correctly remarks of Bulwer's work in general, to mere scrupulous antiquarian (or here we might even say archaeological) detail. Otherwise, one would have to imagine Voltaire dancing on the ruins of Lisbon to find a parallel for Bulwer's fanciful approach to catastrophe. He manages cleverly to work as much vague dread and foreboding as possible out of the coming upheaval without letting it, when it finally comes, actually upset the slick course of his highly sensational and romantic plot. In fact, it proves a useful scene for the final destruction of his Manfredian villain, Arbaces, and a convenient occasion for ridding himself of a supererogatory heroine. Meanwhile our two beautiful lovers, Glaucus and Ione, fine projections of the sentimental Grecian ideals of Bulwer's dandified late Romantic generation, drift out from the wreckage of a world to a long life of the prescribed contemplation of youth in domestic tranquillity. The scenes of gladiatorial combat are more interesting. Yet the interest is sensational (who doesn't enjoy indulging the barbaric instincts vicariously while enjoying the sense of moral superiority that comes from an easy condemnation of customs no longer current). Finally, though the account of early Christianity has pleased some readers as a more serious touch, it is in fact an example of the kind of modernization that Scott usually avoids.[7] Here again, another contemporary fashion is being pandered to, and early Christians become the vehicle for the kind of heavy Evangelical rhetoric pleasing to early Victorian ears even in sensational novels.

Bulwer is obviously small historical game and worth mentioning only because Pompeii presents such a gross example of dishonesty in avoiding a general view of human history by elaborating Scott's tendency to romance and distance. The weakness of a much greater novelist's much greater work, Dickens' *A Tale of Two Cities,* as a major work of historical fiction is a

---

7. Bulwer's preface misleadingly defends his gross "translating" of the past into accessible form by quoting Scott as his authority. Yet Scott had sufficient interest in the past for its own sake. Bulwer also admits disarmingly that he seeks the "poetry of life" more than its "prose."

far more important failure. The well-known relation between this treatment of the French Revolution and Carlyle's "wonderful book" has opened the way for numerous studies of the relation between a great Victorian novelist and a great historian.[8] But all comparison really ends in the perception that Carlyle has written a great work of history which could also be read, if it were not intended as actual history, as the greatest epic historical novel in English and Dickens has written a good novel but one that fails alike as history or historical fiction. In the figure of Mirabeau, Carlyle found an entry for his personal feelings and perceptions into the real course of this political Vesuvius. If he is, in Lukács's distinction, more a figure of elevated tragic drama than a character from the realistic novel, he at least allows Carlyle to let us sympathize directly with a man who faces the Revolution with neither fear nor malice but with an honest desire to make the best of a bad situation. In Mirabeau's fall in the effort to halt the onrushing catastrophe, Carlyle can at least show us one way of living through a revolution with dignity and heroic strength. Mirabeau faces history, is finally overwhelmed by it, but stands as a practical model of leadership which may avert a repetition of such a social devastation. By contrast, Sydney Carton, the man who stands up to the implacable force of knitted destiny in *A Tale of Two Cities,* is not a historical figure but a talisman. His selfless and not very ordinarily motivated act serves as a propitiatory sacrifice. By it, the normal heroes, the reformed French aristocrat, Charles Darnay, and his bride and lovely child, are disentangled from the complicated net which the Revolution has cast about them and restored to the customary future for the Waverley hero of domestic contemplation. One should even perhaps see Carton as an interesting variation on Scott's technique: here a secondary hero (who is indeed in other respects a useless and destructive character) serves to placate historical

8. Most recently, two full-length studies, Michael Goldberg, *Carlyle and Dickens* (Athens: University of Georgia Press, 1972), and William Oddie, *Dickens and Carlyle: The Question of Influence* (London: Centenary Press, 1972). Fleishman, *English Historical Novel,* p. 116, rather overstates Dickens' merits as a historian in placing *A Tale of Two Cities* "on a par with Carlyle's work as historical art" (p. 116).

vengeance rather than the usual villain (Dickens throws in Madame Defarge's well-deserved death as well).

What is most interesting about this novel and reveals Dickens' genius working at a distinguished level even when it refuses thoroughly to master a problem is the degree to which the threat of destructive historical process is generalized and made truly terrible. Whereas Bulwer's escape from disaster seems frivolous, Dickens' is in terrible earnest and, in the end, not entirely convincing. Like Carlyle, Dickens attempts to present the greatest social upheaval of centuries with concrete detail that will bring it home as living reality, not mere statistical result. But where Carlyle accumulates an epic variety of revealing detail in order to make a whole, if preternaturally vivid, canvas, Dickens characteristically blows up a few characters and incidents into lurid, and sometimes eccentric, symbols. The technique, of course, serves him very effectively in his great novels of social perception and discussion. But the method is less easily adapted to a combined social and historical perspective. The overwrought (and at base melodramatic) treatment of Madame Defarge, in whose deliberate knitting all the latent vengeance of historical grievance is to be fused, is at once unconvincing as a way of talking about history and too persuasive as an emotional symbol.[9] As a result, the sense of inevitability that emerges in Carlyle from real understanding of the complexity of the historical process is in Dickens rendered into a paranoid vision of fear. When Darnay leaves England for the Paris of the Terror we are no longer in a historical world but in a world in which history is endowed with the malevolent ineluctability of a nightmare, a magnetic and destructive "Lodestone Rock" which pulls in its victims to their end. If Dickens cannot quite make the characters who figure in this nightmare credible, he makes the nightmare world itself truly terrifying.[10] The magical release from this world by a secular

9. Only one of many such obvious symbols; for example, the impersonal, numbered Jacques used to stand for the aggrieved people.
10. Students of feminism may pursue further the deeper fears released by the Revolution, especially the correspondence between Madame Defarge and the "sharp female newly born," *La Guillotine*. Similarly, social fears emerge in Darnay's trial as fear of an inversion of society: the felons seem to be replacing the judges, Dickens tells us.

sacrifice along the Christian model is then a release from a vision of history, not merely a personal escape into domesticity.[11] By the two-cities theme Dickens is able to elevate the disingenuousness of Scott's retreat from history from a personal to a national level. England, that place of Pickwickian bankers, comic body snatchers, and riots only against spies and villains, is herself freed from the threat of history in that other city by one selfless act. Dickens, in effect, plays capitally on his countrymen's fears that it could happen here, building them up into intolerable strength only to assuage them through the magical romance of his plot. It is a powerful expression of the fear of history and a clear personal philosophy; but it is not a novel that faces honestly and directly individual man's relation to historical process as we ordinarily experience it.

Inasmuch as English writers showed no faintheartedness in gratifying the popular taste for historical romantic fiction, we could prolong the examination of the limitations of Scott's successors indefinitely. In Thackeray's *Henry Esmond,* for instance, there might be seen in detail, and perhaps in its finest expression, the prevalent tendency to flee from history into a defensive and seemingly secure private world; and if Thackeray does not show the mere ironic contempt for history that Fleishman rightly criticizes Lukács for finding in him, he shows little interest in taking seriously the problems of man's relation to history. This splendid novel rather relates a personal and private destiny decided against a perfect re-creation of a past culture in a parody of a past style. The historical setting provides a useful distant perspective in which to view a personal theme, love versus ambition, but not a subject in itself. Perhaps better than Scott himself, Thackeray evokes a wonderfully real historical world; and he tells a good tale of one man's life by various loves possessed. But he does not bring the two together except by the age-old theme of the vanity of ambition.[12]

11. The problem of secular Christianity in *A Tale* is well treated by Fleishman, *English Historical Novel,* esp. pp. 119–122.

12. Fleishman tries ingeniously, but to me not convincingly, to argue that Thackeray makes of the retreat from history a positive statement about history. This ignores Esmond's motives, which are personal throughout. Nor can one really see in his retreat to America a positive social act; America, like Waverley-Honour, is simply a fine estate re-

Or there are the more obvious weaknesses — as well as real strengths of imaginative fertility and descriptive vitality — of Reade's adolescent favorite, *The Cloister and the Hearth:* that world of true hearts and true love, endless hairbreadth escapes from ever present medieval mortality, Felliniesque variety of humanity, and, alas, boy-scout morality. Too good for their age, Gerard and his Margaret bring modern virtues into a barbaric time. The result is that we are given the pleasure, much as we are in Bulwer, of both enjoying the lusty barbarities of the past and of condemning them in our modern superiority; but Gerard's relation to history is not so much a confrontation of personal value with historical barbarity as an endless series of evasions by narrow escapes engineered by the author for our titillation. In the end, we are asked to respond not so much to the powerful theme of a man fighting history as to the sentimental one of star- and vow-crossed lovers. Adventure and sentiment take the place of serious engagement in a potentially interesting theme.

But perhaps most indicative of the general failure are the problems that emerge even in the work of the greatest of English realists when she moves toward direct grappling with public historical process. I mean, of course, George Eliot, who not only tried the genre explicitly in *Romola* but who in *Middlemarch* came as close as any English writer of the century to the comprehensive historical vision of the great continental masters.

If *Middlemarch* is a great novel but not quite a masterpiece of historical fiction, it is not for the author's want of sophistication in approaching the special problems of the historical novel. In an episode in *Romola* she observes a street character trying to puzzle out a placard bearing Savonarola's predictions for the future. When the ending, "Haec autem omnia erunt temporibus nostris," is finally translated to him, "and all these things shall happen in our times," his reply is the normal human one: "Why,

---

moved from historical reality, even more so by its American location (that the life of the gentry loyalist is threatened in eighteenth-century America is not hinted). Thackeray's own perspective on the world he presents, from Marlborough to Mrs. Steele, is more that of the social satirist than of the historian. The social renunciation here is a far cry from the alienation from history of a Tolstoy.

what use would they be else?" The concern, here comically expressed, with the uses of history to the individual and, in turn, the uses of the individual to history is fundamental to George Eliot's approach to history. Rather than merely appropriating some version of Scott's solution to this problem, in both *Romola* and *Middlemarch* George Eliot makes the problem itself a central, if not the central, issue of her stories. The earlier *Romola* (1863), set in distant Renaissance Florence and merging, in the manner of Scott, great personages and private heroes and heroines, has generally received only faint praise for success in parts, mostly for its carefully researched reconstruction of the Florentine Renaissance at a moment of crisis and for the author's isolated moral reflections. The first should perhaps not be passed over as lightly as it usually is. If we compare George Eliot's reconstruction of Florence, even admitting its occasional touch of the lamp, to the historical world we are given by Bulwer or even Dickens or Scott we must recognize an important improvement not just in antiquarian accuracy but in social conception. While Scott can give us both a feeling for the romance of the past and valid symbols of the underlying class struggles which shape the future, George Eliot gives us the cultural texture of an entire civilization at a point of crisis. We have already that sense of modulated response to historical movement across all classes and all kinds of persons, the effect of a single wind touching various responses according to the instruments it reaches, which gives to *Middlemarch* its amazing comprehensiveness. That quality Ruskin praised in Browning's "The Bishop Orders His Tomb at Saint Praxed's Church," of bringing home the major cultural and social forces operating on an entire age through the fine selection of detail in the case of one individual, is everywhere George Eliot's principle of operation. For instance, we are made almost effortlessly to see the parallels in the crises in *Romola*: the crisis in the great world of Florence between pagan Renaissance sensual liberation and the moral regeneration promulgated by Savonarola[13] and the parallel private crisis in Romola's life be-

13. Fleishman, *English Historical Novel,* p. 13, defines the contrast as between Middle Ages and Renaissance; though George Eliot shows the ways in which Savonarola represented a throwback to medieval asceticism, she generally sees him rather as a progressive moral spirit,

tween intellectual individualism and moral duty; and George Eliot finds an effective symbol, much in the manner of Browning, in the casket in which her husband tries to cover up the crucifix of Romola's dead brother with his own unsatisfactory wedding gift: a picture of themselves as innocent Bacchus and Ariadne. The concoction becomes at once a symbol of the confused soul of Renaissance Florence and of that of her individual citizens. The life of the individual is woven securely into the larger fabric of social vision.

George Eliot's problems are thus not in the historical vision which she, with no doubt more sociological ideas and historical training than English novelists before her, brings to her chosen historical epoch. In this she has already in *Romola* something like the clear-sighted social vision of a Stendhal or a Balzac. The problem is rather in just the area where she is most honestly exploratory: working out the specific relations between her characters' lives (as opposed to their place in a given social and cultural milieu) and the larger movement of history. The problem of the book is the familiar one in George Eliot: the destiny of a sympathetic, high-minded, and ardent female heroine. But unlike the heroine's destiny in a more narrowly focused work such as *The Mill on the Floss,* in *Romola* it is specifically seen as the working out of her individual appointment with history. It is enough for a low character simply to assert his purely individual concerns against history; but for Romola, as for Dorothea after her, there is the need to find oneself in finding one's relation to the greater world of society and history where the individual fate touches on the common fate of all. In such a heroine, the Waverley hero suffers a double and very serious transformation. First, and far from insignificantly, he is sexually transposed. Second, his relation to history is changed: while the Waverley hero's weakness and strength was in his casual relation to history, events that he is accidentally drawn into and may conveniently exit from, Romola, like her author, positively seeks a relation to history and cannot easily escape her own conscience even if she can physically escape history itself. The result is a twofold open-

perhaps even too much as an Evangelical; on the whole, her treatment of Savonarola's movement is exceptionally favorable.

ing of the problem of the individual and history temporarily
closed by Scott: the author abandons the stratagem by which she
and her character may be released from the adverse effects of
history and stands heroically to face a life in history, good or bad.
Yet by choosing a female heroine she complicates the new problem she poses. Romola is neither a Saint Theresa nor a George
Eliot who chooses deliberately to adopt a direct relation to the
world; rather, she accepts the traditional relation to society
through marriage and then, with all the hindrances and excuses
of her position, attempts to establish some independent relation
to historical existence outside marriage. The problem, thus posed,
is perhaps insurmountable; certainly, it receives no adequate
solution in *Romola,* where the plot of Romola's ethical growth is
never really merged with the plot of Florence's history. Her one
act in the context of Florentine history, the plea with Savonarola
to involve himself in politics for the sake of saving her innocent
Italian godfather, Bernardo del Nero, from the smallness of
party malice, comes rather as an act of moral judgment than as
an engagement with history. The effect is rather to draw her away
from history: "Romola was feeling the full force of that sympathy
with the individual lot that is continually opposing itself to the
formulae by which actions and parties are judged" (chap. 60).
To fill the need for some effective action, the author then invents
a rather incredible episode of saintly aid to a Mediterranean
village struck by plague: Romola is wafted to this destiny not by
the winds of history but by the waves of a benevolent sea; far
from Florence, the village and her actions bear no relation to the
historical world otherwise so solidly there. The expedient is poor
and reveals the genuine problem (which is confronted honestly
in *Middlemarch*) of finding substantial historical life for a yearning married heroine.

Yet the problem goes deeper than that of finding something to
do, some dying pig to help inter or smoke, and beneath the
surface it really cuts two ways. There is plenty for women to do,
but such danger in their doing it. History is not so much hard to
get involved in as hard to avoid getting dirtied by. The lesson
can be read between the lines in the treatment of Romola's poor
villain husband Tito, fated, in the manner of Scott's villains, to
pay the price for more serious historical involvement while our

female Waverley escapes relatively unscathed. A man of good temper but given to self-interested self-deception, Tito gradually falls to the lowest villainy in his private affairs. What is less convincing is that George Eliot makes him, as he falls in character, better and better equipped to play a part in the historical affairs of Florence. The moral (one again gaining credence today) is that those who "play the game," that is, do get involved in history directly, are either already corrupt or will shortly be so or dead.[14] This is out-Machiavelliing Machiavelli, who is indeed brought in at times to testify to Tito's superior cunning; and Tito's life and death as a triple agent lend another incredible, Howard Huntish, note to the otherwise convincing view of Florence.

In the unresolved antithesis between Romola as miracle of private goodness and her husband as type of the corruption of those involved actively in the history of the day, there is the failure, and perhaps evasion as well, of *Romola*. Wives, any good feminist would remind us, are in fact responsible for themselves even when married. Romola accepts this advice from Savonarola; later she effectively separates herself from Tito. But there remains the suspicion that Tito was created by the author as scapegoat and that Romola's failure to find a role in history as woman represents something of an evasion of the problem of combining public life and private morality. The lives of emotional women in cities are, as Lukács reminds us in his stringent comments on *Salammbô*,[15] a subject for a study of middle-class decadence just because the enjoyment of leisure for self-analysis is a product of a hidden, but nonetheless real, relation to history. Through a new and more tortuous route Romola arrives at the end where Scott more happily placed his hero: in retirement. Only in the study of Savonarola himself, a man who enters history through

14. William Myers, "George Eliot: Politics and Personality," in *Literature and Politics in the Nineteenth Century,* ed. John Lucas (London: Methuen, 1971), pp. 105–131, argues that George Eliot followed Comte in underrating politics and overrating the influence of individual moral values in historical development. However, *Middlemarch,* though critical of politicians in the narrowest sense, does not present the Reform Bill as a mere "national waste of energy" as Myers asserts (p. 108).

15. Lukács, *Historical Novel,* esp. pp. 188–190.

the back door by thinking he is doing God's unworldly work in
the world, does George Eliot come close to facing directly the
problem she wished to pose. Treated perhaps more sympathetically as a consistent and high-minded reformer than he deserves,
he is yet revealed in all his too human weakness as he fails to
live up to his own conception of his historical role. Unfortunately,
there is little the author can do to place him at the center rather
than the periphery of the novel. He is seen clearly probably because he is seen at some distance and never dwelt upon for too
long.

To turn from *Romola* to *Middlemarch* is of course to turn
from a good novel in an explicitly historical format to a great
novel that is less obviously a historical novel. And, in fact, as a
novel about history it is not as full a success as it is in other ways.
That we can talk about it both as a historical novel and as something else is not, however, in itself a weakness, but rather one
of its greatest strengths. With a feeling for the problems of the
historical novel that came from a major effort in the traditional
genre, George Eliot was able to make the leap in *Middlemarch*
to something greater than the provincial Scott tradition as developed by Bulwer or Ainsworth. First, there is fulfillment in an
English context of what Lukács recognized as the greatest destiny
of historical fiction in a writer like Balzac: to reinfuse the tradition of realism from which the historical novel developed with a
sense of a temporal dimension to all experience on every level.
In this, the great gap between public and private is effectively
replaced by a historical understanding of every aspect of social
life. History becomes history at its most fundamental, the
development of an entire nation or civilization in all its complexity. To this intention, which makes a study of provincial life
as true a picture of the England of 1829–1832 as any study of
great figures of the Reform Bill would be,[16] George Eliot also
added an epic aim: to provide within the scene of one provincial
city as comprehensive a picture as possible of the mutual rela-

16. Jerome Beaty, "History by Indirection: The Era of Reform in
Middlemarch," *Victorian Studies,* 1 (December 1957), 173–179, has
pointed out the close symmetry between the time of the novel and the
period of the Reform Bill, Dorothea and Will's marriage coming in May
1832, the final passage of the bill in June.

tions of all individuals and all classes. While Dickens is content to caricature the popular forces of revolution, or Scott is content to embody the middle class in one Bailie Jarvie, George Eliot gives us a living fabric of society as many individuals all responding throughout the book in personal complexity to the great and small events of their age. Having lived with the town through the long agitation of the Reform Bill we know that history is hardly made, in the political sense, in places like Middlemarch; but we are also left with the conviction that here, if anywhere, is a cross section of history as it really occurs, an infinitely complex interaction of local and general, personal and public, petty and generous, foolish and insightful actions all stirred and stirring the larger currents elsewhere. To know the history of Middlemarch in its fullest significance is to know the history of England or of civilization. Its history is indeed what the author calls it, a "parable" in which may be read concretely a typical historical experience. And she explicitly recommends to us the "efficiency" of "historical parallels" (chap. 35) by which we may generalize this one experience to every sphere of the country: "Thus while I tell the truth about loobies, my reader's imagination need not be entirely excluded from an occupation with lords; and the petty sums which any bankrupt of high standing would be sorry to retire upon, may be lifted to the level of high commercial transactions by the inexpensive addition of proportional ciphers."

As far as we can see into the minutiae of Middlemarch society, or out into the larger political events of the time, one concern marks the history of the age, that central one of the author's century, progress, improvement, reform, development. It is not one simple idea, but rather an expectation from the future, with temperaments and moral issues displayed in differing attitudes toward progress and different functions and roles in the emergence of the future. Caleb Garth improves in the substantial way of upgrading property; Bulstrode hopes to see God's special will in his favor worked out in the movement of history; peasants oppose the railroad, are indifferent to talk of reform far away in a Parliament that hardly concerns their lives, or hope for a French Revolution; professional politicians turn the sentiment for change to personal advantage while Mr. Brooke finds the limitations of his personal enlightenment in his attempt to carry the torch to others through the treacheries of ordinary politics. Everywhere the clash of old and new provides the meeting ground for personal intercourse and the field for ruin or success.

Within this total vision of a society in clumsy, often contradictory, movement forward, the intensive study of the major characters, Lydgate and Dorothea, is then worked out. It is unnecessary to belabor George Eliot's success with Lydgate or her greater achievement and difficulties with Dorothea. Lydgate brings the committed historical hero, the Savonarola character with a direct mission in history, to the center, or nearly to the center, of attention. A young doctor devoted to solving the central problem of medicine of his age, the control of the cholera, typhus, and typhoid fevers which would be the bane of the Victorian age, Lydgate parallels both the greater movement to reform on the national scene and the commitment of individuals like Garth to improvement in the local sphere. His failure to keep his engagement with history, for this, after all the talk of Dorothea's helping him, is what his career amounts to, is presented masterfully as a problem in the relation of personal and public roles. Without ever losing the sympathy which allows her to render his private experience so convincingly, George Eliot has the historian's overview of his career, a subject which, she even admits, is well adapted to betting: "the complicated probabilities of an arduous purpose, with all the possible thwartings and furtherings of circumstance, all the niceties of inward balance, by which a man swims and makes his point or else is carried headlong" (chap. 15). What he, of course, fails miserably to learn is what the Scott tradition so carefully avoided admitting, that an appointment with history may require some rearranging of the usual notions of the private life, may even mean some loss with the gain. Praising the Renaissance physician Vesalius to his lovely young wife as his model, Lydgate lists all his triumphs; only as an afterthought he notes, as if it were a mere historical curiosity, "He died rather miserably." Yet such, as we see it worked out in detail, is Lydgate's own fate, only he is miserable in his failure rather than because of his success. Unlike the Waverley hero, he is not merely a means for the author to explore history as a distant pageant but a character deeply implicated in history; and one who, like most men who try great reforms in history, is a failure through the weakness of his own personality against the complex force of circumstances.

When we turn from Lydgate to the central and magnificent creation of Dorothea and try to place her in the same historical light, we are, unfortunately, forced not to affirm further strengths in this well-praised novel but to throw additional light on long-suspected weaknesses. However subtly, sympathetically, and humorously George Eliot uncovers the combination of right feeling and childish enthusiasm in her portrayal of Dorothea Brooke, she has much the same difficulty with her as she had with Romola in solving the problem of bringing the protected heroine into relation with history and the life of the time. And the difficulty is all the more striking in that George Eliot, this second time, is even more explicit about her heroine's problem in getting in touch. We are told in the "Prelude" and again at the end that her problem is one for which she has history to blame in this age in which "later-born Theresas were helped by no coherent social faith"; and we are told again and again in the course of the story about the special difficulties the higher gentry have in coming out of hiding. Most obviously there is a problem of woman's role: Dorothea aspiring beyond the conventional role her sister Celia endorses yet seeing no clear direction in her society for this. Yet such special pleading, while useful in filling in the historical context to her situation, tends to provide special solutions to Dorothea's problem which don't face the fact of failure within the historical context. As a pendant to Lydgate, Dorothea could be seen abstractly as just such a failure as he, falling short of her own high notions of her historical role because of her inability to adjust her personal life to meet the demands of history. And George Eliot does describe her life in general terms as a failure when set against the historical activity of a Saint Theresa. Yet it is, if a failure, a failure without the distinctive lifetime sting that affects Lydgate. Indeed, at a time when she is best equipped, with her husband's money and her social position, to play a part even as a woman of her time in the life of her time, her greatest deed is merely to offer consolation to Lydgate, her fellow failure. Though we all love her for her personal, private growth, and merely respect Lydgate, we can hardly deny that her historical failures are easily forgiven her by the plot whereas Lydgate's are held for scrupulous payment. Casaubon is conveniently ready to die and she is allowed true love after all. Even as a do-good widow she has Garth's capable help in her projects for community improvement; nor is there a hint that some of her tenants, like Brooke's, saw a greater revolution against her class presaged in the Reform Bill. In the end, as most readers feel, she not only has her cake and eats it too; her relation with Will Ladislaw is somewhat hollow and melodramatic, and his relation to the great world to which they emigrate in the end is even more unconvincing. Like the Waverley hero, Dorothea has her endless domestic happiness after her brief engagement with history. But even more fortunate than he, she can continue to feel that she plays a subsidiary part through her husband's conveniently unclear political career. In fairness to her sense of history, George Eliot undercuts Will's man-on-the-white-horse future by noting that his career as an "ardent public man" was subject to the same frustrations in the ambiguity of progress that we have seen in the progress of reform at Middlemarch: "working well in those times when reforms were begun with a young hopefulness of immediate good which has been much checked in our days" ("Finale"). But the impression remains that Dorothea has done her part in the progress of history through her husband without having to pay the kind of price demanded of Lydgate. And then there is the further ambiguity of those "unhistoric acts" of hers which we hear about but have only seen when, before she married, she could exercise the easy charity of a large landowner. As in *Romola,* the will to goodness — moral desire — seems sometimes to stand in masquerade for real historical involvement.

It would be unfair to a splendid portrait in a magnificent novel to dwell overmuch on these problems in the historical treatment of Dorothea, just as it is unfair to overstress the problems with her love for Will. If the book does fall into difficulties and unclear assertions similar to those in *Romola* in relating a private heroine to history, it remains on the whole a wonderfully comprehensive treatment of the life of a community in a perspective at once individually sympathetic and historically acute. If it still shows some of the problems that beset the English historical novel in general, as a historical novel in the best sense, a novel about people's lives in their relation to history, it stands securely above its predecessors.

What we may fairly conclude, though, is that the problem of the English historical novel, even at its best, lies precisely in the articulation of the relation between individual experience and historical overview. Specifically, the problem amounts to a tendency to avoid or evade a direct confrontation of the two, a desire to talk about history on the one hand and about the individual on the other without fully realizing the consequence of seeing individual life in a historical perspective. For in this perspective individual man seems at best tragically heroic in his fight with a finally unconquerable giant; at worst he seems merely puny and inconsequential. Without hoping to offer any specific explanation for the failure of most English writers of the historically conscious nineteenth century to face man's historical destiny, one may speculate that the difficulty has something to do with the peculiar destiny of England in the nineteenth century. If being at the forefront of history made the English writer especially conscious of history and change, it also gave him a rather special perspective. For a brief period that nonetheless seemed to those who lived in it like a permanent state of affairs, history seemed to be turned largely beneficent. The future, as it appears, despite George Eliot's qualifications, in *Middlemarch,* seemed inevitably an improvement on the past. Even if progress in industry and later in the growth of the second empire brought England new problems, they were problems which Englishmen looked confidently to the future to solve. Although many challenged the overly jejune tone, say, of Macaulay's assertions, few, if any, were willing to deny his essential premise that the recent history of England would show a clear movement for the better, a "great and constant progress." Even critics of the tendency of British progress like Carlyle or Ruskin were hesitant to attack directly the common faith in a better future and the common belief in history. If they worried that history seemed even at its progressive best somehow to fail to satisfy individual values, they were yet unwilling to bring the problem home to its root, to the essential incongruence between individual and historical destiny. Instead history was, to a greater or lesser extent, mythologized so that it could read preferable lessons to the age. Carlyle in *Past and Present,* Ruskin in *Stones of Venice,* or Morris in *News from Nowhere* looked similarly to past or to future history for a realm in which reality and individual value could be, in fact, even more easily related than in real historical time. Or, by a more desperate stratagem, Carlyle created in the figure of Frederick the Great a hero who could wield history to his individual desire, but did so only by creating a hero who had given up most personal values in his quest for mastery over history. Neither myth nor great man faced the real problems of the relation of the individual to history. With less consistency but with growing insight, Tennyson in the two Locksley Hall poems began by linking the individual and historical destiny; then, in his own old age, recanted something of his faith in progress itself but even more his faith that historical prosperity for a nation necessarily brings happiness to the individuals of the nation.

Unlike most literature of the nineteenth century, the success of the historical novel depended upon a confrontation with the problem hidden by the general hope in the benevolence of history's course. Yet, from its beginnings in Scott, the historical novel was peculiarly wedded to the hope in progress. While Scott showed the folly and destructiveness of the past, he always linked the happy destiny of the Waverley hero to the general destiny of English history itself. History showed the nation, like the gentleman hero, emerging from a troubled past into a happier and more prosperous future. That such a perspective, right as it may have been in the particular case of eighteenth-century England, is a liability, not an asset, to the historical novelist has been obscured by the fact that the greatest appraisal of Scott and the historical novel in general has come from a critic, Lukács, whose own perspective continues the belief in progress into our own regressive century. Writing in Russian exile from Nazi Europe at a time when history would seem to justify a belief in progress as little as it ever did, Lukács, oblivious of the tragedy of the individual under the historical triumph of progressive Russian socialism around him, bravely affirms his faith in the inevitable development of history toward a socialist utopia. To him the noblest historical novel is thus the one which, like the work of Scott, affirms progress in history. And the ambiguities of this progress in an individual perspective tend to be ignored. If Lukács is too good a historian to deny that progress has its loss, as well as gain, and too fine a critic not to acknowledge the supremacy of Tolstoy over Scott, he is still too sympathetic with those who share his historical optimism to point out clearly the dangers of the belief in progress to the historical novelist.

The anomalous experience of the English historical novel should perhaps stand as a general corrective example to Lukács's overview of the historical novel. Rather than failing during the later "bourgeois decadence" of the late nineteenth century, the English historical novel showed the seeds of its failure from the beginning. Hoping against hope in the benevolence of history, English writers even at their best tended to evade the great problem of the relation of the individual to history which writers in less happy countries faced directly in their own experience and naturally brought into their novels. Certainly, to look for a moment beyond the classic period of the English historical novel in the nineteenth century and at its modern successors, a new kind of historical novel seems to emerge coincidentally with the loss of faith in historical progress. By the turn of the century neither social nor national progress seemed such a settled thing to many English thinkers. And the effect, when inevitable progress was not merely simplistically turned into an equally inevitable decadence, was to lead writers to re-examine the relation of history and the individual. In the poetry of Hardy and Yeats, for example, there is a new and radical focus on the gap between feeling or heart's desire and historical reality. Even before the First World War brought home most clearly both the decline of England and the horrible sacrifice that history can demand of the individual, novelists who meditated on history were similarly beginning to face more unswervingly the problem of the individual's relation to history. Even H. G. Wells, for example, though dedicated to intelligent progress, no longer tried to evade the grim or absurd realities of history as it had in fact occurred. In *Tono-Bungay,* for instance, the world power of the enterprising Napoleon of salesmanship Teddy Ponderevo reduces to absurdity the notion of great individuals in history; and his pathetic fall, when the bubble of Tono-Bungay collapses under him, is what the man who tampers with history must expect. Far more deeply, Conrad's political novels, especially *The Secret Agent, Under Western Eyes,* and the panoramic *Nostromo,* probed the complacency of the English tradition about the relation of history and the individual. Beyond the apparently settled order of the British imperium, as Marlow pointed out to his more ordinary English listeners in the opening of *Heart of Darkness,* there was a more brutal natural order of history where individual man had to face, without the protection of British ideas of ordered progress, the absurdity of his individual fate in the great perspective of history. In Conrad's world, which Lukács might stigmatize as a fantasy of decadent bourgeois imagination but which I am afraid rings only too true to the realities of history, innocent idiot boys must be sacrificed for obscure and ultimately stupid political aims (one being, indeed, to threaten British security in order to provoke it to reaction), progressive revolution feeds on the broken hearts of individuals, and great schemes for material improvement most often end up in moral disasters which pull even the best men down with them.

With a boyhood directly in the historical ferment of Eastern Europe and a career at the outreaches of European civilization, Conrad may appear the classic exception that proves the rule. But the tradition of the English novel in which he wrote was certainly ripe for his special message by the beginning of the twentieth century. Perhaps even more than in the European genius of Conrad, the tradition of the English historical novel found its twentieth-century restatement and revaluation in a work like Ford Madox Ford's World War I tetralogy, *Parade's End.* Imbued with the tradition of the English historical novel from his earlier, more romantic studies of the England of Henry VIII in *The Fifth Queen,* Ford deliberately turned the tradition on its head as he applied it to contemporary civilization in his masterwork. There Christopher Tietjens, a younger son of old gentry, a lover of eighteenth-century society and eighteenth-century good century, is slowly torn apart and torn loose from his past by the sense, every inch the Waverley hero living on into the twentieth methodical failure of English history as the war develops. Where the traditional hero made, as Tietjens seems to think he is making in *Some Do Not . . . ,* a pleasant excursion into history for the sake of his own education, this hero finds himself drawn into a web of history, dangerous and absurd, from which he can find no escape. What is demanded of him is what was usually not demanded in the nineteenth-century novel, knowledge of his own helplessness before history and heroic assertion against history within the context defined for him by history itself. Understandably, the lesson was one to which neither Tietjens nor his predecessors in the English historical novel came without being roughly pushed by the historical process itself. Here, as everywhere, great understanding asks a great price, and it is perhaps no surprise that few nineteenth-century English writers, in the period which Bertrand Russell has suggested may have been the high point of human civilization, "a brief interlude between past and future barbarism," [17] should have been eager to go out of their way for the painful knowledge of their common human destiny. Once awakened into history, however, it was equally unlikely, much as they might wish to return to a more complacent view of history, that modern writers could continue the attractive, if most often mediocre, historical parade begun by Scott.

17. *The Autobiography of Bertrand Russell* (Boston: Little, Brown, 1969), 3:328.

DAVID STAINES

King Arthur in Victorian Fiction

In 1829 Thomas Love Peacock published the only Arthurian novel of the nineteenth century, his satirical romance *The Misfortunes of Elphin*. Victorian England did witness a revival of interest in the Arthurian legends; poets, playwrights, and painters found inspiration in the story of Camelot, yet the novel, the chief literary form of the century, seemed to avoid this material. Peacock's novel continued to hold its distinctive position by default. The major modern studies of Arthurian literature fail to discuss or name any nineteenth-century work of prose fiction other than *The Misfortunes of Elphin*,[1] and bibliographies of Arthurian literature do not offer any assistance.[2] Arthur's world does ap-

1. Howard Maynadier, *The Arthur of the English Poets* (Boston: Houghton Mifflin, 1907); Margaret J. C. Reid, *The Arthurian Legend* (London: Oliver and Boyd, 1938). Even chap. 5, "Tennyson's Contemporaries at Home," of M. W. MacCallum's *Tennyson's "Idylls of the King" and the Arthurian Story from the Sixteenth Century* (Glasgow, 1894) contains no reference to fictional works.
2. The earliest Arthurian bibliography, incomplete and frequently inaccurate, A. E. Curdy, "Arthurian Literature," *Romanic Review,* 1 (1910), 125–139, 265–278, and two subsequent bibliographies, Clark A. Northup and John J. Parry, "The Arthurian Legends: Modern Retellings of the Old Stories — An Annotated Bibliography," *Journal of English and Germanic Philology,* 43 (1944), 173–221, and Paul A. Brown, "The Arthurian Legends: Supplement to Northup and Parry's

pear, however, in some Victorian fiction, and a bibliographical investigation examining its appearances should be of interest to students of Arthurian literature and to literary historians of Victorian England.

The distinction of Peacock's novel merits a brief study of the plot and the degree of its Arthurian content. *The Misfortunes of Elphin* unites three previously unrelated episodes of Welsh tradition in order to present the career of Taliesin, the famous Welsh bard. Each of the episodes has its source in the many studies of Welsh literature and history published in the early nineteenth century.[3] For Peacock, historical accuracy created through fidelity to his sources is as important as the satiric intent which underlies his employment of the material; his satire presents an accurate account of life in sixth-century Wales.[4]

The opening section of the novel introduces Peacock's great comic creation, Seithenyn ap Seithyn, Lord High Commissioner of Royal Embankment. The prosperity of the plain of Gwaelod, ruled by Gwythno Garanhir, king of Caredigion and father of Elphin, depends upon the security of the embankment. When Elphin protests that some portions of the embankment are rotten, Seithenyn is undaunted:

> "But I say, the parts that are rotten give elasticity to those that are sound: they give them elasticity, elasticity, elasticity. If it were all sound, it would break by its own obstinate stiffness: the soundness is checked by the rottenness, and the stiffness by the elasticity. There is nothing so dangerous as innovation. See the waves in the equinoctial storms, dashing and clashing, roaring and pouring,

Annotated Bibliography," *Journal of English and Germanic Philology,* 49 (1950), 208–216, cite only a few of the works discussed in this article.

3. For a study of Peacock's Welsh sources, see Jean-Jacques Mayoux, *Un épicurien anglais: Thomas Love Peacock* (Paris: Nizet et Bastard, 1933), pp. 392–404.

4. Sir Edward Strachey wrote, "I heard him say that he had great difficulty in getting at the true story of Taliesin's birth, as more than one learned authority had concealed his own ignorance on the matter by saying that the story was too long to be told then; and he was proud of the fact that Welsh archaeologists treated his book as a serious and valuable addition to Welsh history" (quoted in Thomas Love Peacock, *Calidore and Miscellanea,* ed. Richard Garnett [London, 1891], pp. 19–20).

spattering and battering, rattling and battling against it. I would not be so presumptuous as to say, I could build any thing that would stand against them half an hour; and here this immortal old work, which God forbid the finger of modern mason should bring into jeopardy, this immortal work has stood for centuries, and will stand for centuries more, if we let it alone. It is well: it works well; let well alone. Cupbearer, fill. It was half rotten when I was born, and that is a conclusive reason why it should be three parts rotten when I die." [5]

Peacock makes Seithenyn the spokesman for the conservative point of view; despite the sixth-century setting, the eloquent defense of the embankment's deterioration resembles contemporary Tory speeches which acknowledged existing social evils yet decried the possibility of change. The destruction of the kingdom makes the narrator reflect "that our own public guardians are too virtuous to act or talk like Seithenyn, and that we ourselves are too wise not to perceive, and too free not to prevent it, if they should be so disposed."

The second section of the novel depicts the growing love between Melanghel, Elphin's daughter, and Taliesin, the young bard, whom Elphin found as a babe in a coracle on the stream. The description of Taliesin's youth follows the Welsh source, though Peacock injects satire again when he looks back at the seeming ignorance of the medieval world:

They lacked some of our light, to enable them to perceive that the act of coming, in great multitudes, with fire and sword, to the remote dwellings of peaceable men, with the premeditated design of cutting their throats, ravishing their wives and daughters, killing their children, and appropriating their worldly goods, belongs, not to the department of murder and robbery, but to that of legitimate war, of which all the practitioners are gentlemen, and entitled to be treated like gentlemen. (Chap. 6)

At this time Maelgon Gwyneth, the king of a neighboring section of North Wales, comes into Elphin's realm on a hunting party. When Elphin refuses to assert that Maelgon's wife is more chaste

5. Thomas Love Peacock, *The Misfortunes of Elphin* (London, 1829), chap. 2.

and more beautiful than his own, "Maelgon acted as the possessors of worldly power usually act in similar cases: he locked Elphin up within four stone walls, with an intimation that he should keep him there till he pronounced a more orthodox opinion on the question in dispute." When Taliesin asks Melanghèl how he can win her love, he learns that he must rescue her father.

The world of King Arthur provides the setting for the third and final section of the novel. King Melwas abducted Gwenyvar while she was hunting in the woods and refuses to give her back to Arthur. Taliesin learns of the abduction and manages to secure the queen's return. As a sign of his gratitude, Arthur uses his influence and power to obtain Elphin's release. Because of Maelgon's rude actions, Arthur forces him to defray the expenses of Taliesin's marriage.

The Misfortunes of Elphin maintains a precarious balance between romance and satire. Peacock roots his story firmly in the world of Welsh tradition so that his novel has the accuracy and veracity of a Welsh history. At the same time he looks at the seemingly uncivilized aspects of this early society only to point ironically at the conservatism and hypocrisy of his own generation. The historical fiction prevents the satire from becoming indignant invective, and the satire lends charm and a further significance to the historical fiction.

The Arthurian dimension of the novel is limited. Arthur, the rough chieftain of early Celtic legends rather than the stately king of later accounts, appears as a strong and commanding leader. His wife's infidelity is a known fact; even Maelgon refers to it, "Though he is a man of great prowess, and moreover, saving his reverence and your presence, a cuckold, he has not yet favoured his kingdom with an heir apparent." Though Arthur's role is secondary, *The Misfortunes of Elphin* is Arthurian because the setting is the world of Arthur and his Welsh neighbors.

The early nineteenth-century disregard of the Arthurian legends does not change as a consequence of Peacock's novel; no future poet or prose writer even alludes to it. More significantly, no other novel of the whole nineteenth century in England employs the Arthurian world as its setting or the medieval Arthurian legends as its source. There are, however, a few Victorian novels that may be loosely, though perhaps inaccurately, termed Arthurian. A brief survey of these will eliminate the oversight of Arthurian bibilographers and clarify the significance of Arthur's absence from Victorian fiction.

In Mrs. Craik's *Avillion; or, The Happy Isles — A Fireside Fancy* (1853), the first Victorian Arthurian work in prose, Wilfred Mayer's dream vision adds a further conclusion to Tennyson's *Morte d'Arthur,* which provides the tale's epigraph:

> I am going a long way,
> With these thou seest — if, indeed, I go —
> (For all my mind is clouded with a doubt)
> To the island-valley of Avillion.

On their honeymoon voyage, Wilfred and his wife meet a German mystic whose life has become a search for "the land beyond sunset — the Island of the Blest":

> "Men in all ages have believed in the existence of this land. Legends, variously modified by different ages and climes, have all agreed in this universal fact, that far westward, in the midst of the vast mysterious ocean, untraversed and untraversable by man, lies an island, whose dwellers have all joys of humanity without its pain — all the sensuous delights of earth, combined with the purity of heaven. Who knows but that the angels carried God's Eden and planted it there in the midst of the sea?" [6]

In a severe attack of pain, Wilfred seems to die and enter the region of the afterlife; he sees his own death and his widow's mourning; he hears the mystic's voice urging him to reach the Happy Isles. His journey brings him to a new land, "not heaven, but earth — earth with its curse taken away, and made pure and beautiful as it was in the Eden-time." He meets Ulysses, who describes this world, "Here all desires are fulfilled — we have wisdom, peace, virtue, glory, together with every delight of sense exalted into purity. We have no longings unattained — we live a life like that of childhood, one delicious present." When Wilfred

6. Dinah Maria Mulock [Mrs. Craik], "Avillion; or, The Happy Isles — A Fireside Fancy," chap. 2, in *Avillion and Other Tales* (London, 1853).

encounters Galahad, his stay in the region becomes an introduction to the men and women of the Arthurian romances in their new world.

From afar Wilfred sees the castle where Arthur and Morgue la Faye dwell:

> They sat together on a throne, alike, and yet unlike; for she was the most beauteous dame in the whole land of Faërie, while on the face of her mortal brother lingered still the traces of his long warfare on earth. Yet he was a noble king to behold; and as he sat leaning upon Excalibur, his fair hair falling on either side his broad forehead, and his limb showing grand and giant-like through his garments' folds, I felt rising within me the same ardour which had impelled so many brave knights to fight, bleed, or die, for Arthur of Britain. (Chap. 6)

Arthur is an exiled king awaiting the call to return to his earthly domain; he asks Wilfred if his kingdom is expecting him; Wilfred tempers his negative response with the admission, "The world's truths of mystical allegory are enduring as itself. The Round Table has crumbled into dust, and the raven hoots where stood the towers of Tintagel; but still many an old romaunt, and many a new poet's songs, keep up the name and the glory of Arthur." Arthur's present home is not a land of perfection but a world where pain and pleasure are mingled, where "is intermixed just so much of evil and of suffering as will purify and lift us one stage nearer to divine perfection."

In contrast to Avillion is the City of the Dead, a world of suffering and oblivion, which Wilfred visits with his Arthurian guides. In response to Merlin's request that his companions "call one of those who were dearest to thee on earth," Arthur laments, "They were few indeed! . . . Ambition was all to me. I loved my royal kingdom more than any of its subject dwellers — save, perhaps, Guinever and Gawaine." At Arthur's bidding, the phantom of Guinever appears in a nun's habit and wails, "Launcelot! Launcelot!" When Galahad summons his father, "the mailed image of a knight" appears. Launcelot "spoke not, and none spoke with him. Only his son Galahad, with clasped hands, knelt and prayed."

Wilfred's stay in Avillion draws to an end. Morgue tells him that he must leave, though of his own free will; his hesitation to depart disappears when Morgue shows him a vision of his earthly home. Wilfred leaves Avillion and reaches Eden-land, an earthly abode "where men of this modern time may live in peace, and worship God." When Wilfred awakens from his visit to Eden-land, his wife notes that he is calm and relaxed after his one-hour sleep.

In *Avillion* Mrs. Craik displays a familiarity with the Arthurian worlds of Malory and Tennyson as well as other medieval romances. Her employment of names not found in Malory reveals her knowledge of the shorter romances in which such figures as Launfal, Triamour, and Ogier le Danois do appear. She makes no attempt to observe any kind of fidelity to earlier presentations of the Arthurian legends. She borrows directly from Malory, for example, in the description of Galahad, "the tender son, who dying 'kissed Sir Bors and Sir Percival, saying, "Salute my father, Sir Launcelot, and bid him remember this unstable world," ' and then was borne upward by angels." She fashions her presentation of Arthur upon the lament of the dying king in Tennyson's *Morte d'Arthur;* the epigraph is the explicit acknowledgment of her debt. *Avillion* is the product of her familiarity with the legends and her desire to present, through a dream vision, a glimpse of the afterlife of these familiar characters. The tale, a jeu d'esprit or "fireside fancy," marks Mrs. Craik's only attempt to incorporate Arthurian material into her fiction; throughout her long career she never returns to Camelot for her inspiration.[7]

Charlotte Yonge's knowledge of the Arthurian world far exceeds Mrs. Craik's familiarity with the material. In her *Kings of*

7. Mrs. Craik makes use of the Arthurian world in only one other novel, *King Arthur* (London, 1886), which derives its title from the name a couple give to their adopted son: "I have thought of a name. We are Cornish born, as I told you, Dr. Franklin. When I was a girl, my one hero was our great Cornishman, who was also 'Nobody's child' — found by Merlin, they say, as a little naked baby on the shore at Tintagel, but who grew up to be the stainless knight — the brave soldier — the Christian king. My boy shall do the same — in his own way. It does not matter how he was born, if he lives so that everybody will mourn him when he dies. So he shall have my hero's name. He shall be my 'King' Arthur" (p. 58). The novel makes no further attempt to develop or extend the Arthurian reference.

England: A History for Young Children (1848) she refers
directly to Arthur, "The sons of Vortigern, and those noble
Romans, Ambrose and his nephew Arthur, the brave King, of
whom so many stories are told, fought long and gallantly in
defence of their country — but in vain; one county after another
was lost to them, until nothing remained except Cornwall and
Wales." [8] In the monthly journal she edited there are two long
series of studies of the legends.[9] In her most famous novel, *The
Heir of Redclyffe* (1853), the hero, Sir Guy, takes as his model
Sir Galahad; though not paralleling Galahad's life in any way,
Guy's career follows the same principles of truth, selflessness,
and charity that motivated Galahad. Yet Miss Yonge's only
attempt to depict the Arthurian world is her short *History of Sir
Thomas Thumb* (1855):

> On the proposal to draw up a Life of Tom Thumb, to accom-
> pany the graceful Illustrations of this little book, the attempt
> would have seemed a presumptuous interference with nursery
> classics, had it not appeared, on examination, that he, unlike his
> companions in fireside mythology, has never been the theme of
> any cultivated mind, but has been left to the unpoetical English
> tradition. His adventures, as usually narrated, are without variety,
> and, in general, disagreeable; and even the name of King Arthur
> cannot raise him, appearing only as the vulgarized Arthur of
> nursery rhymes.
> Fielding's burlesque only added the evils of the literature of his
> age to the dull poverty of the old story, and thus the field ap-
> peared to be open to an endeavour to weave the traditional mis-
> haps of the pigmy-knight into a tale that might be free from the
> former offences against good taste.[10]

8. Charlotte Yonge, *Kings of England: A History for Young Children*
(London, 1848), chap. 2.

9. An anonymous series of six articles, "The Legend of Sir Galahad,"
appeared in *The Monthly Packet of Evening Readings for Younger
Members of the English Church*, vols. 4–6 (1852–53), and Ellen J.
Millington's series of twenty-one articles, "King Arthur and His Knights,
with the Quest of the Sancgreal," appeared in the same journal, vols. 17–
27 (1859–64).

10. Charlotte Yonge, "Preface," *The History of Sir Thomas Thumb*
(London, 1855).

In her rendition the Arthurian world remains a vague background to Tom's adventures. The narration is populated with the characters of the romances, Arthur, Guenever, Lancelot, Hector, Kaye, Bedivere, Lukyn, Tristrem, Bors, Percival, Gawayne, Merlin, and Mordred, yet they remain indistinct, achieving any degree of personality only through the associations attached to their names. More important to our present purpose, however, than the *History of Sir Thomas Thumb* are the explanatory notes appended to the story, longer, indeed, than the narration: "The Notes may perhaps be thought over numerous, but they were added with the desire of rendering accessible to children some of the choice passages of English fairy poetry, well known indeed to their elders, but to them out of reach, as well as to give a few sketches from the romances of King Arthur's Court, often a subject of much youthful curiosity, not easily gratified" (preface). The notes vivify the characters of the story by recounting many of their adventures directly from the medieval romances. The breadth of Yonge's reading, evident in the many sources cited,[11] proves that she had the knowledge, if not the inclination, to write an Arthurian novel. Yet her career as a novelist never turned to the realm of Camelot.

In *Arthur; or, A Knight of Our Own Day* (1876), Mary Neville creates a modern love story derived not from Malory but from Tennyson. In one of her earlier stories, *Alice Godolphin* (1875), she turned to Tennyson's poetry for four of the thirteen chapter epigraphs. In *Arthur,* fifteen of the thirty chapters take their epigraphs from Tennyson. Her affection for the poet leads her to attempt a modern equivalent to his presentation of the Arthur-Guinevere-Lancelot triangle.

In the little village of Arling, Sussex, the rector, Mr. Helmore, has two daughters — Elizabeth, a woman of common sense and practical intelligence, twenty-three years of age, and Ida, scarcely

11. The medieval sources include Nennius, Geoffrey of Monmouth, Giraldus Cambrensis, *Sir Gawain and the Green Knight,* Chaucer, Gavin Douglas, *Sir Tristrem,* Malory, and the *Roman de Merlin.* More modern sources include Spenser, Shakespeare, Percy's *Reliques,* George Ellis's *Specimens of Early English Metrical Romances,* Joseph Ritson's *Ancient English Metrical Romances,* John Dunlop's *History of Prose Fiction,* Tennyson's *Morte d'Arthur,* and Arnold's *Tristram and Iseult.*

eighteen and weary of village life. Into their quiet existence comes
the family of Sir Henry Atherstone, the owner of Arling Grange,
including his son Captain Arthur Atherstone. At the church
service Elizabeth admires Arthur for his religious devotion, Ida
admires him for his handsome features. Arthur finds himself
attracted to the selfless Elizabeth, though Ida is determined to
win his affection. The young trio is completed by the arrival of
Arthur's best friend, Lord Lancelot Trevor.

In order to secure her marriage to Arthur, Ida plants un-
founded rumors of their engagement in the ears of village gossips.
When Arthur hears of the rumors, he feels morally obliged to
propose. To his sadness and to Elizabeth's poignant disappointment, Ida accepts his proposal. The omnipresent and omniscient
narrator cannot restrain her emotions: "Poor Arthur Atherstone!
he is not the first man who has been made the dupe of a fair,
false woman, and has deemed himself the object of a pure and
true affection, when all the time he is walking unsuspectingly into
the snare laid for him by an artful and designing cupidity." [12]

After their marriage Arthur and Ida move to Brighton, where
Ida enjoys the opportunity to mingle in society; she delights in
the attentions she receives from handsome men, particularly from
Lancelot Trevor. When Arthur's sister becomes critically ill, he
returns to his family and entrusts his wife to Lancelot's care. The
epigraph of the chapter emphasizes the conscious parallel to
Tennyson's characters:

> Then Arthur charged his warrior whom he loved
> And honoured most, Sir Launcelot, to ride forth
> And bring the Queen.

Tragedy reigns in Arthur's family. His father has a paralytic
seizure; his sister dies. When Arthur escorts his parents back to
Arling, he asks Ida, much to her disappointment, to spend the
winter there. To relieve the monotony of Arling, Arthur's mother
invites Lancelot to visit them. The winter proves to be a trying
time for Arthur and his wife. Ida, still enjoying Lancelot's flirtatious advances, ignores her husband. Time, however, is Arthur's

12. Mary Neville, *Arthur; or, A Knight of Our Own Day* (London,
1876), vol. 1, chap. 5.

teacher; he realizes that his wife is not the fine woman he imagined; he accepts her lack of affection for him, though he does not suspect Lancelot's love for her. When Lady Laura, a society gossip from Brighton, insinuates that Ida courts Lancelot's attention, Arthur determines that Ida and Lancelot shall not see each other again. In their final meeting Lancelot confesses his love to Ida and vows to leave England forever. Throughout their interview Arthur is a hidden observer, brought by Lady Laura. Disturbed by the sight, Arthur refuses to believe Ida when she swears that she has loved only her husband.

Finally conscious of the seriousness of her coquetry, Ida flees Arthur. In a chapter whose epigraph reads "Let no man dream but that I love thee still," Arthur finds his wife in a room at the Blue Bell in Keighley; he listens to the tale of her journey, though he never looks at her. He promises her an allotment of two hundred pounds a quarter and explains his arrangement that she live with her sister. Though Ida continually begs forgiveness, Arthur departs for Europe.

At this juncture in the plot, the correspondence between the novel and Tennyson's poetry terminates. Having presented the final meeting of her hero and his wife fashioned after Arthur's parting from his wife in *Guinevere,* Neville introduces a conclusion derived from *The Heir of Redclyffe.* Arthur is dangerously ill with a fever in Le Mans, which is Lancelot's current home. Learning of his friend's condition, Lancelot agrees to nurse him. After two weeks Arthur regains full consciousness. Lancelot explains his relationship with Ida and assures Arthur that his deep affection never met with any reciprocation except a few flirtatious gestures. As Arthur summons his wife from England, Lancelot parts from him in a renewed friendship. Later, in Chartres, Lancelot lies dying of fever. In spite of his affection for Arthur, his hopeless love for Ida prevents him from seeking Arthur's assistance in his illness. Alone, Lancelot dies.

When Arthur and Ida return to Arling, their married life blossoms. Ida seems to be a new woman, no longer reserved and aloof from the people of the village. Only one shadow mars the happiness of Arling Grange: "But in all the brightness and serenity that crowned their after years, there was one name seldom uttered, but never forgotten by Arthur and Ida — one memory that was always kept green in their hearts, with the earnest hope that some day they might again meet that much-wronged friend in a land — 'Where beyond these voices there is Peace' " (vol. 2, chap. 14).

Though Neville employs Tennyson's Arthurian triangle as the basis of her novel, the parallels between her modern figures and Tennyson's medieval characters are sporadic and rarely valid. Arthur Atherstone has neither the stature nor the spirituality of Tennyson's Arthur; Ida is a silly, flirtatious girl, in no way equal to the mature queen of Tennyson's *Idylls of the King;* Lancelot Trevor never reveals any innate nobility corresponding to Lancelot's preeminence among the knights. In addition, the glance backward to the Arthurian era of early England serves no purpose. Near the end of the novel the narrator applauds the heroism of her own time:

> Yes, though some will have it that the race of men have degenerated and become effeminate since the good old days of King Arthur and his Round Table, there are some now living whose faithful hearts and self-denying lives would not have disgraced those brave warriors of old. The "days of chivalry" are not over, and many a deed has been wrought in our formal, uninteresting, and most unromantic clique, termed society, which for true valour and generosity has never been eclipsed by any belted knight of the olden time. Men do not in these days ride about clad in armour, waging war against all forms of oppression and wrong; but the fiercest enemies are those who are invisible, and whose weapons are not of steel or iron, or to be withstood by such. (Vol. 2, chap. 13)

Such sentiments do not follow naturally from the story; no contrast between the past and the present is ever suggested. *Arthur; or, A Knight of Our Own Day* is a silly and sentimental Victorian novel, the unfortunate product of a novelist's adoration and desecration of Tennyson's Arthurian poetry.

Mary Elizabeth Braddon avoids Neville's failure by making the tenuous parallel between the love story in *Mount Royal* (1882) and its Arthurian counterpart always implied and never explicit. She does not employ an Arthurian plot as the basis of her novel, but invokes it only as a suggestive frame of reference.

She sets the story of Christabel Courtenay, an orphaned young woman who lives with her widowed aunt, Diana Tregonell, at Mount Royal, an old manor house "on the slope of a bosky hill about a mile and a half from the little town of Boscastle, on the north coast of Cornwall," so that the characters of her ill-fated love triangle share some affinity with the Arthurian triangle of Tristram-Iseult-Mark, whose legends originated in this area.

As Christabel and her aunt's guest, Angus Hamleigh, share their knowledge of the Arthurian legends in exploring the rugged terrain of Cornwall, their affection grows. The legends are a part of Christabel's being: "To Christabel the whole story of Arthur and his knights was as real as if it had been a part of her own life. She had Tennyson's Arthur and Tennyson's Lancelot in her heart of hearts, and knew just enough of Sir Thomas Mallory's prose to give substance to the Laureate's poetic shadows." [13] Angus, however, refuses to accept Christabel's romantic conception: "The Laureate invented Arthur — he took out a patent for the Round Table, and his invention is only a little less popular than that other product of the age, the sewing-machine. How many among modern tourists would care about Tintagel if Tennyson had not revived the old legend?" (chap. 3). At the same time, Angus, a young man of poor health, does come to see himself as Tristram: "Mr. Hamleigh had been nearly two months at Mount Royal, and he told himself that it was time for leave-taking. Fain would he have stayed on — stayed until that blissful morning when Christabel and he might kneel, side by side, before the altar in Minster Church, and be made one for ever — one in life and death — in a union as perfect as that which was symbolized by the plant that grew out of Tristan's tomb and went down into the grave of his mistress" (chap. 5). The subsequent engagement of Angus and Christabel is terminated abruptly when Christabel hears that Angus has had a sordid love affair with a London actress. Angus accepts the termination only because of his certainty that failing health portends his imminent death.

In an effort to grant her dying aunt some personal happiness, Christabel agrees reluctantly to marry Leonard, Mrs. Tregonell's

13. Mary Elizabeth Braddon, *Mount Royal* (London, 1882), chap. 3.

unrefined and selfish son. Their marriage is doomed from its inception. Though fidelity and obedience mark Christabel's behavior to her husband, love is conspicuously absent from their union. After their honeymoon the couple returns to Mount Royal. When Leonard happens to meet Angus in the coastal area, he invites him to stay with them; thus the Arthurian triangle is complete:

> And to think that she — his dearest, she, all gentleness and refinement, was mated to this coarse clay! Was King Marc such an one as this he wondered, and if he were, who could be angry with Tristan — Tristan who died longing to see his lost love — struck to death by his wife's cruel lie — Tristan whose passionate soul passed by metempsychosis into briar and leaf, and crept across the arid rock to meet and mingle with the beloved dead. Oh, how sweet and sad the old legend seemed to Angus to-day, standing above the melancholy sea, where he and she had stood folded in each other's arms in the sweet triumphant moment of love's first avowal. (Chap. 20)

Though the Arthurian triangle offers an interesting point of comparison to the triangle of the uncivilized and jealous Leonard, the patient-suffering Angus, and the beautiful Christabel, torn between obedience to Leonard and love for Angus, the correspondence always remains allusive and suggestive, never accurate or precise.

As the novel reaches its conclusion, the characters' correspondence to the medieval triangle disappears. Christabel's devotion to her husband does not permit her indulgence in any amorous activity with Angus; Angus is so devoted to Christabel that he shows no interest in any other woman; no second Iseult can or does appear. The sole remaining correspondence is Leonard, who, like Mark in certain medieval accounts, kills his wife's lover; here, however, even this parallel ends. As Christabel slowly realizes the cause of Angus's seemingly accidental death, she plots her husband's murder, only to stop her plan at the last moment when she remembers that vengeance is a divine right. She confronts Leonard with her knowledge of his guilt and demands his departure. The setting regains the peace of the early chapters of the novel, "Very quietly flows the stream of life at

Mount Royal now that these feverish scenes have passed into the shadow of the days that are no more."

Mount Royal succeeds where *Arthur* fails because Braddon wisely employs the Arthurian world as a subtle and rarely sustained allusion. She chooses a Cornish setting full of Arthurian associations. She makes her two principal characters knowledgeable readers of Tennyson, Arnold, and medieval Arthurian authors. Most importantly, she does not try to establish a medieval analogue to the events of her story, nor does she impose a demanding correspondence. She colors her story and deepens its power by the pervasive though implicit Arthurian frame of reference.[14]

After the 1859 publication of Tennyson's *Idylls of the King,*[15] John Henry Shorthouse wrote an essay, "The 'Morte d'Arthur' and the 'Idylls of the King,'" in which he found fault with Tennyson's volume primarily because it overlooked the story of the Grail quest. For Shorthouse, "the chief lay and literary exponent in our days of cultured Anglicanism," [16] the Grail quest is the center of the history of the Round Table. The Arthurian world is the depiction of knighthood achieving its highest spiritual calling: "The chiefest quality of the knightly ideal, and that which shines out of every page of its story, and that without which there can be no perfect knighthood, is religion. This is as necessary to the finished knight as his courage; and for want of this, Sir Launcelot, perfect in all earthly points, is brought to shame and to disgrace. The religion of the knight is that of the Son of God, Jesus Christ the man, our Lord." [17] Though a great admirer of Tennyson,[18] Shorthouse did not find Tennyson's later treatment of the Grail story compatible with his own conception. Whereas

14. In *Armorel of Lyonesse — A Romance of To-day* (London, 1890), Walter Besant presents his love story in a locale similar to the setting of *Mount Royal,* yet he makes no use of the Arthurian associations.

15. The 1859 volume contains *Enid, Vivien, Elaine,* and *Guinevere.*

16. J. Hunter Smith, "Introduction," in *Life, Letters, and Literary Remains of J. H. Shorthouse, edited by his wife* (London: Macmillan, 1905), 1:xv.

17. "The 'Morte d'Arthur' and the 'Idylls of the King,'" *Life, Letters, and Literary Remains,* 2:113.

18. For Shorthouse's admiration of the poet, see *Life, Letters, and Literary Remains,* 1:28, 32. Before he began his Arthurian novel, Shorthouse visited the poet at Farringford (1:181–184).

Tennyson makes Percival the tragic victim of his blind enthusiasm and withholds sympathy for him since he rejects marriage for the ascetic isolation of the cloister, Shorthouse lauds Percival's undying commitment to the Grail. It was only natural, therefore, for Shorthouse to create his own nineteenth-century version of the Grail quest.[19]

In *Sir Percival — A Story of the Past and Present* (1886), Shorthouse makes his female narrator, Constance Lisle, the agent of the spiritual commitment of the hero, Sir Percival Massareen. Constance is imbued with the Arthurian writings of Tennyson and Malory; her surroundings often remind her of Malory's settings:

> I never approached this little church but I was reminded of those mysterious chapels in the forest-wilds of the "Morte d'Arthur," — "an olde chapel in a wast land," as one is called; "an olde febel chappell," — and I could have fancied almost, when the hush of summer noon stilled the sense of the present, and lulled it into dreamland, that this was the very chapel whose door Lancelot had found "wasted and broken, and within he saw a fair altar, richly arrayed with cloth of silk, and a candlestick of silver that bear six great candles." [20]

When Constance meets her distant relation, Sir Percival, she questions his interest in the Arthurian world:

> "Do you like Tennyson, Sir Percival?" I said.
> He looked perplexed for a moment, then he said:
> "Oh, yes. I have read his poems. I like them very much."
> "Do you like the 'Idylls of the King?' "
> "Yes," he said, rather doubtfully; "I don't think I have read them all."
> "You know," I said, "they are taken from the old romance of the 'Morte d'Arthur.' The Duke has a wonderful black-letter copy of it, printed by Caxton. I must ask him to show it to us. You

19. For a study of Tennyson's nineteenth-century version of the Grail quest, see my article "Tennyson's 'The Holy Grail': The Tragedy of Percivale," *Modern Language Review,* 69 (1974), 745–756.

20. J. H. Shorthouse, *Sir Percival — A Story of the Past and of the Present* (London, 1886), chap. 2.

know there is a Sir Percival in it. That is why I should like you to see it."

"No," he said, "I did not know that. What sort of fellow was he?"

"He was one of the best knights of the world, that at that time was," I said, repeating the phrase that was engraven in my memory as in brass, "in whom the very faith stood most in."

"That sounds well," he said. "I am glad he was so good a fellow as that. It is well to have a fellow like that of your name to follow." (Chap. 3)

Their exploration of the Arthurian literary world is an indication of the intellectual and emotional camaraderie between them. Their harmony is interrupted by the arrival of their cousin, Virginia Clare, a strikingly beautiful woman, a vehement socialist, and an agnostic: "All religion . . . has been invented for the selfish satisfaction of the rich." Virginia quickly supplants Constance in Percival's affection.

In time, Virginia comes under Constance's spiritual influence; she feels compelled to nurse an old woman who is dying from an epidemic, and this work of mercy brings about her own death.[21] Meanwhile, Percival moves into London society, where his developing personality does not please Constance, "He was less of a boy, more manly in every way, but he seemed to me to have lost more of the freshness and purity of soul in those few weeks than all the previous years of his chequered youth had stolen from him." In a continuing search for his identity, Percival returns to Constance to propose marriage. Aware that he still loves Virginia, she rejects his offer, promising always to be his sister and his friend.

In the final chapter, "The Finding of the Grail," Percival, now on diplomatic duty in Africa, volunteers for a dangerous mission to rescue a bishop held captive by natives.[22] In a letter to Con-

21. Shorthouse commented on Virginia: "Neither can I see how Virginia can stand for the *flesh;* she is *drawn from the life.* Every word she said has been said to me by girl Agnostics, and one, at least, died exactly as she died — I have no hesitation in saying in the service of God, whom she fancied that she did not know" (*Life, Letters, and Literary Remains,* 1:243).

22. Shorthouse used a historical event as the basis of the final chapter: "It was said, or supposed, at the time, that Mr. Shorthouse knew

stance written just before his own execution, Percival relates his
final earthly moments:

> "The gongs have begun to sound. What is this? Surely this
> cannot be death!
>
> "I see the chase and the dark tower, and the flashing waters of
> the channel gleaming in light, and before me on her horse, be-
> neath the oak-trees, an English girl. Who is this, seated in her
> saddle beneath the rustling branches of the oak? She turns her
> head towards me — Virginia? No, it is Constance — Constance
> with the pleading eyes. And the moment that she turns her look
> on me it all vanishes — the English oaks and ashes, and the groves
> of cactus and of palm — and the walls of the hut burst asunder
> to let in the dazzling light — and down the bright, clear spaces
> of the light files a long procession of noble forms — Constance!
> Constance! Who is this?
>
> And the armies that are in heaven follow Him upon white horses,
> clothed in fine linen   white   and clean." (Chap. 11)

With Percival's letter comes his Victoria Cross, an earlier acknowledgment of his earthly success which complements the
spiritual success of his final mission.

Described by its author as "almost a devotional book," [23] *Sir
Percival* presents a modern Percival who achieves the spiritual
stature of his medieval counterpart. Whereas Tennyson expressed
his own fear of handling the subject of the Grail quest, "I doubt
whether such a subject could be handled in these days without
incurring a charge of irreverence. It would be too much like
playing with sacred things. The old writers *believed* in the San-
greal," [24] and finally wrote a version of the quest which studies
the folly of rash knights who forsake their "allotted field" for a

---

Bishop Hannington — even that he must have had letters from him. He
not only never knew the Bishop, but had never heard of his name till
the sad news of his martyrdom reached this country. He happened
simply to read in a newspaper that there was an outbreak of war in
Africa, and that an English Bishop was in danger, and this fact no doubt
influenced the course of his own fictitious story" (*Life, Letters, and
Literary Remains*, 1:178).

23. *Life, Letters, and Literary Remains*, 1:237.
24. Quoted by Hallam, Lord Tennyson, *Alfred, Lord Tennyson: A
Memoir* (London, 1897), 1:456–457.

distant vision, Shorthouse had no hesitation in asserting his own belief in the Grail by writing a version of the quest which is merely the medieval story retold in a nineteenth-century setting. When he learned of the tragic death of Bishop Hannington, he found an incident to serve as the final moment, paralleling the death in Sarras, for his rendition of the story.[25]

The only other Victorian novel which may qualify for the epithet Arthurian is Charles Welsh Mason's *Merlin — A Piratical Love Story*.[26] Mason follows Shorthouse's pattern and writes a modern version of a medieval Arthurian tale. Again a female narrator, Kate Boventry, tells of her hapless love for Jack Smith. In Mason's novel, however, the correspondence to the medieval account of Merlin and Vivien is at best imprecise and out of place.

When Kate Boventry and Jack Smith meet on a ship, Kate's feeling for him is total revulsion. Even though he saves her life in a pirate attack, she still has little sympathy toward her arrogant protector. As his adoration of her becomes apparent, Kate's attitude softens to an alternation of fascination and repulsion. Smith, whose name is later revealed to be Merlin, has a boat which provides a safe escape to Singapore. Only at this port does Kate learn of his true identity: "he is the most eccentric of men, young as he is; fabulously rich, and smitten with an incredible craze of making people think he is a beggar." Kate's deepening affection leads her to exclaim, "I now for the first time saw and heard Merlin divested of affectation. In his natural self he was certainly the most charming and witty man that I have ever met." Unfortunately the fact that Merlin is secretly married prevents Kate from returning his love.

25. More exalted in spiritual stature than Percival, Galahad became a name equated with human perfection. Thus S. Levett-Yeats's narration of the life and death of Peregrine Jackson, a good and selfless assistant commissioner in Burma, is entitled "A Galahad of the Creeks" (*A Galahad of the Creeks and Other Stories* [London, 1897]); no reference to the Arthurian world occurs in the story. The only other instance of a Victorian novel that employs an Arthurian name properly and does not develop the correspondence is Malcolm K. MacMillan, *Dagonet the Jester* (London, 1886), the account of the hard but ultimately happy life of Dagonet, formerly the master fool of Lord Sandicare of Thorn Abbey.

26. *Merlin — A Piratical Love Story* (London, 1896).

Later, at an art exhibit in London, Kate, accompanied by Sir
Thomas Ugoville, sees a painting, *Merlin and His Vivien,* signed
by the artist, Merlin. Recognizing herself in the picture, Kate
visits the artist's studio where she and Merlin acknowledge their
love. Merlin announces that his wife is dead; at this instant his
-wife appears from behind a curtain. Merlin lifts a revolver to
shoot her, but the gun is empty. His wife falls to the floor, the
empty phial in her hand an indication of her suicide. As she dies,
she whispers to Kate, "Save him! Accuse him not; his will is no
longer responsible for what he does." From that day Kate never
sees Merlin again, though she receives many letters from him.
Meanwhile Ugoville, soon to be Kate's fiancé, receives a painting
from Merlin, the title significantly altered to *Merlin and Vivien.*

Mason's Merlin, a demented genius, bears little resemblance
to any medieval depiction of Merlin except for his all-consuming
love for a woman. The demure and aristocratic Kate Boventry
has none of the seductive wiles of Vivien, and her effect on
Merlin is ennobling rather than degrading. Mason employs these
two names to add a further dimension of mystery to a story
closer in mood to Victorian stage melodrama than to the Arthurian legends. The allusion to Merlin and Vivien is irrelevant
to the situation in the novel; the names, laden with rich associations, do not belong in a melodramatic romance.[27]

This catalogue of nineteenth-century Arthurian fiction only
confirms the absence of Arthur from the novel. With the exception of Peacock's satire, these novels employ the Arthurian world
only as a frame of reference or a basis for suggestive allusion.

27. Other novelists employ Arthurian names with no regard for their
associations. In Charlotte Louise Dempster's *Iseulte* (London, 1875),
the heroine, Iseulte de Bourgonce, is a faultless, indeed superhuman
Florence Nightingale. Similarly, in Thorold Ashley's *Sir Tristram* (London, 1898), the hero is a man of spotless integrity who rises to political
success and eventually weds his childhood sweetheart. Arthur was a
favorite name for heroes of nineteenth-century novels, though no medieval associations were introduced. For example, the hero of Christiana
Jane Douglas's *Arthur* (London, 1870), Arthur Caldicot, is a young
cockney who rises to political power and prestige, though he suffers an
early death. There is also a series of edifying children's tales which frequently employ Arthur as the name of the young hero: *Arthur and
Alice; or, The Little Wanderers* (London, 1817); *Arthur, or, The
Motherless Boy* (London, n.d.); *Arthur: or, The Chorister's Rest*
(London, n.d.).

Significantly it is Tennyson's Arthurian world rather than a medieval version which stands directly behind these writings. Tennyson's *Morte d'Arthur* inspires Mrs. Craik; the *Idylls of the King,* particularly *Guinevere,* serves as Neville's model; *Merlin and Vivien* gives an inappropriate frame of reference to Mason's *Merlin;* and Tennyson's Arthurian poetry offers Braddon a reservoir of allusions. Shorthouse's *Sir Percival* is a deliberate attempt to create a nineteenth-century Grail quest which, unlike Tennyson's account, seeks a modern equivalent for the spirituality of medieval versions. And as Tennyson's Arthurian world is in some degree present in these novels, it is also a cause of Arthur's absence from Victorian fiction.

No Victorian novel chooses Camelot for its setting;[28] only in the early twentieth century is it the locale for fiction.[29] In Victorian poetry, however, the Arthurian legends attained a literary stature denied them since the Renaissance. The seventeenth and eighteenth centuries neglected Arthurian stories in their search for literary materials. Even the Romantics paid little attention to Arthur. Tennyson, however, turned to the Arthurian world throughout his poetic career; the *Idylls of the King* spans sixty years of composition. His unending attempt to recreate the legends led him to publish individual Idylls or groups of Idylls as they were completed. By this method of publication he created a large reading public which awaited his further forays into the realm of Camelot. In addition, his position as poet laureate made

28. A possible exception is Alfred J. Church's *The Count of the Saxon Shore* (London, 1887), which presents a fictional account of the Romans' departure from Britain; Arthur makes a brief appearance in the final chapter. The first American prose work to employ Camelot as a setting is Mark Twain's *A Connecticut Yankee in King Arthur's Court* (1889); Twain turns to Malory to obtain material for a satiric and savage contrast between Arthur's feudal society and the modern industrial world.

29. In the early twentieth century, the following English novels employed Arthurian backgrounds: Warrick Deeping, *Uther and Igraine* (London: Grant Richards, 1903); Clemence Housman, *The Life of Sir Aglovale de Galis* (London: Methuen, 1905); Dorothy Senior, *The Clutch of Circumstance; or, The Gates of Dawn* (London: Adam and Charles Black, 1908); Coningsby Dawson, *The Road to Avalon* (London: Hodder and Stoughton, 1911); Chester Keith, *Queen's Knight* (London: G. Allen and Unwin, 1920). For a study of Arthurian literature in the first half of the twentieth century, see Nathan C. Starr, *King Arthur Today* (Gainesville: University of Florida Press, 1954).

him an influential force in the literary world. His belief that Arthur is "the greatest of all poetical subjects" [30] may have influenced contemporary writers to assign Camelot to the literary domain of poetry. Inspired by Tennyson's early Arthurian poems, the pre-Raphaelites, especially Rossetti, Swinburne, and the young Morris, frequently turned to Camelot for their subjects both in verse and in painting. At the same time the novel was almost completely ignoring Arthur's world. Tennyson's employment of the Arthurian realm complemented the strong desire of the Victorian novel to achieve social realism; Camelot, the setting of medieval romances and now the background of Tennyson's poetry, becomes a setting for fiction only after Tennyson's death and the publication of the complete *Idylls of the King*.[31]

In the second half of the nineteenth century Arthur does appear in a new form of fiction, the many popular versions of Malory's medieval romance. Though Tennyson helps to prevent Arthur from entering the world of the novel, he is directly responsible for the advent of these new abridgments and modernizations of the *Morte Darthur*.

Thomas Wright edited Malory in 1858 in order to offer an antidote for the earlier faulty and out-of-print editions, "It is remarkable that the two popular editions published in 1816 have both become rare, and the want of a good edition of this romance has been generally felt." [32] Wright's second edition appeared in 1866, and two years later Sir Edward Strachey edited a handy one-volume edition in response to the popularity of Tennyson's poetry, "Mr. Tennyson has, I may assume, made every one familiar with the retirement of queen Guenever to the nunnery at Almesbury, and with the death of Arthur; and I venture for the

30. *Alfred, Lord Tennyson: A Memoir*, 2:125.
31. The first complete version of the *Idylls of the King* appeared in volume 8 (1899) of the twelve-volume edition of *The Life and Works of Alfred, Lord Tennyson*, ed. Hallam, Lord Tennyson (London, 1898–99).
32. *La Mort d'Arthure*, ed. Thomas Wright (London, 1858), 1:xiv. A second edition of Wright appeared in 1866 and a third in 1889; the third edition was reprinted in 1893 and 1897. In 1816 R. Wilks published a three-volume *La Mort D'Arthur* and Walker and Edwards published a two-volume *History of the Renowned Prince Arthur*. The following year Robert Southey edited the two-volume *The Byrth, Lyf and Actes of Kyng Arthur* (London, 1817). These three were the only editions between the 1634 edition of William Stansby and the Wright edition.

completion of this sketch to show, though from the present volume, how the old story which the poet chiefly follows relates the death and draws the character of Launcelot." [33] Moreover, Strachey emulated Tennyson's censorious modernization of the text:

> such phrases or passages as are not in accordance with modern manners have been also omitted or replaced by others which either actually occur or might have occurred in Caxton's text elsewhere. I say manners, not morals, because I do not profess to have remedied the moral defects of the book which I have already spoken of. Mr. Tennyson has shown us how we may deal best with this matter for modern uses, in so far as Sir Thomas Malory has himself failed to treat it rightly; and I do not believe that when we have excluded anything that is offensive to modern manners there will be found anything practically injurious to the morals of English boys.[34]

When Strachey wrote a revised introduction to a later edition, he described Tennyson's elevation of Malory, "The morality of 'Morte Darthur' is low in one essential thing, and this alike in what it says and in what it omits: and Lord Tennyson shows us how it should be raised. The ideal of marriage, in its relation and its contrast with all other forms of love and chastity, is brought out in every form, rising at last to tragic grandeur, in the *Idylls of the King*." [35] Before the end of the century, Strachey's revised edition went through five printings[36] and three more scholars turned their attention to new editions of Malory.[37]

33. *Le Morte Darthur,* ed. Sir Edward Strachey (London, 1868), p. xxviii. The first edition, which appeared in March, was followed by a second in August 1868. The latter edition with an added index was published in 1869 and reprinted in 1871, 1876, 1879, 1882, 1884, 1886, and 1889.

34. Ibid., p. xviii.

35. *Le Morte Darthur,* ed. Sir Edward Strachey (London, 1891), p. xxii.

36. 1891, 1893, 1897, 1898, 1899.

37. Ernest Rhys edited a series of selections from Malory: *Malory's History of King Arthur and the Quest of the Holy Grail* (London, 1886); *The Book of Marvellous Adventures and Other Books of the Morte D'Arthur* (London, 1893); *The Noble and Joyous History of King Arthur* (London, 1894). H. O. Sommer's three-volume edition of Malory appeared between 1889 and 1891. Israel Gollancz edited a four-

For knowledge of Camelot, however, the Victorian reading public turned less to the scholarly editions of Malory than to the more accessible modernized versions published after the 1859 volume of the *Idylls of the King*. In 1861 James Knowles brought out the first modern compilation of Malory, *The Story of King Arthur and His Knights of the Round Table,* which passed through seven separate editions before the end of the century. In his introduction he describes the organization of the work: "He [the editor] has endeavoured, nevertheless, at however great a distance, to follow the rule laid down in the 'Idylls of the King'; and has suppressed and modified where changed manners and morals have made it absolutely necessary to do so for the preservation of a lofty original ideal." [38] Tennyson's pervasive influence is evident both in the dedication to him, "This attempt at a popular version of the Arthur legends is by his permission dedicated, as a tribute of the sincerest and warmest respect," and in the volume's ending, which is Arthur's departure on the barge to Avalon; there is no presentation of Lancelot's repentance and death. In the third edition of the volume, Knowles asserts Tennyson's role in the Arthurian revival: "The revival of the Arthur legends, under the influence of the 'Idylls of the King,' has interested so many in the subject, that an outline of the noble story has almost become a necessary item of general information . . . The growing popularity of the Arthur story is surely a wholesome sign of the times, especially as being due to their representative Poet." [39]

In 1868 Edward Conybeare brought out an abridged version of Malory with a prefatory apology:

---

volume edition which Dent published in May 1897; a second edition appeared in November of the following year; a third edition appeared in August 1899.

38. James Thomas Knowles, *The Story of King Arthur and His Knights of the Round Table* (London, 1862), p. iii. The volume actually appeared at the end of 1861. Though Knowles became Tennyson's close friend, he had not met him at the time of the volume's publication.

39. James Thomas Knowles, *The Legends of King Arthur and His Knights of the Round Table* (London, 1868), pp. vii–viii. Knowles retained this altered title in later editions, though he subsequently removed the phrase "of the Round Table."

It would be hard to name any other work which, while containing so many of the elements which render books popular . . . has gained so little popularity . . . Indeed the work in its original form could never be a general favourite at the present day. Its great length, the confusion and want of system in the divisions, and the occasional coarseness are insuperable obstacles to popularity; and in spite of the attention which the Idylls of the King have attracted towards the Arthurian romances, Mallory's book has never become generally known, and though it may be read and esteemed at its true rate by some few, remains essentially unpopular.[40]

Conybeare did, however, include Malory's ending. Three years later, B. Montgomerie Ranking published a modernized *La Mort D'Arthur* as a companion to Tennyson's poetry, "the aim of this little book being to show whence Mr. Tennyson has drawn his inspiration"; the subtitle, "The Old Prose Stories whence the 'Idylls of the King' have been taken by Alfred Tennyson," clarified the editor's intention: "It has been thought not unlikely that many will be glad of a chance of reading the stories on which Mr. Tennyson has, in the main, founded his 'Idyls of the King,' who either have not time or inclination to study the whole works of which these stories form part." [41] In spite of the title of his volume, Ranking also included relevant passages from the *Mabinogion.* Another modernization, *The Life and Exploits of King Arthur and His Knights of the Round Table: A Legendary Romance,* introduced selected passages from the *Idylls* throughout Malory's text.[42] Sidney Lanier's *The Boy's King Arthur* had one major purpose, "We might fairly trace the growth of English civilization by comparing with the earliest conceptions of King Arthur the latest ideal of him in our literature given us by our own great master Tennyson." [43] And Henry Firth's edition, *King Arthur and His Knights of the Round Table,* omitted the adul-

40. *La Morte D'Arthur, The History of King Arthur,* abridged and revised by Edward Conybeare (London, 1868), pp. iii–iv.
41. *La Mort D'Arthur,* ed. B. Montgomerie Ranking (London, 1871), p. 10.
42. Anon., *The Life and Exploits of King Arthur and His Knights of the Round Table: A Legendary Romance* (London, 1878).
43. *The Boy's King Arthur,* ed. Sidney Lanier (London, 1880), p. xx.

terous affairs of Lancelot and Guinevere and Tristram and Iseult "to preserve the consistency of the narrative while purging it of any questionable matter, and 'toning down' motives and conduct, which if painted in their true colours would offend." [44]

These popular editions of Malory gave the reading public further knowledge of the world of Camelot to satisfy an Arthurian interest awakened by Tennyson's poetry. In fostering the development of this new dimension in Victorian fiction, Tennyson saw his country share his own fascination with the wealth of legends buried in medieval Arthurian romances. The *Idylls of the King,* complemented by the popular versions of Malory's romance, prepared readers of novels to appreciate Arthurian allusions which were occurring with increasing frequency in later nineteenth-century fiction. And the accessibility of Malory in a variety of forms was a prelude to the early twentieth century, when Camelot would serve again as the setting for historical fiction.

The importance of Tennyson as the cause of the new interest in Malory and the medieval Arthurian world contrasts with his influential position in making Camelot the province of poetry and not of fiction. Yet the absence of Arthur from the Victorian novel does not justify the absence of the novel in discussions of the Arthurian literature of Victorian England. A bibliographical discussion of nineteenth-century Arthurian material must not limit itself to a few plays, an abundance of poetry, and *The Misfortunes of Elphin;* it must include the few novels which use the world of Camelot as a suggestive frame of reference, though the Arthurian dimension is often indebted to Tennyson rather than medieval authors; it must also include the editions and, more importantly, the many modernizations of Malory which filled the void caused by the absence of Arthurian historical fiction.

In an effort to counteract Christabel Courtenay's romanticism,

44. Henry Firth, *King Arthur and His Knights of the Round Table* (London, 1884), pp. iii–iv. Three other abridged versions appeared before the end of the century: *King Arthur and the Knights of the Round Table: A Modernized Version of the Morte Darthur,* ed. Charles Morris (London, 1892), 3 vols.; *Selections from Malory's Le Morte D'Arthur,* ed. A. T. Martin (London, 1896); *Selections from Sir Thomas Malory's Morte Darthur,* ed. W. E. Mead (London, 1897).

Angus Hamleigh stoops to hyperbole, "The Laureate invented Arthur." Yet Tennyson's influence did determine much of the development of Arthurian literature throughout the century, and his Arthurian world permeates the Arthurian writings of the period. Tennyson is the father of the Arthurian renaissance, a renaissance which restrained itself for a time from entering the world of the novel.

ROBERT LEE WOLFF

Some Erring Children in Children's Literature: The World of Victorian Religious Strife in Miniature

Explorers of the worlds of Victorian fiction have long been conscious of the great number of novels dealing directly with all phases and every aspect of the intense religious controversy that pervaded the period. *Loss and Gain, The Heir of Redclyffe, Scenes of Clerical Life, Lothair, The Autobiography of Mark Rutherford, Marius the Epicurean, Robert Elsmere, The Way of All Flesh* represent only the jagged visible peaks of a huge sunken iceberg of fiction compacted of many hundreds of novels of faith and doubt. Even when novelists did not make a religious theme the center of their story, they could hardly avoid alluding to this central preoccupation of their contemporaries, and making known their views on some burning question that over the intervening century or more may have become obscure or even unintelligible. Anne Brontë's country rector, for example, with his rich silk gown, lavender gloves, sparkling rings, and well-curled hair, who flourishes his cambric handkerchief and preaches on "church discipline, rites and ceremonies, apostolical succession, the duty of reverence and obedience to the clergy,

295

the atrocious criminality of dissent, the absolute necessity of observing all the forms of godliness, the reprehensible presumption of individuals who attempted to think for themselves in matters connected with religion, or to be guided by their own interpretations of Scripture" [1] cries out in these days for a whole battery of exegetical footnotes. It would not be enough to refer to the Brontë children's Methodistical upbringing by Aunt Branwell, to their Evangelical father's irritation with his Puseyite curates, and to their own deeply Evangelical preferences. Readers might still overlook Anne Brontë's sardonic and sweeping indictment of Tractarian beliefs and practices, reflecting the bitterness of a controversy now long dead, but then in the forefront of everybody's thoughts and passions.

It was virtually impossible for a Victorian novelist to be neutral about religious matters, or to refrain from expressing his views in his writing. And, as the stream of children's literature began about 1840 to broaden into a river, which quickly became a flood, many writers of books for the young naturally enough made a case for their own particular religious principles, and sometimes even argued out for a Lilliputian audience the controversies that were agitating Brobdignag.

The quarterlies seldom paid attention to literature for children, but the author of a long article on the subject in the *London Review* for January 1860 fully realized what was happening. Publishers' catalogues, he said, were "formidable and everlengthening"; books professing to be for children were increasing at a higher ratio than any other class of literature, and commanded the surest sale. Reviewing thirteen new books for children, he reserved some of his strongest censure for writers who tried to use their authority as adults to indoctrinate the young: "There are certain truths and opinions which cannot be received to any purpose by a human being, unless they satisfy his judgment, and convince his understanding. Controverted doctrines, and the questions which divide the sections of the Christian Church from each other, are of this class." A child might temporarily acquiesce in a religious point of view urged on him in a story, but later on he would discover "that he has

---

1. *Agnes Grey* (1847), chap. 10.

been taking on trust that which ought to have been the result of independent investigation," and would probably "vibrate strongly in the contrary direction." The very trustfulness of children required adults to exercise their responsibility, and "not to dogmatize to the little ones on any but the great fundamental truths of religion and morality." [2] However sound this psychological judgment may have been, many of the writers of Victorian children's books, including some of the most successful and influential, failed to share it. Perhaps it would have required superhuman restraint not to lecture their readers about a subject so close to their hearts and so fundamental for salvation. Twentieth-century writers on Victorian children's literature have often looked upon their subject as somehow separate from literature written for adults; so they have usually neglected to comment on — or even to identify — the particular sectarian religious position of the author. Yet nothing is more central to the Victorian author's purposes or more essential to a proper appreciation of his writing.

It was, of course, when he allowed his young characters to stray from the paths of virtue that the author of a Victorian book for children most readily showed his religious colors. Low, High, or Broad, he treated a naughty or delinquent child in his pages in accordance with the teachings of his own persuasion, occasionally giving the opposition a sideswipe, explicit or implicit. To renew one's acquaintance with some erring Victorian fictional children is to find oneself studying the macrocosm through the microcosm.

All students of children's literature regard Catherine Sinclair's *Holiday House* (1839) as a children's book that marked a major break from the past. It was inspired, she herself declared, by a conversation with Sir Walter Scott, in which he lamented the degeneration of books for children into a "mere dry catalogue of facts" and predicted that as a result there would be no poets, wits, or orators in the next generation. So she wrote *Holiday House* — set in her native Edinburgh in the years before 1815 — in order to portray "that species of noisy, frolicsome, mischie-

2. *London Review,* 13 (1859–60), 470, 477–478.

vous children which is now almost extinct . . . like wild horses on the prairies rather than like well-broken hacks on the road." Carried away by the novelty of the high-spirited, indeed almost hysterical, pranks of its two chief characters, young Harry and Laura Graham, who grow into their teens in the course of *Holiday House,* the critics have failed to note the deeply Evangelical moral fervor that pervades the story and gives it its main point. As early as 1869, Charlotte Yonge — Keble's disciple and an active Tractarian — who thoroughly disliked and distrusted Evangelical teachings, nonetheless overlooked them in *Holiday House,* declaring "the quaint naughtiness" of Harry and Laura Graham and "their unrivaled power of getting into scrapes" delightful. In 1932 Harvey Darton hailed the book as the first "rollicking" children's story to appear, and in 1963, in an often perceptive survey of English books for children, M. F. Thwaite declared that it marked the end of "the long domination of the moral tale." [3]

Yet *Holiday House* is an exceedingly moral book, and a vehicle for Evangelical teaching. Harry and Laura Graham's kind and protective elder brother, Frank, already at school when the book opens, is always the younger children's and the author's ideal. He reads his Bible assiduously. Everybody prophesies that he will "grow up to be a good and useful man; especially when it became evident that, by the blessing of God, he had been early turned away from the broad path that leadeth to destruction, in which every living person would naturally walk, and led into the narrow path that leadeth to eternal life." Frank has, then, already experienced the "conversion" that the Evangelicals insisted was essential for spiritual rebirth and eventual salvation from eternal hellfire. At school Frank wins all the prizes: for Greek, for Latin, for algebra, for geography, for mathematics, and for general good conduct. He becomes a midshipman, but even before beginning his naval career he severely criticizes the great Admiral

3. Charlotte M. Yonge, "Children's Literature of the Last Century: II, Didactic Fiction," *Macmillan's Magazine,* 20, no. 118 (August 1869), 310; J. Harvey Darton, *Children's Books in England,* 2d ed. (1932; reprint ed., Cambridge: At the University Press, 1958), p. 226; M. F. Thwaite, *From Primer to Pleasure* (London: The Library Association, 1963), p. 143.

Nelson for having said on his deathbed, "I have not been a great sinner." Like all other men, little Frank sententiously points out, Nelson *had* greatly sinned. After two years at sea, Frank — Catherine Sinclair assures us — becomes a general favorite in the mess because of his delight in Holy Scripture.

More important still: it is Frank's long-protracted last illness and edifying death that serve to put an end forever to the persistent naughtiness of Harry and Laura, and to precipitate their conversion too:

> All was changed within and around them — sorrow had filled their hearts, and no longer merry, thoughtless young creatures, believing the world one scene of frolicsome enjoyment and careless ease, they had now witnessed its realities — they had felt its trials — they had experienced the importance of religion — they had learned the frailty of all earthly joy — and they had received, amidst tears and sorrows, the last injunction of a dying brother — to "call upon the Lord when He is near, and to seek Him while He may yet be found."

Laura Graham herself declares that their cruel nursery governess, Mrs. Crabtree, had always sought to lead them in the right path by severity, and their kind grandmama and Uncle David by affection (their mother has died and their father lives abroad). But "nothing was effectual till now, when God Himself has laid his hand upon us."

Holiday House consists of a linked series of stories about Harry and Laura's naughtiness: they destroy the china, the ornaments, the clocks; they set the house afire, and cause the nursery to be flooded; they inconsiderately invite all their friends to tea without permission; they are consistently disobedient and forgetful. Mrs. Crabtree's brutal punishments and Uncle David's tolerance pervade episode after episode. Perhaps this very episodic character of the book (it even includes an interpolated fairy tale told by Uncle David — the first Victorian *Kunstmärchen,* a "nonsensical story about giants and fairies") has itself served to conceal the Evangelical lesson from the modern critic. But the Victorian child could hardly have missed it.

Moreover, Harry and Laura are not wicked, only "thoughtless," "forgetful," "heedless, lively romps." They commit no mean action, never quarrel with each other, regularly say their prayers, and read their Bibles. Above all, they "would not for twenty worlds have told a lie or taken what did not belong to them." For their uncle, Major Graham, as for Catherine Sinclair, lying and stealing are the two most heinous crimes. Catherine Sinclair disapproved of children's stories that by dwelling on untruthfulness and theft taught their readers how to commit these sins. She was heavily emphasizing the difference between the venial and the unforgivable.

Her interpolated fairy tale, overenthusiastically described as "the earliest example of nonsense-literature and a direct precursor" of Lewis Carroll,[4] has its own moral: the greedy, lazy little boy called No-book, invited to visit both the fairy Teach-all and the fairy Do-nothing, naturally prefers the latter's invitation, and wallows in luxury, gluttony, and ease until he is captured by the wicked giant Snap-'em-up, who hangs him on a meathook, preparatory to slaughtering and devouring him. After being rescued by Teach-all, No-book stops overeating, loves his lessons, hates his holidays, joins a Temperance Society (!), and eventually becomes Sir Timothy Bluestocking, who thrashes lazy boys with his stick. Lewis Carroll would have detested the cruel imagery and Evangelical moral of the tale. The story is designed as a direct admonition to Harry Graham, himself a dilatory student and a No-book child. Catherine Sinclair's appreciation of the value of learning, however, was only skin-deep. If one minds one's books and becomes Sir Timothy Bluestocking, the only reward is to thrash lazy boys. Lessons also help a schoolboy avoid making embarrassing and foolish mistakes in geography or arithmetic. In a proper education "no teaching can have greater influence . . . than the incidental remarks of an enlightened Christian." And parents are "appointed by God to govern their children as He governs us."

Holiday House does indeed differ from such didactic stories as Mrs. Sherwood's *History of the Fairchild Family* (1818, 1842, 1847) or *Little Henry and His Bearer* (1814). Harry and Laura never commit the worst sins and are never punished for the ones

4. Roger Lancelyn Green, "The Golden Age of Children's Books," in *Only Connect,* ed. S. Egoff, G. T. Stubbs, and L. F. Ashley (New York: Oxford University Press, 1969), p. 3.

they do commit by severe sermons threatening them with eternal damnation. Readers in 1839 and ever since, however, have been deceived by the manic playfulness of Harry and Laura and by the occasional burst of true humor. Behind Catherine Sinclair's mask lurks Mrs. Sherwood after all. Hardly camouflaged, the underlying principles have changed not at all, and the Evangelical moral lies in wait.

By no means all erring Evangelical children experienced their necessary conversions as easily as Harry and Laura Graham. True, it had cost Frank his life; but he was in any case sure of salvation, and had only gone ahead to the blessed world after death in which he and his brother and sister would eventually meet again. The Evangelicals sought to extract the maximum of pathos from children's deathbeds while simultaneously assuring the weeping reader that the deaths were not tragedies but triumphs. F. W. Farrar's famous Eric, however, has a longer, fiercer struggle than the two Grahams.[5] Like Harry and Laura, Eric never lies or steals (although his inability to exculpate himself from a charge of theft leads him to run away from school); but unlike them, he has not confined his bad behavior to mere pranks and scrapes. "Little by little" he has succumbed to all the pressing temptations at school to commit vicious actions. He smokes, drinks, neglects his prayers, keeps evil company, uses bad language. Not even the deaths of a virtuous friend and an equally virtuous little brother can redeem him, although he grieves over both.

Repeatedly beaten at school in scenes that Farrar records in loving detail, Eric is finally saved only after a climactic and almost fatal lashing delivered aboard the ship on which he had been shanghaied. Then he too has his conversion.

> In the valley of the shadow of death a voice had come to him — a still small voice — at whose holy utterance Eric had bowed his head, and had listened to the message of God, and learned

5. In *Eric; or, Little by Little* (1858). P. G. Scott, "The School Novels of Dean Farrar," *British Journal of Educational Studies,* 19 (1971), 163–182, discusses the verisimilitude of *Eric*; but neither he nor the other recent writers on Farrar listed in his first footnote touch on the conversion. Even Hugh Kingsmill's able essay in his *After Puritanism* (London: Duckworth, 1929), pp. 13–56, only skirts the point.

His will; and now, in humble resignation, in touching penitence, with solemn self-devotion, he had cast himself at the feet of Jesus, and prayed to be helped, and guided, and forgiven . . . Yea, for Jesus' sake he was washed, he was cleansed, he was sanctified, he was justified; he would fear no evil, for God was with him.

In order to be converted, Eric has been broken; he now can die assured of salvation. Though he had been influenced by Frederick Denison Maurice's gentler Broad Church teaching that God would eventually redeem all sinners by his love, Farrar in *Eric* wrote in wholly Evangelical language, putting "justification" by faith in its climactic proper place, and displaying the Evangelical spirit at its harshest and most relentless.

Charlotte Yonge, whose Tractarian beliefs were outraged by *Eric,* did warn girls against it as dealing with "school boy trials," which girls had no business reading about. She also expressed the hope that no mother or boy ever read it (although she knew that thousands did), because it would only make them unhappy or suspicious, and convince them that "the sure reward of virtue is a fatal accident." Conversions are often referred to in Evangelical (or Nonconformist) books written for adults, and are occasionally described: movingly in George Eliot's *Janet's Repentance,* ironically and bitterly in William Hale White's *Mark Rutherford,* with self-deprecatory humor in Edmund Gosse's *Father and Son.* In children's literature, however, conversions are rare, and although they provide the true climax in *Holiday House* and in *Eric,* this has hitherto gone unnoticed.

But the Evangelicals did not have it all their own way on this miniature battlefield. Harriett Mozley, for example, sister of John Henry Newman and wife of Tom Mozley, also a Fellow of Oriel and a Tractarian, struck a double blow against the Evangelicals in 1841, the very year of *Tract XC* itself. The literary distinction of her two books for children, *The Fairy Bower* and its sequel, *The Lost Brooch,* has won the admiration of able critics, who have at times compared her to Jane Austen. But perhaps the novels are likely to arouse more lasting interest as documents in the contemporary religious battles.[6]

6. Kathleen Tillotson, "Harriett Mozley," in Geoffrey Tillotson and Kathleen Tillotson, *Mid-Victorian Studies* (London: Athlone Press,

The Fairy Bower is the story of a lie (the lie that Harry and Laura Graham or Eric would never tell), the sin that (together with theft) appeared so heinous to Victorians of all sects. And the lie is told by a little girl of about twelve, Mary Anne Duff, who allows herself to be given credit for an idea that had actually originated with Grace Leslie, aged nine, the heroine: the idea of decorating a room for a Twelfth Night party with garlands of artificial flowers and many lights, to serve as a "fairy bower" for a pet parrot in his cage. When the decorations prove to be a sensational success, the grown-ups crown Mary Anne queen of the evening. Unwilling to expose the deception, Grace says nothing, much to the guilty Mary Anne's surprise and relief. To avoid telling a lie herself, Mary Anne's cousin, Emily Ward, eventually must reveal that the inspiration had come from Grace. Moreover, Grace's barrister godfather conducts an investigation into the mystery, and during the long period in which the truth is in doubt, Grace's own veracity is under a cloud, while all the personages, children and adults alike, discuss the question as if there were no other possible subject of conversation.

The Duff family is strongly Evangelical, and their five children (the erring Mary Anne is the second, with an older brother and three younger sisters) imbibe firm Evangelical principles from their governess, Miss Newmarsh. She will allow her charges no dancing or games played with dice or cards (indeed she is deeply distressed when they are allowed to *see* a conjuror who does card tricks). She is so strict a Sabbatarian that she follows the custom of the Jews, and will never perform any activity after six o'clock on Saturday evening. For entertainment the Duff children have Bible riddles: "they cap in the Bible, make crambo verses out of it, and play at forfeits with texts." Far from punishing them for their faults, Miss Newmarsh rewards them with additional privileges. She endorses the system at a boys' boarding school where the rules prevent all conversation and constant surveillance keeps the pupils from fighting or cheating. Grace's High Anglican Tory godfather assures Miss Newmarsh that these boys will eventually

1965), pp. 38–48; Margaret Kennedy, "Harriett Mozley: A Forerunner of Charlotte Yonge," in *A Chaplet for Charlotte M. Yonge,* ed. Georgina Battiscombe and Marghanita Laski (London: Cresset Press, 1965), pp. 41–55.

"burst with pent up folly and evil" and be "fit for the gallows."

Evangelical principles lead directly to sin. Mary Anne Duff, Miss Newmarsh's pupil, tells the lie about the fairy bower. As a punishment, Miss Newmarsh decrees that for three months Mary Anne "is to lie in bed of a morning a quarter of an hour later than her sisters, and to sit up later at night," so that she may have "leisure to reflect upon her sin." Naturally enough, it is into the mouth of Mary Anne that Harriett Mozley puts an Evangelical speech denouncing country parsons, the backbone of her own High Church party:

> "in the country, [says Mary Anne] all clergymen are old and dull . . . and all the people who live there call them your reverence, and bow down before them almost as the Catholics do before their *priests,* and the squire of the village pays them the same respect . . . so that everybody thinks all they do and say quite right, and nobody dares speak of them as we do of our preachers . . . country parsons are old-fashioned ignoramuses; they sit with the squire drinking wine after dinner, or play at backgammon night after night . . ."

Mary Anne's father, a successful businessman, lives with his family at "Winterton," a London suburb modeled on Clapham: the Low Church Duffs know nothing about the countryside and its clergy, but even their twelve-year-old daughter is ready with the standard Evangelical claim that there has been no change in the rural church since the eighteenth century.

The Duffs' other daughters also are warped by their Evangelical training. Mary Anne's younger sister, Fanny, embarks upon a superheated girlhood friendship with Isabella Musgrove, the fourteen-year-old daughter of a new-made peer. The foolish girls declare that they love one another as lovers do, and plan to run off to live together in solitude. The socially climbing Duffs welcome the friendship only because Isabella's father is a lord. Fanny's twin, Constance, is the most aggressively pious of all the children. In her diary she writes edifying comments on the unhappy "fall" of her sister, Mary Anne, never, as Miss Newmarsh points out, reproaching her — except to compare her to Peter denying the Lord. At the Duffs' house visiting children get drunk at a dinner party and smash the crockery, a destructive act that even Harry and Laura Graham performed while wholly sober.

The Lost Brooch reintroduces the same characters more than six years older. Constance Duff, Miss Newmarsh's most promising pupil, now takes the center of the stage. When she mislays her coral brooch she declares that it has been stolen, and, "almost in a state of monomania," insists on blaming the theft upon an innocent servant-girl, Jessie. With true Evangelical fervor, Constance is planning to found a new women's penitentiary and wants Jessie to become its first inmate. Without perceiving her own cruelty, she hounds her victim, trying to prevail upon Jessie's employer to discharge her, threatening her with the police. The other young people, led by Grace Leslie, intervene to thwart the miscarriage of justice. They obtain evidence that the brooch is still in Constance's own workbox and cause her dramatically to rediscover it. But even when faced with the proof of her own responsibility for the whole sorry episode, Constance is wholly without remorse. Her position — as summarized by a sardonic High Church cousin — is that

> "if a person was unspiritual, it did not matter whether he were a murderer or a thief, or simply unspiritual, for . . . all were in the same condition; and if *she* [Constance] thought, much more pronounced, a person unspiritual, he or she *was* unspiritual; and that further she did pronounce Jessie . . . unspiritual; therefore Jessie was so; and it was impossible for her to injure Jessie by any thing of any kind she could say against her; therefore she had not injured the said Jessie, and she did not think better or worse of her than she did before. Q.E.D."

But there is more to Constance's accusation than this self-righteous working of her Evangelical conscience. She persecutes Jessie in part because Jessie had refused her invitation to attend a religious meeting of Dissenters. As a devout member of the Church of England, Jessie had wanted nothing to do with such a meeting. But Constance, like many Evangelicals, finds more spiritual affinity with Dissenters than with her fellow Anglicans and now, at sixteen, prefers the Quakers to any other sect. Against her High Church cousins and Grace Leslie, Constance argues for the Evangelical tenets of justification by faith and imputed righteousness: "My sins are washed away by His blood, and my heart renewed by His spirit; I renounce my own righteousness, and His righteousness is imputed to me." Faith in Christ alone brings regeneration, and only the "inner witness" can assure a believer that he does in fact believe.

The young Tractarians reply that by attending Dissenters' meetings Constance is disobeying the authority of the Church of England and fostering division within it: "If you profess to be of the church," her own brother tells her (he has been saved from Miss Newmarsh's blight by Eton and Oxford), "you must submit to her teaching." Constance retorts that her opponents are always talking about the Church, while she speaks only "of those who love the Lord Jesus." By her arrogation to herself of the right to pronounce on spirituality or its lack, on innocence or guilt, the extreme Evangelical Constance has come to think of herself as infallible. She has caused much misery, of which she is blindly oblivious.

The pious Constance makes a thoroughly dishonest proposal to raise money to pay the debts of a young spendthrift and professed convert by advertising in a religious magazine (probably the Evangelical *Record,* where such advertisements in fact appeared), soliciting cash contributions for his personal benefit. Constance's twin, Fanny, embarks upon a sentimental attachment for this wicked young man quite as silly as her childhood passion for Isabella. The Duffs, hypocritical and sanctimonious as always, have allowed Fanny to be adopted by a rich worldly woman, upon the pretext that Fanny will do her spiritual good. They are quite able to overlook the obvious fact that Fanny will inherit her money. Though far richer than their High Church cousins, somehow the Low Church Duffs give away only a fifth as much to charity. And while the High Church cousins give to their parish and neighborhood good causes in proper Tractarian style, the Duffs give to "Bible, Tract, Missionary, Jews' Societies."

At nine or ten, in *The Fairy Bower,* Grace Leslie is regular and devoted in her habits of study and deeply fond of her widowed mother, whom she tries to protect against the world. Already she ponders in bed at night about her own "past and present being; the existence and character of God; the true meaning of eternity," and that central question of the nineteenth century: how to reconcile the existence of an all-loving, all-powerful God with the concept of eternal punishment. Thus philosophical, Grace is also well read enough to respond in kind when publicly addressed in extempore verse by her erudite god-father. When he calls her a Grace and a Muse she twice caps his verses aptly, but, reassuringly, fails on a third occasion to do so. Kind, considerate, naturally pious, searching her soul before she acts, determined to do what is right, she is preternaturally good. But she becomes credible in her setting: a world where some children show "a deep sense of religion" at four and others are steeped in "sensibility," weeping at captive butterflies or screeching helplessly when their mothers are unwell. By contrast Grace, with proper presence of mind, goes quietly upstairs and fetches the necessary medicine. Unlike the Duffs, spoiled by their Evangelical governess and neglectful mother, Grace is taught her daily lesson by her mother in person: fortunately, Harriett Mozley declares, Mrs. Leslie has never studied education. But in *The Lost Brooch,* while many of the other children have grown into the young people that they had promised to become, and still seem as sharply and convincingly characterized as they were in *The Fairy Bower,* Grace at sixteen is static, only the embodiment of the virtues she had displayed at ten.

This indicates the weakness of *The Lost Brooch* as a novel and of Harriett Mozley's own position. She successfully satirized the Evangelical enemy but failed to come down positively in favor of a Tractarian program. She seems in fact to have had some doubts about the Tractarian position, and she gradually backed away from it in later years, as her brother went over to Rome and her husband flirted with the same idea. At any rate, she knew she hated the Low Church enemy.

All this Charlotte Yonge fully realized. She thought *The Fairy Bower* and *The Lost Brooch* full of "wonderful cleverness and irony," books "such as only a Newman could write." Though "nowhere inculcating any distinctively High Church doctrines," she accurately noted, "yet there can be no doubt that they did their part toward the Church movement by manifesting the un-loveliness and unsatisfactoriness of this particular phase of sub-urban Evangelicalism." And Harriett Mozley's own husband,

Tom, wrote that *The Lost Brooch* was the greatest "shew-up" of
Evangelicalism yet attempted. The list of subjects favored by
Anne Brontë's Puseyite rector for his sermons indicates that,
except for apostolic succession and church rites and ceremonies,
he too, like Harriett Mozley, was negative, not positive, perpetually on the anti-Evangelical warpath. In Mary Anne and Constance Duff she was portraying in fiction written for children two
young girls guilty of precisely the sins Anne Brontë ironically
listed in *Agnes Grey*: "the reprehensible presumption" of thinking for themselves "in matters connected with religion," and even
of flirting with the "atrocious criminality of dissent."

   In their children's fiction, other High Church writers, including
Charlotte Yonge herself in her dozens of novels, almost never
touched directly on matters of theology. Yet Tractarian teachings
are nevertheless conveyed. In one of the most spirited and delightful of her books for children, *Countess Kate* (1862) (vintage Charlotte Yonge in every respect, with a thirteen-year-old
heroine said to be a self-portrait of the author at that age), she
preached her principles in their full strictness and yet took a
more tolerant attitude toward rebellion and resistance than in
any of her other tales. *Countess Kate* is a "family romance" in
the historical, cultural, and even psychoanalytical sense of the
term. Early orphaned and brought up amidst a family of five
cousins in a simple rural parsonage by an affectionate widowed
uncle whom she calls papa, Kate Umfraville at thirteen unexpectedly becomes Countess of Caergwent and must go off to London
to be looked after by two maiden great-aunts. Mingled with her
despair at having to leave her beloved family and her chagrin at
the harshness of her new way of life is an exhilarating sense of
her own new social importance.

   Obedience, humility, unselfishness: these are the qualities that
the high-strung, intelligent, emotional little girl lacks. From
Kate's own age of thirteen on, Charlotte Yonge herself had
learned these lessons from her mentor, John Keble, the original
Tractarian. Keble had left Oxford in 1836 for the Hampshire
parish of Hursley, close to the house of Charlotte's parents,
whose intimate family friend and counselor he became. While he
lived, he read each of her books before she sent it to the publishers. They reflect his indoctrination in Tractarian ideas and

practices, and *Countess Kate* is typical. In London, in her aunts' confined household, Kate may not make any noise, has no real companionship, little exercise, and insufficient love. Some of the commands she must now obey are outrageous: in her new dignity as Countess Kate, she may not even refer to her beloved uncle as papa, as she has done since infancy. Her tantrums, her near-despair, her occasional pleasures which render her almost as hysterical with joy as her frustrations do with sorrow, her bitter decision to run away, and the final happy resolution of her problems are wholly convincing.

The degeneration of her character in her wretchedness is characteristically Yongeian. Obedient and wholly truthful at first, Kate makes her initial slip when she disobeys orders and allows a playmate to call her by a nickname instead of Lady Caergwent and then fails to report her delinquency. Thereafter — as with Eric, but on a miniature scale — it is downhill "little by little" for Kate. Soon she acts in "direct defiance" of her aunts' commands; she grows deceitful; but she never tells an outright lie. Well read in children's fiction, Kate is steeped in the conviction of her own guilt. Dramatically she declares, "It's the fashionable world. It's corrupting my simplicity. It always does. And I shall be lost!" And, leavening the lump of moral instruction with humor and natural youthful conversation, Miss Yonge makes Kate owlishly tell one of her cousins, "You little know, in your peaceful retirement, what are the miseries of the great," to which he promptly responds, "Come, Kate, don't talk bosh out of your books."

In the end, despite her naughtiness, Kate is rescued from the managing great-aunt, who is reduced to tears and even makes a form of apology. The ways of grown-ups must not be questioned, and Kate has indeed been a grave offender. But an impartial adult judge accuses the aunt of having kept the child a "state prisoner" and of alienating her from her true friends. The aunt, who has always disliked Kate's side of the family and has sometimes found the child intolerable, is nevertheless made to admit, in saying farewell, "There were faults on both sides, Katherine." So Charlotte Yonge struck a rare balance and proclaimed that, whereas the child must submit, the adult must supply love and understanding. Yet the only overtly Tractarian cause espoused in *Countess Kate* is the favorite one of improving the fabric of a church: on the very first page, Kate wishes for money so that her "papa's" church may be made beautiful. At her first opportunity after she has become a countess she begs a new acquaintance to contribute to building a new aisle in her uncle's church and triumphantly comes away with a five-pound note for the purpose.

Harry and Laura Graham are naughty Evangelical children portrayed by an Evangelical author. So is Eric, only he is wickeder. They have to undergo their conversions, and if necessary to suffer and die in the process. Mary Anne and Constance Duff are erring Evangelical children portrayed by a High Church antagonist. They get away with their delinquencies: Mary Anne rewarded for a lie, Constance unredeemably impenitent for her arrogance, both handicapped forever by their faulty Evangelical upbringing and full of the fatal propensity to think about moral and theological questions independently of — and even outside — the sheltering Church. But Kate Caergwent is a naughty Tractarian child portrayed by a Tractarian author. So she need not undergo a conversion, need not have her spirit broken or lose her life. She must learn through suffering what Grace Leslie knows instinctively: how to submit. But the lesson is taught by Kate's experience of life itself, and not by preaching.

"The true meaning of that — to her — most awful word — Eternity; the fearful sense of the doctrine of eternal punishment; the difficulty of reconciling it with the love of the Almighty Creator of the world . . .": these are the knotty problems that Grace Leslie keeps turning over and over in her mind as she lies in bed at the age of nine. They trouble Grace, High Anglican though she is, and they torture many another character in fiction as they did men and women in real life, especially those of stern Evangelical or Nonconformist upbringing. It was, of course, Frederick Denison Maurice, with his insistence that God loved all human beings, and his message that the idea of eternal hope should replace that of eternal punishment, who brought the first message of comfort to those so sorely tried.

While Maurice's Broad Church followers hardly formed a party as such, since their very latitudinarianism prevented them from becoming sectarians like High Churchmen or Low Churchmen, they did, of course, write books for children. But the reader will not find in the famous children's books written by Maurice's famous disciples — Charles Kingsley's *Water-Babies* (1863), Thomas Hughes's *Tom Brown's Schooldays* (1857), or George MacDonald's *At the Back of the North Wind* (1871) and other allegories — unregenerate children who are spared the agonies of Eric.[7]

But in *The Rival Kings* (1857) and *Castle Blair* (1878), two splendid children's books by two extraordinary artists, Annie Keary (1825–1879) and Flora Shaw (1852–1939), a careful listener can still detect the overtones of Maurice's merciful teachings. Although a generation separated the two women and their social backgrounds were dissimilar, their lives had many points in common. Both were spinsters, Annie Keary all her life, Flora Shaw until she was fifty. Annie Keary, handsome and gentle, lost her only serious lover. Flora Shaw, a noted beauty and conversationalist, shied away from youthful marriage and preferred the friendship of older men: Ruskin, Meredith, Charles Eliot Norton. For long periods in their lives, both women, observantly and tolerantly, took care of large families of other people's children, who long remembered their sympathy and tenderness: "better and more precious than a thousand well-ordered Kindergartens," as one of Annie Keary's grateful nephews later wrote.

Both writers were tormented by the central problem that troubled Grace Leslie: the seeming incompatibility of an all-loving God with the doctrine of eternal hellfire. The product of a strongly Evangelical upbringing, in which the annual meeting of the Church Missionary Society in Hull was the greatest entertainment of the year, Annie Keary was comforted when Maurice's teachings first reached her in the late forties. "Almost all the orthodox held the opposite view," but she persisted; she wrote to Charles Kingsley and received a sympathetic answer. Its "beautiful words" seemed to roll a cloud "away from her vision of God." At sixteen Flora Shaw, whose background was also Evangelical

---

7. MacDonald as a child in Calvinist Scotland cried out that he did not want God to love him if God did not love everybody, and in his novels for adults, notably *Robert Falconer* (1868), expounded God's plan for setting sinners free from hellfire. But he did not purvey these doctrines in his books for children.

but less doctrinaire, went through a major religious crisis precipitated by a railway accident in which several friends were killed. She refused to believe that God could possibly have damned the victims. "For ten years," her biographer writes, "she was subject to torturing religious doubts and misgivings, and only painfully arrived at a philosophy which, while it rejected many of the beliefs of her childhood, including that of eternal punishment, left her with a belief in the moral government of the world." [8]

The striking parallels between the lives and religious experiences of the two writers go far to explain the even more extraordinary resemblances between *The Rival Kings* and *Castle Blair*. The delinquencies of the children in both books wholly dwarf those of Harry and Laura Graham, Eric, Mary Anne and Constance Duff, and Kate Caergwent. It is no longer mere naughtiness, or the corruptions of boarding school life, or even lying or religious arrogance and self-satisfaction, or insubordination and petty deception with which we have to do; it is nothing less than sheer hatred, running its disastrous course through the hearts of children. The heightening of the passions and the mounting tension of the plots make the two narratives far more exciting than most Victorian children's stories. In both cases, adults are virtually helpless, and the ultimate lesson is one of Maurician, Broad Church forgiveness.

In 1857, when she sat down to write *The Rival Kings,* Annie Keary had just completed, with her sister Eliza, the first children's version of Norse mythology in English, *Heroes of Asgard and the Giants of Jotunheim.* She was still caring for the three small sons of her widowed brother. Perhaps the effort to adapt for children the semisavage Norse myths, full of violence, direct action, and unrestrained passion, suggested to her that intense hatred and the catastrophes to which it leads were not the sole property of heroic past ages but could be seen every day around the domestic hearth. From observing her own young nephews she may have become aware that, even in the best-brought-up youngsters, with the best religious training, savagery lay not far beneath the surface. Whatever its immediate inspiration, *The Rival Kings*

---

8. Eliza Keary, *Memoir of Annie Keary by Her Sister,* 2d ed. (London, 1883), and E. Moberly Bell, *Flora Shaw (Lady Lugard, D.B.E.)* (London: Constable, 1947), provide the biographical data.

is extraordinary because its children move so unmistakably in their own emotional world.

Next door to the comfortable rectory in a remote Welsh seaside village, where the Lloyd family lives with five children, there moves an English farmer's family, the Fletchers, with three children of their own, coarse and given to anti-Welsh remarks. Before long, Maurice Lloyd, the rector's eldest son, aged about twelve, grows obsessed with his dislike for young Roger Fletcher. Three additional children, the Maynes, recently orphaned, join the Lloyd household. Despite their best intentions, the young Lloyds, especially Maurice, find it impossible to be truly friendly and sympathetic to the newcomers. And the Maynes — stunned by grief, strangers in a household that cannot seem like home to them, despite the kindness of the senior Lloyds and the initial efforts of the Lloyd children — cling to one another and grow increasingly wretched. Each attempt at reconciliation only deepens the dislike between the "rival kings," Maurice and the eldest Mayne boy, Walter. Clever, sneering Walter, wholly different in temperament to the extroverted, bumptious, bossy but well-meaning Maurice, makes an ally of Maurice's deadly enemy, Roger Fletcher, who is somewhat older.

On an excursion to an isolated rocky island, Maurice suffers the humiliation of rescue from a cliff top by Roger Fletcher and Walter Mayne, who make it impossible for him to thank them properly. He fails to report the incident to his parents, and thereafter his miseries increase. His favorite younger sister recites to Maurice a hymn including the verses "He who ruleth well his heart, / And keeps his temper down / Is greater, acts a wiser part / Than he who takes a town." But Maurice ignores the message. Mrs. Lloyd, an attentive and loving mother and foster-mother, writes two stories for the children, especially designed to awaken Maurice before it is too late. In the first, a little boy's ill temper and impetuousness lead to the death of a younger sister, which he vainly regrets all his life. Mrs. Lloyd drives home the moral,

"It is almost too shocking to hear of a brother being the cause of his sister's death; but do not you know that you can do people far greater injury than killing their bodies? You can help the devil to destroy their souls; and there are few weapons stronger than angry words to do this. Think what far more dreadful remorse must be felt if one day, when all secrets are known, one brother or companion should say to another, 'It was your temper, your angry words and overbearing ways that first awoke hatred in my heart, and separated my soul from God.' "

But Maurice visibly hardens himself "in a self-justifying humour," and his mother feels almost sorry "that she had given him the opportunity of slighting another warning."

Her second story is an allegory about two princely brothers and two rival fairies, Discord and Love, who bear them company. Discord's favorite words are *I* and *mine* and *It is my right;* Love's are *You, Yours,* and *I will give up.* The secret of happiness is to refuse to wear Discord's clothes — *Habits of Self-Indulgence* — (covered with prickly little "I's" that prevent anybody coming close), and to put on Love's *Habits of Self-Denial,* the most beautiful clothes in the world, which must be earned by self-sacrifice. This story only confirms Maurice's conviction that "the Fletchers are impossible to like." He fails utterly to see that anyone wearing Discord's clothes cannot love anybody else. The only way to love people because one knows one ought is to believe in the love of "Him who said 'Ye are my friends if ye do whatsoever I shall command you. This is my commandment, that ye love one another as I have loved you.' " But when a pet bird of the youngest Mayne child is killed, in part through Maurice's fault, Mr. Lloyd punishes Maurice. The Lloyd children naturally support their brother; Walter Mayne repeatedly overhears them denouncing him as unwanted and goes through with a fantastic plan he has hatched with Roger Fletcher to take his little sister and brother and run away to live on the island like the happy castaways of whom he has read.

Once on the island the Mayne children and Roger discover that there is nothing to eat. Their boat drifts away; they are isolated for several days by a storm. Only then, sobered by his parents' alarm for the missing children, does Maurice learn the truth about himself. Suddenly he sees that his innocently meant commands *had* been "overbearing." He regrets that he did not report his own near fall to death on the earlier island excursion. "He knew that, if he had continued his old habit of confessing all his faults to his parents, they could not have remained ignorant of what was going on in the family . . ."

The starving little castaways, meanwhile, are terrified and remorseful. But when his younger sister asks Walter Mayne, "if God sends for us now, shall you not be afraid to go?" Walter replies, "I think we ought not to be. Papa would not have liked us to be afraid to come to him if we had been ever so naughty, and God loves us even better than Papa did, and He has promised to forgive us when we are sorry, for Jesus Christ's sake, who was always an obedient child." And so, after deceit, lies, overbearing bossiness, and concentrated hatred have endangered several lives and thrown a loving family into the deepest anxiety, comes the reassuring message of eternal hope, instead of eternal damnation. God here is not the terrible Low Church God but the merciful Broad Church God.

The Maynes and Roger Fletcher are rescued in the nick of time. Maurice Lloyd spends hours daily during Roger Fletcher's long convalescence amusing him and making friends with him. Both Maurice and Walter have learned to distrust their own wills and to go for help to Christ. Self-sacrifice, not self-will, has become the ruling principle. Annie Keary, comforted by Frederick Denison Maurice and Charles Kingsley, had warned her readers that when a determined child conceals the truth, his parents, no matter how devoted and well intentioned and religious, lose their power to help. Hatred can precipitate a fatal or near-fatal catastrophe. But a loving paternal God will forgive a repentant sinner. For a child tormented by thoughts of eternal hellfire, *The Rival Kings* would have brought latitudinarian reassurance about salvation along with its unexceptionable Christian lesson.

If Maurice and the little Lloyds and Maynes of *The Rival Kings* have pushed the grown-ups into the background, Murtagh Blair and his younger brother and sisters in *Castle Blair* are virtually autonomous. Inhabiting a world of their own on their uncle's Irish estate, they create their own society, make their own rules, manage their own lives, adopt the cause of the Irish tenantry, and develop a running feud with their uncle's land agent, which steadily mounts in ferocity. The Blairs revel in their free-dom out-of-doors, manage their intrigues cleverly and enterpris-ingly, work themselves into a frenzy of hatred, and display a ruthless inability to consider any interests but their own. Their parents are in India, their uncle indifferent and preoccupied. A young woman of eighteen, their cousin Nessa, serves as the sole intermediary between them and the adult world. One looks in vain for other nineteenth-century fictional children with the same terrifying single-mindedness and independence. Not until Richard Hughes's *High Wind in Jamaica* (1929) and William Golding's *Lord of the Flies* (1950) does one meet the counter-parts of the Blairs.[9]

The externals of *Castle Blair* — the ice-cold stream up which the children wade to the island, the hut, the pleasant village, and the affectionate relationship between the villagers and the chil-dren — were all remembered from Flora Shaw's own childhood holidays spent on her grandfather's estate near Dublin. But Mr. Plunkett, the landlord's agent, so effective in his job, so awkward and ruthless in dealing with the children, was an invention. The unruly young Blairs steal apples from their uncle's garden, and when Plunkett rebukes them Murtagh calls him no gentleman and, "with concentrated passion in his voice," contemplates killing him someday. Actual theft and prospective violence are present from the start. In their hut the children conceal a young village girl who has lost the money to pay Plunkett the rent and who fears that her drunken stepfather will beat her to death. Plunkett and the villagers are sure the child has been kidnapped; her mother mourns her as if she were dead. A peasant's attempt to assassinate Plunkett turns the children's romantic good deed into a local scandal. When he discovers that the children have hidden the girl, Plunkett "manages to make everything seem wicked" and so makes Murtagh "wicked in reality." He finds the problem of right and wrong so taxing that he wishes he were dead. Then, for the first time, his charming young cousin Nessa has a religious word for him: "You know we are not perfect . . .

9. In the two twentieth-century books, as in *The Rival Kings* and *Castle Blair,* an island figures largely.

We are quite sure to make mistakes, but . . . we ought to . . . go on trying and trying to the end; and then God *is* kind; he will let us have done most good by the time we have to stop."

After a series of increasingly hostile encounters, Plunkett orders workmen to tear down the children's cherished hut (built by their own father in his childhood), and shoots their beloved dog. So Murtagh steals Plunkett's gun and gives it to a would-be assassin. At the last possible moment Murtagh seizes the gun, it goes off, Plunkett fires in turn and wounds Murtagh. Murder has been narrowly avoided, but hatred has led to kidnapping, theft, arson, the killing of a beloved pet, two attempted assassinations, and the near-fatal wounding of the hero. Only after Plunkett has given the bereft Winnie a new dog and both he and Murtagh have admitted their mistakes and forgiven one another does Nessa venture the final (it is only the second) religious comment in the book. Even if people are wicked, Murtagh says, he now realizes that it does no good to hate them, to which Nessa answers, "If God were to hate us when we are wicked, what should we do? It often comes over me with a sort of rush of gladness, how that when we make mistakes, and get tired, and go wrong, He is still there watching over us, loving us all the time, never getting impatient. And you know . . . we are told to try and be as like God as we can."

So, more than twenty years apart, two talented Victorian maiden ladies, each of whom had taken the responsibility for bringing up small children, portrayed the terrible dangers that may arise from hatred. With loving grown-ups rendered powerless in both cases, Maurice Lloyd and Murtagh Blair miraculously escape the consequences of their actions. Without the necessity of a "conversion," the two boys have learned that hatred does no good. Writing in 1857, Annie Keary was still too much an inhabitant of the mid-Victorian world to tell her story without repeated religious commentary, whereas Flora Shaw was of a different generation and, by 1878, could reduce her religious message to two short admonitions. But both writers had overcome their own youthful Evangelical despair at the prospect of eternal punishment and had won through to confidence in Frederick Denison Maurice's all-loving God who forgives even the

Performing Heroinism: The Myth of Corinne

> It is an immortal book, and deserves to be read three score and
> ten times — that is once every year in the age of man.
>
> Elizabeth Barrett (age 26) on *Corinne*[1]

> The hour of agony and revolt ... passes away and does not re-
> turn; yet those who, amid the agitations ... of their youth, be-
> took themselves to the early works of George Sand, may in later
> life cease to read them, indeed, but they can no more forget them
> than they can forget *Werther.* George Sand speaks somewhere
> of her "days of *Corinne.*" Days of *Valentine,* many of us may in
> like manner say, — days of *Lélia,* days never to return!
>
> Matthew Arnold (age 55)[2]

Let us try to take *Corinne* seriously; it was *the* book of the
woman of genius. At least a few chapters and scattered passages,
as well as the complex scheme of the novel that Mme de Staël
had the brilliance but not the talent to write, should be familiar
to anyone pretending to an interest in the traditions of women's
literature; they are already familiar to historians of Romanticism.

Published in 1807, *Corinne* was the work of a woman known

1. *Elizabeth Barrett to Mr. Boyd,* ed. Barbara P. McCarthy (New
Haven: Yale University Press, 1955), p. 176.
2. "George Sand," *Complete Prose Works of Matthew Arnold,* ed.
R. H. Super (Ann Arbor: University of Michigan Press, 1960), 8:220.

in Europe and America as the author of *De la littérature,* which
established Mme de Staël's name forever as the one which "still
rises first to the lips," in George Eliot's words, "when we are
asked to mention a woman of great intellectual power." [3] To take
Corinne seriously is to perceive its place in Mme de Staël's
thought about literature and culture, but to read the novel itself
is also to encounter a predecessor of those "Silly Novels by Lady
Novelists" which George Eliot so wittily demolished. *Corinne*
stands alone in Mme de Staël's oeuvre in its silliness as in its
enormous influence upon literary women. For them, the myth of
Corinne persisted as both inspiration and warning: it was the
fantasy of the performing heroine. [4]

Let us try to take *Corinne* seriously, in order to comprehend
George Eliot's expressed and unexpressed conceptions of heroinism in such a scene as this, from *The Mill on the Floss:*

> "Take back your *Corinne,*" said Maggie ... "You were right
> in telling me she would do me no good; but you were wrong in
> thinking I should wish to be like her."
>
> "Wouldn't you really like to be a tenth Muse, then, Maggie?"
> said Philip ...
>
> "Not at all," said Maggie, laughing. "The Muses were uncom-
> fortable goddesses, I think — obliged always to carry rolls and
> musical instruments about with them ..."
>
> "You agree with me in not liking Corinne, then?"
>
> "I didn't finish the book ..." (Book 5, chap. 4)

At this point of *The Mill on the Floss,* the reader is just as
surprised as Philip Wakem to discover that Maggie Tulliver,
whom we have known up to now as a sensitive, misunderstood
child, is not to turn into a mature woman of intellectual distinction and wide ambition — a *femme supérieure,* like Mme de
Staël or George Eliot herself — but instead into a merely pretty

---

3. "Woman in France," *Westminster Review,* 62 (1854), 450.

4. Which was not, of course, the only kind of heroic, central, female
figure that women writers created, starting in the eighteenth century.
Traveling, loving, and educating heroism are other aspects of a very
broad subject which I am exploring in my forthcoming book, *Literary
Women.*

and dangerous flirt who steals a rich, good-looking suitor away from her cousin Lucy. Swinburne could not bear it. No such "abyss of cynicism" on the subject of female character had been sounded by the wickedest of French novelists — not by Stendhal, Mérimée, or Laclos. "My faith will not digest at once," he wrote, "the first two volumes and the third volume of 'The Mill on the Floss'; my conscience or credulity has not gorge enough for such a gulp." [5]

The myth of Corinne bridges the abyss in *The Mill on the Floss,* even though Maggie Tulliver is not allowed to say whether she likes the heroine of Mme de Staël's novel, which George Eliot read in her adolescence or early twenties.[6] *Corinne* served as a children's book for a special kind of nineteenth-century child: girls of more than ordinary intelligence or talent and rising ambition to fame beyond the domestic circle. Reading *Corinne* made an event of their youth (for some, a catalyst to their own literary talent) which in later years they could not wholly reject unless they were willing also to deny their own enthralling, painful awakening as women of genius — their own "days of *Corinne*," in George Sand's phrase. For the aspiration to glory which is a happy and a wholesome thing in the development of a gifted young man was very different then (perhaps still is today) for such a young woman. In her case, exceptional qualities and ambitions cut cruelly across the normal process of female maturation. That, at least, was the dilemma of Corinne as Mme de Staël, with daunting lucidity, expounded it; and she left it, incidentally, unresolved.

"I didn't finish the book," Maggie Tulliver continues:

As soon as I came to the blond-haired young lady reading in the park, I shut it up, and determined to read no further. I foresaw that the light-complexioned girl would win away all the love from Corinne and make her miserable. I'm determined to read no more books where the blond-haired women carry away all the happiness.

5. *A Note on Charlotte Brontë* (1894; reprint ed., New York: Haskell House, 1970), pp. 32–34.
6. *The George Eliot Letters,* ed. Gordon S. Haight (New Haven: Yale University Press, 1954–55), 1:71, 2:3.

The business of dark hair versus light is not at all trivial in *The Mill on the Floss,* where much of Maggie's childhood anguish is represented by her inability to manage her unruly mop of dark hair; and the inhibiting forces of conventional femininity are represented by the hatefully neat blond curls of her cousin Lucy. In *Corinne,* hair color is momentous: Corinne represents the passionate exuberance of dark-haired Latin culture, and Lucile, her blonde rival, stands for the subdued and inhibited sensibility of Nordic culture, along with all that is implied by the home, the wife, and the private virtues in English society.

Maggie goes on to mention Rebecca in *Ivanhoe* and other dark-haired non-Anglo-Saxon heroines in Scott (who knew all about *Corinne*)[7] as examples of "the dark unhappy ones" that "I want to avenge." Philip takes her light words seriously:

> "Well, perhaps you will avenge the dark women in your own person, and carry away all the love from your cousin Lucy. She is sure to have some handsome young man of St. Ogg's at her feet now; and you have only to shine upon him — your fair little cousin will be quite quenched in your beams."
>
> "Philip, that is not pretty of you, to apply my nonsense to anything real," said Maggie, looking hurt. "As if I, with my old gowns and want of all accomplishments, could be a rival of dear little Lucy."

Pretty or not, Philip has made a fair summary of the rest of the novel, except that Maggie's convenient death in a flood is designed to smooth over, both practically and morally, her ugly revenge on blondes in the person of "dear little Lucy." Corinne, incidentally, also dies at the end, making her faithless lover and her blonde rival wretched with regret, after subversively coaching their little daughter to carry on her own tradition of feminine genius. Mme de Staël's is a funnier revenge of feminine spite, but perhaps preferable to George Eliot's.

For literary women, Corinne was the female Childe Harold, and Byron owed something, as he and his contemporaries recog-

---

7. *Sir Walter Scott on Novelists and Fiction,* ed. Ian Williams (London: Routledge & Kegan Paul, 1968), p. 293.

nized, to Mme de Staël. Just as the Byronic hero became a myth wider than any single literary creation because Byron's own life entered into its making, so Mme de Staël's legend became part of the literary myth she created in *Corinne*. After its publication, when she was universally referred to by her heroine's name, the myth and the writer became inseparable.

In the eyes of literary women, hers was a woman's life unique in history for its great public swathe. Mme de Staël was the first woman of middle-class origins to impress herself, through her own genius, on the major public events of her time — events political, literary, intellectual, in every sense revolutionary. Her position and wealth came initially from her father, who was Jacques Necker, citizen banker of Geneva and finance minister to Louis XVI. But after her marriage to a Swedish diplomat (the only trivial event of her life), she became a power in her own right. Gibbon, Jefferson, Schlegel, Sismondi, Constant, Narbonne, Goethe, Talleyrand — the extraordinary gallery of great men who pass through her life story as friends, colleagues, lovers, dependents, correspondents were drawn to Mme de Staël by her mind, her talk, and her writings.

She was indeed one of the greatest talkers ever to dominate a salon. But there were so many talking women in the history of the French salon; more important, Mme de Staël was a professional writer, whose books changed the world. Her studies of Rousseau, of Peace, of Fiction, of the Passions in the 1790s; of Literature Considered in Its Relation to Social Institutions, in 1800; and of Germany, of Suicide, of the French Revolution in the 1810s brought her persecution by an emperor and "a degree of homage," as one of her nineteenth century biographers put it, "never before paid to any woman who was not a queen." [8] As early as the 1790s the rarity of her accomplishment entered the consciousness of literary women, as Fanny Burney, Hannah More, Mary Berry, and Maria Edgeworth testify.[9] Her presence

8. Lydia Maria Child, *The Biography of Madame de Staël* (Edinburgh, 1836), p. 68.

9. See R. C. Whitford, *Madame de Staël's Literary Reputation in England,* University of Illinois Studies in Language and Literature, 1918; Robert Arthur Jones, "Madame de Staël and England," unpublished thesis, University of London, 1928; these and other studies discuss Mme

in England (an émigrée in 1793) provided an impetus to the feminist ferment of that remarkable decade, as well as, in the person of a minor member of her entourage, a husband for Fanny Burney. But it was only with *Corinne,* in 1807, that the myth floated free — the myth of the famous woman talking, writing, performing, to the applause of the world.

As early as 1808 Jane Austen was recommending *"Corinna"* (in one of the quickly available English translations) to a gentleman of her acquaintance who was stone deaf — with what accents of irony one can only imagine. Mary Godwin picked up *Corinne* as soon as her first illegitimate baby (by Shelley) was born. Catharine Sedgwick, the American novelist, made a pilgrimage to Mme de Staël's grave at Le Coppet and was surprised to find that the author of *Corinne* had actually been silenced by her death in 1817. The poetesses of the 1820s in England and America were identified by their large public with Corinne, and for good reason. "That book," wrote Felicia Hemans, "has a power over me which is quite indescribable; some passages seem to give me back my own thoughts and feelings, my whole inner being, with a mirror more true than ever friend could hold up." And on the American frontier, young Harriet Beecher read *Corinne* and a life of its author, registered "an intense sympathy" with them both, and set out on her own literary career.

By the early 1830s young Elizabeth Barrett had already read *Corinne* three times over, and George Sand was writing *Lélia.* By the early 1840s Margaret Fuller was being called the "Yankee Corinna" by Emerson and everyone else — and the Victorian apotheosis of the Corinne myth was under way. (It would last as long and spread as far as the Maine of Sara Orne Jewett and the Missouri of Kate Chopin.)[10] Because of the myth, Charlotte

---

de Staël's effect on her English contemporaries, but do not carry the story into the Victorian era.

10. *Jane Austen's Letters,* ed. R. W. Chapman (New York: Oxford University Press, 1952), p. 242; *Mary Shelley's Journal,* ed. Frederick L. Jones (Norman: University of Oklahoma Press, 1957), p. 39; C. M. Sedgwick, *Letters from Abroad to Kindred at Home* (New York, 1841), 1:260; Henry F. Chorley, *Memorials of Mrs. Hemans* (London, 1837), 1:296; Charles Edward Stowe, *The Life of Harriet Beecher Stowe* (Boston, 1889), p. 67; *Barrett to Mr. Boyd,* p. 176; Pierre Reboul, critical edition of *Lélia* (1833; Paris: Garnier, 1960); Margaret Fuller, *Memoirs*

Brontë cast the hero of *Villette* as a Napoleon, in his opposition
to intellectual and strong-minded women; for Napoleon, who
censored, banned, and exiled Mme de Staël for her writings,
entered too into the myth of Corinne. "He resembled the great
Emperor," wrote Brontë of her Paul Emanuel; ". . . would
have quarreled with twenty learned women . . . would have exiled
fifty Madame de Staëls, if they had annoyed, offended, out-
rivalled, or opposed him."

The Corinne myth was "perilous stuff" to women, to use Bulwer's phrase for Byronism, and like the Byronic hero Mme de
Staël's heroine often makes her most significant presence felt in
literature by the force of resistance she evokes. So Maggie Tulliver
insists that she does not want to be a Corinne, and Lucy Snowe,
the supreme antiheroine of Victorian fiction, rejects all the excel-
ling, all the public display that the myth implies. But in Charlotte
Brontë's youthful imagination, Corinne herself had stalked un-
trammeled and unrepressed in the person of Zenobia Percy,
Countess of Northumberland. With flashing eyes and raven hair,
with her velvets, plumes, and crowning turban, Zenobia is "the
prima donna of the Angrian Court, the most learned woman of
her age, the modern Cleopatra, the Verdopolitan de Staël." At
eighteen Brontë wrote the figure into her Angria tales, those
fantasies which served to nourish her mature fiction and also to
exorcise from it such perilous stuff as the myth of Corinne.[11]

There is a hero in *Corinne,* and he is dealt with — actually,
set up — in the first of the novel's twenty books. There we find
an English nobleman progressing in distracted and melancholy
fashion, during the winter of 1794–95, across the continent
toward Italy, in what is a kind of pre-Romantic ruined fragment
of the grand tour which such men made throughout the eigh-

(London, 1852), 1:67–68, 286–287; 2:172–173; Sara Orne Jewett, annotated copy of *Corinne, ou l'Italie* (New York, 1862), in Houghton
Library, Harvard University; Per Seyersted, *Kate Chopin: A Critical
Biography* (Baton Rouge: Louisiana State University Press, 1969), pp.
25–26, 62.

11. *Villette,* chap. 30; Fannie Elizabeth Ratchford, *The Brontës' Web
of Childhood* (New York: Columbia University Press, 1941), p. 87;
Charlotte Maurat, *The Brontës' Secret,* trans. Margaret Meldrum (New
York: Barnes & Noble, 1970), pp. 76–77.

teenth century. He is a Scottish peer called Oswald lord Nelvil — an orthography which has always made trouble, though it is a fair representation of what the French ear hears when the name Neville is pronunced. Such trivia as spelling and the distinction between England and Scotland meant nothing to Mme de Staël, but it was very important to her that her hero be a Briton, an exemplar in emotive and moral tone of the new sensibility and culture then sweeping down like a tidal wave out of the north to engulf the Francophone, Latin civilization of the Age de Lumières.

Mme de Staël makes Oswald "interesting" by giving him noble birth, unrevealed past, and unexplained gloom; but she must also make him worthy of such a heroine as Corinne. The matter is efficiently dispatched in book 1: Oswald steers a ship through a storm, calming both the elements and the spirits of lesser men about him; and then he saves a whole community from destruction by fire. These "scenes" are all the reader has to cling to, later on, when Corinne loses her heart to the hero. Mme de Staël tosses them at us and later looks back at them with an air of saying: however weak and vacillating, however dull and priggish is my Oswald, remember that he has demonstrated that physical courage and protomilitary leadership which alone are lacking to the heroism of the woman of genius.

And the fire scene is our first indication that the more stupid the narrative in *Corinne,* the more interesting are the ideas which drive it forward. For no apparent novelistic reason Mme de Staël sets fire to Ancona, a city she describes as divided equally among people of the Roman Catholic, Greek Orthodox, and Jewish faiths. Lord Nelvil risks his life to save the Jews, barricaded in their quarter at nightfall and blamed by the Christians of the city for the conflagration that threatens them all. Oswald's indignant and generous rejection of superstition is that of a Briton and a Protestant, as well as a hero. So ends book 1, entitled "Oswald," and so ends our interest in that gentleman.

Book 2, the most important of the novel, is "Corinne au Capitole." It establishes the ultimate fantasy of the performing heroine with a brio, a luster, and a folly beyond the possibility of future novelists to exceed. All this takes place in the Capitol of the capital of the world. Oswald awakens to the brilliant sun of

Rome and to the ringing of bells and booming of cannons which announce that, that very day, there will be carried in triumph to the Capitoline Hill, there to be crowned with the laurel wreath of genius, as Petrarch and Tasso were before her, the most famous woman of Italy: "Corinne, poëte, écrivain, improvisatrice, et l'une des plus belles personnes de Rome." [12]

All of Rome seems to have turned into the streets for the occasion. The babble of the populace arouses Oswald's curiosity about a woman whose nationality, past, and even real name are unknown (but not her age: she is twenty-six, a year older than he) — and predisposes him to admire Corinne before he sees her. "In England he would have judged such a woman very severely, but in Italy he could ignore social conventions and take an interest in the crowning of Corinne similar to that of an adventure in Aristo" (book 2, chap. 1). This love affair begins with a clashing of cultures as well as a clanging of bells.

Music sounds. A parade of Roman and foreign dignitaries marches by. Then come the four white horses which draw the chariot mounted with an antique throne, on which, in a noble attitude, sits Corinne. Young girls dressed in white walk by her side, but Corinne herself is no maiden: she is a mature woman of what we would call solid build. Mme de Staël insists on her beautiful arms and asks us to think of Greek statuary, just as George Eliot does with the "large round arm" of Maggie Tulliver at the time of that heroine's apotheosis: "the dimpled elbow . . . the varied gently-lessening curves down to the delicate wrist . . . the firm softness. A woman's arm touched the soul of a great sculptor two thousand years ago, so that he wrought an image of it for the Parthenon which moves us still . . . Maggie's was such an arm as that" (book 6, chap. 10).

12. *Corinne ou l'Italie* (Paris, 1839), p. 21. In my translations I have tried to capture the style of *Corinne,* which seems to me to have the flat-footed grace and dignity of a sprightly elephant — not what Sainte-Beuve means, perhaps, when in his preface to this edition he praises the style of *Corinne* for "la majesté soutenue" (p. vii). The startling modernisms in my translations are inspired by the original, but this sentence defeats me, for who would believe me if I had Mme de Staël call Corinne "one of the beautiful people" of Rome? For her style at its best, and for her most eloquent feminist statement, see "Des femmes qui cultivent les lettres," part 2, chap. 4, of *De la littérature.*

Corinne is robed in white like the Domenichino sibyl, with a blue drapery flowing from her shoulder and an Indian shawl wound round her head and through her beautiful black hair. It is an "extremely picturesque" costume, Mme de Staël points out, "but not so far out of fashion as to be liable to the charge of affectation." For an idea of the style, do not look at the Gérard portrait of Mme de Staël in the garb of Corinne, which is simply too depressing, but instead look at Dorothea Brooke in *Middlemarch* as posed by George Eliot (not on the Capitoline, for times by then had changed) in a museum in Rome: "standing against a pedestal near the reclining marble; a breathing blooming girl, whose form, not shamed by the Ariadne, was clad in Quakerish grey drapery; her long cloak, fastened at the neck, was thrown backward from her arms, and one beautiful ungloved hand pillowed her cheek, pushing somewhat backward the white beaver bonnet which made a sort of halo to her face around the simply braided dark-brown hair" (chap. 19).

"Vive Corinne! vive le génie! vive la beauté!" cheers the marvelously responsive Italian crowd: long live genius, long live beauty, long live Corinne. And Oswald loves. Or, to be more precise, he suddenly experiences a transforming shock that runs like a thrill of electrical energy (the image is Mme de Staël's) from this moment to the end of the novel, a shock to his soul and to his cultural prejudices. All Oswald's British respectability, dignity, impassivity, and taciturnity; all his essentially religious deference to the sacred idols of *the home* — privacy, discretion, solitude, patriotism, paternal ancestry — are shaken by a threefold experience: Italy, its climate and culture; applause by the masses of spiritual rather than military genius; and the woman of genius. As Mme de Staël puts it: "The admiration of the populace grew ever greater the closer she came to the Capitol, that place so rich in memories. This beautiful sky, these enthusiastic Romans, and above all Corinne herself electrified the imagination of Oswald."

For what Oswald is made to love in Corinne is not the woman in the genius but, if the expression is pardonable, the whole package: the woman of genius at the moment and in the place of her greatest public triumph. It isn't easy, and in fact it does not work out very well, but at least it must be said that what

Mme de Staël puts at issue is no simple *amour* but the total transformation of cultural attitudes (and perhaps civilization itself)
by the romance of the woman of genius.

At last the procession reaches the Capitol. Senators, cardinal,
academicians are seated, as well as a spillover crowd. Corinne
touches her knee to the ground before taking her seat and
listening to the speeches and odes recited in her praise. Then
she rises to improvise on the theme of "the glory and the happiness of Italy" — almost a chapter-length of throbbing prose
(book 2, chap. 3). It is the first of many such improvisations
which are dotted through the novel and which were rendered
into English, in the most widely read translation of *Corinne,* by
the English poetess Letitia E. Landon, herself a disciple of
Corinne, known as L. E. L. and as the author of a poem in the
Corinne tradition called "The Improvisatrice." [13]

The final chapter of book 2 deals with the actual crowning. A
senator rises with the laurel wreath. Corinne detaches her turban,
letting her ebony curls flow free, and advances her bare head
with a smile of undissimulated pleasure on her face: no longer a
modest woman, for she has just spoken very well indeed; no
longer a fearful woman, but an inspired priestess dedicated to the
cult of genius. Music sounds, the crown descends, Corinne's eyes
fill with tears — and my own emotions are at this point too
strong to permit me to continue with what is almost a literal
translation of the passage. I have been following Mme de Staël's
scenario very precisely, for the steps in Corinne's triumph were
very precisely observed not only by Oswald but by writers after
her: first the gossip overheard by a skeptical stranger, then the
fanfare, then the procession, then the distant view — oh so
lovely, so unusual — of the heroine, then the formal praises; only
then the actual performance (very difficult for a novelist to make
convincing); and at last the crown. Reading this material with a
woman's eye makes it hard to keep a straight face; but I am
bound to say that *Corinne* is one of very few works by women

---

13. *Corinne; or, Italy,* trans. Isabel Hill "with metrical versions of the
odes by L. E. L." (London, 1833); *The Poetical Works of L. E. Landon,*
with preliminary memoir by William B. Scott (London [1880]), pp.
11–14.

which is trivialized rather than honored by being read as a woman's work.

What contemporary readers saw in the triumph of Corinne was not the adolescence of Maggie Tullivers to come but a remarkably courageous celebration of the rights of spiritual genius and intellectual freedom, in defiance of the spreading imperial rule of a military genius named Napoleon. "Corinne is the sovereign independence of genius even at the time of the most absolute oppression," wrote Sainte-Beuve, "Corinne who has herself crowned in Rome, in the Capitol of the eternal city, where the conqueror who exiles her will not set foot." [14] That Napoleon was a man and Mme de Staël a woman was a matter of historical accident and did not affect the emperor's decision to exile the author of *Corinne*. That the claim for art over force, for mind over might, was made — in somewhat original and Romantic terms — by a woman, and in a woman's novel, was a historical accident with major literary repercussions. But the politicizing of genius, that is, the demonstration of genius by means of public acclamation, by an actual crowning, was Mme de Staël's principal intention, before self-aggrandizement, before feminism, when she wrote book 2 of *Corinne*.

Literary women, however, dearly wanted that crown: some formal, palpable, public tribute to female genius. The most charming of all Victorian crowning scenes, because the one which most consciously records a young woman's reactions to *Corinne,* is in book 2 of *Aurora Leigh.* There Mrs. Browning's heroine, an aspiring poet, playfully makes herself a poet's crown for her twentieth birthday: not of bay leaves, the classical laurel ("The fates deny us if we are overbold"), but of "that headlong ivy! not a leaf will grow / But thinking of a wreath." In the midst of her solitary playacting, Aurora finds that she is being observed by "My public! — cousin Romney — with a mouth / Twice graver than his eyes" (2.39–60).

The very name of "poet," for Aurora Leigh, "Is royal, and to sign it like a queen" is what she yearns to, but dares not do, for " 't is too easy to go mad / And ape a Bourbon in a crown of

14. Preface to *Corinne* (see above, note 12), pp. iii–iv; see also his three essays on Mme de Staël in *Les grands écrivains français par Sainte-Beuve (XIXe siècle)*, ed. Maurice Allem (Paris: Garnier, 1932).

straws" (1.940–941). These images of crowns and queens (and even Bourbons) traveled across the ocean to the poetry of Emily Dickinson, who revered Mrs. Browning herself as "the Head too High to Crown" and wrote wistfully, in the accents of the girl poet Aurora Leigh,

> I'm saying every day
> "If I should be a Queen, tomorrow" —
> . . . . .
> If it be, I wake a Bourbon,
> None on me, bend supercilious — [15]

George Eliot is always trying to put a golden halo on Dorothea Brooke's head, and, in a different mood, she pins a gold star on Gwendolen Harleth's archery dress (*Daniel Deronda,* book 1, chap. 10). She also has a "star of brilliants" descend from the royal box on the brow of Armgart, the prima donna in her verse play of that title. The singer is accused of enjoying the "ecstasy" of satisfied ambition. "Why not?" Armgart asks,

> Am I a sage whose word must fall like seed
> Silently buried toward a far-off spring?
> I sing to living men . . .
> . . . If the world brings me gifts,
> Gold, incense, myrrh — 'twill be the needful sign
> That I have stirred it as the high year stirs
> Before I sink to winter.[16]

I think it must be said that women writers who have attempted the literary portrait of genius have insisted more than men on showing it off at the moment of public acclaim; and that the literary result is more often raw fantasy than finished art. But the compulsion to write public triumphs, in the nineteenth century, surely resulted from the impossibility of ever having them in real life. The sort of experience that only moderately distinguished women today consider routine — making speeches, chairing

---

15. *The Complete Poems of Emily Dickinson,* ed. Thomas H. Johnson (Boston: Little Brown, 1960), no. 373 (cf. no. 312); Rebecca Patterson, "Elizabeth Browning and Emily Dickinson," *The Educational Leader* (Kansas State Teachers College), 20 (1956), 46.

16. "Armgart," *Poems* (New York: John W. Lovell, n.d.), p. 43.

meetings, lecturing, arguing in court — was absolutely closed to
Jane Austen, the Brontës, indeed to Mme de Staël, and was only
beginning to be conceivable at the time of George Eliot or
George Sand.

In the performance of Corinne, Mme de Staël apparently intended to summarize all the gifts of genius by which women of
her own time and before lay claim to fame — all gifts but one
significant by its absence: Corinne is not a novelist. She is an
improvisatrice, that is, a maker and reciter of spontaneous verses,
because Mme de Staël heard Isabel Pellegrini recite to great
applause when on her own Italian tour of 1804–05.[17] Improvisation was an Italian tradition (it referred to poetry before music)
which impressed all eighteenth-century travelers, and particularly
one like Mme de Staël — for its Romantic spontaneity, its popular appeal, and its near domination by women. She herself was no
poet, spontaneous or otherwise, but she had her heroine choose
a poet's name: that of Corinna, the Greek lyric poetess reputed
to be the teacher of Pindar.[18] For Corinne has the problem professional women have always had with the social implications of
a maiden or a married name; her own real name, which turns out
in book 14 to be miss Edgermond, simply will not do.

When Mme de Staël herself performed in public, it was as a
talker and provoker of serious talk by others. Her eccentric use
of the social institution of the salon as a medium of education or
philosophical discussion rather than conversation aroused amusement in France, surprise in England, and consternation in Germany. Much of the fluency, the brilliance, the intensity, and, alas,
the bore of her own manner she did indeed transfer to her heroine: "I see her, I hear her, I feel her," cried Napoleon on St.

17. J. Christopher Herold, *Mistress to an Age: A Life of Mme de
Staël* (New York: Bobbs-Merrill, 1958), p. 312.
18. Mme de Staël's note 11 (p. 516) to book 14 of *Corinne.* The
Greek Corinne or Corinna was better known to the eighteenth century
and is mentioned by Richardson in *Sir Charles Grandison,* ed. Jocelyn
Harris (London: Oxford University Press, 1972), 1:431, 481, a work
which I suspect had much to do with shaping Oswald's Italian romance
in *Corinne;* cf. Robert de Luppé, *Les idées littéraires de Madame de
Staël* (Paris: Librairie Philosophique, 1969), pp. 19–23, 30–33.

Helena when he attempted to reread *Corinne*; "I want to flee
from her, I throw away the book." [19] Women readers of *Corinne*
who attempted to re-create and to direct in their own person a
similarly high-minded level of social discourse — Margaret Fuller in Boston, George Eliot in her Sibylline mood at The Priory,
Kate Chopin in St. Louis — seem to have patterned themselves
after this aspect of Mme de Staël's heroine; but intellectual talk
is only a small part of Corinne's performance. She is also a great
tragic actress, midway in the novel acting a scene (in her own
translation) from *Romeo and Juliet*; and Mme de Staël's model
here was the great Mrs. Siddons, whom she had seen act in
England and in the novel sends Corinne to see for herself (book
17, chap. 4).

For Corinne's gifts as a dancer, and for the famous scene in
which she dances a tarantella, Mme de Staël had in mind similar
performances by her beloved friend Juliette Récamier and by the
German novelist Julia von Krüdener.[20] Corinne is, like them, a
woman of social and intellectual standing who accedes to her
admirers' request to dance, in a ballroom, not a minuet or
gavotte (not, Mme de Staël writes, one of the French dances
remarkable for elegance and intricacy) but a peasant dance of
passion and spontaneous genius. "Corinne made the spectators
feel what she was feeling, as if she had improvised, as if she had
played on the lyre or done sketches" — the last two, incidentally,
among Corinne's other talents: "Everything was language for her
. . . and I know not what impassioned joy, what imaginative sensibility, electrified all the witnesses of this magic dance, and
transported them to an ideal existence where one dreams a happiness not of this world" (book 6, chap. 1). The tarantella scene
suggests both the glamour and the risk that attend the woman
who gives herself spiritually and physically to a wide public,
while offending, exciting, and perhaps losing the single lover who
awaits her in the privacy that is a romance. George Eliot used

19. Las Cases, *Mémorial de Sainte-Hélène* (Paris: Garnier, 1961),
2:173.
20. Mme de Staël's note 14 (*Corinne*, p. 513); M. Levaillant, *The
Passionate Exiles*, trans. Malcolm Barnes (New York: Farrar, Straus,
1958), pp. 15–18.

just such a dance scene to open *The Spanish Gypsy,* her verse drama about a heroine in the cause of social justice. And Ibsen turned the scene around, for the purposes of feminist rebellion, in *A Doll's House.*

Poet, *improvisatrice,* dancer, actress, translator, musician, painter, singer, lecturer — Corinne is all of these, as well as a published author of various unspecified volumes. That Mme de Staël (and her followers) was primarily concerned with literary genius is clear from her emphasis on the imaginative quality, the spontaneity and depth of soul, rather than the perfection of a craft, conveyed by Corinne with all her gifts. But as a woman writer concerned with the theme of fame, Mme de Staël was impelled to bring her heroine's genius out of the study and into the public eye, where she could be shown in the act of swaying the multitude; and as a novelist, Mme de Staël was perhaps the first to discover that book writing is an antinovelistic subject.[21] Many a novelist after her, attempting to make heroism out of literary genius, has discovered that the best way to do it is to exchange his own art for another, one offering more colorful scenes and costumes, more exciting apprenticeships and rivalries, more dramatic public response to turn to narrative purposes.

The poet at least can be made to talk like a poet. (How does a novelist talk? Certainly not like Stephen Dedalus.) The composer's music can be evoked in words, as Proust and Mann have done, and the artist's works can be described, as well as his models, his studio, his *Marble Faun.* But the successful novelist, as the dreary ending of *David Copperfield* showed long ago, has only royalties, reviews, and second marriages. (And the unsuccessful novelists who abound as heroes of second-rate novels in our own time bring teaching positions and psychoanalysis to fiction, not works in progress.)

"My story is a simple one," Virginia Woolf once said in a lecture (not a novel) about her profession. "You have only got to figure to yourselves a girl in a bedroom with a pen in her hand. She has only to move that pen from left to right — from ten

21. For a relevant glance at her predecessors, see Pierre Fauchery, *La destinée féminine dans le Roman européen du dix-huitième siècle, 1713–1807: Essai de gynécomythie romanesque* (Paris: Armand Colin, 1972), p. 438.

o'clock to one." [22] Woolf made Lily Briscoe in *To the Lighthouse* a painter rather than a novelist, painting probably being the most popular of the mysteries that novelists have always used as substitutes for their own; and women novelists have done so almost from their beginning. The heroine of *The Tenant of Wildfell Hall* is posed before her easel, with brush and smock, for other characters to marvel at; although her dry rejoinder to the hero (when he tries to rhapsodize over her talent), that she paints because she needs the money she gets selling her work, indicates that Anne Brontë cared more for the feminist than for the artist, and may have been thinking more of the painter-heroine of Mary Brunton's *Self-Control* (1811) than of Corinne. But her sister Charlotte worked within Mme de Staël's myth.

Charlotte Brontë makes a serious claim for the imaginative genius of Jane Eyre (and clearly for her own) when she unties her heroine's portfolio of watercolors and spreads them out for Rochester's examination.

> "Were you happy when you painted these pictures?" ...
>
> "I was absorbed, sir: yes, and I was happy. To paint them, in short, was to enjoy one of the keenest pleasures I have ever known."
>
> "That is not saying much. Your pleasures, by your own account have been few; but I daresay you did exist in a kind of dreamland while you blent and arranged these strange tints. Did you sit at them long each day?"
>
> "I had nothing else to do, because it was the vacation . . ."
>
> "And you felt self-satisfied with the result . . . ?"
>
> "Far from it. I was tormented by the contrast between my ideas and my handiwork: in each case I had imagined something which I was quite powerless to realise." (Chap. 13)

All the Brontës had a little painterly talent, Emily, who never wrote about it, most of all. But those familiar with the Brontë story recognize in this dialogue a reference not to painting but to the protonovelistic activity that filled the sisters' few free hours when in service as governesses or teachers: the imagining of such serial fantasies as could hardly be spread out for Rochester's

22. "Professions for Women," *The Death of the Moth and Other Essays* (London: Hogarth, 1942), p. 149.

appraisal. Instead, Charlotte Brontë offers a few extraordinary
paragraphs of prose fantasy, which purport to be paintings:

> The first represented clouds low and livid, rolling over a swollen
> sea ... One gleam of light lifted into relief a half-submerged mast,
> on which sat a cormorant, dark and large, with wings flecked with
> foam: its beak held a gold bracelet, set with gems, that I had
> touched with as brilliant tints as my palette could yield, and as
> glittering distinctness as my pencil could impart. Sinking below
> the bird and mast, a drowned corpse ... a fair arm ...
>
> The second picture contained for foreground only the dim
> peak of a hill, with grass and some leaves slanting as if by a
> breeze. Beyond and above spread an expanse of sky, dark blue
> as at twilight: rising into the sky was a woman's shape to the bust,
> portrayed in tints as dusk and soft as I could combine. The dim
> forehead was crowned with a star; ... the eyes shone dark and
> wild; the hair streamed shadowy, like a beamless cloud torn by
> storm or by electric travail. On the neck lay a pale reflection like
> moonlight ...
>
> The third showed the pinnacle of an iceberg piercing a polar
> winter sky: a muster of northern lights reared their dim lances,
> close serried, along the horizon. Throwing these into distance,
> rose, in the foreground, a head, — a colossal head ... Two thin
> hands, joined under the forehead, and supporting it, drew up
> before the lower features a sable veil; a brow quite bloodless,
> white as bone, and an eye hollow and fixed, blank of meaning but
> for the glassiness of despair ... (Chap. 13)

No wonder Rochester inquired if Jane Eyre was happy while
painting these pictures! But their fantasy content, fascinating as
it is, is not so important novelistically as the touches of information about the painter's craft which make this imaginative
material workable as pages of a novel. Charlotte Brontë establishes the creativity of her heroine, not just her mere sensibility,
by making her art into a performance — and making her beloved
the audience.

One of the oddest things about *Corinne* is that it is a guidebook to Italy just as much as a guide to the woman of genius, and
Mme de Staël called the novel *Corinne, ou l'Italie* to signify its
double usefulness. From her view of Italy as *the* place for the

woman of genius resulted much Victorian Italophilia, as Mrs. Browning and Margaret Fuller testify.[23] But the guidebook aspect of *Corinne* also affected the myth of the performing heroine in a curious and apparently accidental way, by associating art criticism with woman's genius. Literary criticism was of course Mme de Staël's own field, and she had strong views, enunciated as early as her *Rousseau* (which may be the first work of that kind ever published by a woman), that women should follow her lead into the study of *la littérature*. To the visual arts she herself was notoriously indifferent; when she went to Italy, the classical scholar A. W. von Schlegel, then a member of her entourage, had some difficulty persuading her to share his enthusiasm for the study of works of painting, sculpture, and architecture. But heroines of novels are subject to special conditions.

Little as Corinne, with her draperies and her lyre, could be shown performing as a novelist, even less could she be made to huddle over a desk in a study, compiling from notes and books the kind of massive analyses of literature and culture for which Mme de Staël was celebrated. Instead, Corinne becomes a tour guide to culture, a *Reiseführerin*. In most of the novel she is shown leading Oswald past the Tombs, Churches, and Palaces of Rome (that is the title of book 5) or Vesuvius and the Environs of Naples (book 10). Corinne lectures, inspires, directs the eye and the mind; she is an improviser in motion before a beautiful and changing scene; she thus served as model for the career of Anna Brownell Murphy Jameson, who, in the 1840s and 1850s, became the first and most widely read woman art historian and critic in England (and America). Mrs. Jameson's influential books on art, informally presented as handbooks, memoirs, and companion guides, were openly (and respectfully) directed to a semieducated female audience — someone like Dorothea Brooke, who "fed on meagre Protestant histories and on art chiefly of the hand-screen sort," can see in the Roman art galleries only "long vistas of white forms [with] marble eyes" (*Middlemarch,* chap. 20).

The influence of *Corinne* is everywhere present, in explicit

23. For the important ideas on women and culture that are also in *Corinne,* see my article "Madame de Staël and the Woman of Genius," *The American Scholar,* Spring 1975.

citation and implicit reference, in the book with which Mrs. Jameson began her fame — an odd little hybrid work of 1826, still redolent of period charm, called *The Diary of an Ennuyée*. Something like a novel, something like a diary, something like a travel book, something like a guide to Italian art, the *Diary* purports to be a melancholy young woman's account of her progress through Italy, her heart riven by an unhappy, undefined love (of which she dies at the end) and her pen drawn by every work of art she can set eyes on. There is something very odd about the circumstances of this anglicized Corinne. The narrator-guide is an anonymous young woman, not married, who travels about freely and respectably without her family. What justification can there be for so much female independence combined with such good connections? Who was she to visit Canova's studio without a chaperone? to stroll with the Countess Bubna on the Corso? come upon "the old poet" Rogers in the gardens of the Villa Albani? There is something so charmingly girlish, so naively humble, and withal so self-assured about the diarist that it is with mingled relief and disappointment that we learn the actual circumstances of the young lady's Italian tour. Anna Murphy did indeed go to Italy most respectably though without relatives or husband: she went as governess to a wealthy English family.[24] In real life, in the early nineteenth century, there were no jobs open to women as art critics, as guides, or as Corinnes.

"A wild desire for an existence of lonely independence" was the typical reaction of women readers, in this case young Fanny Kemble, to books like *Corinne* and its imitations published in England in the 1820s and 1830s.[25] "Mrs. Jameson's 'Diary of an Ennuyée,' which I now read for the first time," Kemble continued, "added to this desire for isolation and independence such a passionate longing to go to Italy, that my brain was literally filled with chimerical projects of settling in the south of Europe, and there leading a solitary life of literary labour, which, together

24. Anna Jameson, *The Diary of an Ennuyée* (Boston, 1858), pp. 52, 191–192; Clara Thomas, *Love and Work Enough: The Life of Anna Jameson* (Toronto: University of Toronto Press, 1967), pp. 23–25.

25. Lionel Stevenson, *The English Novel: A Panorama* (Boston: Houghton Mifflin, 1960), pp. 183–184; Jones, "Madame de Staël," pp. 153–177.

with the fame I hoped to achieve by it, seemed to me the only worthy purpose of existence." [26]

That reads like a fair summary, and for good reason, of the story of *Aurora Leigh*. But Elizabeth Barrett Browning, a precocious poet, provides less remarkable evidence of the power of the myth of Corinne than does Fanny Kemble, who was a unique case among respectable, educated Victorian women: Miss Kemble had wide fame and public applause within her grasp, from an early age, as an actress. A member of a solidly established theatrical family — her aunt was the Mrs. Siddons that Mme de Staël admired, her father the actor-manager of Covent Garden — Fanny Kemble triumphed on the stage as Juliet at the age of nineteen. But she disliked "the theatrical profession," found everything about the stage "more or less repugnant," and always wanted to be remembered as an author (as she mainly is today).[27]

In the novels women wrote after Mme de Staël, the actress did not become the principal descendant of her performing heroine, for reasons supplied not only by Zola's *Nana,* but also by Fanny Kemble's *Record of a Girlhood* or by a woman's novel like *Villette.* "It was a marvelous sight: a mighty revelation," Charlotte Brontë wrote in the course of her unconventional tribute to the actress as artist (the chapter given to the performance of Rachel, called Vashti in *Villette*). But she adds immediately: "It was a spectacle low, horrible, immoral." Vashti partakes of the divine fire, she is a woman of genius; nevertheless, "Vashti was not good, I was told; and I have said she did not look good; though a spirit, she was a spirit out of Tophet. Well, if so much of unholy force can arise from below, may not an equal efflux of sacred essence descend one day from above?" (chap. 23).

The answer to Charlotte Brontë's prayer was the opera singer.

When the first chords of the orchestra summoned Consuelo to her place, she rose slowly; her mantilla fell from her shoulders, and her face finally appeared to the nervous and impatient spectators . . . But what a miraculous transformation had taken place in this young girl, a moment before so pale and worn . . . ! Her

26. Fanny Kemble, *Record of a Girlhood* (London, 1878), 1:202–203.
27. Ibid., 2:13–14.

large brow seemed bathed in a celestial fluid . . . her calm glance
spoke of none of those trivial passions which aim at ordinary
success. There was instead something grave, mysterious and profound . . . which commanded respect . . .[28]

From George Sand's *Consuelo* (1842) to Willa Cather's *Song of
the Lark* (1915), the prima donna justified the myth of Corinne;
the miracle of operatic performance served as could no other to
show off a woman's genius. For a great voice does indeed trans-
port an audience to an ideal existence (as Mme de Staël wrote
of Corinne's tarantella), and it excuses any degree of hyperbole.
There is only one voice like it in a century, as Flora Tristan, the
French feminist, could write of her opera singer heroine;[29] and
the reader cannot quibble with Willa Cather's snobbery (though
we may be troubled by its vehemence) when she says of Thea
Kronborg that "she is uncommon, in a common, common
world." [30]

For the feminist — and there was no more radical disciple of
Mary Wollstonecraft than Flora Tristan[31] — the opera singer
makes a heroine who is strong, willful, and grand; an international traveler; a solitary, but with a subservient entourage in
attendance. Men adore her, but there is no other kind of heroine
(not even the saint) who can so plausibly be made a chaste as
well as a mature and desirable woman. George Sand keeps Consuelo a virgin, even a married virgin, for more than a thousand
pages. And George Eliot has her prima donna, in *Armgart,* reject
a nobleman's proposal of marriage in coldly elitist terms:

Armgart   . . . . seek the woman you deserve,
             All grace, all goodness, who has not yet found
             A meaning in her life, nor any end
             Beyond fulfilling yours. The type abounds.
Graf.   And happily, for the world.
Armgart.   Yes, happily.

28. George Sand, *Consuelo* (Paris: Garnier, 1959), 1:73 (trans.
E. M.).
29. Flora Tristan, *Méphis le prolétaire* (Paris, 1838), 1:9–14.
30. Willa Cather, *The Song of the Lark* (Boston: Houghton Mifflin,
1943), p. 268.
31. Flora Tristan, *Promenades dans Londres* (Paris, 1840), pp.
302–323.

> Let it excuse me that my kind is rare:
> Commonness is its own security.[32]

Mme de Staël had put the matter even more dryly in her first defense of literary women. "Many men prefer," she wrote in her study of Rousseau, "wives who are solely involved with household cares . . . and incapable of understanding anything else. It's a matter of taste; and anyway, as the number of distinguished women is very small, those who don't want one have a wide choice." [33]

Corinne is not French or Genevese, but Anglo-Italian; Consuelo is *La Zingara,* not a Frenchwoman; Thea Kronborg is of immigrant family, not of the old Virginia stock of the Cathers. And the singers in George Eliot's work as well — Tina in "Mr. Gilfil's Love-Story," Mirah in *Daniel Deronda,* the prima donna in *Armgart* — are Italian, Jewish, German, anything but Staffordshire ladies nervous about their respectability. But it was George Eliot who dispensed with the safety screen of otherness and domesticated the performing heroine. No woman writer after Mme de Staël strove harder to spotlight, in the beam of glory, the isolate woman of genius: the "cygnet," in George Eliot's metaphor from the "Prelude" to *Middlemarch,* "reared uneasily among the ducklings in the brown pond." Her heroines are never silly, whatever other adjective we may wish to apply to them; when they fail, they are painful failures. Much anguish in George Eliot's personal life underlay the pain, but the kind of heroism found in her novels belongs to a tradition of women's literature that began long before and continued long after her.

That the heroine of George Eliot's first novel is a Methodist preacher rather than an opera singer hardly disguises the fact that Dinah Morris, in *Adam Bede,* is a true descendant of Corinne. She is seen first from a distance, seen to be admired by a skeptical, upper-class stranger who comes riding into *Adam Bede* at the start of the novel for the single purpose of succumbing to the magic of Dinah's performance.

32. George Eliot, "Armgart," p. 53.
33. *Lettres sur les écrits et le caractère de J.-J. Rousseau* (Paris, 1814), p. 154 (trans. E. M.).

Dinah's clothes are Quaker gray, not sibylline draperies and turbans; her listeners are yokels and milkmaids, not Roman noblemen; her setting, the village green, not the Capitoline Hill; her vehicle, a wheelwright's cart drawn under the maple tree to serve as pulpit, not a chariot drawn by four white horses; her music is not a fanfare but a hymn; her advance praises are given not in formal odes but in the gossip of carpenters and innkeepers; and the subject of her improvisation is not the civilization of Italy but the gospel of Jesus Christ. Nevertheless, Dinah fascinates, "for there is this sort of fascination in all sincere unpremeditated eloquence, which opens to one the inward drama of the speaker's emotions." So thinks the stranger, who many early readers of *Adam Bede* must have thought would become an Oswald in the course of the novel — "the stranger, who had been interested in the course of her sermon, as if it had been the development of a drama." He rides off, however, "while Dinah said, 'Let us sing a little, dear friends'; and as he was still winding down the slope, the voices of the Methodists reached him, rising and falling in that strange blending of exultation and sadness . . ." (chap. 2).

The *Times* this week (July 1974) carries a front-page photograph of a woman in clerical robes newly ordained as an Episcopalian minister, though in the teeth of episcopal opposition. No other advance in the current cause of "women's liberation" could be more astonishing or more thrilling to the Protestant women novelists of the past century. For them, preaching was the most familiar career; the one offering the most obvious opportunities for public performance of an inspirational nature; the one most absolutely closed to women. They saw their fathers, brothers, and suitors go into the church as a sexual at least as much as a spiritual prerogative (as Mary Garth points out to Fred Vincy, with considerable acerbity, in *Middlemarch*). The Gaskell and Brontë and George Eliot and Harriet Beecher Stowe heroines who speak religious and moral truths to eager, instantly converted listeners are spokesmen of views deeply held and maturely ruminated by the novelists; but they are also fulfillments of a compelling female fantasy. Of all the preaching heroines, the most clearly professional is Little Eva at the end of *Uncle Tom's Cabin*: her name is short for Evangeline; her destiny, to play the evangelist, is thwarted by death, as her creator's (whose father and seven brothers were ministers) was thwarted in life by her sex.

Dinah Morris gives up her preaching career, at the end of *Adam Bede,* with a flutter of glad submission, for George Eliot, as her readers have always been surprised to discover, was no feminist. That is, her aim as a novelist was not to argue for a diminishing of the social inhibitions and a widening of the options that affect the lives of ordinary women; instead, like Mme de Staël, George Eliot was always concerned with the superior, large-souled woman whose distinction resides not in her deeds but in her capacity to attract attention and arouse admiration. Her heroines are not intellectuals (any more than Corinne is centrally an intellectual); they do not enjoy using their minds or working for those acquirements which George Eliot herself so remarkably achieved. Instead, as Lucy marvels at Maggie Tulliver for having absorbed "Shakespeare and everything" since she left school, it seems to be the result of "witchcraft," part of her "general uncanniness" (book 6, chap. 3). In one way or another, George Eliot's heroines are women of genius noticed by the world.

Dorothea Brooke, in *Middlemarch,* is the worst kind of product of the myth of Corinne (and the worst sort of influence on novelists like Doris Lessing), for she is good for nothing *but* to be admired. An arrogant, selfish, spoiled. rich beauty, she does little but harm in the novel. Ignorant in the extreme and mentally idle (without feeling any of the guilt of Jane Austen's heroines for their failure to read), Dorothea has little of interest to say, but a magnificent voice to say it in: "What a voice! It was like the voice of a soul that had once lived in an Aeolian harp" to Will Ladislaw (chap. 9); and to Caleb Garth, whose musical tastes are less romantic, "Bless me! it reminds me of bits in the Messiah" (chap. 56). She also has what must be the most stunning wardrobe in Victorian fiction. Here is one of Dorothea's typical Corinne-like entrances:

> When the drawing-room door opened and Dorothea entered, there was a sort of contrast not infrequent in country life when the habits of the different ranks were less blent than now. Let those who know, tell us exactly what stuff it was that Dorothea

wore in those days of mild autumn — that thin white woollen stuff soft to the touch and soft to the eye. It always seemed to have been lately washed, and to smell of the sweet hedges — was always in the shape of a pelisse with sleeves hanging all out of the fashion. Yet if she had entered before a still audience as Imogene or Cato's daughter, the dress might have seemed right enough: the grace and dignity were in her limbs and neck; and about her simply parted hair and candid eyes the large round poke which was then in the fate of women, seemed no more odd as a head-dress than the gold trencher we call a halo. By the present audience of two persons, no dramatic heroine could have been expected with more interest . . . (Chap. 43)

Merely pretty and well-dressed women, in novels by Mrs. Gaskell and Mrs. Stowe, make some of the most attractive heroines in fiction (I would particularly recommend Nina, the charming southern belle in *Dred* [1856], Stowe's little-known second slavery novel). But in George Eliot, as in Charlotte Brontë, prettiness is a focus of anguish, not of heroinism; and in their earliest novels it inspires some moments of malice too strong for anything in their religion or their morality to control. In *Jane Eyre* the venom discharged upon the showy beauty Blanche Ingram, Jane's putative rival for Rochester's affections, is made a trifle more palatable to the reader, rather than less, because envy of the spoiled rich combines with envy of the spoiled beauty in Brontë's mind. But nothing excuses George Eliot's vindictiveness toward Hetty Sorrel in *Adam Bede,* made worse by all the words about tolerant understanding that George Eliot mouths but does not heed herself, as a novelist.

A minor but interesting gauge of the maturity that both George Eliot and Charlotte Brontë achieved in their last novels is the peace they were able to make with merely pretty women characters, a peace with honor and with irony much the equivalent of the one Dickens made in *Our Mutual Friend* with his dandy heroes. Ginevra Fanshawe in *Villette* is a triumph of tolerance carried to the pitch of good humor and affection; she shows Charlotte Brontë's admiration for that particle of grit at the base of every "merely pretty" woman's power to charm. And George Eliot repeated the triumph with her Gwendolen Harleth in *Daniel Deronda,* a character created, I daresay, with a conscious bow to Charlotte Brontë's last novel; for George Eliot estimated *Villette* at its true value.[34]

Both Brontë's Ginevra and George Eliot's Gwendolen are spoiled and shallow beauties, coarse-minded and ignorant flirts, wretchedly brought up to be family tyrants and shameless fortune hunters. Cut loose from religion, morality, and even nationality, they wander through continental resorts in search of social position, and they teeter not far from the edge of the abyss of high-grade prostitution. Each has just enough intelligence to admire a finer quality of being, as represented by Lucy Snowe or Daniel Deronda. But Gwendolen Harleth is the richer and deeper creation, because George Eliot used her to sound out the sources and test the implications, in the widest sense, of the myth of Corinne.

Gwendolen is and is not a heroine; she is a victim and also a villainess; she is an irritation as well as a focus of concern in the novel; but the one thing she is not is an idealized self-portrait of the novelist. By the 1870s (when she was in her fifties) George Eliot had at last lived down her own days of *Corinne*. Yet none of her novels is so imbued as *Daniel Deronda* (1876) with the idea of performing heroinism, with the life given over to the impulsions of genius, with the challenge of the arts and the perils of public admiration. With mature wisdom, and drawing on wide (non-English) experience, George Eliot wrote in *Daniel Deronda* what might have been, but it is something superior to a merely clever satire of *Corinne*. To the ideal of female glory she brought a sense of artistic standards on the one hand, and on the other — for the first time in her work — a realistic and tolerant appraisal of the difficulties of a woman's life.

Much of the technical apparatus that Mme de Staël had developed and George Eliot had often used herself for the establishment of a heroine is drawn upon for the first scene of the novel — an odd scene, wrenched confusingly out of the narrative chronology in order to make our first sight of Gwendolen Harleth a distant one, in the Corinne tradition. Gwendolen is placed in the center of a mixed and admiring crowd; the first of her actions

34. George Eliot, reviewing the cheap edition of *Villette*: "which we, at least, would rather read for the third time than most new novels for the first" (*Westminster Review*, 65 [1856], p. 301).

is a performance; she is first observed through the appraising eye and resisting consciousness of a distinguished stranger, a visitor from another world: Daniel Deronda, the hero of the novel. But George Eliot's aim here is to criticize female fantasy rather than reinforce it. Thus she makes the setting as sordid and trivial as it is glamorous, a German gambling casino; and Gwendolen's showing off of her beauty, her poses, and her spirit at the gambling table are observed by the stranger with a mix of emotions in which admiration plays the least role. Deronda feels grief, pity, and disgust — and he certainly does not fall in love. "The darting sense that he was measuring her and looking down on her as an inferior, that he was of a different quality from the human dross around her, that he felt himself in a region outside and above her, and was examining her as a specimen of a lower order" (book 1, chap. 1) — this reversal of relative position between the admired and the admirer, and with little admixture of sexual attraction, is the kind of education to reality to which Gwendolen is submitted throughout the novel.

But there is no vindictiveness in George Eliot's treatment of the girl, and, what would be worse, no mealymouthed, pitying condescension. Instead Gwendolen is presented with wry sympathy as representative of a common kind: "The Spoiled Child," as George Eliot entitles book 1 (Gwendolen's book) of *Daniel Deronda*. She is not a genius, not even a girl of talent, but one of thousands of pretty girls whose idle and selfish youth, whose deferential families and servants, whose school successes, and whose early triumphs among the neighbors and suitors in the restricted province of their immediate circle give them a thirst for admiration which they assume will be quenched forever, and by the world at large. The accidental encounters (such as the first, with Deronda) that make up Gwendolen's destiny are George Eliot's device to bring her up against the standards and ideals of that wide world of which she has no imagining and which takes no account of her. And "The Spoiled Child" is not so far from "Corinne au Capitole" as one might think.

George Eliot directs our attention to a source of the performing fantasies in women's literature more durable and more dangerous even than societal restrictions on women's careers. That is, the admiration on which little girls are fed, in treacly spoonfuls, from their earliest years. Little boys, who also come in for their share, are made to outgrow the poisonous food; but throughout female youth, often to the brink of marriage, girls are praised for cuteness, for looks, for dress, for chatter, for recitations, for jangling rhymes, for crude sketches, for bad acting, for wretched dancing and out-of-tune singing. They are praised, fondled, and petted for giving pleasure with the amateur entertainment girls are required to provide in the domestic circle, just as Corinne provides it for all of European civilization on the Capitoline Hill.

Television may one day prove to be an invention as liberating for women as was the typewriter, by providing not jobs but something to look at in the home other than little girls. But in the past, and as far back as we have biographical records of literary women, the warpage of gifted girls by an excess of domestic admiration is supported by a mass of depressing evidence. A century before Mme de Staël, Lady Mary Wortley Montagu was toasted, feasted, and caressed by the Whigs of the Kit-Cat Club for her "wit and beauty" when she was seven years old [35] — and a Corinne in the making. Mme de Staël herself sat from the age of six by her mother's side in their Paris salon, and early received praise for her conversational talents; the component of admiration in her father's affection counted undoubtedly for even more. "To see his daughter was his only and dearest relaxation," recorded de Staël's principal girlhood friend. "He never criticized her, let her talk freely, enjoyed the wit she displayed, applauded her enthusiastically, caressed her, and left her content and with refreshed spirits" [36] — and left her, too, not just with an Oedipus complex of such dimensions as to stimulate Napoleon's derision but also with a lifelong greed, as reflexive as that of a salivating dog, for the food of applause.

An excess of early praise for amateur accomplishment may have done more than all the hardships of a woman's lot to separate minor from major accomplishment among literary women. The biographical data that we have about women poets suggests that they are the most liable to early spoiling, especially

35. Robert Halsband, *The Life of Mary Wortley Montagu* (New York: Oxford University Press, 1960), p. 4.
36. Herold, *Mistress to an Age,* p. 36.

if they are pretty as well as gifted, for the making of verses leads to recitation, and so to the kind of praise that tends to flatter a girl's charms rather than refine her compositions. Felicia Hemans provides the type of those facile, shallow poetesses of the nineteenth century: a golden girl of precocious talent, she was fussed over and fondled by all who knew her in her earliest years, and, having survived her, lamented as did Henry Chorley that "she did only a partial justice to her powers." [37]

Sisters under the skin of Felicia Hemans, for all their separation in time and place, were Elizabeth Barrett and Sylvia Plath, both pretty and precocious, both saved from mediocrity by a miracle — perhaps in the shape of a younger brother who displaced them from the center of the adoring family circle. The career of Sylvia Plath, in our own time, suggests that American ingenuity has merely institutionalized, not invented, the species of shallow and premature glory that menaces female talent. Plath was a published poet at eight, was showered with prizes throughout her school years. Her professional career might well have ended where it began, with her selection through *literary* competition to serve as an editor of a fashion magazine — and to be dressed up, made up, danced with, feted, and photographed as the presumed reward for *literary* ability. "I was supposed to be the envy of thousands of college girls all over America," Plath wrote with self-disgust at the start of *The Bell Jar,* "when my picture came out in the magazine." (chap. 1.)

But what of the writer who is gifted and plain, the case of the great majority of the literary women of history, especially among Victorian novelists? I would guess that the onset of adolescence brings a shock of an especially female kind, for then such a girl discovers that the ecstasy of admiration which was hers as a child, as reward for performance, is now withdrawn from her plainness and given instead, by inexorable right, to the beauty. Beauty alone draws the eyes of the world, is the grim lesson of female maturity; beauty alone is drawn by four white horses in triumph to the Capitoline Hill to be crowned as "Miss Universe"; beauty alone — "this tall dark-eyed nymph with her jet-black

37. *Memorials of Mrs. Hemans,* 1:23.

coronet of hair" that Maggie Tulliver so implausibly becomes in adolescence (book 6, chap. 2) — has a line of partners waiting to dance with her in the brilliantly lit drawing room at Park House and draws all the attention to her stall at the bazaar in the baronial hall of St. Ogg's. That is why "the culmination of Maggie's career as an admired member of society" is not the day she sings an aria, or makes a speech, or publishes a book, but is "certainly the day of the bazaar, when her simple, noble beauty, clad in white muslin of some soft-floating kind," etc., etc. (book 6, chap. 9). The gulf in *The Mill on the Floss* that made Swinburne gag was surely the revenge of female fantasy on the tortures of female adolescence for the gifted but plain girl. Maggie really does want to be something other than a Corinne; and she is quite right in her opinion that "the Muses were uncomfortable goddesses."

Gwendolen Harleth, however, does want to be a Corinne, and thinks it will be both easy and delightful as a way of life. Her piano playing has never been criticized in the drawing room. Her face looks exceptionally pretty when she sings, everyone has told her, and her voice keeps pretty well in tune. In parlor charades her acting has always been much in demand. Brought up to be a lady, she has a beauty and a style which are beyond question very fine. Therefore, when family reverses make her think of looking out for herself, Gwendolen decides that she will be an artist — or rather that, without condescending to try (or certainly to work), she already is one. Note George Eliot's careful switch of tenses in the following passage from *Daniel Deronda*:

> ... the dawning smile of self-contentment rested on her lips as she vaguely imagined a future suited to her wishes: it seemed but the affair of a year or so for her to become the most approved Juliet of the time; or, if Klesmer encouraged her idea of being a singer, to proceed by more gradual steps to her place in the opera, where she won money and applause by occasional performances. Why not? At home, at school, among acquaintances, she had been used to have her conscious superiority admitted; and she had moved in a society where everything, from low arithmetic to high art, is of the amateur kind politely supposed to fall short of perfection ... The self-confident visions that had beguiled her were not of a highly exceptional kind ... (Chap. 23)

U. C. KNOEPFLMACHER

The Counterworld of Victorian Fiction
and *The Woman in White*

"The novel is born at the same time as the spirit of rebellion and expresses, on the aesthetic plane, the same ambition." In *The Rebel,* Albert Camus devotes a special section to the novel as the archetypal form of "the literature of rebellion, which begins in modern times." Pointing to the scarcity of works of fiction found in "the literature of consent, which coincides, by and large, with ancient history and the classical period," Camus regards the novel as the product of a more recent and more defiant romantic imagination: "there are no more fascinating heroes than those who indulge their passions to the fullest." Camus's specimens of rebellion in the novel are taken, unsurprisingly, from Russian, French, and modern American fiction. Beyond a brief allusion to Heathcliff, "who wanted to go beyond death in order to reach the very depths of hell," the English Victorian novel is pointedly ignored.[1]

At first glance, Camus's omission seems justified. There are no Stavrogins or Julien Sorels in the masterpieces of Victorian fiction; those few heroes and heroines who do "indulge their pas-

1. Albert Camus, *The Rebel* (New York: Vintage Books, Random House, 1956), pp. 258, 259, 263.

351

sions to the fullest" are handled with circumspection by novelists who insist on dissociating themselves from their creatures' excesses. Recent critics such as Raymond Williams and J. Hillis Miller have correctly stressed the communal emphasis of Victorian fiction, its exaltation of a collective conscience, its distrust of escapism, isolation, and defiance — those same impulses which Camus regards as endemic to creative rebellion. The Victorian novel is uneasy about revolt; *Mary Barton, The Tale of Two Cities, Felix Holt* attest to that uneasiness. Dickens and George Eliot disarm all that threatens to undermine their precarious faith in a beneficent social order bonded by love: Oliver Twist must be preserved from his contaminating contact with Fagin's anarchic underworld; Maggie the rebel must expiate her desire to flee St. Ogg's. One side of the Victorian novelist rejects the escapism or aggression that the other side indulges. Even Heathcliff, the sole English representative of that romantic "intelligence in the service of nostalgia or rebellious sensibilities" which Camus claims to find in all novels,[2] is muted in his Manichaean role when replaced by the tamer Hareton and the second Catherine.

Does the Victorian novel, then, belong to Camus's "literature of consent" rather than to his "literature of rebellion"? I think not. It will be my contention in this essay that beneath the moralism and the collective ethic of love invoked by most Victorian novelists to protect themselves and their readers from impulses antagonistic to society lurks a vital "counterworld" that is asocial and amoral, unbound by the restraints of the socialized superego. Just as the figures of Heathcliff and the first Catherine dominate *Wuthering Heights* despite Brontë's attempts at counterbalance, so does the power of most other great Victorian novels reside in the sometimes concealed, sometimes more overt traces of an anarchic "intelligence" (or emotional affect) opposed to the lawful, ordered Victorian values to which novelist and reader tacitly agreed to subscribe.

This subversive counterworld (usually restricted to characters whom the novelist tries to keep at a distance either by casting them in the role of villains or by placing them in subsidiary roles)

2. Ibid., p. 264.

does not merely exist as a sanctioned vehicle for the criticism of established values and institutions. Mrs. Gaskell may enlist the figure of John Barton in her polemic against the unfairness of the Manchester masters, yet her interest in the quasi-Dostoevskian mentality of this dark, rebellious, homicidal figure of negation clearly outweighs his serviceability as a spokesman for the oppressed. George Eliot and Trollope are hardly uncritical of the provincial societies whose strong communal bonds they nonetheless endorse; yet it is in their treatment of figures that both they and their invented societies reject — a Bulstrode or a Melmotte — that each author reveals a paradoxical fascination, even empathy, with the ruthlessness of a power-hungry and unrestrained egotism. Dickens' well-documented attraction to criminal minds and Thackeray's empathy with the destructive logic of Becky Sharp are inevitably checked, but the asocial energies of such creatures survive despite the attempts at dissociation made through a protesting narrator or through the blunting effects of characterization and plot.

In the ensuing discussion, I intend first to sample some of the ways in which nineteenth-century English novelists repudiate yet indulge rebellious attitudes at odds with the dictates of accepted behavior, and then shall analyze Wilkie Collins's *The Woman in White* (1859–60) as a unique instance of a mid-Victorian novel in which the author openly acknowledges an anarchic and asocial counterworld as a powerfully attractive alternative to the ordered, civilized world of conventional beliefs.

Though pre-Victorian, Sir Walter Scott's *Ivanhoe* (1820), a novel specially dear to the Victorian imagination, provides some interesting paradigms for the later treatment of the alienated outcasts and rebels whose prominence increases so markedly as the English novel progresses from *Oliver Twist* (1837–1839) to *Lord Jim* (1900). Like many a Victorian novelist after him, Scott is fascinated by the convulsions of a chaotic social order; like his successors, he is also deeply ambivalent about the figure of the social rebel. In *Ivanhoe,* England's lawlessness can be repaired only by the reinstatement of the king, who prefers to participate in the Ashby tournament disguised as the Black Knight. Richard acts as the novel's deus ex machina, as a potential healer and restorer of authority; paradoxically, however, it is this "rash and romantic" monarch's earlier abdication of his power that has created the very vacuum he must now again fill. Even after his return, Richard continues to cherish his anonymity, the duels and combats he participates in, the outdoor meals he partakes with Robin Hood's outlaws.

As soon as the unruly Black Knight chooses to resume his responsibilities as a ruler he can restore a social identity to his disenfranchised subjects: the pardoned outlaws return from the forests to which they had been driven; the Saxon nobility gains an access to Norman law. The Ivanhoe who is awarded Rowena ceases to be "El Desdichado," a nameless knight-errant at odds with his own father. Chaos and alienation give way to the normality of civilized order. Significantly enough, however, Scott refuses to integrate all characters into the world that so readily absorbs his conventional lovers. Rebecca the Jewess and Brian de Bois-Gilbert remain fixed in their respective roles of Outsider and Rebel. And the considerable appeal which these two figures of alienation hold for Scott greatly qualifies his assent to the restoration of order in a fictive world which he considers, despite its medieval trappings, as a not-so-covert analogue to civilization "in our own days, when morals are better understood." [3]

Scott's empathy for the "fair and wise" Rebecca requires no documentation. The Jewess is a prototype for all those later outsiders who act as discerning but passive spokesmen for their creators — George Eliot's Philip Wakem, for instance, a figure who guardedly identifies with Maggie Tulliver's rebellious impulse "to avenge Rebecca and Flora MacIvor and Minna," the neglected dark-haired heroines of Scott's romances.[4] Like Philip or like Conrad's Marlow, that other seer who understands yet shies away from the impulses of the rebel, Rebecca remains a passive bystander; her intelligence is that of the critical observer. Her detachment permits her to detect contradictions to which Richard and Ivanhoe, the Christian knights, are totally immune. She sees that "the fantastic chivalry of the Nazarenes" represents

3. *Ivanhoe: A Romance,* with an introduction by George Burke Johnston (New York: Harper and Row, 1965), p. 398.

4. *The Mill on the Floss,* ed. Gordon S. Haight (Boston: Riverside Edition, Houghton Mifflin, 1961), p. 261.

a perversion of their avowed religion of love. She censures the gigantic, blood-bespattered Black Knight, who greedily "rushes to the fray as if he were summoned to a banquet"; she rebukes Ivanhoe for his own "impatient yearning after action." But the young man cannot bear her criticism. He retorts that only someone as "passive as a priest, or a woman" could fail to appreciate the laws of chivalry: "Thou art no Christian, Rebecca; and to thee are unknown those high feelings which swell the bosom of a noble maiden when her lover hath done some deed of emprize." [5]

Rebecca's logic not only makes her Ivanhoe's superior but also elevates her above Rowena, the "noble maiden" Ivanhoe so readily invokes; moreover, as a genuine healer, she also acts as a direct foil to Richard, the potential healer who slaughters enemies with his battle-ax. Still, Ivanhoe's remark about Rebecca's passivity is justified. She is impotent. Her earlier self-denigration as a "poor Jewess" immediately curbed the sexual "emotion" with which Ivanhoe had "hitherto gazed on the beautiful features." [6]

Yet Scott offers Rebecca the opportunity to live in an alternate world more suited to her true powers and to a lineage that "belongs to another climate." If Ivanhoe manages to remain faithful to Rowena, Brian de Bois-Gilbert (like Scott) immediately senses Rebecca's superiority to her blonde rival. Nor is Bois-Gilbert deluded by the chivalric codes that bind Ivanhoe and Richard. Though ostensibly a Templar, he is a secret skeptic and nihilist who is willing to renounce his religion and the deficient society into which Ivanhoe and Rowena become integrated. Aware that Rebecca's paralyzed intelligence cannot thrive in the conventional world he secretly despises, Bois-Gilbert proposes their joint exile into a roomier and freer alternative, a counterworld: " 'Listen to me, Rebecca,' he said, again softening his tone; 'England — Europe — is not the world. There are spheres in which we may act, ample enough even for my ambition. We will go to Palestine, where Conrade Marquis of Montserrat is my friend — a friend free as myself from the doting scruples which fetter our free-born reason: rather with Saladin will we league

5. *Ivanhoe,* pp. 225–255.
6. Ibid., p. 241.

ouselves than endure the scorn of bigots whom we contemn. I
will form new paths to greatness." [7]

Bois-Gilbert's seductive voice is that of the Romantic rebel,
the confirmed Manichaean. It is a voice that Scott soon silences.
Bois-Gilbert's cynical willingness to dissolve all bonds and
pledges, to flee to an exotic counterworld of Saracens and Christian renegades, though worthy of Rebecca the princess in exile,
must be branded by her as "an empty vision of the night." Scott
refuses to pursue this darker vision. Through Rebecca, he manages both to entertain and to deny the allurement of "spheres" in
which men and women may move free from restraint and contradiction. In the three decades after *Ivanhoe,* most of Scott's
Victorian successors followed his precedent: Dickens disengages
Oliver from Fagin's grasp; Charlotte Brontë forces Jane to resist
the blandishments of an illicit life with Rochester; George Eliot
compels Maggie Tulliver to return to the circumscribed world
from which she had fled with Stephen Guest. In the 1860s and
1870s, when escapism from a defective society is entertained
more openly, the alternative of a freer Manichaean counterworld
nonetheless continues to be resisted. The characters in Dickens'
and George Eliot's last novels recognize, with Bois-Gilbert, that
"England — Europe — is not the world." Yet the private society
that forms around Boffin as an alternative to the Veneering world
or the public mission to Palestine on which Mirah and Deronda
embark (in a curious reversal of Bois-Gilbert's intended voyage)
only constitutes a wishful extension of the same quasi-Christian
morality of self suppression and love advanced in the earlier
fiction of Dickens and Eliot. Even in the 1880s and 1890s, when
this morality breaks down, the yearning after a freedom from
"doting scruples" is still treated as a self-destructive deviance:
Dr. Jekyll, Dorian Gray, Sue Bridehead, Kurtz cannot survive in
their antisocial spheres of action.

Only through idealization — the same idealization that would
convert rebels such as Jane Eyre and Maggie Tulliver into figures
of self-denial — can Scott combat the allurement of the antagonistic and escapist impulses he attributes to Bois-Gilbert. Indig-
nantly rejecting the proffered role of rebel, Rebecca chooses

7. Ibid., p. 356.

instead to place her trust in Providence, as well she might. For Bois-Gilbert is soon vanquished, not by Ivanhoe's feeble spear, but by the artifice of a "providential" event, an apoplectic heart attack: "Unscathed by the lance of his enemy he had died a victim to the violence of his own contending passions." [8] Uncontaminated by such passions, Rebecca renounces Ivanhoe to Rowena: the dark-haired outsider bows to the conventional heroine. Dedicating her future life to serve God by helping the distressed, Rebecca takes a path followed by later Victorian heroines who combat their alienation through a self-renouncing life of usefulness.

Ivanhoe furnishes a crude paradigm for some of the ways in which later novelists would handle their simultaneous yearning and resistance toward the alien's counterworld. The three types through which Scott indulges yet purges his social alienation recur in different combinations in the seventy years of fiction from Dickens to Conrad. Ivanhoe-Richard, Rebecca, and Bois-Gilbert represent a self-division that would persist in the figures of (1) outsiders whose temporary social estrangement ends with their reintegration in the community, (2) outsiders whose more passive alienation prevents such a communal reintegration, and (3) outsiders whose more active and hostile alienation converts them into professed enemies of the community's values.

Historically, Scott's tentative fascination with a counterworld was soon to find a more thorough expression in those early Victorian novels that reflect a bolder interest in the figures of the pariah and the outlaw. Harrison Ainsworth, Scott's immediate heir in the realm of historical fiction, romanticized the exploits of Dick Turpin in *Rookwood* (1834), while Bulwer-Lytton dealt with a highwayman in *Paul Clifford* (1830) and made a murderer the hero of *Eugene Aram* (1834). Yet out of these Newgate novels only one stands in relief in its powerful empathy with the defiance of the social outcast: *Oliver Twist* (1837–1839).

In Dickens' novel the merry Sherwood outlaws of *Ivanhoe* have become transmuted into the sinister trinity of Fagin, Sikes, and Monks. No returning king can relocate these outcasts into

8. Ibid., p. 408.

society. Although Mr. Brownlow is instrumental in restoring
Oliver's identity, he possesses none of the authority that Scott
attributes to Richard: it is Fagin who, from his prison cell, bestows
on Oliver the papers that will move the boy back into a world of
respectability. Critics such as J. Hillis Miller are undoubtedly
correct when they stress the analogy Dickens intends between
"the alienated consciousness of the orphan" and the "alienated
consciousness of the outcasts of London." [9] But the analogy
breaks down: the scenes of Sikes's death and of Fagin's trial
carry a far greater authorial investment than the tame concluding
reclamation of a young Christian gentleman. Like Scott, who must
destroy Bois-Gilbert, Dickens must purge himself of his fascination with what Graham Greene has called "the eternal and alluring taint of the Manichee." [10] But, unlike Scott, Dickens allows
his engagement with a lawless counterworld to dominate his
novel. The conclusion of *Oliver Twist* may be as artificially contrived as that of *Ivanhoe*; certainly Oliver's final dissociation
from Fagin ("Oh! God forgive this wretched man!") rings almost as hollow as Rebecca's protestation to Bois-Gilbert. Yet the
triumph of the machinery of respectability and goodness cannot
detract from Dickens' real empathy with the defiance of the
criminal at bay: "roused into new strength and energy," the all-
powerful Sikes can be defeated only by Nancy's spectral eyes;
"surrounded by a firmament, all bright with gleaming eyes," the
cowering Fagin experiences no remorse, only a fear of the gallows.[11] Dickens, who once speculated that he might easily have
become a little robber, clearly prefers the unregenerate Dodger
("I wouldn't go free now, if you was to fall down on your
knees") to the reclaimed Charley Bates.

   To Thackeray, Dickens' sympathy for potent criminals seemed
as unsatisfactory as Scott's curtailment of Rebecca's power. Re-
sorting to parody, he mocked both Scott and Dickens by award-
ing Rowena's husband to Rebecca in *Rebecca and Rowena*

   9. *The Form of Victorian Fiction* (Notre Dame: University of Notre
Dame Press, 1968), pp. 94–95.
   10. "The Young Dickens," in *The Lost Childhood and Other Essays*
(London, 1951), p. 57.
   11. *Oliver Twist,* ed. Peter Fairclough, with an introduction by Angus
Wilson (Baltimore: Penguin Books, 1966), pp. 451, 466.

(published in 1850, but written almost a decade earlier) and by exalting criminal life with tongue in cheek in *Catherine* (1839), a novella written under the pseudonym of Ikey Solomons, the fence on whom Dickens had based Fagin. In these burlesques Thackeray not only teases his predecessors for sentimentalizing outcasts and rebels but also laughs at the readers who had concurred in this sentimentalization. By insisting again and again on the artifice involved in a parody of fictive excesses, he denies his own involvement. Yet despite his ironic disavowals, Thackeray exploits the stereotypes he wants to subvert. Although he undercuts his own sentimental attraction to "Rebecca, that sweetest creature of the poet's fancy" in *Rebecca and Rowena*,[12] his intention to "right" her fate nonetheless seems sincere. And though he purports that *Catherine* is meant as a "cathartic" to purge once and for all the absurd taste for Newgate fiction, Thackeray (who continued to exploit the figure of the rogue in *Barry Lyndon* in 1844) obviously cherishes the opportunity to depict real rogues, "not dandy, poetical, rose-water thieves; but real downright scoundrels, leading scoundrelly lives." *His* criminals, he insists, do not quote Plato like Bulwer's Eugene Aram or chant romantic ballads like Ainsworth's Dick Turpin; his heroine, "Mrs. Cat," will not die "white-washed" like Dickens' Nancy.[13]

Thackeray continued his ironically self-protective presentation of outsiders and rebels in *Vanity Fair* (1847–48). There, too, the voice that mocks the reader for sentimentalizing the outcast is ever present. At first the novelist seems on the side of the rebellious Miss Sharp, who defies the self-righteousness of Miss Pinkerton. We prefer this dark outsider to the bland Amelia, who regards Becky's *"Vive Bonaparte"* as "the greatest blasphemy Rebecca had as yet uttered."[14] But Thackeray soon tempers our enthusiasm for a heroine whose actions betoken her refusal to be cast in the role of noble outsider so readily adopted by her namesake in *Ivanhoe*. Skillfully Thackeray reverses the accepted stereotypes: Becky the anarchist covets the respectability of a stall in Vanity Fair; Amelia the outcast remains as sheltered and

12. *Thackeray's Works,* Kensington Edition (Boston, 1891), 24:82.
13. Ibid., 19:221.
14. *Vanity Fair,* ed. Geoffrey Tillotson and Kathleen Tillotson (Boston: Riverside Edition, Houghton Mifflin, 1963), p. 19.

uncomprehending as Amelia the insider; Dobbin the chivalrous
exile finds no comfort in his reintegration into society with his
Rowena-type wife. No counterworld exists except in the imagination of sentimentalists like Miss Briggs: in a world uniformly
governed by covetousness and aggression there is no need to
assign a special sphere to the rapacity of a Fagin or the unscru-
pulousness of a Bois-Gilbert.

The early work of Wilkie Collins becomes meaningful when
set against the background I have been tracing. To Collins, who
began his career with a historical romance entitled *Antonia; or,
The Fall of Rome* (1850), a portrait of a decadent society unable to withstand the more vital barbarians who live outside the
bounds of Roman law, Scott remained "beyond all comparison
the greatest novelist that has ever written . . . the Prince, the
King, the God Almighty of novelists." [15] Yet in his second full-
length novel, *Basil: A Story of Modern Life* (1852), Collins
aligned himself with the more recent revival of Newgate fiction.
Accusing those critics who had deplored the prurience of *Anto-
nina* of practicing a morality that "stops at the tongue," Collins
provided his detractors with further fuel by openly defying convention in his characterization of the all-powerful Robert Man-
nion, the master criminal who dominates the lurid plot of his
second novel. The critics responded by charging that *Basil*
illustrated the "aesthetics of old Bailey" in its "vicious atmosphere." [16]

Unlike Dickens, who would later urge his friend to respect the
sensibilities of his Victorian audience,[17] Collins never disguised
his fascination with the amorality of the counterworld. In *A*

15. Quoted in Robert Ashley, *Wilkie Collins* (London: Arthur Barker,
1952), p. 109.
16. Quoted in Kenneth Robinson, *Wilkie Collins: A Biography* (New
York: Macmillan, 1952), p. 71.
17. See, for instance, Dickens' concern about Collins's proposed
dramatization of *Armadale*: "Almost every situation in it is dangerous.
I do not think any English audience would accept the scene in which
Miss Gwilt in widow's dress renounces Midwinter" (July 9, 1866, *Letters
of Charles Dickens to Wilkie Collins: 1851–1870,* ed. Laurence Hutton
[London, 1892], p. 132). Collins, in turn, felt misgivings about Dickens'
prudery: he claimed that since the portrayal of Nancy in *Oliver Twist*
Dickens "never afterwards saw all sides of a woman's character — saw
all round her" (Robinson, *Wilkie Collins,* p. 258).

Rogue's Life: From His Birth to His Marriage, a five-part novella published in *Household Words* in 1856, three years before the serialization of *The Woman in White* in *All the Year Round,* he depicted with great relish a transported young convict's supposed confessions. Like the satirical Becky Sharp, Frank Softly (who starts his career as the caricaturist Thersites Junior) shares his creator's delight in puncturing the pretensions of conventional society. Like Becky also, this remorseless pícaro goes unpunished: although transported to Australia, he becomes "a convict aristocrat — a prosperous, wealthy, highly respectable mercantile man." [18] His memoirs end abruptly at this point, for, as he explains, he cannot "be expected to communicate any further autobiographical particulars" now that his identity has merged with that of his readers: "No, no, my friends! I am no longer interesting — I am only respectable like yourselves." [19]

In *A Rogue's Life,* Collins follows Thackeray's precedent whenever he teases the appetite for sensationalism of readers who belong to the same middle-class society that exiles Frank. Yet unlike the Showman who discourages us from empathizing with Becky Sharp or the moralist who asks us to look askance at the misconduct of Arthur Pendennis (like Frank Softly, the ne'er-do-well son of a respectable physician), Collins delightedly enters into Frank's shady activities, his contact with underworld figures such as Mr. Ishmael Pickup, a Jewish art dealer who commissions the young man to forge old masters, and Doctor Dulcifer, a suave coiner who has advanced from the adulteration of wine to "The more refined pursuit of adulterating gold and silver." [20] Like Captain Wragge in *No Name* (1862), another colorful confidence man, Dulcifer easily evades the punitive retribution he would have received at the hands of most other Victorian novelists.

In his later career Collins continued to antagonize reviewers offended by his markedly sympathetic treatment of the villains and villainesses who had become his trademark. Increasingly sarcastic, he defended the characterization of figures such as the

18. *A Rogue's Life: From His Birth to His Marriage* (New York, n.d.), p. 202.
19. Ibid., pp. 203–204.
20. Ibid., pp. 121–122.

voluptuous Miss Gwilt in *Armadale* (1866) by protesting that
his work could be considered "daring" only if "estimated by the
clap-trap morality of the present day." [21] The clumsiness of such
pronouncements, however, belies the subtlety with which he had
undermined this morality in the counterworld of his masterpiece,
The Woman in White.

Like the novels discussed above, *The Woman in White* depicts
a collision between a lawful order in which identities are fixed
and an anarchic lawlessness in which these social identities can
be erased and destroyed. In the novel's "Preamble," the chief narrator, Walter Hartright, draws an analogy between his chronological documentation of "an offence against the laws" and the
presentation through successive witnesses made by a prosecutor
in a court of justice. [22] The reader of the novel's strands of narrative is thus invited to preside as judge and juror; we are asked to
sift and assess the depositions made by a series of witnesses.
Hartright's intended analogy between legal truth and his narrative truth, however, is subverted as soon as we are drawn into
the story's incidents. A trial involves the knowledge of the offense
and the offender; it relies on a detached, ex post facto analysis of
events. But the narrative strips that Hartright has assembled
draw us into the same time scheme of characters wholly unaware
of their future; for a long time we share their ignorance of the
offense alluded to in the "Preamble" and adopt their false sur-
mises, their uncertainties, their surprise. We become engaged in
the narrative, not as impartial and objective judges but as subjective participants in a mystery — a mystery based on the irrational
suspicions of the same figure who has posed in the "Preamble"
as a rational accuser before a rational court of law.

Hartright is the novel's prime orderer. Determined to restore
Laura Fairlie's identity, he fulfills the same function as Scott's
Richard and Dickens' Mr. Brownlow, those other agents for
social reintegration. But Hartright's role is strangely qualified.
Near the end of the novel, this fighter for the cause of truth

21. *Armadale* (New York, 1874), p. 9.
22. *The Woman in White,* ed. Kathleen Tillotson and Anthea Trodd
(Boston: Riverside Edition, Houghton Mifflin, 1969), p. 1. Further references to this work will be given in the text.

admits that he has resorted to fiction in his presentation of the
facts: to protect all characters, including himself, he has assigned
them fictive names. The admission is significant: by giving the
name of Petrarch's beloved to Laura Fairlie, the conventional,
blonde, disingenuous heroine so unfairly treated by the villainous
Sir Percival Glyde, and by calling attention to his own sound
heart, Hartright resorts to obvious conventional precedents.[23]
The stereotypes he adopts, however, are as inadequate as his
analogy to a trial. The dutiful Laura who respects her father's
wishes when she renounces Walter soon ceases to fit her assigned
part as she becomes engulfed in the anarchic reality that prevails
at Blackwater Park; she becomes so like the deranged outcast
Anne Catherick that the keeper of the insane asylum cannot tell
the two apart. Even Hartright ruefully admits that Laura no
longer resembles the conventional beauty he fell in love with at
Limmeridge House: the "terror" that she has undergone has set
its "profaning marks" on her face; her "fatal resemblance" to the
madwoman who proves to be her sister has become "real and
living" (p. 341).

Laura's disenfranchisement converts her into Anne Catherick's
double, a persecuted alien. But Hartright's own belief in "law
and reason" is affected by the madwoman whose touch sends an
illicit thrill through his "bosom." On first meeting the apparition
in white, Walter so identifies with her plight that he lies to the
lawmen who want to return her to the asylum. On meeting her
again in the churchyard, he reads in the "dark deformity of her
expression" his own irrational feelings of hatred for Sir Percival
(p. 77). His alienation is hers: she hides to escape confinement
by those who brand her as insane; he flees to Honduras to avoid
being overcome by madness and despair. Away from the civilized
world he survives fever, murder, and drowning — all emblems of
the death wish that almost destroys the less hardy Laura.

When Hartright returns to England to restore Laura's identity,
he must resort to methods that lie outside the "law and reason"
to which Collins's Victorian readers presumably gave their assent.

23. Hartright's unsubtle use of Petrarch differs markedly from Collins's subtle use of Dante, traced by Peter Caracciolo in "Wilkie Collins'
'Divine Comedy': The Use of Dante in *The Woman in White*," *Nineteenth-Century Fiction*, 25 (1971), 383–404.

He considers wearing a disguise; he resorts to intimidation. Sir Percival the hunter of Anne and Hartright the hunter of Sir Percival's Secret resemble each other more and more. But Walter's true antagonist turns out to be Count Fosco, like himself an avenger with genuine motives for his revenge. Fosco taunts Marian Halcombe: "Warn Mr. Hartright! . . . He has a man of brains to deal with, a man who snaps his big fingers at the laws and conventions of society, when he measures himself with ME" (p. 433). Yet the count fails to reckon with Hartright's own alienation, his ability to operate outside "the laws and conventions of society." Walter soon learns that to reinstate Laura he cannot work within the legal fabric of society; it is the villains, Glyde and Fosco, who can avail themselves of the law. He therefore relies on the primitive habits he has acquired by walking with stealth: "I had first learnt to use this stratagem against suspected treachery in the wilds of Central America — and now I was practising it again, with the same purpose and with even greater caution, in the heart of civilised London!" (p. 357). At the end Hartright resorts to even more uncivilized tactics: by betraying Fosco to members of the counterworld, the anarchists who belong to a secret terrorist society, he not only succeeds in dislodging the count but also becomes responsible for his assassination.

Hartright's confederate and fellow guardian of the sentimental Laura, the ugly, dark-haired Marian Halcombe, is also led to adopt the lawless tactics of the outsider. Although it is she who first invokes convention to part the young drawing master from her half-sister, she is herself unconventional, a descendant of both Scott's and Thackeray's Rebecca, whose passionate intelligence always breaks through the observances of etiquette. After she forces herself to acknowledge Sir Percival's handsome looks and his seemingly "considerate and unselfish" behavior, she immediately disclaims, "I hate Sir Percival! I flatly deny his good looks. I consider him to be eminently disagreeable" (p. 147). Aggressive and direct, she displays none of Laura's submissive acquiescence. Incensed at a fat servant who tells her that the keeper shot a wounded dog, she exclaims, "I was almost wicked enough to wish that Baxter had shot the housemaid instead" (p. 158). On seeing the marks on Laura's wrists, she does not shrink from the thought of murdering Sir Percival: "They say we are either better than men, or worse. If the temptation that has fallen in some women's way, and made them worse, had fallen in mine, at that moment — Thank God! my face betrayed nothing" (p. 232).

If the Walter Hartright who skulks around London is hardly the civilized man of feeling who renounced Laura Fairlie to Sir Percival, the Marian Halcombe who spies on Fosco and Sir Percival by lying on a roof in a dark, rain-drenched cape is hardly the same Victorian lady whose delicacy prevented her from further inquiry into Sir Percival's reputation. Collins delights in portraying the metamorphoses of beings forced to shed their civilized identities. But just as Walter and Laura revert to their stereotypical roles after Fosco's defeat, so does Marian Halcombe again become a subsidiary figure, the kindly maiden aunt of Laura's and Walter's child. Collins deliberately toys with the artificiality of this return to convention; he makes it clear that the unconventional sensibility that Marian displayed makes her a potential fellow rebel of Count Fosco, Marian's stout admirer. If Laura, the sentimental heroine with the Petrarchan name, is the heroine of Hartright's narrative, a narrative that concludes on the side of convention and law and order, Marian Halcombe is the heroine of the novel that Fosco would have written if his notion of "truth," and not that of Hartright, were allowed to dominate. The Italian count, too, knows his Petrarch when he calls Marian "my adored enemy."

Long before we sense Fosco's infatuation with Marian, an infatuation that prompts his only acts of imprudence, we are made aware of Marian's acute interest in the foreign nobleman: "he excites my strongest interest . . . I wonder if he will ever come to England? I wonder if I shall like him?" (p. 147). When Laura describes Madame Fosco, her aunt, Marian deplores the absence of any allusion to the count, "who interests me infinitely more." When the party arrives at Blackwater Park, Marian records her impressions, quickly disposing of the wife as a mere example of the count's power of taming this "once wayward Englishwoman." She is mesmerized by the husband who "has interested me, has attracted me, has forced me to like him" (p. 167), and her elaborately detailed description of the count, his pet animals, his vests, his corpulence, permits the reader to share her fascination as well as her flattered response to his quick recognition of her own fine intelligence.

Collins skillfully encourages the reader to regard this unconventional pair as the true protagonists of his novel, far more deserving of our sympathy and interest than Hartright and his insipid Laura. We are made to entertain the union between these two characters far more seriously than the union between Rebecca and Bois-Gilbert. Like Scott, Collins has Marian reject her kinship with the Rebel; unlike Scott, however, Collins does not endorse the rejection. Quite the contrary, he makes it clear that Marian's sudden revulsion over the count's "horrible admiration" (p. 432) involves a repression of her own asocial impulses. It is neither Fosco's actions against Laura nor the "glib cynicism" she professes to find in his philosophy that causes Marian to recoil; what so unsettles her is the discovery that Fosco has invaded the privacy of her diary, read her innermost thoughts, and concluded that a civilized English lady is a fellow anarchist, "a person of similar sensibility" (p. 262). She denies this judgment and insists that she be vindicated, that Hartright pursue revenge for her sake. She prefers the safety of the stereotype of self-renouncing friend, Hartright's desexualized "sister."

Through the figure of Fosco, however, Collins makes the reader see that Marian is only a step away from the count's licentious counterworld. To Fosco, renunciation is a meaningless act, at odds with true instinct: he deplores that his lawful wife should but get "the shillings and pennies" of his affection, while "the gold of my rich nature" is poured hopelessly at Marian's feet, but he accepts his faithless impulses with ease: "Such is the world, such Man; such Love. What are we (I ask) but puppets in a show-box?" (pp. 475–476). Regarding moral strictures as but an artificial superimposition on the true nature of human beings, Fosco considers a ménage à trois; he views the ugly woman whom Hartright can see only in a formal and socialized role as a "magnificent creature who is inscribed in my heart as 'Marian' — who is known in the colder atmosphere of Society, as 'Miss Halcombe' " (p. 475).

In *The Woman in White* that colder atmosphere prevails, but not until Collins has given a fuller hearing than any of his English predecessors to the antisocial voice of the Rebel. Fosco's long exposition of his philosophy to Marian stresses a logic that Dickens had suppressed in *Oliver Twist* and that Thackeray had employed only for satirical purposes in *Vanity Fair,* namely, that crime can pay. Fosco asks Marian: "Which gets on the best, do you think, of two poor starving dressmakers — the woman who resists temptation, and is honest, or the woman who falls under temptation, and steals? You all know that the stealing is the making of that second woman's fortune — it advertises her from length to breadth of good-humored, charitable England — and she is relieved, as the breaker of a commandment, when she would have been left to starve, as the keeper of it" (p. 181).

Fosco's point is borne out by Anne Catherick's mother. She has yielded to the money of Sir Percival and to the good looks of Philip Fairlie, the blond father absurdly trusted by Laura as the truest and best of men. But her goal is respectability. Like Becky Sharp standing in her booth in the charity bazaar, Mrs. Catherick exults in her acceptance by the same society that denies Laura her identity: "I stand high enough in this town, to be out of your reach. The clergyman bows to me" (pp. 383–384). Yet this prospective member of the Dorcas Society can also write to Hartright, "If I was a young woman still, I might say 'Come! put your arm round my waist, and kiss me, if you like.' . . . and you would have accepted my invitation" (p. 417). As Fosco recognizes, social decorum is but a veneer.

There is much of Collins' own bohemianism in Fosco's quick rejection of Hartright's high-sounding words; using the same vocabulary that Collins employed in the diatribes against his reviewers, the count vows: "Your moral clap-traps have an excellent effect in England — keep them for yourself and your countrymen, if you please" (p. 467). The name Fosco may mean "dark" or "sinister," but there nonetheless is a clear logic in the man who delights in stripping Laura Fairlie of her respectable identity. Like Scott and Dickens before him, Collins kills off his version of the rebel. Significantly, though, the forces of law and reason cannot punish the count; he is murdered by the anarchists that Hartright has unleashed. The enormous corpse is surrounded by a wailing group of Frenchwomen who lift their "hands in admiration, and [cry], in shrill chorus, 'Ah, what a handsome man!' " (p. 495). Madame Fosco pays her own tribute when she writes a biography which, like Collins's own "public" biography of his father, contains only praise of the dead man's "domestic virtues, the assertion of his rare abilities." On the last page she writes: "His life was one long assertion of the rights of the aristocracy, and the sacred principles of Order" (p. 496).

Despite Collins's irony, Madame Fosco's tribute is not incorrect: the aristocratic Fosco has asserted certain principles of order at variance with middle-class Victorian morality. Fosco sees a universe that is not governed by the Providence that Hartright and Marian invoke after the fashion of Dickens and Scott: "Mind, they say, rules the world. But what rules the mind? The body. The body (follow me closely here) lies at the mercy of the most omnipotent of all mortal potentates — the Chemist. Give me — Fosco — chemistry; and when Shakespeare has conceived Hamlet, and sits down to execute the conception — with a few grains of powder dropped into his daily food, I will reduce his mind, by the action of the body, till his pen pours out the most abject drivel that has ever degraded paper. Under similar circumstances, revive me the illustrious Newton" (pp. 477–478).

In *The Woman in White* Collins deftly undermines the fictional conventions he purports to follow. Although, like his predecessors, he portrays the eventual triumph of order, he forces the reader to admit the justice of Fosco's anarchic belief in the frailty of our social identities. Only through evasion and incomprehension can men and women manage to resist the truths of a darker counterworld: like so many Conradian heroines, the well-meaning Mrs. Michaelson stays protected in her orderly world; surrounded by her husband's sermons, she never sees the truths that Marian Halcombe rejects.

Collins compels us to empathize with the man who so clearly prefers animals to humans. (Fosco's horse is called Isaac of York; his favorite white mouse may well be called Rebecca.) The foreign count's denial of the Victorian morality of renunciation and his absolute freedom from scruples are those of Bois-Gilbert, Fagin, and Becky Sharp. But it is noteworthy that Collins also had to go outside English fiction for a precedent: the eccentric Isidor Ottavio Baldassare Fosco is an adaptation of Count Mosca of *The Charterhouse of Parma,* another middle-aged nihilist who openly defies conventional morality. In *The Rebel* Camus asks why a figure like Count Mosca should appear so much more familiar than "our professional moralists." [24] The answer, clearly understood by Collins though rejected by Marian Halcombe, is obvious: beneath our acceptance of the social codes by which we live lurks the nihilism of the amoralist.

24. *The Rebel,* p. 260.

PHILIP FISHER

City Matters: City Minds

A famous sentence by Marx states that the making of the five senses is a project of all history down to the present. This formation is neither smooth nor a question simply of gains in precision, inclusiveness, and nuance. Clumsiness, blindness, losses, a trade between perceptual growth in one direction and atrophy in another, between subtlety and crude approximation, between vaguely seen novelty and no longer noticeable cliché: Marx's history accounts for the balanced structure, construction, and destruction of the power to be aware of experience.

Where conditions of experience alter suddenly, the making and unmaking of the senses becomes in itself a crisis available to consciousness. In its overt form this crisis becomes the subject of art, its "matter," and appears as a "problem." The city, which was surely the major revolution in the structure of experience in modern history, first appeared in the content of poetry, painting, and, of course, the novel as the "problem of the city." Matter for description, argument, polemic, the city as an object out there, a landscape, a life structure subject to breakdown or reform, was totalized by contrast, most often to rural life. As a matter the city was visible precisely because it was placed and rhetorically accounted for by alien and archaic forms of mind, minds risking but ultimately defeating the reconstruction the city implies.

371

Wordsworth's sonnet on Westminster Bridge landscapes the city
with a rural frame, captures the city across from the self as a view
or prospect. The city is significantly asleep, still, not itself, and
the observer, in order to frame the scene, does not stand within
it at all but in midair, on a bridge outside and over against it as
a whole. The miracle is to have located the Archimedean point
— in midair, the Archimedean moment — sleep, and the stance
of landscape so that through these three alien unrealities the city
can be seen compositionally. By negation the archaic mind finds
peace, the inverse of the characteristic noise of the city, composition, the inverse of the fragmentation and disorder, flow and
heart, the inverse of the shock and heartlessness that usually
characterize the city's tone. The gift of the city as matter results
from the contrasting mind that reads backward. The descriptive
convention of the "approaching traveler" who first sees smoky
hints in the distance, then the shapes of the whole infernal city,
then the human confusion of the outskirts, and finally enters
with his portable outside-observer's consciousness, collapses the
visited city into a distasteful spot on the wide and enduring earth,
a spot permanently in the distance even when seen for a time in
almost photographically horrible close-up. Commenting on the
many mid-century set-piece descriptions of the city, momentary
totalizing excerpts like those in Carlyle's *Sartor Resartus* or the
opening of *Bleak House*. George Levine has written that the
view is from above, from a tower whose remoteness makes details comprehensible but at the price of nonparticipation and a
generalized, literary language.

As matter totalized within an outside mind the city is the subject, the antagonist even, of that classical nineteenth-century
form, the novel of entrance, in which the individual immigrant
biography condenses the slower, less recordable transition of the
society as a whole. *Great Expectations* and *Jude the Obscure,*
Melville's *Pierre* or James's *The Ambassadors* in America, landscape and totalize the city as Wordsworth did on Westminster
Bridge, and except for the case of Jude, the city is before the outsider as something to "choose." The city entered is a topic for
virtuoso description and allegorical indictment, for conscious
statement and apostrophe. Stephen Marcus's recent book *Engels,
Manchester and the English Working Class* limits itself to the

deliberate "pictures" of the city and becomes, for that reason, a work about allegory, isolated images that miniaturize theory. At their most condensed such descriptions become ultimately binary, contrastive, that is, they become metaphoric, and the stock details for approaching "infernal Manchester" have often been catalogued. The archaic religious and rural vocabularies and moral stances, the landscaping of the city seen at entrance, the totalizing pictorial indictment, the sociological and reformist city, the city in metaphor — these are the signs of the city captured within still-undisturbed remnants of trusted perceptual systems. Wordsworth trusts by negation and is relieved to find on Westminster Bridge that the city answers at certain moments to the arrangement of the senses known as "scene" and "landscape."

To trust that the city or the psychology of the city in the decisive period of adjustment — the nineteenth century — can be completely explored by locating specific descriptive moments like those in de Tocqueville, Mrs. Gaskell, Carlyle, or Dickens, or by examining statements where the city is the conscious topic, or by locating emblem characters for the city like Jo in *Bleak House* is no more adequate than to imagine accounting for religious consciousness in the literature of the century by looking first at novels written by clergymen, then at novels with clergymen as characters, and finally at novels within which a certain number of scenes are set in church or where churches are directly described at key moments. The emblem character Jo is less an account of the city than the jigsaw puzzle procedure of *Bleak House* — the odd islands that snap into place against one another as new information is announced. The character island Nemo is in fact the father of Esther and under the earlier name Hawden the former lover of Lady Dedlock. Ruskin noticed that the reading of novels in and of itself is more decisive than either their content or procedures. Such reading becomes dietary in the city because it educates the mind for the alternations of boredom and violent sensation that the city mind ends by craving. Ruskin described as well the central topic of violence and death, the almost erotic savoring of death in city novels, but in his moral vision he took for fact what is a technique. Evidently, he said in a famous phrase, it is the fate of most citizens to die "like rats in a drain." Raymond Williams, describing the same violence, converts the literary fact into an experience of structure by saying that the need for complete actions in a setting where fragments of action are common puts a special mark on violence, the last completely localized action.

Where is the account of the crowd more decisively given — in Engels' famous description? in the picturesque street scenes of Zola's Paris novels or in Baudelaire's poetry where, as Benjamin has said, the crowd is so important that it never appears directly but hangs like a veil between the writer and everything he sees, where the streets in the early morning look as they do because the crowd is not yet there? As Hauser has pointed out, it is in impressionism, where the images are rural landscapes, that the new technology of experience, the new arrangement of the senses, can be found. Impressionism sees any part of the world through "the eyes of the townsman and reacts to external impressions with the over-strained nerves of modern technical man. It is an urban style because it describes the changeability, the nervous rhythm, the sudden sharp but always ephemeral impressions of the city."

On the one hand are the direct image traces like Wordsworth's lines on Westminster Bridge and on the other hand are the implicit but deep dislocations of a poem like Baudelaire's on the rotting carcass of a horse, where poetry and beauty take a step into the city by practicing their power to subdue anything and convert even the most repulsive of matters into beauty by means of an art surface, and immunize the human powers of experience against the repulsion and dread, against the grotesque observation, the isolated death that are familiar experience patterns in the city. The figure cut off by the frame at the edge of so many canvases since Manet, the body half seen, half nothing as though it were coming around the corner of a building, records more of the conditions of city experience than the thousands of architectural, composed city engravings of the century. Such engravings and descriptions are symptoms of confidence in direct perception, lacking as they do the doubled stance, the hesitations or self-consciousness about the techniques that account for description.

At the risk of using an awkward term I would like to introduce the idea of reperception, which stands to perception as recognition does to cognition, as representation does to presentation, as remark does to mark. Reperception is a secondary act of capture that records not a doubling of material as metaphor or contrast does, but a slippage in confidence and certainty about seeing itself. Three modes of reperception reappear constantly in the literature of the city mind. First, reperception as a doubled vision of the experience with the two visions separated in time. Many critics have described the Dickensian plot as a device to present as isolated, mysterious, and inscrutable what will later be, with information added, reseen as a web of connections. Both the preliminary mystery and the later relationships are excessive to the point of stylization. Too many connections call connection itself into doubt in a final way that is more threatening than the early isolation, always pregnant with hints and possibilities of connection. In the same way Joyce's theory of epiphany reperceives objects habitual perception has overlooked. The time of habit and the time of epiphany, once again separated into before and after moments that complete one another. In painting this separation of time is converted into a separation of viewing distance: the canvas seen close up is strokes and spots, dabs of color juxtaposed, but at a distance shapes and objects appear, a "second" painting is there for experience. This built-in reperception became standard in the impressionist era.

The second major device of reperception does not separate times or distances of experience but builds into the act of seeing a self-conscious account of the struggle to see and comprehend. James's Strether in Paris, Rilke's Malte Brigge, also in Paris, make overt the process of sight which then becomes a second matter alongside the story content of the novel itself. The final form of reperception, perhaps the most essential of all, filters perception through transformed ways of seeing usually dismissed as defective, overloaded, or peripheral. Illness and fever, the special alertness of the hunted man, hallucinatory, mad, or obsessed angles of vision — from the London experiences De Quincey described in the *Confessions of an English Opium Eater,* through the special narrative uses of illness in *Bleak House,* through Dostoevski's record of St. Petersburg through the feverish center of Raskolnikov, or Hardy's melodramatic Christminster reperceived by the ill and dying Jude, the decisive accounts of the city have characteristically been given by filtration through states of mind dramatically opposed to the reflective mind of the observer who, in the set-piece descriptions of the city, judges and places from the outside as Wordsworth, Carlyle, Engels, or de Tocqueville did.

The stance of reperception is within the city, not across from it. Deliberately it is off balance, as though possession of the world and self-possession — health, sanity, objectivity — were always simultaneously at stake. By the time of Eliot's early city poetry, "The Preludes" and "Rhapsody on a Windy Night," the motifs of reperception, once so odd that they had to be justified by locating them within an aberrant figure, are normalized. A woman is seen with an eye that "twists like a crooked pin." Objects and persons exchange characteristics, even parts. The street with all "its muddy feet" is joined harmoniously to the feet in a way the bodies above the feet no longer are so that the feet are now parts of the street's body. Parts are seen autonomously as wholes, acting independently — "short square fingers stuffing pipes." In turn the detached parts are collectivized as repetitions of one another. The hands are raising shades in a thousand furnished rooms. The streets and fogs are animated, alternately playful and sinister, but always intelligent and purposeful. But the people are drained, passive. The wind wraps old newspaper scraps around a leg that has less vitality than either wind or paper. These hallucinatory cityscapes repeat in a morbid, sinister tone the techniques of Dickens' comic descriptions. Parts of the body have autonomous powers, buildings and rooms are animate characters, experience in repetition takes on an independent life, the borders between persons and possessions are fluid, disturbing. Dorothy Van Ghent in her famous article "The View from Todgers" analyzed and catalogued the devices of what I am here calling Dickens' reperception.

As a complement to the study of direct perception — what I have called the matter of the city — the study of reperception attempts to articulate the latent, often structural impulses of the city mind, the stance within the city. Earlier works like Hillis Miller's study of Dickens, Fanger's work on Dickens, Balzac, and Dostoevski, and more recently Raymond Williams' *The Country and the City* have outlined novelistic and poetic categories internal to the city mind, categories that account for a "poetics of the city," as Fanger has called it. The impulse behind any such poetics is to separate and radicalize within the literature of the city (as distinct from the literature about the ciy) the half-articulated components that are continuous with modernist writers like Eliot, Rilke, Biely, Joyce, Dreiser, Dos Passos, and Kafka, writers for whom the city is never a problem or a matter but a structure of consciousness.

The fusion of novelistic and poetic reperceptions is a decisive fact of the city mind. Techniques are cross-registered, and the sociology of these experiences outside literature — Le Bon's *The Crowd,* Simmel's "The Metropolis and Mental Life," Benjamin's uncompleted study of Paris in the nineteenth century — points to a flooding of categories within art and at the border between institutions like the newspaper or the arcades, behavioral categories like the crowd, the stranger, the observer-artist, and techniques of language and representation within literature itself.

The act of perception within the city becomes reperception first of all with the recording of the process of contamination by which the very stance of distanced observation is acknowledged as a danger. The observer no longer follows what he observes, he shadows it, to use detective language, and is himself turned into a shade. Two famous passages, Engels' description of a crowd and Wordsworth's account in *The Prelude* of his feeling of annihilation amid the strangers on a London street show clearly the distinction between the observer and the shadow. In Engels the details are framed by the device of impersonal observation: "one notices . . ." And within the characterization expressions of surprise, contrast, and indignation frame morally the behavior of those on the street. "They rush past one another as if they had nothing in common or were in no way associated with one another. Their only agreement is a tacit one: that everyone should keep to the right of the pavement, so as not to impede the stream of people moving in the opposite direction. No one bothers to spare a glance for the others." Beneath the words "no" or "only" the structure of outraged values appears intact. In Engels the action of the city on its victims is described by a voice aware of and loyal to a humanity neither the city nor its victims any longer consider. Three parties are present, one protests from the tower where he remains unscarred. In Wordsworth the third figure vanishes.

> How often in the overflowing streets
> Have I gone forward with the crowd, and said
> Unto myself, the face of everyone
> That passes by me is a mystery.
> Thus have I looked, nor ceas'd to look oppress'd
> By thoughts of what, and whither, when and how,
> Until the shapes before my eyes became
> A second sight procession, such as glides
> Over still mountains, or appears in dreams;
> And all the ballast of familiar life,
> The present and the past; hope, fear; all stays,
> The laws of acting, thinking, speaking man
> Went from me, neither knowing me, nor known.

No passage includes a more subtle version of the derealization of the self under those conditions in which, as Baudelaire said, we are "wounded by mystery." The strangers passing refuse to return and accumulate — memories and experiences — until they become "selves." As they are phantoms, the poet's own memory fades. His purchase on himself declines as his purchase on them does. The self of memory, continuity, recurrent images, scenes, and people becomes unstable, and the only name for this perception is the reperceptive name, hallucination.

The vocabulary of detection — mystery, shadowing a suspect, hunting and being hunted — a vocabulary to which I will later return, suggests at once the sinister danger of knowing within this setting, a danger of knowing no less present in Pip's London journey, Strether's experiences in Paris, or Bloom's June day in Dublin. A recurrent image for the danger of pursuit and following in the poetry of the city is the peculiar one of the follower poet as pharaoh, the pursued as the Jews, the buildings and fog as the temporarily parted sea in which the shadow will be drowned. In Mrs. Browning's "Aurora Leigh" the distance of the observer — seated and secure — is maintained as it is in Engels' crowd scene.

But sit in London as the days decline
And view the city perish in the mist
Like Pharaoh's armaments in the deep Red sea,
The chariots, horsemen, footmen, all the host,
Sucked down and choked to silence — then, surprised
By a sudden sense of vision and of time
You feel as conquerors though you did not fight.

(III.195–201)

The word "sit" makes the city a landscape seen from the indoors, a refuge the flood will never reach. Yet the image of anxiety — that the city is a magical, momentary suspension of nature that will one day reclose over the city — is an image that makes of any crowd in the streets pharaohs. In Apollinaire the motif for London is, in the English translation, striking as a world from which the safe inside perspective has vanished.

One half foggy night in London
A street boy who resembled my beloved
Accosted me, and the look he threw me
Made me shut my eyes with shame.

I followed this boy
Who whistled, hands in pockets.
We seemed between the houses
On the opened floor of the Red Sea
He the Jews, Me Pharaoh.

The reclosing of nature is of course the conceit of the beginning of *Bleak House* and again the opening chapter on the Thames of Conrad's *Heart of Darkness,* in both of which the final stages of civilization bend back to reecho the mud, primitive chaos, and violence of the earliest stage. The Red Sea recloses over the fictional human parting of nature. It was in Baudelaire that the heroics of pursuit within the parted river were best expressed. The drowning of space, like those streets Wordsworth spoke of as "overflowing," is the signal for an almost comic urban heroism. In English the lines from "Les sept vieillards" read:

> One morning when mist in the gloomy streets
> Made the houses seem taller, like the two
> Quays of a swollen river; when — decor
> In harmony with the state of my soul —
>
> A foul, yellow fog inundated all space,
> I went steeling my nerves like a hero
> Disputing with my soul, already weary,
> Along the neighborhood jarred by heavy carts . . .

The pursuit in which the follower is as imperiled as the one followed, the rescuer always aware that he is at a higher level about
to sink himself — the psychology of Strether's pursuit of Chad
through Paris — translates into the metaphoric anxiety of the
flooded city. But whether it is the crowd that is drowned or the
self drowned by the crowd — as in Eliot's line "A crowd flowed
over London Bridge," where the crowd mimics the water flowing
under London Bridge — the images become metaphoric substitutes for one another. When Wordsworth says "How often in the
overflowing streets / Have I gone forward with the crowd" the
pair are fused. In Zola's *L'assommoir* the entire city of Paris is
miniaturized in the laundry. Water and alcohol flood the city,
which becomes a city of drains, gutters, downward flow, circulation; a city in which the flood of workers enters in the morning
only to drain back at night; a city in which everyone drowns and
sinks. The metaphor of the drowned man haunts the background
of both Joyce's *Ulysses* and Eliot's *The Waste Land*.

In Wordsworth's overflowing streets the tone of all experience
is the tone of mystery. The word "mystery" itself suggests the
connection between the unfamiliar and the detective form, but it
is essential to see that the melodramatic mystery of crime and
detection is an emblem of the permanent, porous, and ungraspable events and persons within which the self moves. In the city,
as in the opening of his poem "Les sept Vieillards," Baudelaire,
creating a more hysterical version of Wordsworth's "second sight
procession," sees mystery circulating like sap through the veins of
a giant. Within the crowd the unknown becomes the unreal until,
under the flow of derealized images, mysteries, the self observing loses its own laws, its own past and familiarity and within a
derealized outer life drowns into selflessness. The image of hal-

lucinated life, of states of mind no longer exceptional, in which the outer world and the dream world, subjective and objective, inside and outside, merge and weaken in the face of one another, Wordsworth's second stage, is the state of excitation made into a poetic program by Rimbaud and represented through the character of the sick dreamer in Dostoesvki's city novels. At the two poles, that of the unique visionary artist, the too precise individual, and that other scrap of the community, the crowd, the alternative state to boredom is the intoxicated, dreamlike overstimulation of what Wordsworth so precisely called "shapes" and "spectres." The combination of intoxicated dreaming and the dreams of illness, the external world of shades and a growing emptiness of the internal world, are precisely the motifs of Hardy's Jude within Christminster.

What might in Baudelaire or Eliot, in Dostoevski's doubles, in the eerie supernaturalism of the ghost-story sections of Rilke's *Notebooks of Malte Laurids Brigge,* and in the hallucinated Nighttown section of *Ulysses* seem an aberrant, almost Gothic use of lives crossed between real and unreal, living and dead, interior and exterior, is in fact the strident representation of Wordsworth's state, the ordinary state of the mind surrounded by presences without familiarity or obvious meaning. At the climax of the first section of *The Waste Land,* the crowd flowing over London Bridge is the living who seem dead. The corpse planted in the garden like a seed will grow death, sprout, and "live." The confusions and intermixtures of living and dead record for Eliot how the city, unlike the sea, where the sailor actually dies, can only be imagined through paradoxical spiritual categories.

What appears within the city novel as the story of the double, that new character like "the stranger" essential to the syntax of the city novel, is a special case of the derealization of boundaries. The double, halfway between a self and an other, is experienced with the intimacy of the self, but the danger and unpredictability of the other. Jekyll and Hyde, Dostoevski's many doubles, even James's great city story "The Jolly Corner," image the escape of the self from the self, the hallucination of oneself as a specter. Outside the body as antagonist and persecutor the double contests the self as though it were a territory to be plundered or surrendered.

The power of Raskolnikov's crime even in its planning stage, like the power of Richard Carstone's obsession with the chancery suit in *Bleak House,* is to expose the self at every moment to the urgency of projection, hallucination, spiritual duel, doubling, confusion of scene with interior mood — a state of permanent, anxious enchantment. What Hillis Miller and Dorothy Van Ghent have described in Dickens' novels as the animation of the world of objects, the collaboration of rooms with personalities, the fairy-tale life of the world, are only partly comic, magical versions of what in Dostoevski or Rilke's *Notebooks* results from an atmosphere saturated with crime and illness.

The answering state within the self in which apparition, doubling, exchange between interior and world, between perception and imagination, standardizes itself as the norm of perception is illness. Within *Bleak House* the illness and confusion that make perceptible the world are insulated and kept at the periphery of the novel. When ill, Jo "identifies" Esther and Lady Dedlock, and when dying, the heat of his fever is the means to identify himself as the hunted one, the extra man with no place in the world yet completely guilty and responsible for it. The metonymic substitute for the irrational labyrinth of the city, the chancery suit, interiorizes itself as suspicious, feverish anger in both Gridley and Richard Carstone. Ever more solitary, each dies of the illness the chancery–city world creates.

The choice in Dickens to locate the narration within health only momentarily touched by illness (Esther Summerson outside the city in a refuge) rather than in Richard Carstone, ill within the city, was a choice not followed in later city novels. In Hardy's Jude drink and illness, in Dostoevski's Raskolnikov illness and the intensity of crime, in Rilke's Malte illness and its mystical cousin, poetic seeing, become the norms through which the city becomes visible. Even in Joyce's *Portrait of the Artist,* a novel of development attuned to the patches of experience within the city, the "artist" is first seen hunted, hiding threatened beneath a table, then ill, blending fever and world until in the infirmary he *hallucinated* to reperceive Parnell's death as the climax of his own illness.

Perhaps the central text in city consciousness, one whose motifs reappear again and again in poetry and the novel is the brief London section of De Quincey's *Confessions of an English Opium Eater.* Ill and hungry in a world porous with mystery, living with unfathomable strangers — are they father and daughter, master and servant? — in an abandoned house where old papers are the blankets for the young boy and girl who sleep together for warmth on the floor, collapsing in the streets from hunger and illness, aided by a young prostitute whose last name he never learns although he hunts her through the labyrinth of streets certain she is one street away; detective, ill poet, outcast, stranger within a melting and inscrutable set of arrangements: De Quincey models at the very outset of city literature the tone of sinister but poetic mystery, the mood of being haunted by the city, ensnared by its ungraspable order, pursuing desire and beauty in tainted forms, even the inconclusive dissolve that replaces an ending which later seemed the special contribution of Kafka to city poetics. The city with its answering internal illness is finally in De Quincey an equivalent to the dreamlike opium world he enters once he leaves the city.

What is left open-ended in De Quincey by an act of flight that abandons the unanswered questions and the unsolved identities of his London experience was more often located within a frame, that of the detective form, designed to permit a temporary experience of mystery, but then a resolution that dissolved the unknown through an intellectual act of connection. In *Bleak House* the many detective characters guide the master detective, the reader, who, better than Bucket or Tulkinghorn or Mrs. Snagsby, connects and infers until a web replaces a set of knots. The deep atomization of experience that makes detection a fundamental social act lies far beyond the local gaps that we call crimes or mysteries.

Within city experience the expectation that either in time or in space experience will be continuous is squeezed down until in either direction anticipation and memory are devalued. The power to predict and await is condensed, and the virtue of events and persons lies in being either self-explanatory — available in pure present time — or coated with a mystery valuable in its own right. At the extreme each person would pass any other only once — a life literally among strangers; and at any one place only one event could be remembered to have taken place. Instead of sharpening the uniqueness of the moment, as Pater imagined, the effect would be to isolate and erase the self's power to have and remember any experience whatsoever. Raymond Williams has written of the speech of Dickens' characters as the rapid, compressed, self-enacting of people who pass one another in the streets, quickly trying to set an image of themselves on another mind in the urgent moment of passing. Like the cocktail party, that urban invention which stimulates within a house the circulation of a crowd in the street, each person is given a brief moment to present himself, to enact himself and fix himself within another's experience as a certain unique flavor. The numbers and competitiveness of rapid selves creates what Simmel calls a specialization of uniqueness, commonly described in Dickens as "eccentricity." What from a literary point of view can appear a comic device, from the angle of social analysis counts as an alarmingly successful, pungent, brief self-enactment designed for conditions in which only such instantaneous offering can any longer work, conditions where "getting to know someone" is replaced by "getting a fix on someone."

Such characters amount to an instantaneous form of personality, portable, on tap at a moment's notice, universally distributable. (Very little variation occurs in the self-presentation of characters in Dickens when it is an entirely different person to whom the capsule is offered.) Simmel has written of the desperate search for unique, identifiable traits in the city — the bizarre variations of "Oh, that's who you are, the man with the largest collection of bottlecaps . . . the man who swims in the river every New Year's morning . . ." This cultivated specialization is performed repetitively like an actor with only one part, one set of lines for his lifetime. The performance of self within the city under conditions of brief random contacts underlies the most common metaphor for the city since Wordsworth's London book of *The Prelude*: the city is a theater containing within itself other theaters, professional or amateur, indoor or outdoor.

The role of the self-actor of a deliberately minimized vivid part that is not so much spoken but shouted is forced upon the urban character by the brevity of his average contact experience. At the same time he is forced for most of his hours into a spectator's role while the innumerable others whom he has never contacted and thus does not recognize pass before his eyes as exotic, self-acting strangers or as a depressingly blank, uniform "them." Exoticism and boredom, again Ruskin's basic dichotomy, are the two poles of the spectator's range of feeling. The innumerable varieties of the spectator that appear in the novel are the complementary figures to the peculiar eccentrics often at either its periphery or, as is true of Dickens, at its center. The flaneur of Baudelaire, that ambulatory dandy whose consciousness is a portable kaleidoscope, the observers of James and Conrad, the walkers in the city like Joyce's Stephen and Bloom, the dreamers of Dostoevski, the entire tribe of artists with notebooks (Rilke's Malte, Joyce's Stephen of the final section of *The Portrait,* Sartre's Roquentin) all project the assumption that the forced mode of the spectator can itself become as spiritually complex as the mode of the performer.

Where character in this charged instantaneous "take" cannot be seized in its unique taste to be arranged later panoramically in a gallery (as novels and notebooks are often galleries of eccentrics, of epiphanies, of instantaneous flavors) the alternative is to take precisely the mystery of the stranger (the single alternative character to the performer: both stranger and performer appear opposite the spectator) and making that mystery itself his "character." De Quincey relates falling asleep at the roadside, only to awake to find himself stared at by a stranger. Whether the stranger is a robber or merely curious he cannot tell. If a robber, does he imagine De Quincey too poor to rob? Is he, years later, among the readers of the passage De Quincey writes about the experience? This stare of the two strangers, neither of which can "place" the other or even guess limits to the roles, becomes their relation, one of mysterious mutual inspection.

With the appearance of the "stranger" in the novel the economy of forces and destinies no longer works itself out within a circle or social set of recurrent, socially related figures. Dickens expands the circle until, magically, it takes in a crowd of figures all technically related, all recurrent. In *Crime and Punishment* the circle of families exists alongside decisive singular experiences with strangers like the young prostitute seen in the park or the young girl who leaps past Raskolnikov into the river. An

enchantment falls over these figures who "interrupt" for a paragraph or two the closed economy of the circle, an enchantment
like the mystery described by Baudelaire in "Les sept vieillards."

In the categories I am using, this mystery of the stranger unites
the fat man riding in the coach with Esther Summerson in *Bleak
House,* a man she later learns was not a "stranger" at all, but her
benefactor, and the girl seen at the water's edge by Stephen Dedalus in *A Portrait of the Artist* and, above all, that permanent
stranger, Lord Jim. How to experience, order, recognize, and
represent the stranger is an essential technical matter in the novel
of the city that neither embraces variety while disarming it
through the category of the picturesque, nor rejects the stranger
completely as Wordsworth did in the London book of *The Prelude,* where the city of strangers must be fled because a procession of the unknowable, the unrepeating unfamiliar, undermines
memory and self-recognition and turns the world into a dream.

In Dickens the stranger is a toy; not a mystery, but a secret, a
puzzle we suspend ourselves in front of, confident the solution is
twenty or two hundred pages away, but certain to arrive. The
peculiar fat man with Esther in the coach will, since attention is
paid to him at all, turn out to be "someone." Even the dead law
clerk Nemo will only temporarily be "no one," although we experience him in time as the quintessential forgotten nobody of
urban rooming houses. That Dickens later dispels strangeness is
not an assurance, but a reassurance, a security after the fact of
isolation and puzzled anxiety.

The rhythm of mystery and solution when the reader is alert
to a puzzle that hints something more is going on, his willingness
to suspend himself in that state, then relax once given an answer,
translates a life rhythm more and more dominant in urban experience. The city, Simmel has shrewdly seen, intellectualized
men by demanding more and more consciousness, more alertness
and inference, more balance and tolerance for the unexpected,
more processing of the immediate environment. The novel
trained and fed this psychology of detection with its intellectual
keenness, its suspicion, its playfulness and speculation in the face
of what it sees, but created simultaneously an emotional passivity
that amounts to a reserve in the face of what can't be anticipated
or understood until the moment it is unexpectedly revealed. In

achieving *this* training the novel in Dickens, James, Conrad, and Joyce carried to a spiritualized level the rhythm of obscurity and illumination.

In *The Crowd* the psychology Le Bon traces through the crowd repeats in surprising ways the urban psychology of those three varieties of the individual: the stranger, the observer, and the performer. The very grammar of experience used by Dickens and Baudelaire, Eliot, Joyce, Rilke, and Dostoevski for interior states suggests that their apparently solitary characters might best be described as the "scene of a crowd," just as a place is the "scene of a crime" even when the crime is not visibly taking place. This atom of a crowd, forever walking, rapid and compressed as a self-formula, is as Le Bon described him, appealed to through images, susceptible only to experience that is theatricalized. Experience irrupts into him and he must stylize himself to irrupt into the consciousness of others.

The violence of this entrance has been described by Raymond Williams as the essence of the new urban art created by Dickens where, "for him, in the experience of the city, so much that was important and even decisive could not be simply known or simply communicated, but had to be revealed, to be forced into consciousness." This subtle version of the common theory that modern art dealt with a material that could not be phrased, made orderly, exchanged, and communicated, but had to enter consciousness in an act of violence, of shock, of subversive unfamiliarity, throws the burden of disorder onto the forbidden and unthinkable material. But in *The Crowd* Le Bon suggests the more permanently subversive idea that the need for experience to arrive violently in the mind is a characteristic of the urban mind rather than of the mind's attempt to catch up with materials temporarily forbidden. For Le Bon the representation of ideas in dramatically intimate ways replaces the earlier desire to prove them. Ideas are theatricalized, often by a magical leader, then are transferred by a sweeping contagion. They leap into consciousness in exaggerated forms, shock by their intensity and emotional purity, and triumph through the prearranged passivity of the audience. Material dominates which can overleap the field of representation and minimize the need to reason about the material, anticipate material or remember material — that is, to the extent that the material can become instantaneous, pure presentness.

Where the detective form consciously rehearses the destruction and fantasy reconstruction of composed experience, a deeper training would practice the toleration of disintegrated parts. Such a format would, like the art surface of the poetry of ugliness, convert to pleasure the materials of anxiety. Adjacent to art, the newspaper is in itself an image of the city, a miniaturized sample of the total life world, not seen in relation but in simple juxtaposition. Column by column, weighted without account of importance, the heroic and the trivial repose side by side: a fire in a vacant warehouse, the scores of baseball games, a bomb killing twenty in a foreign airport, a movie star's divorce, a traffic jam caused by an unexpected snowstorm, the birth of quintuplets in Australia. The front page of a newspaper is itself a crowd, a present together mass of individuals, strangers to one another. The front page trains the rapid alternations of experience, the panoramic mentality that permits an article on starvation in Africa to run down one column next to a six-column advertisement for the grand opening of a restaurant on Long Island, and neither space contaminates the other, neither suggests nor should suggest outrage or moral indignation. The newspaper is a training ground for the crowd and the city, the place where the habits of perception and imperception are formed and steadied. Explicitly the newspaper is an image of the total structure of the city itself. It accounts for the deaths, births, marriages, condition of money, weather, recent games, and amusements. It is a throwaway daily epic — an image of the cacophony of the city. The only modern novel deeply epic, *Ulysses,* overlays city map and newspaper as two images for life spatialized. Joyce not only makes of the newspaper a constant prop, he models a chapter on the format of a newspaper, connects both main characters as contributors to the newspaper, and accepts its comic miniaturization of the city day as the skeleton for a modern epic.

Walter Benjamin, writing on the decline of storytelling, has suggested that the creation of the novel was a halfway stage between storytelling and that final devaluation of experience, the newspaper. In Benjamin's theory, for the newspaper what was once experience becomes stripped, nonrelational, reduced to information, servicing the city mind by insulating it by training the mind to receive events packaged so as to isolate them from private experience.

The newspaper is itself a picaresque form, a reminder that the most decisive city novels, alongside those rooted in the detective form, are modified variants of the picaresque, the noncumulative, successive adventures of a central figure. The city, after all, is not a society, but a folded road. Its deep image in Dickens, seen in anxiety, not comedy, is that special, folded road, the labyrinth.

MARK R. HILLEGAS

Victorian "Extraterrestrials"

In my judgment, the most important kind of Victorian "science fiction" (the phrase wasn't, of course, coined until the 1920s) was the journey to another world in space.[1] Stories of aliens and other worlds had then and still have a very great fascination, and for this I believe there must ultimately be a psychological explanation, first attempts at which having already been made in Robert Plank's *The Emotional Significance of Imaginary Beings* (1968) and Carl Jung's book on flying saucers (1958). Whether or not one accepts the theories of these and other psychologists, the fact seems indisputable that many people have had a deep need to find that we are not alone. And today this need manifests itself not only in endless books, fiction and nonfiction, about "extraterrestrial" life (the word, incidentally, is used by H. G.

1. General information on nineteenth-century science fiction can be found in J. O. Bailey, *Pilgrims through Space and Time* (1947; reprint ed., Westport, Conn.: Greenwood Press, 1972); David Ketterer, *New Worlds for Old: The Apocalyptic Imagination, Science Fiction, and American Literature* (Garden City, N. Y.: Doubleday, Anchor Press, 1974); H. Bruce Franklin, *Future Perfect: American Science Fiction of the Nineteenth Century* (New York: Oxford University Press, 1966); Robert M. Philmus, *Into the Unknown: The Evolution of Science Fiction from Francis Godwin to H. G. Wells* (Berkeley: University of California Press, 1970).

Wells in *The War of the Worlds*) but also in extensive undertakings with sophisticated arrays of radio telescopes to pick up signals from planets circling distant suns. So far we haven't had word; and, as Sir Francis Crick pointed out at an international symposium held in the USSR in September 1971, we may never have: at the moment we don't know enough about the chemistry of life even to guess whether or not life is unique to Earth.[2] If it should turn out after all that ours is the only inhabited world in an exceedingly vast universe, then childhood's end will have really ended, but differently from Arthur Clarke's vision. Meanwhile, though, we go on listening for signals, writing stories, and spinning theories. The Victorians were not much different.

And before the Victorians others also traveled space in their imaginations. Sources for the imaginary journey to another world are ancient, at least as early as Lucian's *Icaromennipus* and *True History*; but, as Marjorie Nicolson showed in her *Voyages to the Moon*,[3] no real development of the form could take place until the moon and planets were proven worlds. Under the impact of the discoveries of the new astronomy of the seventeenth century, writers began to consider the problems of the journey in space, and within a short time three major voyages were described: Kepler's *Somnium* (1634), Bishop Godwin's *The Man in the Moone* (1638), and Cyrano de Bergerac's *Voyages to the Sun and Moon* (1650). They influenced subsequent stories into the nineteenth and sometimes even the twentieth century.

Although many of the conventions of the journey through space were established in the seventeenth century, such voyages were not characterized by elaborate attention to technical and scientific details until the 1820s and 1830s. One reason was that science and technology had not advanced far enough for writers and their readers to understand completely the difficulties involved in space flight or to have much knowledge of the physical nature of the moon and planets. Another reason was that writers

2. Carl Sagan, ed., *Communication with Extraterrestrial Life* (Cambridge: MIT Press, 1973), p. 52.

3. *Voyages to the Moon* (New York: Macmillan, 1948). This is, of course, the pioneer study of the "cosmic voyage," the term that Professor Nicolson coined more than thirty years ago. Needless to say, I am greatly indebted to her book for an understanding of these voyages, especially those prior to the beginning of the nineteenth century.

of early voyages, especially in their descriptions of other worlds, adapted literary traditions of fantasy, including the utopian. As scientific and technological advances forced greater attention to plausibility, the older traditions of fantasy were usually forgotten.

This change came about in the course of the nineteenth century, first of all because it was a period of tremendous scientific activity, with new concepts in chemistry, physics, astronomy, geology, and biology. The birth of historical geology and the formulation of the theory of evolution had, of course, the most obvious impact. But major contributions were also made in other sciences. Development of the atomic theory was followed by formulation of the periodic table of elements. Such basic ideas in chemistry as valency and the use of structural formulas were established, and chemists succeeded not only in isolating an enormous number of organic substances but also in synthesizing many of them. Modern bacteriology began when fermentation and putrefaction were proven to be caused by living microorganisms and certain diseases by specific microbes. Helmholtz stated the principle of conservation of energy about 1840, and within a few decades the laws of thermodynamics were set forth. The theory of electromagnetic waves was developed by Clerk Maxwell, and light was shown to be one manifestation of this phenomenon. During the last four decades of the century, chemistry, physics, and astronomy employed the important new tool of spectrum analysis. In astronomy, emphasis shifted from the gravitational astronomy dominant in the eighteenth century to two new forms, sidereal and descriptive.[4] Astronomy seems especially to have caught the public's imagination.

But as important in impact on the popular mind as the great progress in pure science were the technological applications which, it hardly needs stating, completely changed the conditions of human life in the nineteenth century. The advances were many

4. See the discussions of nineteenth-century science in W. C. Dampier, *A History of Science and Its Relations to Philosophy and Religion, with a Postscript by I. Bernard Cohen* (Cambridge: Cambridge University Press, 1966); Charles Coulston Gillispie, *The Edge of Objectivity: An Essay in the History of Scientific Ideas* (Princeton: Princeton University Press, 1960). A useful but long-out-of-print book is Agnes M. Clerke, *A Popular History of Astronomy during the Nineteenth Century,* 4th ed. (London: A. & C. Black, 1902).

and spectacular: the railway, steamship, electric motor and dynamo, telegraph, photographic process, electric light, phonograph, telephone, and countless others.[5] Technological progress was extremely important in gaining acceptance for science as Madeleine Cazamian pointed out in 1923 in *Le roman et les idées en Angleterre: L'influence de la science (1860–1890)*. There were no better agents of popularization, she noted, than steam transportation and the electric light.

It is not surprising, then, that as early as the 1820s and 1830s imaginary journeys to other worlds began to appear which at least made a try at a new plausibility, chiefly by elaborate attention to the details of the space vehicle and its means of propulsion, but also to the description of the wonders of space. Writers began to send their travelers through space in airtight cars containing apparatus to generate oxygen, remove deadly carbon dioxide, and provide heat. Requirements for food, water, and clothing during the long period the travelers were sealed inside their ships now had to be worked out with more precision. Writers were also careful to describe devices that would propel a ship through the vacuum of space: usually antigravity or projectile. Extensive references to the physical nature of the heavenly bodies were increasingly incorporated; descriptions of collisions with meteors and the brightness of the stars in space became standard conventions.

Three very minor stories, written early in the century, deserve mention, chiefly as forerunners of Jules Verne's stories. The first, George Tucker's *A Voyage to the Moon* (1827), seems to have been the earliest to work out the details of the journey through the cold, airless void of space and so to have inaugurated a long series of stories employing the device of antigravity. Aside from a brief statement as to its lesser gravitation, Tucker's description of the moon shows no attempt at scientific plausibility and is instead a pale reflection of *Gulliver's Travels*, conventional utopias, and the fantastic worlds seen by seventeenth-century cosmic voyagers. The next attempt at realism, Poe's "Hans Pfaall," made its appearance a short time later (in the June 1835

---

5. See J. D. Bernal, *Science and Industry in the Nineteenth Century* (1953; reprint ed., Bloomington: Indiana University Press, 1970).

Southern Literary Messenger). Poe, who understood the change
that the story of space travel was starting to undergo, discussed
the new realism in his notes and found the old, familiar moon
voyages wanting because they lacked "plausibility." Even
Tucker's *Voyage to the Moon* was unsatisfactory because the
means of flight was "more deplorably ill conceived than are even
the *gansas* of our friend Signor Gonsales" (in Godwin's story).
Although he boasted of his own scientific accuracy, Poe did not
write a first-rate tale. "Hans Pfaall" is partly a parody of the
seventeenth- and eighteenth-century lunar voyage, partly a plausible account of space travel (by balloon, since Poe posited a
slight atmosphere in space); and the combination is not successful. Finally, a very ephemeral piece should be mentioned here,
though it is not precisely a journey to another world. During
August and September 1935 a series of articles in the New York
Sun employed scientific verisimilitude to perpetrate one of the
most famous newspaper hoaxes of all times — Richard Adams
Locke's "Great Astronomical Discoveries Lately Made by Sir
John Herschel at the Cape of Good Hope." Better known today
as the Moon Hoax, the story told how life had supposedly been
seen on the moon by Herschel through a new type of telescope
that brought the moon to within an apparent distance of forty
feet. The great public interest in the story and the widespread
acceptance of its truth have too often been described to require
repetition here. It is sufficient to note that the only thing in
modern experience comparable to the Moon Hoax was Orson
Welles's 1938 radio dramatization of H. G. Wells's *The War of
the Worlds*. Aside from these three, there are no journeys of any
significance until Verne's trip around the moon.[6]

With Verne's two-part saga *From the Earth to the Moon*
(1865) and *Round the Moon* (1870) we get plausibility with a

6. Among the lesser stories of voyages are George Fowler, *A Flight
to the Moon* (Baltimore, 1813); Anon., *Adventures in the Moon and
Other Worlds* (London, 1834); Anon., *A Fantastical Excursion into the
Planets* (London, 1839); J. L. Riddell, *Orrin Lindsay's Plan of Aerial
Navigation ... and His Wonderful Voyage around the Moon* (New
Orleans, 1847); Sydney Whiting, *Heliondé; or, Adventures in the Sun*
(London, 1855); Anon., *The History of a Voyage to the Moon*
(London, 1864).

vengeance.[7] I don't suppose anyone has ever managed to pack so much information into a story of space travel: essentially it is a work of scientific and technological popularization and prophecy, set in a slight though adequate narrative framework. Both parts were immensely popular when they appeared,[8] and rumor went round that Sir John Herschel had supplied Verne with his "velocities, parabolas, and mathematics." Very much impressed, the reading public thought that someone should actually make the trip, and the tale influenced other tales for at least the next fifty years.

According to the story, the members of the Baltimore Gun Club, artillerists and ballistics experts left unemployed after the Civil War, plan to shoot a projectile to the moon. Over five million dollars to finance the undertaking is raised by subscription from people all over the world. Inquiry of the Cambridge Observatory yields precise information for launching the projectile from its great gun, the Columbiad, which is cast in the soil of Florida; and, to observe the progress of the projectile through space, a giant reflecting telescope is constructed on Long's Peak. As work on the project nears completion, the witty Michel Ardan arrives from France and asks that the shape of the projectile be changed from spherical to cylindroconical so that he can ride in it. Two members of the Baltimore Gun Club, the sober Yankees President Barbican and Captain Nicholl, agree to forget their rivalry and accompany Ardan. The projectile, with oxygen equipment and supplies for a landing on the moon, is unfortunately deflected from its course by a near collision with a

7. Two different but useful approaches to the work of Verne can be found in Kenneth Allott, *Jules Verne* (New York: Macmillan, 1941); Jean Chesneux, *The Political and Social Ideas of Jules Verne,* trans. Thomas Wikeley (London: Thames and Hudson, 1972). A survey of the many unexpected significances in the work of Verne which have been seen in recent years by French critics can be found in Marc Angenot, "Jules Verne and French Literary Criticism," *Science Fiction Studies,* 1 (Spring 1973), 33–37.

8. The earliest translation listed in the catalogue of the British Museum is by Louis Mercier and Eleanor King and is dated London, 1873. It is given the title *From the Earth to the Moon Direct in Ninety-seven Hours and Twenty Minutes; and a Trip around It.* Something of the interest it generated is suggested by the fact that at least three editions, presumably the same translation, are listed for the next four years; and then in 1877 a new translation by T. H. Linklater appeared.

meteor and after circling around our satellite returns again to Earth and crashes into the Pacific Ocean. Barbican, Nicholl, and Ardan, unharmed, are rescued by the crew of the United States corvette *Susquehanna*.

The new descriptive astronomy, with its investigation of the physical nature of celestial bodies, and the new sidereal astronomy, with its fathoming of the size and shape of the universe of stars, were the aspects of nineteenth-century scientific advance which most stimulated Verne's imagination in *From the Earth to the Moon* and *Round the Moon*; they are crammed with names and facts drawn from the progress since the late eighteenth century: Herschel's discovery of the movement of stars inside the galaxy, Flammarion's suggestion, after Hansen, that there might be an atmosphere on the opposite side of the moon, Nasmyth's interpretation of the moon's rills, Beer and Mädler's famous map of the moon, Lord Rosse's giant Parsonstown telescope, Laplace's nebular hypothesis.

Nowhere does Verne more skillfully employ his knowledge of astronomy to achieve plausibility than in his description of the passage from sunlight into shadow as the projectile circles the moon. Because of the lack of atmosphere, the change from light to darkness is immediate, with no twilight transition. While Ardan is looking at the moon's surface it suddenly vanishes. "Melted, disappeared!" he exclaims. The temperature inside the car, previously kept comfortable by the sun's radiation, drops rapidly. Ice forms on the inside of the windows and the travelers burn their precious gas to provide heat. On one side of the ship the stars shine with extraordinary brilliance; on the other there is inky black nothingness where the darkened moon blots out the heavens. The three men stand spellbound before the windows of their ship as they watch the brilliant, silent panorama of the stars:

> Indeed, nothing could equal the splendour of this starry world, bathed in limpid ether. Its diamonds set in the heavenly vault sparkled magnificently. The eye took in the firmament from the Southern Cross to the North Star . . . Imagination loses itself in this subline infinity amidst which the projectile was gravitating, like a new star created by the hand of man. From a natural cause,

these shone with a soft lustre; they did not twinkle, for there was no atmosphere . . . These stars were soft eyes, looking out into the dark night amidst the silence of absolute space.[9]

Verne's greatest indebtedness to nineteenth-century astronomy appears in his description of our satellite, where there are numerous and detailed references to the great selenographers and their discoveries. Woven into his moon story are the contributions of such outstanding students of the moon as Schröter, Lohrman, Gruithuisen, Julius Schmidt, Beer and Mädler, the elder Herschel, and Nasmyth. As the projectile moves along an orbit at times only fifty miles from the surface of the moon, the three travelers look through telescopes and see the craters, the mountains, the so-called seas, the plains, the rifts, and the rills — whose names are romance itself — but their observations show no fantastic moon-world in the seventeenth-century tradition.

Since the books are carefully researched, the travelers can only discover that the moon is a lifeless world. The projectile passes close enough to our satellite to determine whether anything moves on her surface, and no movement is seen. Nor is there any evidence of intelligent life in the form of building or ruins: "And what have we seen? Everywhere and always the geological works of nature, never the works of man." To cater to the desire for inhabitants of the moon, Verne includes two hasty, unconfirmed observations which point to life. Once, while the projectile is passing through the shadow of the moon, the dark gloom is penetrated by the sudden, terrifying appearance of an erupting volcano, followed by the ejection of a flaming meteor. For one instant the great meteor lights up the hemisphere never before seen by man. In this incident Verne follows the theory of nineteenth-century astronomers like Hansen and Flammarion, and the travelers think that they see "real clouds in the midst of a very confined atmosphere," "real oceans," and "large dark masses, looking like immense forests." It is such a brief glimpse, however, that it could well have been "a mistake, an optical illusion," and later,

9. *From the Earth to the Moon, Including the Sequel, Round the Moon,* trans. Louis Mercier and Eleanor King, revised by Carter Hull (New York: Didier, 1947), pp. 244–245.

when they discuss their observations, they do not refer to the incident. After the projectile has passed back into sunlight, Verne again teases the reader with another unverified observation, this time indicating life in the past. Ardan thinks he sees the ruins of a fortress and town; but, since he observes everything with so much "imagination in his glance," his two companions are skeptical. In this incident Verne apparently had in mind Gruithuisen's famous announcement in 1822 that he had detected a fortress-city on the moon, and elsewhere he refers directly to Gruithuisen's discovery.

It was not because he did not know the fantastic traditions of the seventeenth- and eighteenth-century cosmic voyage that Verne wrote a tale of space travel so completely dominated by the effort to achieve scientific and technological plausibility. On the contrary, his knowledge of the early history of the cosmic voyage is evident as his characters discuss famous early voyages like Godwin's *Man in the Moone* and Cyrano's journey to the moon and as they explain Kepler's theory about the formation of lunar craters. Verne also knew the stories by Locke and Poe, and in several places the moon saga seems indebted to Poe's "Hans Pfaall," particularly for the facetious tone that occasionally appears alongside the new realism. Every now and then elements of the old fantasy seem ready to appear, especially in such episodes as the humorous encounter of the travelers with the bouleversement and their experiences with the exhilarating sensations of space travel. But whenever this happens the trio in the projectile turn to adjust their oxygen supply and measure the temperature of space, and we realize that this is a new age.[10]

10. The Baltimore Gun Club makes a reappearance with an unsuccessful attempt to right Earth's axis in Verne's *Purchase of the North Pole* (Paris, 1889). Verne's only other novel about space travel, besides the moon saga, is *Hector Servadac* (Paris, 1877). This novel, one of Verne's dullest, presents a close-up of the solar system as seen by men carried off on the comet Gallia, which has collided with Earth and swept up a fragment of its surface from Gibraltar to Malta. Verne may have taken the idea from Edward Everett Hale's story about an artificial satellite, "The Brick Moon," which appeared in the *Atlantic Monthly* in 1870 and 1871. A novel derived from Verne's moon story is Paschal Grousset's bizarre but entertaining *The Conquest of the Moon* (English trans., London, 1889), the story of men accidentally carried off when,

Journeys to the planets largely replaced journeys to the moon during the 1880s and 1890s. Our barren, airless satellite was hardly a suitable subject for the writers of ultrarealistic interplanetary voyages which appeared in ever increasing numbers after 1880. The authors of these stories responded to recent theories and discoveries and appeared to be unaware not only of the seventeenth-century doctrine of a plurality of worlds (it was unable to survive in a more scientifically aware and sophisticated age and died a natural death in 1853 with the Whewell-Brewster debate) but also of the long tradition of the cosmic voyage before the advent of the new plausibility. In this period the influence of *From the Earth to the Moon* and *Round the Moon* was extremely great, and most writers imitated Verne in the elaborate use of scientific and technical details, especially for the narrative of the journey through space.

Mars was the favorite destination of space travelers in the eighties and nineties.[11] Interest in Mars had been growing steadily since Sir William Herschel related the periodic expansion and contraction of the Martian polar caps to the Martian seasons. "The analogy between Mars and the earth," Herschel wrote in 1784, "is perhaps the greatest in the whole solar system." Descriptive astronomy, concerned with the physical nature of the worlds in space, turned to observing the planet, and each favorable opposition in the nineteenth century brought forth new information and more detailed maps. And then, in 1877, obser-

---

brought to Earth by the attraction of a great electromagnet, the moon is suddenly allowed to snap back. Grousset even models the boisterous, farcical meetings of his Luna Company after those of the Baltimore Gun Club.

11. See my short article about the theme of the advanced Martians: "The First Invasions from Mars," *Michigan Alumnus Quarterly Review,* 66 (Winter 1960), 107–112. In the 1880s and 1890s there were also stories of journeys to worlds at earlier stages of development — usually either Venus or Jupiter — such as Wladislas Lach-Syrma, *Aleriel* (London, 1883); John Jacob Astor, *A Journey in Other Worlds* (New York, 1894); Gustavus Pope, *A Journey to Venus* (Boston, 1895). They are all very insignificant, the theme never really receiving the kind of extensive development as the journey to the advanced Mars. Of course, the ultimate development of the idea of Venus as a primitive world comes in the twentieth century with C. S. Lewis's *Perelandra*: a theological variation, since Tor and Tinidril, the Adam and Eve of the new world, do not fall.

vation of the planet reached a sensational climax with Giovanni Schiaparelli's detection of the canals and Asaph Hall's discovery of the two moons, Deimos and Phobus.

The public was especially fascinated by Schiaparelli's canals. The Italian astronomer observed Mars from the clear atmosphere of Milan and concluded that what had been taken for Martian continents were actually islands separated by a network of straight lines, running sometimes to a length of three or four thousand miles. He called them *canali* because he thought that they were "grooves" in the planet's surface, and the Italian word was mistranslated as "canals." Although professional astronomers were generally skeptical about the existence of the markings, the public enthusiastically responded to the implication that intelligent life had produced artificial waterways on Mars, and the oppositions of Mars in 1882, 1884, 1886, and 1892 were newsworthy events. Some indication of the extent of public interest in the subject can be found in an anecdote that begins a discussion in the October 1896 *Edinburgh Review* of three books on Mars — Flammarion's *La planète Mars et ses conditions d'habitabilité,* Schiaparelli's *The Planet Mars,* and Lowell's *Mars*:

> A lady of the inanely inquisitive kind having met an eminent astronomer, implored permission to ask him *one* question. "Certainly, Madam," he replied, "if it isn't about Mars." It *was* about Mars. That was the time of the great Mars boom when public imbecility and journalistic enterprise combined to flood the papers and society with "news from Mars," and queries concerning Mars, most exasperating to grave thinkers and hard workers in science.[12]

While the detection of the canals was the chief cause of the excitement over Mars as a habitable world, Schiaparelli's discovery only furnished the capstone to a theory that Mars was a planet much older than Earth, with inhabitants superior to man. The major source of this idea was the nebular hypothesis, according to which the outermost planets were the oldest because they were formed first, the innermost planets the youngest because most recently created. On the older Mars, intelligent

12. *Edinburgh Review,* 184 (October 1896), 368.

life would have had a chance to evolve beyond that of Earth.
The discovery of the great system of canals seemed to offer
proof that Mars was just such a world: a planet scientifically,
technologically, and socially far advanced.

In concluding this summary, I need only note that discussion
of the idea of an advanced Mars reached its climax in the books
written by the American astronomer Percival Lowell, surely the
most energetic exponent of the theory. Lowell believed that the
general physical conditions of Mars were hospitable to our form
of life but that it was an aging world where water had retreated
through cracks and caverns into the interior. Irrigation had become an "all-engrossing" pursuit of the Martians, who must have
united into a supranational community to perform the tremendous engineering feat of constructing the planet-wide canal
system. They were evidently far ahead of us:

> A mind of no mean order would seem to have presided over the
> system we see . . . Party politics, at all events, had no part in
> them; for the system is planet-wide. Quite possibly, such Martian
> folk are possessed of inventions of which we have not dreamed,
> and with them electrophones [telephones] and kinetoscopes
> [motion pictures] are things of a bygone past, preserved with
> veneration in museums as relics of the clumsy contrivances of the
> simple childhood of the race. Certainly what we see hints at the
> existence of beings who are in advance of, not behind us, in the
> journey of life.[13]

Here, of course, is a classic statement of the idea of Mars as a
scientifically, technologically, and socially advanced world-state
— in short, a vision of utopia. It is not hard to understand the
shape this vision took, since popular excitement about scientific
and technological discovery continued strong during the last
two decades of the century. Ordinary people still eagerly read
inexpensive encyclopedias and books on science, fashionable
people milled to hear lectures by eminent scientists, and scien-

13. *Mars,* 3d ed. (Boston, 1897), p. 209. The first edition was published in 1895. Lowell also wrote *Mars and Its Canals* (1897) and *Mars
as the Abode of Life* (1907). Portions of these books were first delivered
as lectures at the Massachusetts Institute of Technology and the Lowell
Institute. He also contributed numerous papers to periodicals and the
journals of scientific societies.

tific discoveries and new inventions were fully reported in the newspapers. And in addition to the application of steam to machinery, which had come in the first half of the century, the second half saw the application of the discoveries of scientists like Volta, Ohm, Oersted, Ampere, Faraday, and Clerk Maxwell and the birth of an age of electricity. It was only natural that writers of Martian stories would transfer the promised new age to the planet supposedly far advanced beyond Earth.

Perhaps as many as a dozen or more Martian romances appeared in the 1880s and 1890s which incorporated the idea that Mars was an older world whose civilization surpassed Earth's,[14] but not all of them carried the theory to the extremes that Lowell proposed. The culmination of the story of the superior Martians came, of course, with Wells's *The War of the Worlds;* but before turning to it, I think four earlier works merit brief discussion. Wells's accomplishment can best be appreciated when set against that of his predecessors.

The first Martian romance, Percy Greg's *Across the Zodiac* (1880), is one of the most carefully worked out journeys to another world between Verne's lunar voyage and Wells's *The War of the Worlds,* but it is very minor as literature. In *Across the Zodiac* a strange metal manuscript, found in the crater formed after a meteor crashes on a Pacific island, tells how the unknown narrator discovers the electrically generated antigravity force, Apergy, builds a spaceship propelled by this force, and travels to Mars, where he lives for a time. Great attention is given to the ship and to the journey through space, and Mars is the planet as described by the astronomy of the day, although Schiaparelli's canals are not specifically mentioned. Martian

14. Among them are Henry Gaston, *Mars Revealed* (San Francisco, 1880); Hugh MacCall, *Mr. Stranger's Sealed Packet* (London, 1889); Robert D. Braine, *Messages from Mars by the Aid of the Telescope Plant* (New York, 1892); William Simpson, *The Man from Mars, His Morals, Politics, and Religion* (San Francisco, 1893); John McCoy, *Prophetic Romance, Mars to Earth* (Boston, 1896). George du Maurier's *The Martian* (London, 1896) is the story of Barty Josselin, whose mind is occasionally inhabited by a spirit in the process of being reimbodied on Earth after life on Mars. At one point Josselin receives a revelation of Mars and its inhabitants: a physically inhospitable world, "far advanced in its decadence and within measurable distance of its unfitness for life of any kind."

civilization is what ours will be when science and technology are victorious. Greg provides his Martians with most nineteenth-century inventions and those which were to come in the foreseeable future: submarines, telephones, concrete houses, automobiles, automation, and many others. But Martian society is not utopian, for although the material side of life has long been perfected people are not really happy. The book could be seen as a foreshadowing of twentieth-century antiutopias.

A more readable Martian novel, Robert Cromie's *A Plunge into Space* (1890), which appeared when interest in Mars was nearing a climax, expands the idea that the planet is an old world at the height of its evolutionary development. Electrically generated antigravity force, similar to the Apergy of *Across the Zodiac,* propels Cromie's travelers through space. The canals are mentioned, though explained away as "simoons crossing the great central continent of Mars." But Cromie does follow theories that Mars was a worn and aged world where evolution had run its course. Water is scarce, and the planet is covered with vast deserts, the air thin though breathable. Instead of the rugged mountains, the stormy oceans, the giant forests, the sturdy animals of our own earth, the explorers find on Mars only gently sloping hills, quiet, shallow lakes, delicate flowering plants, dainty and sensitive animals. The Martians themselves have evolved beyond men, and their civilization is what we would expect: scientifically, technologically, and socially advanced; and the bound giant electricity does everything for them that nineteenth-century prophets foresaw it would one day do for the men of Earth. But the utopian society of Mars turns out to be dull and uninteresting to the travelers, who after a short time yearn for their own less perfect but more exciting planet.

Popular interest in Mars and its canals reached a peak with the favorable opposition of August 1892. Gustavus Pope's lengthy *Journey to Mars* (1894) appears to be a direct response to this occurrence, as this passage from his introduction indicates: "The last opposition of the planet was of special interest, and awakened a degree of public attention never before known; the press teemed with articles on the event. The telescopes of all the great Observatories of Europe and America were nightly pointed to the skies, and while cities and villages were quietly sleeping, the patient astronomer, seated in his chair or perched on his ladder, was keeping his lone watch on our brother world." [15] Pope takes his stand with those who believe in the canals: "The recent observations of Mars during its opposition in August, 1892, seem to confirm the existence of these lines, particularly the observations conducted at the great Lick Observatory in California." This inept novel contains the first expression of the theme of Martian migration to the more hospitable Earth. A party of Americans on an Antarctic expedition are rescued from an ice cave by Martian explorers who have landed at the South Pole — a beginning similar to that of Kurd Lasswitz's thousand-page Martian novel, *Auf zwei Planeten* (1897). As in Lasswitz's novel, Pope's terrestrial men are taken in an antigravity spaceship to Mars, where they see a technologically advanced civilization. The canals turn out to be not waterways at all but vast linear cities from one to two thousand miles long and fifteen to twenty miles wide, built in this way to offer protection against the great swarms of meteors that constantly bombard the planet. The story ends when the visitors return with a group of colonists fleeing the doomed planet, whose moons are about to fall.

In 1898 the Martian romance reached the climax of its development in English with the publication in book form of H. G. Wells's *The War of the Worlds*.[16] While there are several parallels between Lasswitz's novel, published less than a year before, and *The War of the Worlds* (both tell of the invasion of Earth by vastly superior Martians), the similarities are probably only coincidental and may be attributed to the fact that the two authors were acquainted with the tradition of the Martian story and knew the current theories about the habitability of the planet. "Men like Schiaparelli watched the red planet," writes the narrator in *The War of the Worlds,* and writers like Greg, Cromie, Pope, Lasswitz, and Wells followed the discussions of life on Mars. Although the German novel was not translated into Eng-

15. *Journey to Mars* (New York, 1894), p. 10.
16. *The War of the Worlds* had appeared serially in *Pearson's Magazine* in England and *Cosmopolitan* in America, both serializations beginning in April 1897.

lish until a few years ago (and then only in an abridged version)[17] and hence had little influence in England and America, it deserves brief discussion since it represents the most extensive fictional use ever of the idea of the advanced utopian Martian world.

In *Auf zwei Planeten* the men of Earth first learn of the Martian landing when a German balloon expedition discovers a strange circular building at the North Pole. The polar building and a space station hovering one earth-radius above form the first foothold of the invading Martians, who have come to Earth in spherical antigravity ships steered by rockets. As the landing proceeds, a Martian airship is attacked by an English warship. News of this hostile act reaches Mars, and a party of Anti-Baten ("Ba" is the Martian word for Earth) develops on Mars. When the English reject the Martian demands for satisfaction, the Martians reduce them to subjection in a one-sided war which lasts only a few days, and the Martians then establish a protectorate over Earth in order to educate humanity to their level of culture. Terrestrial men visit Mars and observe the advanced civilization. As Martian rule becomes despotic, mankind unites in a desire to free itself, and a group of engineers in America secretly studies the invaders' technology in order to build airships and weapons. A surprise attack which captures the polar stations and other installations drives the Martians from Earth and precipitates a crisis on Mars in which the pro-Earth party (Philobaten) gains control. A peace treaty is concluded, and Earth, now united as a world-state, begins a new era of peace and freedom.

Never before had the theories put forward by men like Percival Lowell been incorporated so successfully into the Martian romance. The Mars of *Auf zwei Planeten* is an older world than Earth, with a thinning atmosphere and a diminishing supply of water. Forced to unite politically and socially by the hostility of their aging planet, the Martians have brought their technology and science to a level of development centuries ahead

17. *Two Planets,* abridged by Erich Lasswitz, trans. Hans H. Rudnick, afterword by Mark R. Hillegas (Carbondale: Southern Illinois University Press, 1971).

of ours. At a time when the men of Earth are just entering a new era of technology, the Martians look back not only to the age of steam but to the age of electricity as an old inheritance. The canals, such a mystery to terrestrial astronomers, were constructed ages before to carry water from the melting snows of the polar caps to the desert regions. Martian cities are linear, built along the sides of the great canals. The main highways and the canals, which run in straight lines through the middle of the cities, are spanned by permanent fixed buildings devoted to commerce, industry, and professional services. Bordering the central commercial strip are areas of luxuriant vegetation — parks and gardens with trees that grow to enormous heights because of the lesser gravitational attraction. In these park areas are located the private dwellings of the Martians, buildings which can be taken during the night to any part of the Martian world the owner chooses. The limited supply of water is used to maintain the park areas and not to raise foodstuffs, for chemists have perfected the manufacture of proteins and carbohydrates out of rocks, soil, water, and air without the use of plant cells. Energy to run the complex technology comes from the sun in the form of electricity generated by great solar condensers installed on rooftops and on the great desert plateaus. Electric motors power the gigantic conveyor-belt highways, as well as the small personal vehicles which accommodate a few passengers at a time. Movies, radio, television, and the *Retrospektiv,* an instrument for viewing past events by capturing light waves in their journey through space, have been perfected, while automation is everywhere employed and makes life effortless for all classes of Martians.

The ultimate nineteenth-century development in the story of interplanetary travel and the idea of advanced Martians is, as I have said, Wells's *The War of the Worlds* (1898).[18] It has a plot superficially similar to *Auf zwei Planeten,* but Wells elevates his material to the level of literature: a novella (and also a horror story) as good in its way as the best of his scientific romances and stories, including, in my opinion, even *The Time*

18. An extended discussion of the literary meaning and significance of *The War of the Worlds* can be found in Bernard Bergonzi, *The Early H. G. Wells* (Manchester: Manchester University Press, 1961).

Machine.[19] As a story of aliens and travel between worlds, it is much more original and inventive than *The First Men in the Moon* (1901), where Wells returns to the older traditions of the voyage to other worlds.

In *The War of the Worlds,* the Martians, with "minds that are to our minds as ours are to the beasts that perish, intellects, vast and cool and unsympathetic," look longingly at our young world and decide to take it from us. The inevitable cooling of Earth, which physicists in the nineteenth century predicted from the second law of thermodynamics, has already proceeded far on Mars, and the invaders are driven from their planet. "The last stage of exhaustion," wrote Wells, "which to us is still incredibly remote, has become a present-day problem for the inhabitants of Mars." Hurtling through space come the Martians to put us to rout with their superior machines, their heat ray, their poison gas, only to die suddenly and unexpectedly from terrestrial diseases to which they have long before lost immunity.[20] With both Lasswitz and Wells the war between the planets is prophetic of the holocaust of World War I and its airplanes, submarines, and poisonous gas.[21]

There are, however, major differences between the two stories. One of the most striking is the nature of the invaders and their civilization. Unlike the hideous creatures of *The War of the Worlds,* the Martians of *Auf zwei Planeten* are physically identical to us except for their brighter eyes, which flash moral and intellectual superiority. Martian civilization for Lasswitz is merely a projection of the best of human society, whereas Wells's Mars is so far advanced that its culture, like the physical form of

19. Limitations of space preclude consideration of *The Time Machine,* ancestor of all stories of time travel. It is an outgrowth of nineteenth-century discussion of non-Euclidean geometry and speculation that time might be the long-sought-for fourth dimension. I do not consider travel in time the same as travel in space, but that is, of course, the splendid metaphor which forms the basis of Wells's novella.

20. The idea that terrestrial men might have diseases to which Martians would have no resistance is present in Greg's *Across the Zodiac,* where a fatal illness is transmitted by earthly roses.

21. I. F. Clarke, in *Voices Prophesying War* (London: Oxford University Press, 1966), has seen *The War of the Worlds* as belonging to the tradition of future war stories that began after the Prussians quickly overwhelmed the French in 1870–71.

its inhabitants, is totally different and nonhuman.[22] Wells's invaders plan to conquer our world and crush its population in preparation for the Martian migration: human beings will be kept only to provide the blood which the Martians inject for food. On the other hand, the invaders in *Auf zwei Planeten* are culture bearers who wish to elevate humanity to their own level. Lasswitz's novel, much longer than Wells's, is also a great deal more detailed in its description of Martian technology and culture. Lasswitz, for example, devotes considerable attention to the problems of space travel, a subject on which Wells hardly touches. Whereas the spaceships in *Auf zwei Planeten* are the familiar antigravity spheres of many Martian stories, Wells employs Jules Verne's gun and projectile.

The most important difference can be found in the way Wells transforms the Martian story. *Auf zwei Planeten,* though a well-written, well-conceived work and the first to carry out the idea of a Martian invasion, is in other respects not greatly different from earlier works like *Across the Zodiac*. Wells's story, however, transforms the Mars novel into another kind of imaginative writing. His purpose is not to present a technological utopia but instead to portray human fear and terror when immensely intelligent and hostile beings from another world suddenly and unexpectedly invade our quiet earth.

When the first projectile falls flaming from the sky and buries itself in the peaceful Surrey countryside, there is no indication of the terrible events that will follow. Wells makes the arrival seem real and natural — the sand and gravel thrown aside on the heather of the common, the crowd that gathers to see the

22. The Martians are, of course, what men might be after a million years of evolution. As all Wellsians know, he had worked this idea out much earlier in his article "Man of the Year One Million," which appeared in the November 1893 *Pall Mall Budget*. In *The War of the Worlds* he refers to himself as "a certain speculative writer of quasi-scientific repute," writing long before the Martian invasion, "who pointed out that the perfection of mechanical appliances must ultimately supersede limbs; the perfection of chemical devices, digestion; that such organs as hair, external nose, teeth, ears, and chin were no longer essential parts of the human being, and that the tendency of natural selection would lie in the direction of their steady diminution through the coming ages." Only the hand and brain, he contended, had a strong case for survival.

strange meteor, including a few small boys who throw stones at the dark object in the pit. Even after the Martians demonstrate their hostility by destroying the deputation that comes to meet them with white flags in hand, the people of England go about their everyday affairs with infinite complacency, "serene in their assurance of their empire over matter." And then the war begins; the soldiers with their useless guns are annihilated, and the Martians march slowly and relentlessly on London. As a roaring wave of fear sweeps through the greatest city in the world, its social organization collapses. London's populace pours out of the city — "a stampede gigantic and terrible — without order and without goal, six million people, unarmed and unprovisioned, driven headlong." It is the rout of civilization, and the description of the panicked refugees on the crowded roads is vivid and intense. Wells heightens the credibility of the story by the skillful use of such episodes as the narrator's six-day imprisonment in the ruined house with the curate and his encounter with the surviving artilleryman. One of the most awesome scenes in the book comes at the end, when the narrator visits the ruins of London. It is not difficult to see why *The War of the Worlds* has been the source of countless imitations.[23]

The superiority of *The War of the Worlds* as imaginative literature not only to *Auf zwei Planeten* but to other stories of the sort is best illustrated by Wells's treatment of the conventions of the Martian romance. Instead of describing the physical conditions on the planet from which the invaders come, he makes their actions on earth and the objects brought by them reveal the nature of their world. Their extraordinarily advanced technology is indicated by the devices they use, such as their walking tripods and spidery handling machines, which on first impression seem to be living organisms.[24] The thin atmosphere on Mars is indicated

23. It also produced an immediate sequel in Garrett Putnam Serviss's "Edison's Conquest of Mars," published serially in the New York *Evening Journal,* beginning early in 1898. The *Journal* and the Boston *Post* had also previously published "unauthorized, lurid versions" of *The War of the Worlds.* A fascinating account of the misuse of Wells's story and his response to the incident can be found in David Y. Hughes, "*The War of the Worlds* in the Yellow Press," *Journalism Quarterly,* 43 (Winter 1966), 639–646.

24. A story obviously related to *The War of the Worlds* is Wells's "The Crystal Egg," first published in the *New Review* in 1897. In the

by the "pulmonary distress" of the Martians in our own air. The lesser gravitational attraction on Mars is shown when the Martians, whose weight is three times greater here, vainly strain to raise themselves up on their delicate tentacle-hands.[25] The short-lived yet prolific red weed which comes with them explains the red color of Mars. Details are filled in by a few, brief passages such as the following:

> The secular cooling that must some day overtake our planet has already gone far indeed with our neighbor. Its physical condition is still largely a mystery, but we know that even in its equatorial region the mid-day temperature barely approaches that of our coldest winter. Its air is much more attenuated than ours, its oceans have shrunk until they cover but a third of its surface, and as its slow seasons change huge snow-caps gather and melt about either pole and periodically inundate its temperate zones.[26]

Wells's narrator explains that Mars, older, farther from the sun, and smaller than Earth, is "not only more distant from life's beginning but nearer its end." Life began on Mars while Earth, formed later according to the nebular hypothesis, was still molten. Looking sunward from their dying planet, the Martians see "a morning star of hope, our warmer planet, green with vegetation and gray with water, with a cloudy atmosphere eloquent of fertility, with glimpses through its drifting cloud wisps of broad stretches of populous country and narrow, navy-crowded seas."

Something needs to be said about the Selenites in Wells's *The First Men in the Moon* (1901). The Selenites are a major con-

---

story Mr. Cave is able to see by means of a mysterious crystal much the same world from which the invaders come: the Martians themselves, "large-headed creatures" fitted with "two bunches of prehensile organs"; the machines like living organisms; and the red weed. Implied or directly expressed in "The Crystal Egg" are contemporary speculations about Mars, for the planet Mr. Cave observes is an old, eroded world, red in color, with a thin atmosphere and canals to conserve the scarce supply of water.

25. Lasswitz's Martians also have difficulty with Earth's greater gravitation and heavier, moister air.

26. *The War of the Worlds,* in *Seven Science Fiction Novels of H. G. Wells* (New York: Dover Publications, n.d.), p. 310.

tribution to the literature of other worlds and the only original part of Wells's story; otherwise, though well written, it is a traditional lunar voyage. The indebtedness of *The First Men in the Moon* to earlier works, all the way back to Kepler's *Somnium,* has been thoroughly traced by Nicolson in her *Voyages to the Moon.*[27]

In *The First Men in the Moon,* two Englishmen, Bedford and Cavor, travel to our satellite in a sphere coated with the antigravity substance Cavorite. They are captured by the Selenites and carried into caverns beneath the moon's surface after they become intoxicated from eating the plants that spring to life as the frozen air thaws and dawn comes to the crater in which they have landed.[28] Bedford eventually escapes and returns alone in the sphere to Earth, while Cavor is taken deeper into the moon, where he observes the tremendously specialized lunar society and for a time is able to send back reports by wireless to Earth before the Selenites silence him forever. Enormous shafts penetrate to the great cities lying above the Central Sea, two hundred miles below the surface of the moon; and it is down one of these shafts that Cavor is taken in a kind of balloon.

The Selenites are one of Wells's greatest inventions. Almost all writers who described, either in fiction or in serious works, intelligent life on other worlds imagined it to be anthropoid in form. Wells, drawing on his study of biology, went a step further and conceived intelligent life which had evolved out of a nonanthropoid form, in this case the insect. "He does not mention the ant,"

27. *The First Men in the Moon* is linked by Nicolson to earlier voyages to the world underground, of which there are two kinds. One is the journey into the hollow earth, that is, an earth formed like an eggshell and habitable on both inner and outer surfaces (for example, Baron Ludwig Holberg's *A Journey to the World Underground by Nils Klim* [1741] or Captain Adam Seaborn's *Symzonia* [1820]). The second is the journey to gigantic caverns or pockets in the earth's crust (for example, Robert Paltock's *The Life and Adventures of Peter Wilkins* [1751], Verne's *A Journey to the Center of the Earth* [1864], or Bulwer-Lytton's *The Coming Race* [1871]). Nicolson finds both varieties developing from the seventeenth-century cosmic voyage, but I believe they become something essentially different from the journey into space.

28. See the informed and sensitive reading of this section of the novel in Norman Nicholson, *H. G. Wells* (Denver: Alan Swallow, 1950), pp. 23–25.

Bedford says in relating the messages from Cavor, "but through-out his allusions the ant is continually brought before the mind, in its sleepless activity, its intelligence, its social organization, and more particularly, the fact that it displays, in addition to the two forms, the male and the female, produced by almost all other animals, a great variety of sexless creatures, workers, soldiers, and the like, differing from one another in structure, character, power and use and yet all members of the same species." [29] A few writers after the advent of the theory of evolution may have suggested that rational life on other worlds would take different forms from that on Earth, but nothing equal to the intelligent anthill inside the moon had ever been conceived. The theme of biological innovation is a persistent one in Wells's early stories and scientific romances. *The Island of Dr. Moreau* shows man himself attempting to replace evolution by vivisection and sur-gery; *The War of the Worlds* presents man after one million years more of evolution; and *The First Men in the Moon* portrays in-sects who have evolved intelligence.

The nineteenth-century story of life on other worlds thus cul-minates in Wells's Martians and Selenites, and from them are descended the horrible, often crudely portrayed creatures of a great deal of science fiction in the twentieth century, the beings lovingly called Bug Eyed Monsters by the "fans." An unsympa-thetic analysis of the phenomenon appears in C. S. Lewis's *Out of the Silent Planet* (1938), where Ransom, who has been kidnapped to Malacandra (Mars), overhears talk of the *sorns,* one of the three intelligent species of the unfallen planet, and is filled with terror. The familiar passage describing his reaction deserves quoting yet again, for it offers an assessment of the impact of Wells's conception of extraterrestrial life. Ransom "had read his H. G. Wells and others": "His universe was peopled with horrors such as ancient and medieval mythology could hardly rival. No insect-like, vermiculate or crustacean Abominable, no twitching feelers, rasping wings, slimy coils, curling tentacles, no monstrous union of superhuman intelligence

29. *The First Men in the Moon,* in *Seven Science Fiction Novels of H. G. Wells,* p. 595.

Contributors

HENRY AUSTER Department of English
University College, University of Toronto

DAVID BROWNELL Department of English
St. John's University

JEROME H. BUCKLEY Department of English
Harvard University

PHILIP FISHER Department of English
Brandeis University

BARBARA CHARLESWORTH GELPI Department of English
Stanford University

MELVYN HABERMAN Department of English
University of California, Santa Barbara

MARK R. HILLEGAS Department of English
Southern Illinois University at Carbondale

ROBERT KIELY Department of English
Harvard University

U. C. KNOEPFLMACHER Department of English
University of California, Berkeley

HARRY LEVIN Department of Comparative Literature
Harvard University

JOHN MAYNARD Department of English
New York University

J. HILLIS MILLER Department of English
Yale University

ELLEN MOERS Department of English
Brooklyn College and Graduate School of The City University of
New York

WINSLOW ROGERS Department of English
University of Missouri — St. Louis

415

DAVID STAINES Department of English
   Harvard University

RICHARD C. STEVENSON Department of English
   University of Oregon

DONALD D. STONE Department of English
   Queens College, City University of New York

ROBERT LEE WOLFF Department of History
   Harvard University

The seventh volume in this series, *Shakespeare: Not of an Age,* will be edited by Gwynne B. Evans; the eighth, *Studies in Biography,* will be edited by Daniel Aaron.

Morton W. Bloomfield
Jerome H. Buckley
Harry Levin

— *Editorial Board*